Mastery Study Guide

MW00610583

■ Introduct
PSYCHOLOGY

Exploration and Application

SIXTH EDITION

Dennis Coon
Santa Barbara City College

Prepared by
Tom Bond
Thomas Nelson Community College

Bill Cunningham
Thomas Nelson Community College

West Publishing Company

Minneapolis/St. Paul   New York   Los Angeles   San Francisco

WEST'S COMMITMENT TO THE ENVIRONMENT

In 1906, West Publishing Company began recycling materials left over from the production of books. This began a tradition of efficient and responsible use of resources. Today, up to 95% of our legal books and 70% of our college texts and school texts are printed on recycled, acid-free stock. West also recycles nearly 22 million pounds of scrap paper annually—the equivalent of 181,717 trees. Since the 1960s, West has devised ways to capture and recycle waste inks, solvents, oils, and vapors created in the printing process. We also recycle plastics of all kinds, wood, glass, corrugated cardboard, and batteries, and have eliminated the use of Styrofoam book packaging. We at West are proud of the longevity and the scope of our commitment to the environment.

Production, Prepress, Printing and Binding by West Publishing Company.

 *PRINTED ON 10% POST CONSUMER RECYCLED PAPER*

Table of Contents

Acknowledgements

With this edition a co-author, Bill Cunningham, has been added. We would like to thank Steve Schonebaum and Dennis Ralling, our editors at West Publishing, for their patience, understanding, encouragement, and willingness to help us solve problems. In addition, without the initial encouragement and friendship of Clyde Perlee, Editor in Chief at West Publishing, none of this would have been possible.

We could not have put together this *Study Guide* nor would we have wanted to without the fantastic Coon text. Dennis and Sevren Coon have been a continuing source of warmth and support. We wish each of you could get to know them personally.

Tom Bond
Bill Cunningham

To the Student

GENERAL INTRODUCTION

This *Study Guide* is essentially self-explanatory. It is designed to help you learn as much as possible about the interesting field of psychology. At the same time we want you to have every opportunity to succeed in your efforts. If you use this *Study Guide* in the way we have intended for you to, you will probably achieve both of these goals and enjoy the process.

ABOUT THIS *STUDY GUIDE*

If you turn to any chapter in this *Guide* you will quickly see the general structure. Each chapter is divided into six sections:

KEY TERMS, CONCEPTS, AND INDIVIDUALS — This is just a list of the main terms, ideas, and individuals contained in the material in the chapter. These terms and ideas will be tested and reinforced in the other sections.

LEARNING OBJECTIVES — Each learning objective relates to the essential information in the text. Knowledge of all of the learning objectives will ensure that you know the chapter well. Write in the spaces provided. This gives you practice in mastering the material. Be sure to do all of the objectives before proceeding to the self-quizzes.

DO YOU KNOW THE INFORMATION? — This section contains different kinds of self-quizzes (multiple choice, true-false, and/or matching) to give you feedback regarding your basic knowledge of the material.

CAN YOU APPLY THE INFORMATION? — This section contains more self-quizzes, but these quizzes require that you apply the concepts. We have tried to make the questions challenging, but fun. We hope you will find an item every once in a while that will tickle your fancy.

CHAPTER REVIEW — This section is a fill-in-the-blank review to be used shortly before a test. It will give you a good review by focusing on the key terms and concepts presented in each chapter.

ANSWER KEYS — These keys give you the correct answer, the objective being tested, and the corresponding page in the text. Use the answer keys wisely. Don't cheat yourself by looking up the answer ahead of time.

USING THIS *STUDY GUIDE*

While no one study technique works equally well for each student, our best students from over the years have related the following method which has proved most successful for them. First, one should read quickly through the objectives in this *Study Guide*. Then with the *Guide* open beside the textbook, read the chapter while noting either by underlining or highlighting the material which relates to each objective. Next, write the answers to the objectives in the *Study Guide*. Then use the self-quizzes to test your knowledge of the concepts. Finally, use the Chapter Review shortly before a test.

LET US HEAR FROM YOU

This *Study Guide* is written for you. We are interested in your comments and suggestions. This is not just lipservice. Please let us hear from you. It need not be a formal letter; just drop us a note. Only through your critical comments can the *Study Guide* really be improved. The best revision comes from the input of the users.

Tom Bond and Bill Cunningham
Department of Psychology
Thomas Nelson Community College
P.O. Box 9407
Hampton, Virginia 23670

Chapter 1

Psychology and Psychologists

KEY TERMS, CONCEPTS, AND INDIVIDUALS

definition of psychology
  what is behavior
  empirical evidence
impediments to inquiry
anthropomorphic fallacy
  animals in research
goals of psychology
  control
Wilhelm Wundt
  introspection
structuralism
  Edward Titchener
functionalism
  William James
behaviorism
  John Watson, B.F. Skinner
women in psychology
  Margaret Washburn
gestalt psychology
  Max Wertheimer
psychoanalysis
  unconscious, Sigmund Freud
  behavior is determined
humanism
  Carl Rogers, Abraham Maslow

free will vs. determinism
  self-actualization
eclectic approach
cognitive and psychobiological perspectives
psychiatrist, psychologist, psychoanalyst, counselor
clinical vs. counseling psychologist
  APA professional code
basic vs. applied research
  developmental psychologist
  learning psychologist
  personality psychologist
  sensation and perceptual psychology
  comparative psychologist
  physiological psychologist
  social psychology
SQ3R method
  study hazards
  test-taking skills
  critical thinking skills
pseudo-psychologies
  palmistry, phrenology, graphology, astrology
  uncritical acceptance
  fallacy of positive instances
  P.T. Barnum Effect

LEARNING OBJECTIVES

To demonstrate mastery of this chapter you should be able to:
1. List two reasons for studying psychology.
    a.

    b.

1

2.   Define psychology.

3.   Describe what behavior is and differentiate overt from covert behavior.

4.   Explain what empirical evidence is and give an example of it.

5.   Identify the point at which psychology became a science and what sets it apart from other fields.

6.   Give two reasons why the study of some topics in psychology is difficult.
      a.

      b.

7.   Explain what the anthropomorphic fallacy is and how it can lead to problems in psychological research. Explain why and how animals are used in research and define the term "animal model" in your discussion. List two ways in which psychological research may benefit animals.

8.   List and explain the four goals of psychology and its ultimate goal, including why the word "control" has a special meaning for psychologists which is distinct from the everyday meaning of the word.
      a.

      b.

      c.

      d.

9.   Explain the sentence "Psychology has a long past but a short history."

10. Describe the school of psychology known as structuralism including:
     a.   where and when it was established

     b.   who established it (the "father" of psychology)

     c.   the focus of its study

     d.   research method and its drawback

     e.   its goal

11. Describe the functionalist school of psychology including:
     a.   its founder

     b.   its goal

     c.   major interests

     d.   impact on modern psychology

12. Describe behaviorism (S-R psychology) including:
     a.   its founder

     b.   why its founder could not accept structuralism or functionalism

     c.   its emphasis

     d.   Skinner's contribution

e.   role of cognitive behaviorism

f.   therapeutic outgrowth

13.   Characterize the representation of the sexes in early psychology and explain the reason for the discrepancy. State the ratio of the sexes receiving doctorates in psychology today. Name the first woman to receive her doctorate in psychology.

14.   Describe the Gestalt school of psychology including:
       a.   what the word Gestalt means

       b.   who founded it

       c.   its goal

       d.   its slogan

       e.   areas of interest

15.   Describe the psychoanalytic school of psychology including:
       a.   who founded it

       b.   point of departure

       c.   four contributions to psychology

       d.   method of psychotherapy

       e.   psychoanalytic psychology today

16. Describe the humanistic school of psychology including:
    a. how its approach differs from psychoanalytic and behavioristic thought

    b. who its major representatives are

    c. position on "free will" (as contrasted with determinism)

    d. psychological needs

    e. interest in an objective, behavioral science

    f. subjective factors

    g. concept of self-actualization

17. Describe the eclectic approach.

18. List and briefly describe the five major perspectives in modern psychology (especially cognitive and psychobiological).
    a.

    b.

    c.

    d.

    c

19. Characterize the differences in training, emphasis and/or expertise among psychologists, psychiatrists, psychoanalysts, and counselors.

20.   List the three points in the professional code for psychologists established by the APA.
      a.

      b.

      c.

21.   Identify the largest areas of specialization among psychologists. Name the major source of employment for psychologists.

22.   Differentiate basic from applied research.

23.   Write a brief summary of each of the following areas of specialization in psychology:
      a.   clinical and counseling

      b.   developmental

      c.   learning

      d.   personality

      e.   sensation and perception

      f.   comparative

      g.   physiological

      h.   social

i.   industrial

j.   school

k.   experimental

* * * * * * * * * *

The following objectives are related to the material in the "Applications" and "Exploration" sections of your text.
24.   Explain what SQ3R means and describe what each of the steps in the method involves and how they can be applied to using Coon's textbook.

25.   Name two keys to note-taking and tell how to effectively use notes.
a.

b.

26.   List five things you can do to make your study habits more productive.
a.

b.

c.

d.

e.

27.   List two possible reasons why people procrastinate, and describe two ways to combat procrastination.
why it occurs?
a.

b.

how to combat it?
a.

b.

28.   List six ways to improve your performance on objective tests.
      a.

      b.

      c.

      d.

      e.

      f.

29.   List four ways to improve your performance on essay tests.
      a.

      b.

      c.

      d.

30.   Explain what critical thinking is by listing and then applying six questions which should be considered when evaluating information.

31.   Indicate the foundations and fallacies of each of the following pseudo-psychologies:
      a.   palmistry

      b.   phrenology

      c.   graphology

      d.   astrology

32. List and explain the three reasons why pseudo-psychologies continue to thrive even though they have no scientific basis.

a.

b.

c.

SELF-QUIZZES

Do You Know the Information?

Multiple Choice

1. Your author states that psychology should be studied because
    (a) a person can hardly be considered "educated" without knowing something about the field of psychology.
    (b) we are in the midst of a psychological revolution.
    (c) it helps us better serve as informal therapists.
    (d) it allows us to become one with the universe.

2. Psychology is
    (a) the study of the behavior of animals.
    (b) the study of the mind of man.
    (c) the scientific study of human and animal behavior.
    (d) the scientific study of organisms.

3. Which of the following is an example of *covert* behavior?
    (a) talking   (c) glaring
    (b) thinking   (d) laughing

4. Empirical evidence is evidence that
    (a) relies on authority for its veracity.
    (b) is as good as a professional psychologist's opinion.
    (c) is gained through direct observation and measurement.
    (d) None of the above answers is true.

5. Psychology became a science when
    (a) psychologists began performing experiments.
    (b) the first psychological laboratory was built.
    (c) behaviorism became the major school of psychology.
    (d) philosophy was downgraded to an art.

6. Some questions about behavior go unanswered because
    (a) ethical standards may be violated in conducting the research.
    (b) a suitable method is lacking.
    (c) of practical concerns.
    (d) all of the above are true.

7. The temptation to attribute human thoughts, feelings, and motives to animals is called the
    (a) fallacy of overgeneralization.   (c) rattomorphic view.
    (b) anthropomorphic fallacy.   (d) cynical veterinarian syndrome.

8. Which of the following statements about using animals in research is *false*?
    (a) Psychological research may help protect endangered species.
    (b) Animal models may provide the only information on a subject.
    (c) Animals are used to discover principles which help to solve human problems.
    (d) Animals are helpful research tools, but they are substantially different from humans and the knowledge gained
        from such research cannot be applied to humans.

9. Which of the following is *not* a goal of psychology (immediate or ultimate)?
    (a) predict   (d) describe
    (b) control   (e) judge
    (c) understand   (f) gather knowledge for the benefit of humanity

10. Probably the most misunderstood goal of psychology is
    (a) control.   (c) understanding.
    (b) prediction.   (d) description.

11. Psychology is said to have a long past but a short history because
    (a) the experimental techniques used by psychologists were developed by philosophers.
    (b) introspection was not an accepted method of investigation until the early 20th century.
    (c) psychology's past includes philosophy which is hundreds of years old, whereas psychology's history is only
        about 100 years old.
    (d) the word "past" is more ambiguous in its meaning than the word "history."

12. In the history of psychology very few women were credited with accomplishments or even mentioned because
    (a) there were very few female psychologists, about one in every 100.
    (b) there were no women who were awarded doctorates.
    (c) men dominated the academic life in the late 1800s.
    (d) there were really no well-known female psychologists.

13. The first woman to be awarded a doctorate in psychology was
    (a) Ladd-Franklin.   (d) Martin.
    (b) Washburn.   (e) Navratilova.
    (c) Calkins.

14. A person who blends ideas and perspectives from different schools of thought could be called
    (a) Freudian.   (c) eclectic.
    (b) clinical.   (d) philosophical.

15. Which of the following *are not* considered to be one of the five major perspectives in modern psychology?
    (a) structuralism   (e) psychodynamic
    (b) functionalism   (f) humanism
    (c) behaviorism   (g) cognitive
    (d) Gestalt   (h) psychobiological

16. The APA professional code for psychologists does *not* stress
    (a) performing only recognized psychoanalytic therapy.
    (b) confidentiality in professional endeavors.
    (c) high moral and ethical standards.
    (d) protection of the client's welfare.

17. The largest area of specialization in psychology is
    (a) counseling.
    (b) comparative and experimental.
    (c) clinical.
    (d) industrial.

18. The greatest number of psychologists
    (a) are in private practice.
    (b) are Rolfers.
    (c) work in hospital settings.
    (d) are employed by educational institutions.

19. A recent study shows that one of the major problems with students' note taking is
    (a) most students don't review their notes on a regular basis.
    (b) students don't listen for the key points.
    (c) students try to write down what an instructor says verbatim.
    (d) students try to figure out in advance what is going to be said and write down incorrect information.

20. Which of the following is *poor* advice to follow when trying to improve scores on objective *or* essay tests?
    (a) Check for spelling and grammatical errors last.
    (b) Skip items you are uncertain about.
    (c) Don't change your answer on multiple-choice tests. Your first answer is usually correct.
    (d) Read the directions carefully.

21. Which of the following pseudo-psychologies analyzes a person's personality by studying his or her handwriting?
    (a) phrenology
    (b) palmistry
    (c) graphology
    (d) astrology

22. Which of the following is not a reason why pseudo-psychologies continue to thrive even though they have no scientific basis?
    (a) the P.T. Barnum Effect
    (b) the fallacy of positive instances
    (c) uncritical acceptance
    (d) they make good philosophical points

Can you differentiate psychologists from psychiatrists, psychoanalysts and counselors? Place an "x" in the appropriate column(s).

	1	2	3	4	5	6	7	8	9
psychologist									
psychiatrist									
psychoanalyst									
counselor									

1. first undergoes analysis before treating others
2. must have a medical degree (M.D.)
3. may teach, do research, act as a consultant to business or industry
4. has either a Ph.D. or an M.D.
5. may do psychotherapy
6. may prescribe drugs
7. exclusively uses Freudian theory
8. looks for physical causes of psychological difficulties
9. at one time limited practice to less serious adjustment problems

Matching *(Each will have more than one answer. Use the letters on the right only once.)*

_____ 1. behaviorism
_____ 2. functionalism
_____ 3. Gestalt
_____ 4. humanism
_____ 5. psychoanalytic
_____ 6. structuralism
_____ 7. cognitive
_____ 8. psychobiology

A. Freud
B. tries to explain behavior by using physical mechanisms
C. study of conscious experience
D. functions of the mind
E. the whole exceeds the sum of its parts
F. one outgrowth was behavior modification
G. goal was to develop a sort of "mental chemistry"
H. free will as opposed to determinism
I. shouldn't analyze psychological phenomena; study wholes
J. less interested in an objective, behavioral science
K.   founder wanted to make psychology more scientific
L.   centers on thinking, language, problem-solving, creativity
M. goal — to learn how thought, perception, habits, and emotions aid human adaptation
N. unconscious
O. self-image, self-evaluation, frame of reference, self-actualization
P. importance of childhood for later personality development
Q. emphasized stimulus-response relationships
R. introspection
S. computer models of thinking
T. spurred the development of industrial psychology

Fill in the Blank

1. "I am interested in behavior and how people grow and change from conception through death. I am a(n) _____ psychologist."

2. "I do psychotherapy to try to help people with emotional or behavioral disorders. I am a(n) _____ psychologist."

3. "I am interested in racism, conformity, attitudes, and in the behavior of people in groups. I am a(n) _____ psychologist."

4. "I used to study the bumps on a person's head to discover aspects of their personality. I was a _____."

5. "I am interested in improving learning and motivation in the classroom. I am a(n) _____ psychologist."

6. "I read the lines on your hand to foretell your future and evaluate your personality. I am engaged in _____."

7. "I am interested in all aspects of a person's job and work environment. I am a(n) _____
   psychologist."

8. "I am interested in how your brain and nervous system affect your behavior. I am a(n) _____
   psychologist."

9. "I learn about you and your personality by analyzing your handwriting. I am a _____ ."

10. "I am interested in questions about animal behavior. I am a(n) _____ psychologist."

11. "How do we come to know the world? I am interested in information processing. I am interested in
    _____ and _____."

12. "I apply scientific research methods to study human and animal behavior. I am a(n) _____
    psychologist."

Can You Apply the Information?

1. Which of the following is an acceptable example of behavior?
   (a) looking
   (b) daydreaming
   (c) thinking
   (d) all of these

2. Which of the following is an example of empirical evidence?
   (a) The results of a controlled experiment reveal that children who are reinforced for aggressive behavior act more aggressively.
   (b) The Methodist minister said, "After 30 years of religious study I am convinced that there is life after death."
   (c) A person argues that a seven-month-old fetus has better chance of survival if born than an eight-month-old fetus.
   (d) none of the above

3. The statement "our dog is jealous of our new iguana" reflects
   (a) the views of the functionalist school.
   (b) the anthropomorphic fallacy.
   (c) a philosophical inquiry.
   (d) a lack of humanistic concern.

4. The woman did not receive help when she was attacked because there were many potential helpers standing around. This statement best exemplifies which of the four goals of psychology?
   (a) prediction
   (b) control
   (c) understanding
   (d) description

5. The school of psychology that would probably have the *least* interest in the study of a person's experiences after being declared clinically dead would be
   (a) psychoanalytic psychology.
   (b) behaviorism.
   (c) structuralism.
   (d) humanism.

6. "I believe that a person can be motivated by unconscious forces but also that one strives for self-actualization. I am using behavior modification to help a student who suffers from overwhelming test anxiety. I see myself as _____."
   (a) a humanist
   (b) psychoanalytically oriented
   (c) a behaviorist
   (d) eclectic

7. The psychotherapist *most* likely to be interested in the repressed aspects of your toilet training would be a
   (a) psychologist.
   (c) psychoanalyst.
   (b) psychiatrist.
   (d) gestalt therapist.

8. Which of the following is the *best* example of "basic" research?
   (a) a study of the aerodynamic characteristics of a car being designed for maximum gas mileage
   (b) the effects of differing levels of high density lipoproteins on the recurrence of heart attacks
   (c) the effect of immediate versus delayed feedback of test results on student performance
   (d) the effect of lysergic acid diethylamide (LSD) on the Asiatic elephant

9. The "Learning Checks" in your text serve what purpose in the SQ3R method?
   (a) review
   (c) question
   (b) read
   (d) recite

10. Ralph wants to make his study habits more productive. Which of the following would best help him?
    (a) quit studying on his bed where he sleeps and sometimes eats
    (b) study for longer stretches of time with fewer breaks which interrupt his concentration
    (c) once something is learned, quit studying it because this may lead to confusion
    (d) quit asking himself questions over the material which may be nothing like what the test questions will be

11. The headlines in the tabloid claim that an airplane missing since 1942 has just landed and that it contained the skeletal remains of all of the passengers and crew. Which among the following questions would be *least* appropriate to ask regarding this claim?
    (a) Has any other independent researcher or observer verified the claim?
    (b) How many people were supposedly on board?
    (c) What claim is being made?
    (d) How much credence can the claim be given?

Chapter Review

1. One reason for studying psychology is that you can hardly consider yourself _____ without knowing something about the field. Another reason is so we can know _____ better.

2. Psychology is the _____ study of _____ and _____ behavior.

3. Running, thinking, laughing, and learning are all examples of _____. Hidden behaviors are called _____, and visible behaviors are called _____.

4. Evidence gained by direct observation and measurement is said to be _____. Whenever possible, psychologists settle differences by collecting _____.

5. Psychology became a science when psychologists began to perform _____, make _____, and seek _____. What sets psychology apart from other fields is that it applies the _____ method to questions about _____.

6. The study of some topics in psychology is difficult. Many psychological questions may remain unanswered because of _____ or _____ concerns. More frequently, there is just the lack of a suitable _____.

7. The _____ fallacy is the tendency to attribute human thoughts, feelings, and motives to animals. Animals are used in experiments to discover _____ that help solve human problems. Also, they sometimes serve as _____ to provide the only information on a subject. Behavioral research has provided ways to avoid the _____ of animals. Such research has also aided the successful care of _____ species.

8. The goals of psychology are to _____, _____, _____, and _____ behavior. Its ultimate goal is to gather _____ for the benefit of _____. One of psychology's goals, _____ behavior, is satisfied when we explain _____ a phenomenon occurs.

9. _____, another goal, is rarely as precise as it is in other sciences like chemistry.

10. _____ is the goal of psychology that is frequently questioned and misunderstood probably because it sounds like a threat to personal _____. To most psychologists, it simply means altering _____ that influence behavior in predictable ways.

11. Psychology's past is long because it includes _____ which is centuries old. Psychology's history is short. It began in the year _____ in _____, Germany. There _____ established the first psychological laboratory. He is considered the "father of psychology." He wanted to study _____ _____ by analyzing it into basic elements. To do this he developed an investigative method known as _____. The method unfortunately could not answer psychological questions if two people disagreed. His ideas eventually served as the basis of the school of psychology known as _____, because they dealt with the structure of mental life.

12. James is associated with the _____ school of psychology. He was interested in how the mind _____ to adapt us to changing demands. The functionalists sought to learn the ways in which thought, perception, habits, and emotions aid human _____. Functionalism had a direct impact on the development of _____ and _____ psychology.

13. Watson is associated with the _____ school of psychology. He considered introspection _____. He placed much importance on the relationship between _____ and an organism's _____. As a means of explaining most behavior, Watson adopted Pavlov's concept, the _____ _____.

14. One of the most widely known and influential modern behaviorists was _____. He believed that behavior is shaped and maintained by its _____. He emphasized stimulus-response relationships and ignored _____ and _____ experience. In fact, he thought that the mind could not be studied _____. To counter such a view, _____ behaviorism combines thinking and environmental control to explain behavior. A particularly valuable product of behaviorism is a form of therapy called _____ _____ which is based on learning principles.

15. There were _____ women in psychology in its early years largely because men _____ academic life in the late 1800s. Today for every 100 doctorates awarded in psychology, roughly _____ will be awarded to women. The first woman to be awarded a doctorate in psychology was Margaret _____.

16. The German word _____ means form, pattern or whole. This school of psychology, founded by _____, sought to study experience as _____. These psychologists differed from the structuralists who sought to analyze or break down conscious experience. This viewpoint is particularly influential in the areas of _____ and _____.

17. _____ psychology was established by Freud. According to him, many areas of thoughts, conflicts, and desires are unknown to us and are termed _____. He also maintained that personality development was greatly influenced by a person's _____. The method of psychotherapy that he developed was called _____. His fourth major contribution was his insistence that all actions are _____. This school of psychology today is more commonly referred to as _____ psychology. It focuses on the internal _____, _____, and _____ forces that influence our behavior.

18. The school of psychology that was developed to counter the negativity of behaviorism and psychoanalysis was _____. Two of its major proponents have been _____ and _____. This school of psychology rejects the Freudian idea of the _____ and the behavioristic idea that people are controlled by the _____. This school emphasizes the human ability to make choices, the concept of _____ _____. This concept is the opposite of _____ which holds that behavior is largely determined by forces beyond our control. This school is less interested in attempts to treat psychology as an _____, _____ science. According to this school all humans have a need for _____ - _____, the need to develop to our fullest _____.

19. If a psychologist is not loyal to just one theoretical viewpoint but draws from many theories, he or she can be called _____. The five major perspectives evident in psychology today are the _____, _____, _____, _____, and _____ views. _____ psychologists study thoughts, language, consciousness, etc. _____ believe that eventually we will be able to explain all behavior by reducing it to _____ mechanisms.

20. The label "_____" refers to a person who has master's degree or a doctorate in his or her specific discipline. A _____ must have a medical degree. If both of these people are providing psychotherapy, the former is probably a _____ _____. The latter is trained to look for the _____ causes of psychological disorders.

21. A _____ has to have either an M.D. or a Ph.D. and has been extensively trained in _____ theories. To be a _____, a person must typically have a _____ degree. At one time these professionals handled _____ problems that did not involve serious mental disorder. Today however, the distinctions between them and _____ psychologists is becoming blurred because they are both doing psychotherapy.

22. The professional code for psychologists established by the APA stresses high levels of _____ and _____, high _____ and _____ standards, _____ in professional work and _____ of the client's welfare.

23. The largest subareas of specialization in the field of psychology are _____ and _____, but more psychologists are employed by _____ institutions than any other single employer.

24. Research that is performed just for the sake of knowledge is termed _____. However, if the information gained from the research is to be put to immediate use the research is called _____.

25. A(n) _____ or a(n) _____ psychologist does psychotherapy. Psychologists who are interested in basic questions about animal behavior are called _____ psychologists. Investigating how people grow and change over time would make a person a(n) _____ psychologist.

26. If you believe that all other areas of psychology will ultimately be explained by reference to the action of nerve cells or parts of the brain you are probably a(n) _____ psychologist.

27. _____ psychologists are interested in people in a group setting. A(n) _____ psychologist would be interested in the improvement of the work environment and in the selection, evaluation, and training of job applicants.

28. "I am interested in detecting and treating learning disabilities, counseling students with vocational or emotional concerns, and improving learning and motivation in the classroom. I am a(n) _____ psychologist."

29. A(n) _____ psychologist applies scientific research methods to study human and animal behavior.

30. SQ3R stands for _____, _____, _____, _____, and _____. The textbook is organized around this method.

31. Effective note-taking requires _____ _____. To use your notes most effectively you should _____ them _____.

32. To make study habits more productive you should study in a _____ _____ and do nothing else there, use _____ practice, try memory aids such as _____, _____ yourself, and be sure to _____ the material beyond bare mastery.

33. Many students procrastinate because they equate school performance and _____ _____ or because they tend to be _____ and expect the impossible from themselves and thus end up with all-or-nothing work habits. Procrastination can be lessened by better _____ _____ and more effective _____ _____.

34. On objective tests, one should _____ the directions carefully and read all of the possible _____ before selecting one. You should _____ items you are unsure about and _____ certain alternatives. Be sure to answer every question unless there is a penalty for guessing. _____ your answer if you feel you need to.

35. On essay tests, one should also _____ the directions carefully, think about your _____ before beginning writing, get to the _____, and then _____ over your paper for grammatical and spelling mistakes.

36. Critical thinking refers to the ability to _____, _____, _____, _____, and _____ information. One should consider _____ claims are being made, what _____ has been made, _____ performed it, how good was it, and can they be _____ . How _____ are the investigators, do their findings appear to be _____, and how much _____ can the claim be given?

37. _____ - _____ are dubious and unfounded systems superficially resembling psychology. _____ claims that lines in the hand are indicators of personality and a person's future.

38. _____ is the theory of personality based upon the location of bumps on the _____. Brain research revealed that many areas listed as controlling one characteristic were actually responsible for something drastically different.

39. Despite the fact that it scores close to zero on tests of accuracy in rating personality, handwriting analysis or _____ is used in this country to evaluate job applicants by over 500 companies.

40. _____ is based on the assumption that the position of the stars and planets at the moment of a person's birth determines personality characteristics. It has been repeatedly shown to have no scientific _____ .

41. Pseudo-psychologies continue to survive and be popular because of _____ _____ by people, the fallacy of _____ _____, and the _____ _____ _____ Effect.

42. The _____ of _____ _____ occurs when a person tends to remember or notice things that confirm his or her expectations and to forget the rest.

43. The _____ _____ _____ _____ is a personality description written in such vague generalities that everybody can find something in it to believe.

ANSWER KEYS

Do You Know the Information?

Multiple Choice

1. (a) obj. 1, p. 1
2. (c) obj. 2, p. 2
3. (b) obj. 3, p. 2
4. (c) obj. 4, p. 2
5. (a) obj. 5, p. 3
6. (d) obj. 6, p. 5
7. (b) obj. 7, p. 5
8. (d) obj. 7, p. 6
9. (e) obj. 8, p. 6
10. (a) obj. 8, p. 6
11. (c) obj. 9, p. 7
12. (c) obj. 13, p. 11

13. (b) obj. 13, p. 11
14. (c) obj. 17, p. 13
15. (a,b,d) obj. 18, p. 13
16. (a) obj. 20, p. 16
17. (c) obj. 21, p. 16

18. (d) obj. 21, p. 16
19. (a) obj. 25, p. 20
20. (c) objs. 28-29, p. 22
21. (c) obj. 31, p. 26
22. (d) obj. 32, pp. 26-27

	1	2	3	4	5	6	7	8	9
psychologist			X		X				
psychiatrist		X	X		X	X		X	
psychoanalyst	X		X	X	X	X	X		
counselor			X		X				X

obj. 19, pp. 14-15

Matching

1. F,K,Q; obj. 12, p. 9
2. D,M,T; obj. 11, p. 8
3. E,I; obj. 14, p. 10
4. H,J,O; obj. 16, p. 12
5. A,N,P; obj. 15, pp. 11-12
6. C,G,R; obj. 10, p. 7
7. L,S; obj. 18, p. 13
8. B; obj. 18, p. 13

Can You Apply the Information?

1. (d) obj. 3, p. 2
2. (a) obj. 4, p. 2
3. (b) obj. 7, p. 5
4. (c) obj. 8, p. 6
5. (b) objs. 10-16, pp. 7-12
6. (d) obj. 17, p. 13
7. (c) obj. 19, pp. 11-14
8. (d) obj. 22, p. 16
9. (d) obj. 24, p. 19
10. (a) obj. 26, p. 20
11. (b) obj. 30, p. 24

Fill in the Blank

1. developmental; obj. 23, p. 17
2. counseling or clinical; obj. 23, p. 15
3. social; obj. 23, p. 17
4. phrenologist; obj. 31, p. 25
5. school or educational; obj. 23, p. 15
6. palmistry; obj. 31, p. 25
7. industrial; obj. 23, p. 15
8. physiological; obj. 23, p. 17
9. graphologist; obj. 31, p. 26
10. comparative; obj. 23, p. 17
11. sensation, perception; obj. 23, p. 17
12. experimental; obj. 23, p. 15

Chapter Review

1. educated, ourselves (p. 1)
2. scientific, human, animal (p. 2)
3. behavior, covert, overt (p. 2)
4. empirical, data (p. 2)
5. experiments, observations, evidence, scientific, behavior (p. 3)
6. ethical, practical, method (p. 4)
7. anthropomorphic (p. 5); principles, models, killing, endangered (p. 6)
8. describe, understand, predict, control, knowledge, humanity, understanding, why (p. 6)
9. Prediction (p. 6)
10. Control, freedom, conditions, (p. 6)
11. philosophy, 1879, Leipzig, Wundt, conscious experience, introspection, structuralism (p. 7)
12. functionalist, functions, adaptation, educational, industrial (p. 8)
13. behaviorist, unscientific, stimuli, responses, conditioned response (p. 9)
14. Skinner, consequences (p. 9); thought, private, scientifically, cognitive, behavior modification (p. 10)
15. few, dominated, 50, Washburn (p. 11)
16. Gestalt, Wertheimer, wholes, perception, personality (p. 10)
17. Psychoanalytic, unconscious (p. 11); childhood, psychoanalysis, determined, psychodynamic, motives, conflicts, unconscious (p. 12)
18. humanism, Maslow, Rogers, unconscious, environment, free will, determinism, objective, behavioral, self-actualization, potential (p. 12)
19. eclectic, behavioristic, humanistic, psychodynamic, cognitive, psychobiological, Cognitive, Psychobiologists, physical (p. 13)
20. psychologist, psychiatrist, clinical psychologist, physical (p. 14)

21.   psychoanalyst, Freudian, counselor, master's, adjustment, clinical (p. 15)
22.   competence, responsibility, moral, ethical, confidentiality, protection (p. 16)
23.   clinical, counseling, educational (p. 16)
24.   basic, applied (p. 16)
25.   clinical, counseling (p. 16); comparative, developmental (p. 17)
26.   physiological (p. 17)
27.   Social(p. 17); industrial (p. 15)
28.   school (p. 15)
29.   experimental (p. 15)
30.   survey, question, read, recite, review (p. 18)
31.   active listening, review, periodically (p. 20)
32.   specific place, spaced (p. 20); mnemonics, test, overlearn (p. 21)
33.   personal worth, perfectionistic, study habits, time management (p. 21)
34.   read, alternatives, skip, eliminate, change (p. 22)
35.   read, answer, point, check (p. 22)
36.   evaluate, compare, analyze, critique, synthesize, what, test, who, repeated, trustworthy (reliable), objective, (p. 24); credence (p. 25)
37.   Pseudo-psychologies, Palmistry (p. 25)
38.   Phrenology, skull (p. 25)
39.   graphology (p. 26)
40.   Astrology, validity (p. 26)
41.   uncritical acceptance (p. 26); positive instances, P.T. Barnum (p. 27)
42.   fallacy, positive instances (p. 27)
43.   P.T. Barnum Effect (p. 27)

Chapter 2

Research Methods in Psychology

KEY TERMS AND CONCEPTS

the fallacy of common sense
scientific method
   hypothesis
   operational definition
naturalistic observation
   observer effect and observer bias
correlational study
   coefficient of correlation
   causal relationship
experiment
   independent, dependent, & extraneous variables
   experimental and control groups
     random assignment
   field experiment

statistical significance
replicability
placebo effect
endorphins
single and double blind arrangements
experimenter effect
self-fulfilling prophecy
clinical method, case study
survey method
   representative sample
   courtesy bias
critical reading of the popular press
ethics of research
using animals in research

LEARNING OBJECTIVES

To demonstrate mastery of this chapter you should be able to:

1. Explain the problem with using common sense as a source of information.

2. List the five steps of the scientific method.
   a.   d.

   b.   e.

   c.

3. Define the term "hypothesis" and be able to identify one. Explain what an operational definition is.

4.   Explain the purpose of theory formulation.

5.   Describe the technique of naturalistic observation including both the advantages and limitations of this method. Include the terms observer effect and observer bias.

6.   Describe what a correlational study is and list three advantages and disadvantages of such a method. Explain what a correlation coefficient is, how it is expressed, what it means, and how it is related to causation.

7.   List and describe the three variables in the experimental method.
      a.

      b.

      c.

8.   Explain the nature and the purpose of the control group and the experimental group in an experiment.

9.   Explain the purpose of randomly assigning subjects to either the control or the experimental group.

10.   Identify three advantages and two disadvantages of the experimental method.

         advantages   *disadvantages*

   a.   a.

   b.   b.

   c.

11.   Explain the purpose of the field experiment.

12.   Explain what statistically significant results are.

13.   Explain why replicability is so important in science.

14.   Explain what a placebo is, how effective it is, how it probably works, and what its purpose in an experiment is.

15.   Explain what single-blind and double-blind experimental arrangements are.

16.   Explain the nature of the experimenter effect and how it is related to the self-fulfilling prophecy.

17.   Briefly describe the clinical method of research including two advantages and three disadvantages. Give an example of a case in which the clinical method would be used.

18.   Briefly describe the survey method of investigation including an advantage and a disadvantage. Define the term "courtesy bias."

* * * * * * * * *

The following objectives are related to the material in the "Applications" and "Exploration" sections of your text.

19.   List seven suggestions that your author gives to help you become a more critical reader of psychological information in the popular press.

a.

b.

c.

d.

e.

f.

g.

20.   List and describe the three areas of ethical concern in psychological experiments, and explain the position of the APA in terms of ethical guidelines.

a.

b.

c.

21.   Briefly describe the polarity that exists in the debate concerning animal research. Describe the middle ground of the debate.

SELF-QUIZZES

Do You Know the Information?

Multiple Choice

1. Common sense is often a very poor source of information because
    (a) most of the pseudo-psychologies rely on it.
    (b) it was the very reason for the beginning of the scientific revolution.
    (c) it can prevent people from seeking better information or seeing the truth.
    (d) of all of the above.

2. Which of the following is *not* one of the steps of the scientific method?
    (a) experimentation   (c) hypothesizing
    (b) inference   (d) defining the problem

3. A hypothesis
    (a) is a guess that has been tested.   (c) proves or disproves a correlation.
    (b) is like a theory.   (d) is a tentative explanation of an event.

4. Without theory formulation
    (a) research would yield a mass of disconnected observations.
    (b) experiments could not be conducted.
    (c) hypotheses would be useless.
    (d) experiments would be useless.

5. If a researcher is taking copious notes while watching her subject behave in its own environment the researcher is probably engaged in
    (a) a survey.   (c) computing a correlation coefficient.
    (b) the experimental method.   (d) naturalistic observation.

6. The observer effect occurs when
    (a) a subject's behavior is changed because of an awareness of being observed.
    (b) observers see only what they expect to see.
    (c) observational records are objectively biased by the observer.
    (d) fewer questions than expected are stimulated.

7. An advantage of the naturalistic observation method of study is
    (a) the causes of an observed behavior can be determined.
    (b) the subject is studied in its customary environment.
    (c) powerful controlled observations can be made.
    (d) information regarding large numbers of subjects can be gathered.

8. A coefficient of correlation is a number which
    (a) expresses the degree and nature of the relationship between two events.
    (b) shows the degree to which one event causes another.
    (c) indicates the extent of control in the experimental method.
    (d) is frequently used when doing a case study.

9.   In the experimental method the variable which is manipulated is the
     (a) dependent variable.
     (b) variable that is "tried" on the control group.
     (c) independent variable.
     (d) extraneous variable.

10. Outside variables which can contaminate an experiment and which the researcher wishes to remove are called
     (a) controlled.
     (b) random.
     (c) extraneous.
     (d) artificial.

11. The purpose of the control group in the experimental method is to
     (a) be subjected to the independent variable.
     (b) serve as a point of reference to which to compare the experimental group.
     (c) be manipulated by receiving the dependent variable.
     (d) allow surveys to be taken.

12. In order to control differences in personal characteristics of subjects in the control and experimental groups that could influence the outcome of the experiment
     (a) all of the relevant characteristics of the subjects are controlled by testing and then the subjects are divided equally into the two groups by characteristics.
     (b) the researcher hand picks each subject and uses very large groups.
     (c) more than one experimental group is used.
     (d) subjects are randomly assigned to each group.

13. The experimental method may be criticized as a research technique because it
     (a) involves too many variables.
     (b) often appears artificial.
     (c) may involve observation.
     (d) all of the above.

14. Statistically significant results are
     (a) less likely to occur in field experiments than in a laboratory.
     (b) likely to occur in about 5 experiments out of 100.
     (c) those in which differences in the groups would be unlikely to occur by chance alone.
     (d) the only ones reported in psychology journals.

15. A key element in the scientific pursuit of truth is the
     (a) random assignment of variables.
     (b) ability to make critical judgments.
     (c) correlational method combined with observation.
     (d) ability to replicate observations or experiments.

16. In an experiment to test the effects of a drug, the control group is given a placebo
     (a) so that each group will be exactly alike except for the drug.
     (b) because the experimental group has been given a placebo plus the drug.
     (c) to test the effect of the dependent variable.
     (d) to control for a single-blind design.

17. A double-blind research design is used to
     (a) control for the experimenter effect.
     (b) insure that the experimenter does not influence the subjects.
     (c) control for the placebo effect.
     (d) do all of the above.

18. If subjects in a psychological experiment respond to subtle cues from the experimenter about what is expected of them, this is called
     (a) cue-dependent submission.
     (b) experimental expectation.
     (c) the experimenter effect.
     (d) cheating.

19. In order to take advantage of situations where important information can be gathered about topics that could not be studied any other way, which method of investigation would be employed?
    (a) clinical
    (b) naturalistic observation
    (c) survey
    (d) experimental

20. The research methods in which little control is possible are
    (a) survey, naturalistic observation, clinical.
    (b) correlational, experimental, survey.
    (c) naturalistic observation, correlational, survey.
    (d) correlational, clinical, naturalistic observation.

21. The method of investigation which is designed for the gathering of information from large numbers of people is
    (a) the experimental method.
    (b) naturalistic observation.
    (c) the survey method.
    (d) the clinical method.

22. In order to be able to distinguish the difference between wishful thinking and science, an informed reader should
    (a) discriminate between inference and observation.
    (b) look for errors in distinguishing between correlation and causation.
    (c) be skeptical.
    (d) pay attention to all of the above.

23. Ethical or moral questions raised by certain psychological research
    (a) have largely gone unanswered.
    (b) have produced a spate of laws sponsored by the Department of Health, Education and Welfare.
    (c) prompted the APA to adopt research guidelines.
    (d) have been deemed to be irrelevant because of the pursuit of knowledge.

24. The more moderate view of the role of animals in research includes which of the following positions?
    (a) Animals should never be purposely killed in the conduct of an experiment.
    (b) Human welfare should take precedence over that of animals.
    (c) Animal research is necessary at times, but they should always be humanely treated.
    (d) Ronald McDonald should be tarred, feathered, and driven out of town in a cattle truck.

True-False

_____ 1. The accuracy of any naturalistic observation may be diminished because the observer may report biased observations.

_____ 2. Coefficients of correlation vary between 0 and +1.

_____ 3. A correlational study is one that determines the degree of correlation between two traits or behaviors.

_____ 4. Correlation does not prove causation because by its very nature correlation can only show that two events are related.

_____ 5. One advantage of the experimental method is that causal relationships can be identified.

_____ 6. Many researchers feel that a major disadvantage of the experimental method is that there are too many controls.

_____ 7. The survey method is the method used to bridge the gap between the artificiality of the lab and the real world.

_____ 8.   A placebo is a substance which has no direct chemical effect itself.

_____ 9.   Research indicates that placebos do nothing physically; the effect of the placebo is imaginary.

_____10.   The way a sample is chosen can either make or break a survey.

_____11.   Since most surveys primarily measure attitudes, it is essential that the information gathered be truthful.

Can You Apply the Information?

1.   George's dog Gus wandered away from home. This disturbed George so he decided to try to find a way to teach Gus a lesson. The next time Gus wandered away George called and called his name. Finally Gus came to George who was waiting with a rolled up newspaper. George smacked Gus a couple of times and said, "That'll teach you not to wander away again!" The next time Gus got out and wandered away George could not coax him home by calling but had to go out and find him. The dog no longer responded to George's calling. (Smart dog!) George's plan was an example of
(a) using naturalistic observation.   (c) using common sense.
(b) problem solving by correlation.   (d) reverse psychology.

2.   You are a psychologist and have been conducting research on aggression in children. Your studies have focused on modeling and aggression, the effects of TV on aggression, and the effects of punishment on aggression. You have performed many studies and have collected much data but you feel as if there is no unifying idea in all your data. You can't see the proverbial forest because of the trees. According to the scientific method your next step would probably be to
(a) develop a theory.   (c) conduct research on one specific idea.
(b) propose a different, totally new hypothesis.   (d) give up and have a good cry.

3.   George pondered, "I'll bet if I reward instead of punish Gus when he responds to my call, he'll begin to respond faster and more often." George's statement is an example of
(a) an observation.   (c) defining the problem.
(b) a theory.   (d) a hypothesis.

For questions 4-7, choose the letter of the research technique from the list below which would most effectively give you answers to each question.

(a) naturalistic observation   (d) clinical method
(b) correlational method   (e) survey method
(c) experimental method

_____ 4.   You are a doctor interested in the gastrointestinal tract. You have the opportunity to observe a person whose surgeon did a poor job repairing a gunshot wound to the stomach. The patient was left with a fistula (a hole from a hollow organ to the surface of the body). What does the process of human digestion in the stomach really look like?

_____ 5.   Is there any relationship between unemployment and the number of admissions to psychiatric hospitals?

_____ 6.   What kinds of breakfasts are eaten by lower, middle, and upper income families?

_____ 7.   Does eating breakfast enable children to do better in school?

8. This is your first trip with the Lewis and Clark expedition to explore and map portions of the U.S. One day your party hears thunder and you overhear the person next to you say, "Ugh! I hate rain. Rain causes mosquitoes. Whenever it rains we start getting more mosquitoes." You laugh to yourself because
   (a) the person obviously has used the clinical method instead of observation.
   (b) this is an example of confusing causation and correlation.
   (c) there are too many extraneous variables to draw a valid conclusion.
   (d) his observation was caused by the self-fulfilling prophecy.

9. A researcher notes that the amount of ice cream consumed and the number of drownings are correlated +.66. The researcher may conclude that
   (a) as the amount of ice cream consumed decreases, the number of drownings also decreases.
   (b) ice cream causes people to drown.
   (c) as the amount of ice cream consumed increases, the number of drownings decreases.
   (d) there is very little relationship between ice cream and drownings.

10. In an experiment involving the effects of certain kinds of practice on the acquisition of piano-playing skill, the researcher is worried that one student may have certain advantages over another. To control for some of these advantages (such as age, sex, previous musical training, manual dexterity, and pitch discrimination) the researcher has each student fill out a detailed questionnaire so that each group can be made roughly comparable to the others. The researcher
    (a) appears to have thought of most of the important extraneous variables.
    (b) can't do this type of research on this problem.
    (c) should use naturalistic observation.
    (d) needs to use random assignment of groups instead.

11. You are a physician and have a patient with chronic, intractable pain. The patient is rapidly becoming addicted to the morphine derivative that you have prescribed. Which of the following statements is most applicable?
    (a) The pain is most likely psychosomatic.
    (b) A fourth surgical procedure is definitely indicated.
    (c) Send the patient to a psychotherapist.
    (d) This might be a good time to try a placebo.

For questions 12-20, use the following paragraph as a basis:

Children who watch an aggressive program on television are more aggressive in free play than children who do not watch the aggressive program. In this experiment eighty 6-year-old children are randomly assigned to two groups. One group watches a 30 minute program that has been previously rated as aggressive. The other group watches a 30 minute program that has been previously rated as unaggressive. Both groups of children are then observed through a one-way mirror in a lab for 15 minutes of free play. The number of aggressive acts (which have been previously operationally defined) is counted.

Using the above paragraph place the correct letter from the following in the appropriate blank.
(a) experimental group   (d) independent variable
(b) dependent variable   (e) control group
(c) hypothesis   (f) extraneous variable

_____12. number of observed aggressive acts

_____13. watched unaggressive television program

_____14. aggressive TV program

_____15. Children who view aggressive TV are more aggressive than children who view nonaggressive TV.

_____16. viewed aggressive TV show

_____17. amount of time the TV is watched

18. This is an example of
    (a) a field experiment.
    (b) a controlled experiment.
    (c) naturalistic observation.
    (d) a clinical study.

19. If the researcher knew which children had seen the aggressive TV program, this could serve as the basis for
    (a) the experimenter effect.
    (b) a negative correlation.
    (c) the placebo effect.
    (d) the dependent measure.

20. In order to minimize bias
    (a) the person observing the children should administer the independent variable.
    (b) one group of children should listen to taped violence.
    (c) the observer measuring the dependent variable should not know which group each child was in.
    (d) the children should understand the hypothesis.

Chapter Review

1. We can be prevented from seeking better information or seeing the truth by a set of blinders called
   _____ _____. As an alternative to this and to avoid faulty observa-
   tions, many scientists make use of the _____ method. This method ideally includes the
   following steps:
   (a) _____
   (b) _____ _____ _____
   (c) _____ _____ _____
   (d) _____
   (e) _____ _____

2. A _____ is a description or explanation of an event or observation that is tentative
   because it has not yet been adequately tested. _____ definitions state the exact procedures used to represent a concept. They are important because they allow _____
   concepts to be tested in "real world" terms.

3. In order to summarize a large number of observations in a way that accounts for existing data, predicts new
   observations, and guides further research, psychologists formulate _____. Good
   ones should be _____.

4. _____ _____ involves studying subjects in their
   customary environment. One of the advantages of this research method is that the behavior of the subject is
   observed in a _____ _____. One disadvantage is that the presence of an
   _____ may change the behavior of the _____. This is called the
   _____ effect. In addition, the observer may be _____, and it is difficult to
   determine the _____ of the observed events.

5. A _____ study is one that determines the degree of relationship between two traits, behaviors, or events. This type of study can be done in the _____ or in the _____ _____ and it allows for _____. On the negative side, little or no _____ is possible, relationships may be _____, and a researcher cannot confirm _____-_____ relationships.

6. Coefficients of correlation vary between _____ and _____. If the number is _____ or close to it, there is a weak or nonexistent relationship. A positive correlation would be a number above _____ and indicates that _____ in one measure are matched by _____ in the other. In a negative correlation, _____ in the first measure are associated with _____ in the second, and vice versa. Correlational studies help us discover _____, but correlation does not demonstrate _____.

7. To identify cause-effect relationships an _____ must be conducted. The three variables are the _____, _____, and _____ variables. The variable which is manipulated, applied or changed by the experimenter is the _____ variable. Measures of the outcome of the experiment are called _____ variables. _____ variables are not allowed to affect the outcome of the experiment by making the conditions the same for both groups.

8. In the simplest psychological experiment there are two groups of subjects. The _____ group and the _____ group are treated exactly alike except for the _____ variable. The _____ group is exposed to this variable and the _____ group is used to establish a point of reference to which to compare the other group. Subjects are assigned to each group _____ so that each subject has an equal chance of being a member of either group. This helps ensure that subject differences are balanced across the two groups.

9. The experimental method is advantageous because it allows you to establish _____ and because everything but the independent variable is _____. Also, there is no need to wait for the _____ event to occur. On the negative side, the experimental method is somewhat _____. Some _____ behavior is not easily studied in the lab. This criticism may be overcome by conducting a _____ experiment.

10. When a difference like that observed between the experimental and control groups would occur very rarely by chance alone, the results of such experiments are called _____ _____. A key element in the scientific pursuit of truth is the ability to _____ observations or experiments.

11. A substance which is basically inert but has a tremendous psychological impact is called a _____. The effect of the _____ is not imaginary because experiments have shown that pain-killing, opiate-like drugs are released in the _____. A _____ is used in an experiment to insure that both groups are treated exactly alike except for the _____ variable.

12. A psychologist is doing research on a drug that is usually given in injection form. To control for the effect of the injection itself (the _____ effect) all subjects would be given an _____. Thus the subjects do not know who received the drug. This experimental technique is known as _____-_____ arrangement and it controls for the _____ effect. The control group would be given the _____ and the experimental group would be given the _____. Thus the subjects would all be _____ as to who actually received the drug.

13.   If the experimenter is also _____ as to who actually received the drug, this would be a _____ - _____ arrangement. This arrangement prevents the experimenter from consciously or unconsciously influencing the subjects' reactions which is called the _____ effect. When a prediction is made that influences the course of events toward fulfilling that prediction, the _____-_____ _____ has occurred.

14.   If a clinical psychologist conducts an in-depth interview with a person to learn as much as possible about the person's background, the psychologist is using the _____ method of investigation. One problem with this research method is that there is little possibility of _____. Another problem is that the researcher may not make _____ interpretations.

15.   A researcher interested in how large segments of the general population feel about the issue of abortion would be likely to use the _____ method of investigation. It is very important when using this method to make sure that the sample of people questioned is _____. Sometimes this method may not be very _____. An example of this is when people show a _____ bias, the tendency to give answers which are agreeable and socially acceptable.

16.   There is much that can be learned from the popular press about psychology. However, much is written that is not scientific, and appears to be based on wishful thinking. One way to discriminate science from half-truths in the popular press is to be a(n) _____ reader. One should also consider the _____ of the information. If an experiment was discussed, a wise reader should be sure to look for a _____ group.

17.   Two more suggestions for being a more critical reader of the popular press are look for errors in distinguishing between _____ and causation, and be sure to distinguish between observation and _____. It is also important for the informed reader to be aware of _____ and to remember that the phrase "_____ _____" is no guarantee of proof.

18.   There are three areas of ethical concern that anyone conducting psychological research should be sensitive to: the use of _____, invasion of _____, and lasting _____ to participants. In response to these concerns the American Psychological Association has adopted guidelines which stress _____ for the people who participate and concern for their _____ and _____.

19.   The argument concerning using animals in research contains diametrically opposite views. The more moderate position holds that animals are necessary in some research, but their use should be _____ and they should be treated _____.

ANSWER KEYS

Do You Know the Information?

Can You Apply the Information?

Multiple Choice

1. (c) obj. 1, p. 30
2. (b) obj. 2, p. 31
3. (d) obj. 3, p. 31
4. (a) obj. 4, p. 32
5. (d) obj. 5, p. 33
6. (a) obj. 5, p. 33
7. (b) obj. 5, pp. 33, 43
8. (a) obj. 6, p. 34
9. (c) obj. 7, p. 37
10. (c) obj. 7, p. 37
11. (b) obj. 8, p. 37
12. (d) obj. 9, p. 37
13. (b) obj. 10, pp. 37, 43
14. (c) obj. 12, p. 38
15. (d) obj. 13, p. 39
16. (a) obj. 14, pp. 39-40
17. (d) obj. 15, p. 40
18. (c) obj. 16, p. 40

19. (a) obj. 17, p. 41
20. (d) objs. 5,6,17, p. 43
21. (c) obj. 18, p. 42
22. (d) obj. 19, p. 46
23. (c) obj. 20, p. 48
24. (c) obj. 21, p. 49

True-False

1. T, obj. 5, pp. 33, 43
2. F, obj. 6, p. 34
3. T, obj. 6, p. 34
4. T, obj. 6, p. 34
5. T, obj. 10, pp. 38, 43
6. F, obj. 10, pp. 38, 43
7. F, obj. 11, pp. 38, 43
8. T, obj. 14, p. 40
9. F, obj. 14, p. 40
10. T, obj. 18, pp. 40-42
11. F, obj. 18, p. 42

1. (c) obj. 1, p. 30
2. (a) objs. 2,4, pp. 31-32
3. (d) obj. 3, p. 31
4. (d) obj. 17, p. 41
5. (b) obj. 6, p. 34
6. (e) obj. 18, p. 42
7. (c) objs. 7-8, pp. 37-39
8. (b) obj. 6, p. 34
9. (a) obj. 6, p. 34
10. (d) obj. 9, p. 37
11. (d) obj. 14, p. 40
12. (b) obj. 7, p. 37
13. (e) obj. 8, p. 37
14. (d) obj. 7, p. 37
15. (c) obj. 3, p. 31
16. (a) obj. 8, p. 37
17. (f) obj. 7, p. 37
18. (b) obj. 11, p. 39
19. (a) obj. 16, p. 40
20. (c) objs. 15-16, p. 40

Chapter Review

1. common sense (p. 30); scientific, observation, defining a problem, formulating a hypothesis, experimentation, theory formulation (p. 31)
2. hypothesis, Operational (p. 31;) abstract (p. 32)
3. theories, falsifiable (p. 32)
4. Naturalistic observation, natural setting, observer, observed, observer, biased (p. 33); causes (p. 43)
5. correlational, lab, natural environment, prediction (p. 34); control, coincidental, cause-effect (p. 43)
6. +1, -1, 0, 0, increases (decreases), increases (decreases), increases, decreases, relationships, causation (p. 34)
7. experiment, independent, dependent, extraneous, independent, dependent, Extraneous (p. 37)
8. experimental, control, independent, experimental, control, randomly (p. 37)
9. causation, controlled (p. 37); natural, artificial, natural, field (p. 43)
10. statistically significant (p. 38); replicate (p. 39)
11. placebo, placebo, brain, placebo, independent (p. 40)
12. placebo, injection, single-blind, placebo, placebo, drug, blind (p. 40)
13. blind, double-blind, experimenter, self-fulfilling prophecy (p. 40)
14. clinical (case study) (p. 41); control, objective (p. 43)
15. survey, representative (p. 42); accurate, courtesy (p. 43)
16. skeptical (informed), source, control (p. 44)
17. correlation, inference (p. 46); oversimplifications, for example (p. 47)
18. deception, privacy, harm, respect, dignity, welfare (p. 48)
19. minimized, humanely (p. 49)

Chapter 3

The Brain, Biology, and Behavior

KEY TERMS AND CONCEPTS

biopsychology
neuron
  dendrite, soma, axon, axon terminals
  action potential
  ion, ion channel
  threshold
    all-or-nothing event
myelin
neurotransmitter
  synapse
neuropeptides
  enkephalins, endorphins
neuron vs. nerve
neurilemma
brain grafts
central nervous system
peripheral nervous system
  somatic system
  autonomic system
    sympathetic branch
    parasympathetic branch
spinal cord
  reflex arc
cerebral cortex, corticalization
brain efficiency
hemispheres
corpus callosum
split brain
hemispheric lateralization
occipital lobes
parietal lobes
  somatosensory area

temporal lobes
frontal lobes—motor cortex
associative areas
neglect
aphasia
Broca's and Wernicke's areas
agnosia, facial agnosia
subcortex
  brainstem (hindbrain)
    medulla
    cerebellum
reticular formation
  midbrain
forebrain
  thalamus
  hypothalamus
limbic system
  hippocampus
ESB
redundancy, plasticity
endocrine system
  hormone
  pituitary
  hypopituitary dwarf
  giantism
acromegaly
thyroid
handedness
brain dominance
  sinistral advantages
techniques to study the brain

RONNIE

STRIPPER or TONER
BETTER HAIR
BLONDE - L.BROWN RED/ASH
TINT

REMEMBER FOR
THUR

LEARNING OBJECTIVES

To demonstrate mastery of this unit you should be able to:

1.   Define biopsychology.

2.   Name the basic unit of the nervous system, state what it is specifically designed to do (see p. 53), and list and describe its four parts.

    a.   c.

    b.   d.

3.   Explain how a nerve impulse (action potential) occurs and how it is an all-or-nothing event.

4.   Describe the effect of myelin on the speed of the nerve impulse.

5.   Describe the difference between the nature of a nerve impulse and the nature of the communication between neurons.

6.   Explain how nerve impulses are carried from one neuron to another.

7.   Explain what determines whether a neuron will have an action potential triggered.

8.   Explain the functions of neuropeptides and enkephalins.

9.   Differentiate a nerve from a neuron.

10.   Explain what determines whether or not a neuron or a nerve will regenerate. Explain how in some cases brain damage can be partially alleviated. Describe the ethical concern related to this intervention and how the dilemma may be resolved.

11.   Chart the various subparts of the human nervous system and explain their functions.

12.   Differentiate between the two branches of the autonomic nervous system.

13.   Explain the mechanism of the reflex arc.

14. Describe the main difference between the brains of lower and higher animals. (See also p. 68.) Name what appears to be the foundation of human intelligence. Describe the main difference between the brains of people who score high on mental tests and those who score low.

15. Complete the following sentence: The cortex is composed of two sides, or _____.
16. Describe the function of the corpus callosum.

17. Explain how and why a brain is "split" and describe what the resulting effects are.

18. Differentiate the abilities of the two hemispheres of the cerebral cortex.

19. Describe the function(s) of each of the following:
    a. occipital lobes

    b. parietal lobes (include the somatosensory areas)

    c. temporal lobes

    d. frontal lobes

    e. associative areas

20.   Explain the relationship between the size of the various parts of the somatosensory and motor areas of the cortex and the degree of sensitivity or importance of the corresponding body parts.

21.   Explain how brain injuries are related to behavioral outcomes. Describe the problem known as neglect.

22.   Describe the cause and effect of the three disorders aphasia, agnosia, and facial agnosia.

23.   List and be able to recognize the three areas of the subcortex.
      a.

      b.

      c.

24.   Explain the function of each of the following parts of the three areas of the subcortex:
      a.   Hindbrain (brainstem)
           1) medulla

           2) cerebellum

           3) reticular formation

      b.   Forebrain
           1) thalamus

           2) hypothalamus

25.   Name the structures that comprise the limbic system and explain its function.

26.   Describe the process of ESB — how it is done, what it can be used for, and what its limitations are.

27.   List five basic functions of the brain.
       a.

       b.

       c.

       d.

       e.

28.   Explain the concepts of redundancy and plasticity. Include the mechanism of plasticity.

29.   Briefly explain the purpose of the endocrine system and name and describe the mechanism by which this system carries out its function.

30.   Describe the effect that the following glands have on the body and behavior:
       a.   pituitary (include a description of giantism, dwarfism, and acromegaly)

       b.   thyroid

       c.   adrenal medulla

       d.   adrenal cortex

The following objectives are related to the material in the "Applications" and "Exploration" sections of your text.

31.   Describe the relationship among handedness, brain dominance, and speech.

32.   Explain how a person can determine which hemisphere is dominant.

33.   State the incidence of left-handedness and discuss the relative advantages and/or disadvantages of being right-handed versus left-handed.

34.   Write a brief sentence describing each of the following brain studying techniques: dissection, staining, ablation, deep lesioning, micro-electrode recording, CT scan, MRI, EEG, MANSCAN, PET scan, MEG scan.

SELF-QUIZZES

Do You Know the Information?

Multiple Choice

1.   Biopsychology is the study of
      (a) the mind.
      (b) the way our behavior is affected by the spinal cord.
      (c) how the brain and nervous system relate to behavior.
      (d) the neuron and the mechanism of nerve transmission.

2.   Impulses are triggered and travel down the
      (a) soma.   (c) axon.
      (b) dendrite.   (d) synapse.

3. An action potential is started when
   (a) sodium moves through the ion channels into the axon.
   (b) the neurotransmitters charge the axon.
   (c) the synapse is crossed.
   (d) the cell's voltage drops below its resting potential.

4. Myelin is a layer of insulation around an axon that
   (a) speeds up the action potential.   (c) protects the nerve.
   (b) aids in axonal regeneration.   (d) both a and c above.

5. Which of the following statements *best* characterizes the difference between axonal and synaptic transmission?
   (a) Synaptic transmission (communication between neurons) is primarily an electro-chemical event.
   (b) The nerve impulse (axonal transmission) is basically a chemical event.
   (c) Axonal transmission is an electrical event.
   (d) Synaptic transmission is basically an electrical event.

6. A nerve impulse crosses the synapse by
   (a) jumping the gap like a spark.
   (b) releasing neurotransmitters.
   (c) stimulating the resting potential.
   (d) moving potassium and sodium ions across a membrane.

7. If enough excitatory messages arrive at a neuron at the same time or in quick succession a neuron's
   _____ is reached and an action potential is triggered.
   (a) potential   (c) resting potential
   (b) level of inhibition   (d) threshold (trigger point)

8. Neuropeptides
   (a) aid in the regeneration of neurons.
   (b) regulate basic processes such as memory, pain, emotion, and pleasure.
   (c) lower the threshold for an action potential.
   (d) are found in the parasympathetic system.

9. The structure found on many nerve fibers outside the CNS which aids in regeneration is the
   (a) telodendria.   (c) myelin sheath.
   (b) neurilemma.   (d) somatos.

10. The peripheral nervous system is divided into two parts, the
    (a) autonomic and the parasympathetic systems.   (c) somatic and the sympathetic systems.
    (b) spinal cord and the parasympathetic systems. (d) autonomic and the somatic systems.

11. Which of the following statements is *correct* concerning the differing functions of the two branches of the autonomic nervous system?
    (a) The parasympathetic system prepares the body for "fight or flight."
    (b) The sympathetic system responds during danger or emotion.
    (c) The sympathetic system is the "status quo" system.
    (d) All of the above statements are correct.

12. Indicate (by circling) which of the following are necessary for a reflex arc.
    (a) connector neuron   (e) spinal cord
    (b) brain   (f) motor cortex
    (c) motor neuron   (g) sensory neuron
    (d) subcortex   (h) effector cells

13. Human intelligence appears to be related to
    (a) the size and weight of the brain.
    (b) the ratio of the mass of brain compared to the mass of the spinal cord.
    (c) the increase in the size and wrinkling of the cortex.
    (d) the proportion of the frontal lobes.

14. The cortex is composed of two sides or _____, which are connected by the _____ _____.
    (a) lobes; limbic system   (c) hemispheres; sympathetic system
    (b) lobes; parasympathetic system   (d) hemispheres; corpus callosum

15. A split-brain individual has a circle flashed to her left brain and a square to her right brain. Which of the following statements describes the results?
    (a) Both sides of the brain are aware of the square and the circle.
    (b) She will draw a circle with her left hand.
    (c) She will draw a square with her right hand.
    (d) She will draw a square with her left hand.

16. Place an "R" in the blank for right hemisphere functions and an "L" for the left as they apply to the "typical" person:
    _____(a) judges time and rhythm   _____(d) arranges blocks
    _____(b) cannot speak   _____(e) recognizes melodies
    _____(c) performs math computations   _____(f) expresses emotion

17. Bodily sensations are channeled to and are registered on the
    (a) parietal lobes.   (c) temporal lobes.
    (b) frontal lobes.   (d) occipital lobes.

18. Which of the following is *not* one of the three areas of the subcortex?
    (a) midbrain   (c) forebrain
    (b) brainstem   (d) subbrain

19. The part of the brain responsible for posture, muscle tone, and coordination is the
    (a) thalamus.   (c) cerebellum.
    (b) limbic system.   (d) medulla.

20. The hypothalamus
    (a) acts as the final sensory switching system.
    (b) controls heart rate and respiration.
    (c) receives and processes visual information.
    (d) is the master control center for emotion and many basic motives.

21. The limbic system is important for
    (a) the production of emotion and motivated behavior.
    (b) the regulation of salt balance in the body.
    (c) the processing and interpreting of auditory information.
    (d) direct control of voluntary muscles.

22. The endocrine system "communicates" with the rest of the body by means of chemicals called _____ which are secreted directly into the bloodstream.
    (a) endocrines   (c) hormones
    (b) corticoids   (d) phermones

23. Which of the following glands is very important for the regulation of the salt balance in the body and the body's ability to withstand stress?
    (a) adrenal cortex
    (b) thyroid
    (c) adrenal medulla
    (d) pituitary

24. Which of the following statements is *incorrect?*
    (a) Almost all right-handers process speech in the left hemisphere.
    (b) Left-handed people who write with a hooked hand are probably right-brain dominant.
    (c) About 15% of left-handers use both sides of the brain for language.
    (d) In the left-handed person, the left hemisphere controls the right hand.

True-False

_____ 1. Neurons are designed to carry and process information.

_____ 2. The soma collects and combines incoming information.

_____ 3. A nerve cell fires with differing intensities.

_____ 4. Neurons (which can also be called nerves) are tiny individual cells.

_____ 5. Sometimes damage to the brain can be partially alleviated by cutting out the damaged portion and allowing healthy new tissue to regenerate in its place.

_____ 6. The reflex arc is the simplest behavior sequence and can occur without any direct participation of the brain.

_____ 7. One of the most important differences in the brains of man and lower animals is the proportion of the brain devoted to the cerebral cortex and specifically to the association cortex.

_____ 8. The hemispheres of the brain are "split" by severing the spinal cord.

_____ 9. Voluntary muscle movements are controlled by the frontal lobes.

_____ 10. The larger the size of the part of the somatosensory area on the parietal lobe, the more sensitive the corresponding body part.

_____ 11. With right hemisphere damage a person could understand what was said, but would not recognize whether it was said in an angry or humorous way.

_____ 12. With aphasia a person has an impaired ability to use language.

_____ 13. The medulla controls vital life functions such as heart rate, swallowing, and respiration.

_____ 14. The reticular formation is responsible for alertness and wakefulness.

_____ 15. The hypothalamus and the reticular formation are parts of the limbic system.

_____ 16. Just as ESB can artifically produce almost all basic behaviors, it can be used to control a person against his or her will.

_____ 17. One of the five basic functions of the brain is to control responses such as reflexes.

_____ 18. With increasing development, an adult's brain exhibits greater plasticity than a child's brain.

_____ 19. One of the benefits of being left-handed is that typically brain injuries aren't as damaging because there is less lateralization.

Matching *(Use the letters on the right only once.)*

_____ 1. dendrites
_____ 2. neuron
_____ 3. neurotransmitters
_____ 4. action potential occurs
_____ 5. enkephalins
_____ 6. nerve
_____ 7. central nervous system
_____ 8. corpus callosum
_____ 9. left hemisphere
_____ 10. occipital lobes
_____ 11. temporal lobes
_____ 12. hands
_____ 13. aphasia
_____ 14. redundancy
_____ 15. pituitary
_____ 16. acromegaly
_____ 17. thyroid

A. problem with language
B. regulates pain and pleasure
C. connects hemispheres
D. auditory area
E. balance and coordination
F. aids process of reorganization and recovery after injury
G. directly regulates metabolism
H. regulates salt balance
I. collect information
J. if threshold is reached
K. brain and spinal cord
L. basic unit of nervous system
M. recognizes melodies
N. natural opiates
O. visual area
P. somatic and autonomic
Q. secretion of too much growth hormone by pituitary late in the growth period
R. carry impulses from one neuron to another
S. large area on motor cortex
T. comprehends language in 95% of people
U. regulates functions of other glands
V. bundle of axons and dendrites

Can You Apply the Information?

1. You stimulate a neuron with a brick. Then you stimulate the same neuron with a feather. The feather stimulates a weaker action potential from the neuron than does the brick.
    (a) True   (b) False

2. You are the first to arrive at the scene of a horrible accident. One of the victims has her arm severed midway between the wrist and the elbow. There are a few very small whitish looking strands protruding from the severed limb. These are most likely
    (a) neurons.   (c) cell bodies.
    (b) telodendria.   (d) nerves.

3. If the victim in question 2 had her arm reattached she would likely soon begin to experience some sensation because of the
    (a) soma.   (c) neurilemma.
    (b) myelin sheath.   (d) plasticity phenomenon.

4. As you sit reading this question the _____ branch of your autonomic nervous system is probably the more active branch. (This assumes that you are not frantically studying for a test.)

   (a) peripheral
   (b) parasympathetic
   (c) somatic
   (d) sympathetic

5. It is possible that Marie Antoinette who was beheaded during the French Revolution could have had a knee jerk reflex elicited immediately after her death.

   (a) True
   (b) False

6. If you were a mad scientist and wanted to operate on the human brain to produce the closest thing to a two-headed person, which brain structure should be cut?

   (a) optic chiasma
   (b) cerebellum
   (c) somatosensory area
   (d) none of the above

7. A right-handed man who has had a split-brain operation is driving down a divided highway in his Geo automatic transmission car. He is staring straight ahead. A car from the other side of the highway (to his left) begins to skid across the median strip toward him. Which of the following statements *best* reflects what the split-brained man will probably be able to do?

   (a) push on the car's accelerator with his right foot to avoid an accident
   (b) yell "Damn! I'm going to die!"
   (c) steer out of the way of the oncoming car
   (d) push on the brake to avoid an accident

8. You lovingly whisper "sweet nothings" into your husband's ear. You angrily yell at your husband. In each case he gets your literal meaning but he just doesn't seem to emotionally respond to the tone of your messages. It is likely that his problem is

   (a) damage to his Broca's area.
   (b) lack of sufficient neurotransmitters.
   (c) damage to the right hemisphere.
   (d) damage to both hemispheres.
   (e) that he has the intelligence of a cucumber.

9. Bob has recovered from a car accident in which he suffered extensive damage to his left hemisphere. He hasn't had problems at work. It is likely that Bob is

   (a) a graphic artist.
   (b) an English teacher.
   (c) a mathematician.
   (d) a free-lance writer.
   (e) president of the U.S.

10. One reason people probably enjoy kissing so much is that

    (a) the neurons from the lips transmit impulses slightly faster than from most other body parts
    (b) the temporal lobes are especially sensitive to the processing of sensory information from the facial region
    (c) there are no myelin sheaths to interfere with the transmission of action potentials to the CNS
    (d) there is a larger area on the parietal lobe for the reception of information from the lips

11. Mary, a 68-year-old widow, had a stoke in her right hemisphere. Although her speech center was undamaged, she never brushes the hair on the left side of her head, and she forgets to wear makeup on the left side of her face. She even forgets to put her left arm through the sleeve of her blouse. What is Mary's condition called?

    (a) contralateral unconsciousness
    (b) hemispheric nondominance
    (c) neglect
    (d) peripheral atrophy

12. If a child is hit in the head in the area of the frontal region and aphasia results, the child will most likely have

    (a) difficulty with complex motor skills.
    (b) difficulty speaking.
    (c) a lower than average I.Q.
    (d) vivid memories produced.

13.   If you *had* to lose one structure in your brain and you were vitally concerned that your body at least stay alive, which brain structure would be the *last* one that you would want to lose?
      (a) cerebellum   (c) medulla
      (b) reticular formation   (d) corpus callosum

14.   Thermal stimulation of a certain part of the brain can make a rat in a 120° cage shiver. Which structure must be stimulated to produce this effect?
      (a) limbic system   (c) cerebellum
      (b) hypothalamus   (d) occipital lobes

15.   You have a child who is struck by a car while riding a bicycle. She suffers brain damage. Why might it be better if she were only seven years old rather than ten?
      (a) Younger children better adapt to the psychological consequences of pain.
      (b) Older children do not develop new neurons as fast as younger children.
      (c) She has greater brain plasticity.
      (d) She has not yet developed hemispheric dominance.

16.   A patient complains to his doctor about being tired all of the time and feeling sleepy. The doctor also notes that the man is 20 pounds overweight and decides to run some tests. The doctor is probably looking for signs of
      (a) damage to the hippocampus.   (c) an adrenal problem.
      (b) a thyroid condition.   (d) acromegaly.

17.   In general, which of the following brain studying techniques would you *not* want used on you?
      (a) ablation   (c) MANSCAN
      (b) CT scan   (d) PET scan

Chapter Review

1.   _____ is the study of how the brain and nervous system relate to behavior.

2.   The basic unit of the nervous system is the _____. It is designed to carry and process _____. The four basic parts of this unit of the nervous system are the _____, _____, _____, and _____ _____.

3.   A nerve impulse or _____ _____ occurs when a brief flow of electrical current is caused by the movement of sodium ions into the axon through the ion channels. A neuron will only carry an impulse if the _____ is reached. This makes the nerve impulse an _____ - _____ - _____ event. Nerve impulses are faster when _____ surrounds the axon.

4.   The nerve impulse is primarily a(n) _____ event. In contrast, neurons communicate with each other _____. The impulse is carried from one neuron to another by means of _____. Some may excite the next neuron or inhibit it. The neuron will carry an _____ _____ if a number of excitatory messages arrive close enough together to reach the _____.

5. Recent research has revealed a new class of neurotransmitters called _____. These important chemicals seem to serve as _____ of memory, pain, emotion, and other basic processes. In addition the brain also produces opiate-like neural opiates called _____. Related chemicals called _____ are released by the pituitary gland. Both of these chemicals serve to relieve _____ and _____.

6. Nerves are not the same as _____ but are bundles of _____ and _____. Most nerves outside the brain and spinal cord also have a thin layer of living cells called the _____ wrapped around them. It is important because it aids _____. Recently there has been research concerning the possibility of repairing damage to the CNS through _____ of healthy _____ cells. The ethical problem heretofore with this procedure was that the cells had to come from a _____ . Recently however, researchers have grown _____ cells in the lab.

7. The _____ and the _____ _____ comprise the central nervous system. The _____ nervous system consists of nerves which carry information to and from the _____ nervous system.

8. The peripheral nervous system (PNS) is divided into two subparts: the _____ system and the _____ system. The latter system can also be further divided into the _____ and _____ branches. Although both branches are always active, the _____ branch is more active during periods of low arousal, while the _____ branch is more active during times of danger or emotion.

9. The cable system of the body that connects the brain to the rest of the body is called the _____ _____. It is responsible for the simplest behavioral sequence that can occur without direct participation of the brain. This behavior sequence is called a _____ _____. There are several mechanisms involved. The incoming stimulus is detected by a _____ neuron and carried to the _____ _____ where the _____ neuron is activated. This neuron communicates information to a _____ neuron which leads back to muscle fibers.

10. As we move up the phylogenetic scale towards man there is an ever-increasing proportion of brain tissue devoted to the _____ _____ and especially to the _____ areas. Human intelligence appears to be related to _____, the increase in size and wrinkling of this portion of the brain. The main difference between the brains of people who score high on mental tests and those who do not is in the _____ of the brain.

11. The cortex is composed of two sides or _____ which are connected by the _____ _____. If this structure is surgically cut, the brain is referred to as "_____." This procedure is typically done to lessen the severity of the seizures associated with _____. After the surgery is performed, it is almost like having two _____ in one body.

12.   The left hemisphere is usually responsible for _____, _____, and compre-
hending _____. In addition, the left hemisphere is better at _____,
judging _____ and _____, and at coordinating complex _____.
In contrast, the right hemisphere can only respond to very simple _____ and cannot
_____. However, the right hemisphere is better than the left at recognizing
_____ patterns, _____ and _____,
and it is involved in the recognition and expression of _____. The right brain is also
better at tasks requiring _____ and "_____ -
_____" skills. Direct studies of brain activity show that _____ hemispheres
are activated for virtually all tasks.

13.   The occipital lobes, which are located at the back of the brain, are responsible for _____. The
area of the brain to which bodily sensations are channeled is the _____ lobe. The temporal
lobes are responsible for _____ and _____ storage. For most people, this lobe
also contains a _____ center. The frontal lobes contain areas which direct the body's
_____ responses and receive information for the sense of _____. All
other areas of the cerebral cortex (including parts of the lobes just described) are called the
_____ cortex. When stimulated, it yields responses more complex than simple
sensations or movements.

14.   The larger the area on the somatosensory portions of the _____ lobes, the greater
the _____ of the corresponding body part. Similarly, the larger the area on the motor
cortex of the _____ lobes, the more _____ the corre-
sponding body part.

15.   Damage to the _____ brain may cause many language-related difficulties. Damage to the
_____ brain may cause a person to get lost while driving or to ignore things in the left half of his
world, a condition known as _____.

16.   Injury to either Broca's area or Wernicke's area may result in _____, an impaired ability
to use _____. Other injuries to the brain may cause a person to be unable to identify
seen objects, a condition known as _____. The inability to identify familiar persons
is called _____ _____.

17.   The subcortex can be divided into three general areas called the _____ or
_____, the _____, and the _____. The first area can be
further divided into three areas: the _____, the _____, and the
_____ _____. The structure that contains centers important for the
reflex control of vital life functions is the _____. The _____ functions
primarily to regulate posture, muscle tone, and coordination although it may play a role in some types of
_____. Among many activities, the _____
_____ is responsible for alertness and wakefulness.

18.   The forebrain is composed of the _____ _____, the _____,
and the _____. The _____ acts as a final switching station for sensory
information. The _____ has been implicated in the control of behaviors such as sex, temperature control, eating, and drinking. It is a kind of master control center for _____
and many basic _____. These two structures and the _____
(which is important for the formation of long term memories) along with several others comprise the
_____ system. This system is important in the production of _____ and
_____ behavior.

19. ESB refers to _____ _____ _____ _____
     _____. This technique refers to the implantation of _____ in the brain. Although ESB has
     had only limited use with humans, it has been used to produce outbursts of _____ and
     _____ behavior.

20. The brain controls _____ _____ _____, keeps track
     of the _____ world, issues commands to the _____
     and _____, generates complex _____ in the light of current
     needs and past experience, creates _____, and _____ its
     own behavior.

21. The brain has an impressive capacity for reorganization and recovery after injury because of
     _____. In response to brain injury, children show a remarkable ability to recover
     due to flexibility or _____. This ability is probably based on increased branching of
     _____.

22. The _____ system is the chemical communication system in the body. The chemicals
     are called _____ and activate _____ in the body. The _____ regulates
     bodily growth and is one of the structures in this system. If too little growth _____ is
     released, a person may suffer growth failure called _____. If too much is released,
     _____ may result. If too much is released toward the end of the growth period, there may
     be excessive growth of the extremities — a condition called _____.

23. Metabolism is regulated by the _____ gland. The _____ glands are located on
     top of the kidneys. The _____ _____ is the source of
     adrenaline and noradrenaline. The _____ _____ secretes a
     _____ which regulates the salt balance in the body.

24. Almost all right-handers and about 60% of left-handers produce speech from the _____
     hemisphere. Right-handed individuals who write with a straight hand, and lefties who write with a hooked
     hand, are probably _____- brain dominant for _____. The prevalence of
     right-handedness in humans probably reflects the left brain's specialization for _____.
     Left-handed people have less brain _____ than righties. Math abilities
     may benefit from fuller use of the _____ hemisphere.

25. There are a variety of techniques both invasive and noninvasive used to study the structure and function of the
     brain. Dissection and staining are used to identify major brain pathways, hence they are good at studying the
     _____ of the brain only and not the _____ of the parts
     studied. _____, on the other hand, is the surgical removal of parts of a functioning
     brain. When followed by a change in behavior, ablation tells something about the
     _____ of the missing part. (_____ _____ is similar
     to ablation except that it occurs inside the brain.) _____-_____ record-
     ings allow the study of single functioning neurons. A CT scan is a specialized type of ____-_____ which
     makes the interior of the brain visible. MRI scans use the response of _____
     atoms in a magnetic field to "peer" into the living brain as though it were _____.
     EEGs are used to measure various _____-_____ patterns which are indicative of a
     number of problems or conditions. A _____ is a cross between an EEG and a MRI.
     Finally, PET scans detect the presence of _____ from radioactive glucose in the
     brain which then allows the measurement of living brain _____.

ANSWER KEYS

Do You Know the Information?

Multiple Choice

1. (c) obj. 1, p. 54
2. (c) objs. 2-3, p. 54
3. (a) obj. 3, p. 54
4. (a) obj. 4, p. 55
5. (c) obj. 5, p. 56
6. (b) obj. 6, p. 56
7. (d) obj. 7, p. 57
8. (b) obj. 8, p. 57
9. (b) obj. 10, p. 58
10. (d) obj. 11, p. 58
11. (b) obj. 12, p. 59
12. (a,c,e,g,h) obj. 13, pp. 60-61
13. (c) obj. 14, p. 63
14. (d) objs. 15-16, p. 63
15. (d) obj. 17, pp. 64-65
16. (a) L, (b) R, (c) L, (d) R,
    (e) R, (f) R obj. 18, p. 65
17. (a) obj. 19, p. 66
18. (d) obj. 23, p. 70
19. (c) obj. 24, p. 70
20. (d) obj. 24, p. 71
21. (a) obj. 25, p. 71
22. (c) obj. 29, p. 73
23. (a) obj. 30, p. 75
24. (b) objs. 31-32, p. 77

True-False

1. T, obj. 2, p. 53
2. T, obj. 2, p. 54
3. F, obj. 3, p. 54
4. F, obj. 9, p. 58
5. F, obj. 10, p. 58
6. T, obj. 13, p. 61
7. T, obj. 14, pp. 63,68
8. F, objs. 15-17, p. 64
9. T, obj. 19, p. 67
10. T, obj. 20, p. 66
11. T, obj. 21, p. 68
12. T, obj. 22, p. 68
13. T, obj. 24, p. 70
14. T, obj. 24, p. 71
15. F, obj. 25, p. 71
16. F, obj. 26, p. 72
17. F, obj. 27, p. 73
18. F, obj. 28, p. 73
19. T, obj. 33, p. 78

Matching

1. I, obj. 2, p. 54
2. L, obj. 2, p. 53
3. R, obj. 6, p. 56
4. J, obj. 7, p. 54
5. N, obj. 8, p. 57
6. V, obj. 9, p. 58
7. K, obj. 11, p. 59

8. C, obj. 16, p. 63
9. T, obj. 18, pp. 64-65
10. O, obj. 19, p. 66
11. D, obj. 19, p. 67
12. S, obj. 20, p. 67
13. A, obj. 22, p. 68
14. F, obj. 26, p. 73
15. U, obj. 30, p. 75
16. Q, obj. 30, p. 74
17. G, obj. 30, p. 75

Can You Apply the Information?

1. (b) obj. 3, p. 54
2. (d) obj. 9, p. 58
3. (c) obj. 10, p. 58
4. (b) obj. 12, p. 59
5. (a) obj. 13, p. 61
6. (d) obj. 16, p. 63
7. (d) objs. 17-18, pp. 64-66
8. (c) objs. 18, 21, p. 68
9. (a) obj. 18, p. 65
10. (d) obj. 20, p. 66
11. (c) obj. 21, p. 68
12. (b) obj. 22, p. 68
13. (c) obj. 24, p. 70
14. (b) obj. 24, p. 71
15. (c) obj. 27, p. 73
16. (b) obj. 29, p. 75
17. (a) obj. 34, p. 79

Chapter Review

1. Biopsychology (p. 54)
2. neuron, information, dendrites, soma, axon, axon terminals (p. 54)
3. action potential, threshold, all-or-nothing, myelin (p. 54)
4. electrical, chemically, neurotransmitters, action potential, threshold (p. 54)
5. neuropeptides, regulators, enkephalins, endorphins, pain, stress (p. 57)
6. neurons, axons, dendrites, neurilemma, regeneration, grafts, brain, fetus, brain (p. 58)
7. brain, spinal cord, peripheral, central (p. 59)
8. somatic, autonomic, sympathetic, parasympathetic, parasympathetic, sympathetic (p. 59)
9. spinal cord, reflex arc, sensory, spinal cord, connector, motor (p. 60)
10. cerebral cortex, association, corticalization, efficiency (p. 63)
11. hemispheres, corpus callosum (p. 63); split, epilepsy, brains (p. 64)

12. speaking, writing, language, math, time, rhythm, movements, language, speak, visual, faces, melodies, emotion, visualization, manipulo-spatial, both (pp. 64-65)

13. vision, parietal, hearing (p. 66); memory, language, motor, smell (p. 67); association (p. 68)

14. parietal, sensitivity P. 66); frontal, important (p. 67)

15. left, right, neglect (p. 68)

16. aphasia, language (p. 68); agnosia, facial agnosia (p. 69)

17. brainstem, hindbrain, midbrain, forebrain, medulla, cerebellum (p. 70); reticular formation, medulla, cerebellum, memory, reticular formation (p. 71)

18. cerebral cortex, thalamus, hypothalamus, thalamus, hypothalamus, emotion, motives, hippocampus, limbic, emotion, motivated (p. 71)

19. electrical stimulation of the brain, electrodes, anger, flirtatious (p. 71)

20. vital bodily functions, external, muscles, glands, responses, consciousness, regulates (p. 70)

21. redundancy, plasticity, dendrites (p. 73)

22. endocrine, hormones, cells, pituitary, hormone, dwarfism, giantism, acromegaly (p. 74)

23. thyroid, adrenal, adrenal medulla, adrenal cortex, hormone (p. 75)

24. left, left, language, language (p. 77); lateralization, right (p. 78)

25. structure, function, Ablation, function (p. 79); Micro-electrode, X-ray, hydrogen, transparent, brain-wave (p. 80); MANSCAN (p. 81); positrons, activity (p. 82)

Chapter 4

Sensation and Reality

KEY TERMS AND CONCEPTS

sensation
data reduction system
transducer
    feature detectors
localization of function
psychophysics
    absolute threshold
    perceptual defense
        limen, subliminal
    difference threshold (JND)
        Weber's Law
visible spectrum
    hue (wavelength)
    saturation (narrow band)
    brightness (amplitude)
cornea, lens, retina
    accommodatin
    hyperopia, myopia, astigmatism, presbyopia
iris & pupil
rods & cones
    blind spot
    fovea
    acuity
    peripheral vision
    maximal color sensitivity
trichromatic and opponent-process theories
    visual pigment
color blindness, color weakness
    Ishihara test
dark adaptation
    rhodopsin & night blindness
sound waves
    compression & rarefaction

frequency & amplitude
hearing structure
    pinna, eardrum (tympanic membrane),
    auditory ossicles, oval window, cochlea
    hair cells
frequency and place theories
deafness: conduction, nerve, and stimulation
    temporary threshold shift
    cochlear implant
    tinnitus
olfaction and gustation: chemical senses
    anosmia
    lock and key theory
four basic taste sensitivities
taste bud
somesthetic senses
    skin, kinesthetic, vestibular
skin receptors, skin sensitivity
pain
    referred system
    warning system
        reminding system
sensory adaptation
    physiological nystagmus
selective attention
sensory gating
    acupuncture, beta-endorphins
controlling pain
    anxiety, control, attention,
    interpretation, counterirritation
space adaptation syndrome
sensory conflict theory

LEARNING OBJECTIVES

To demonstrate mastery of this chapter you should be able to:

1. Explain how our senses act as a data reduction system by selecting, analyzing, and coding incoming information.

   Our senses are narrowly limited in sensitivity

2. Explain how sensory receptors act as biological transducers.

   Each sensory organ is most sensitive to a select range of energy, which it most easily translates into nerve pulses.

3. Explain the concept of localization of function.

   Sensory receptors send messages to specific locations in the brain.

4. Explain the idea behind the statement: "Seeing does not take place in the eyes."

   Each sense organ is merely the first link in a long chain that ends in the cell and fiber forest of the brain.

5. Define sensation.

   The immediate neural response in the brain caused by excitation of a sensory organ.

6. Define the term "absolute threshold."

   The minimum amount of stimulation necessary for a sensation to occur

7. Explain the process of perceptual defense.

   Unpleasent stimuli that raises the threshold for recognition

8. Define limen and describe subliminal perception including its effectiveness.

   limen - threshold a limit
   Subliminal perception is when stimuli is half good/ half bad and forms an impression. Its effectiveness can make something more likeable or not.

9. **Explain Weber's law and the concept of the difference threshold (JND).**

    Weber's law - the amount of change needed to produce a JND is a constant proportion of the original stimulus intensity

    difference threshold - how much a stimulus must change before it becomes a JND.

10. **Describe hue, saturation, and brightness in terms of their representation in the visual spectrum of electromagnetic radiation.**

    hue - color that corresponds to light's wavelengths

    Saturated → hues produced by a narrow band of "pure" wavelengths

    brightness - corresponds to the physical height of light waves.   greater energy ↗ brightness

11. **Explain how the eye focuses and the process of accommodation.**

    - The front of the eye has a clear covering → Cornea
       ↳ bends light rays inward
    - the lens, elastic,
      accomodation → lens being stretched or thickened by a series of muscles, so that more or less additional binding of light occurs

12. **Describe the following four conditions:**

    a. **hyperopia**

    The eye is too short, nearby objects cannot be focused, distant objects are clear.
       'farsightedness'

    b. **myopia**

    eye ball is too long, image falls short of retina distant objects cannot be focused
       'Nearsightedness'

    c. **astigmatism**

    When cornea or lens is misshapen, part of visual field will be focused and part will be fuzzy.

    d. **presbyopia**

    farsightedness due to aging

13. **Explain how the eye controls light.**

    this is a colored circular muscle that expands and contracts to control the size of the pupil

    The iris allows us to move quickly from darkness to brightness, or reverse. In dim light, pupils dialate
       " bright " , " constrict

14.   Describe the functions of the rods and cones.

  – Cones work best in bright light. They produce color sensations and pick up fine details.
  – Rods are unable to detect color, pure rod vision is black and white. Much more sensitive in light, therefore they allow us to see in very dim light.

15.   Explain how the visual area of the brain detects features.

16.   Explain the relationship between the fovea and visual acuity.

  The tightley packed cones of the fovea produce the greatest visual acuity, or sharpness.

17.   Discuss peripheral vision. Include the structures responsible for it and how this type of vision affects night vision.

18.   Discuss the following theories of color vision:
  a.   trichromatic theory

  There are 3 types of cones, each most sensitive to a specific color: red, green, or blue.

  b.   opponent-process theory (include a description of afterimage) → of the other color as system recovers

  Three coding systems (red or green, yellow or blue, black or white) are used by the visual system to analyze color formation.

19.   Describe color blindness and color weakness.

  color blindness – either lacks cones or has cones that do not function normally – see black + white

  ? color weakness –

20. Briefly describe the process of dark adaptation including the function of rhodopsin in night vision and night blindness.

21. Explain the stimulus for hearing.

22. Describe the location and explain the function(s) of the following parts of the ear:
    a. pinna

    b. eardrum (tympanic membrane)

    c. auditory ossicles

    d. oval window

    e. cochlea

    f. hair cells (and include the Organ of Corti)

23. Describe the frequency theory and the place theory of hearing.

24.   List and describe the three general types of deafness.
      a.

      b.

      c.

25.   Describe the factors that determine whether hearing loss will occur from stimulation deafness. (Include a discussion of how temporary threshold shift and tinnitus are related to stimulation deafness.)

26.   Describe the sense of smell including:
      a.   its nature

      b.   how it works

      c.   a description of the lock and key theory

      d.   a description of the condition anosmia

27.   Describe the sense of taste including:
      a.   its nature

      b.   the four basic taste sensations

      c.   the tastes to which humans are most and least sensitive

      d.   how the vast number of flavors is explained

    e.   how it works

    f.   how taste is affected by smell, genetics, and age

28.   List the three somesthetic senses and be able to describe the function of each.
    a.

    b.

    c.

29.   List and be able to recognize the five different sensations produced by the skin receptors.
    a.
    b.
    c.
    d.
    e.

30.   Explain why certain areas of the body are more sensitive to touch than other areas.

31.   Name and describe the two different pain systems in the body.
    a.

    b.

32.   List and discuss the three reasons many sensory events never reach conscious awareness.
    a.

    b.

    c.

33.   Discuss how endorphins explain some of the feelings associated with running, acupuncture, ESB, masochism, and childbirth.

The following objectives are related to the material in the "Applications" and Exploration" sections of your text.

34.   Discuss four techniques that can be used to reduce the amount of pain perceived.

35.   Describe the space adaptation syndrome, and explain how the otolith organs and the semicircular canals of the vestibular system are related to it.

36.   Describe how the sensory conflict theory explains motion sickness.

SELF-QUIZZES

Do You Know the Information?

Multiple Choice

1.   The senses can be said to serve as a data reduction system because
    (a)   each sense only responds to one type of stimulation.
    (b)   many receptors break down information before sending it to the brain.
    (c)   each sensation is directly affected by the area of the brain where it terminates.
    (d)   of all of the above.

2.   When the photoreceptors in the eye convert photons of light into nerve impulses, the photoreceptors have functioned as
    (a)   transformers.   (c)   adaptors.
    (b)   translocutors.   (d)   transducers.

3.   Localization of function means that
    (a)   each area of the body is capable of receiving a single specific type of stimulation.
    (b)   the type of sensation experienced depends ultimately on the type of nerve pathway on which it travels.
    (c)   specific brain areas receive messages from each of the senses.
    (d)   "hearing" takes place in the ears.

4. Sensation may be defined as
    (a) the incoming flow of information.
    (b) the organization of incoming information by the brain.
    (c) feelings made up of the somesthetic senses.
    (d) the transduction of the external world.

5. The absolute threshold is
    (a) the absolute minimum amount of stimulation necessary to be able to detect a difference in two stimuli.
    (b) the minimum amount of stimulus necessary to raise a threshold.
    (c) the difference between physical stimuli and psychological responses.
    (d) the least amount of stimulation necessary for sensation to occur.

6. A visual stimulus that is subliminal is
    (a) basically weak.
    (b) rather ineffective as an advertising medium.
    (c) below the normal threshold for that particular sense.
    (d) all of the above.

7. The dimension of vision known as brightness corresponds to which characteristic of light waves?
    (a) amplitude
    (b) narrowness of the band of wavelengths
    (c) wavelength
    (d) purity

8. The process whereby the lens of the eye is stretched or thickened to focus the incoming image is called
    (a) facilitation.
    (b) accommodation.
    (c) adaptation.
    (d) acuity.

9. Hyperopia is the condition that exists when
    (a) the length of the eye is too short.
    (b) a person cannot focus distant subjects.
    (c) farsightedness exists because of old age.
    (d) a person can see objects close to the eye.

10. The mechanism of the eye that controls the amount of light entering is the
    (a) lens.
    (b) aperture.
    (c) iris.
    (d) diaphragm.

11. The visual receptor primarily responsible for color vision is the
    (a) cone.
    (b) fovea.
    (c) rod.
    (d) pupil.

12. The visual area of the brain detects features by
    (a) working like a camera.
    (b) responding more to color than to black and white.
    (c) being more sensitive to stronger impulses.
    (d) analyzing incoming information into lines, angles, movement, etc.

13. The best night vision is obtained when
    (a) looking at the center of an object.
    (b) a moving object is detected at the center of the visual field.
    (c) the incoming image is focused on the fovea.
    (d) looking slightly to one side or the other of an object.

14. The opponent-process theory of color vision holds
    (a) afterimages are caused by the fatigue of one of the three types of rods.
    (b) there are three paired receptors and while one of the pair is "on" the other is "off."
    (c) there are three types of cones.
    (d) none of the above are correct.

15. A person who has color weakness
     (a) sees the world much like the view presented on a black and white TV.
     (b) has partial color blindness such as red-green color blindness.
     (c) has a rare condition.
     (d) probably also suffers from presbyopia.

16. The increase in sensitivity to light that occurs when one spends time in the dark is called
     (a) light enhancement.   (c) light sensitizing.
     (b) dark facilitation.   (d) dark adaptation.

17. The structures actually responsible for transduction in the ear are the
     (a) ossicles.   (c) tympanic membranes.
     (b) hair cells.   (d) stapes.

18. The oval window is connected to the
     (a) eardrum.   (c) hair cells.
     (b) round window.   (d) ossicles.

19. The frequency theory of hearing holds that
     (a) tones of differing frequencies register on different places on the cochlea.
     (b) pitch is signaled by the area of the cochlea most strongly activated.
     (c) as pitch rises, nerve impulses of the same frequency are fed into the auditory nerve.
     (d) "Hunter's notch" is a result of very low frequency sound waves.

20. The type of deafness that occurs when auditory messages do not reach the brain because the eardrum or the auditory
     ossicles are immobilized is called
     (a) nerve deafness.   (c) brain deafness.
     (b) stimulation deafness.   (d) conduction deafness..

21. Whether or not a person will suffer a hearing loss due to stimulation deafness depends upon
     (a) the loudness of the sound.   (c) the length of exposure to the sound.
     (b) the presence of damage to the hair cells.   (d) all of the above.

22. The lock and key theory is based on the idea that
     (a) only certain tastes are detected by certain taste buds.
     (b) our specific patterns of genetic inheritance hold the keys that will in time unlock our sensitivities to certain
          tastes.
     (c) there are holes on the odor receptors that match the shape of the various odor molecules.
     (d) the taste of bitter was the key to man's survival.

23. Which of the following statements concerning taste is *incorrect*?
     (a) The sense of taste diminishes as we age because taste cell replacement slows down.
     (b) Humans are most sensitive to sour and least sensitive to salt.
     (c) The sense of taste is chemical in nature.
     (d) Subjective flavor is probably one-half smell.

24. Which of the following is considered to be a somesthetic sense?
     (a) the kinesthetic sense   (c) the vestibular senses
     (b) the skin senses   (d) all of the above

25. Which of the following is *not* one of the sensations which has its own receptors?
     (a) cold   (c) hot
     (b) pressure   (d) pain

26. The decrease in sensory response that accompanies a constant or unchanging stimulus is called
     (a) sensory adaptation.
     (b) selective attention.
     (c) sensory habituation.
     (d) response decrement.

27. Our ability to tune in on any one of many sensory messages while excluding others is known as
     (a) sensory selection.
     (b) sensory adaptation.
     (c) selective attention.
     (d) selective sensation.

28. Physiological nystagmus is the process in which
     (a) the eye makes involuntary movements to move the visual image off of the inoperative fovea.
     (b) the tiny muscle movements made by the eye shift the visual image from one receptor to another and prevent adaptation.
     (c) the eye counteracts negative afterimages.
     (d) the eye selectively attends to only important stimuli.

29. Using the concept of sensory gating, Wall and Melzack explain the phenomenon of acupuncture as
     (a) a patient's subjective response to the placebo effect.
     (b) a subtle hypnotic suggestion.
     (c) one pain message closing the "gate" to pain transmitted by another fiber.
     (d) due to the release of endorphins in the brain.

30. One possible explanation for the phenomenon known as the runner's "high" is
     (a) a well functioning vestibular system.
     (b) selective attention of pleasure signals from the muscles.
     (c) sensory adaptation to the pain from running.
     (d) the release of endorphins in the brain.

31. Which of the following can be used to reduce a person's perception of pain?
     (a) Apply a brief, mildly painful stimulus to another part of the body.
     (b) Shift the focus of attention away from the painful stimulus.
     (c) Seek some degree of control over the stimulus.
     (d) All of the above are true.

32. The sensory conflict theory holds that the dizziness and nausea of the space adaptation syndrome result from
     (a) a mismatch of information from the vestibular system and the eyes and body.
     (b) when the ampullae of the semicircular canals misfires.
     (c) when the "flaps" or "floats" of the otolith organs are overstimulated.
     (d) none of the above statements are true.

True-False

_____ 1. The reason why seeing does not occur in the eyes only is that what we call vision involves structures and processes from the eyes all the way to the brain.

_____ 2. Perceptual defense occurs when the absolute threshold is lowered.

_____ 3. If the cornea or the lens is misshapen, the resulting condition is a partially focused field and is called astigmatism.

_____ 4. The fovea is packed with rods.

_T_ 5. The rods are mainly responsible for our ability to see in dim light.

_T_ 6. Because rods are most sensitive to blue-green lights, many police cars have blue emergency lights for use at night.

_F_ 7. The Ishihara test is a test for nystagmus.

_T_ 8. If a room is illuminated with red light the process of dark adaptation is speeded up because the rods do not respond well to this wavelength of light.

_T_ 9. Anosmia is a "smell blindness" for only one type of odor.

_T_ 10. It is quite possible that if two children of the same sex and from the same family are opposite in their tastes for certain foods, these differences in taste can be due to genetics.

_F_ 11. The sense that signals balance is called the kinesthetic sense.

_T_ 12. The sensitivity of a certain area of the skin roughly corresponds to the number of receptors in that area.

_F_ 13. The most frequently found receptor in the skin is for temperature.

_T_ 14. In terms of pain, the reminding system is carried on small nerve fibers and the pain is slow, nagging, aching, and widespread.

Matching (Use the letters on the right only once.)

_T_	1. nerve deafness		A.	external ear
_G_	2. myopia		B.	corresponds to wavelength
_J_	3. olfaction and gustation		C.	space adaptation syndrome
_A_	4. pinna		D.	difference threshold
_I_	5. perceptual defense		E.	conduction deafness
_H_	6. cochlea		F.	most frequently found receptor in the skin
_F_	7. pain		G.	nearsightedness
_D_	8. JND		H.	contains the ultimate receptors for hearing
_B_	9. hue		I.	when the absolute threshold is raised
_E_	10. middle ear		J.	chemical senses
_Q_	11. endorphins		K.	phosphenes
_O_	12. limen		L.	stimulates the auditory nerve directly
_M_	13. Vitamin A		M.	necessary for the production of rhodopsin
_C_	14. motion sickness		N.	sharp kind, bright, fast, from specific body areas
_N_	15. warning system		O.	defined as threshold or limit
_P_	16. kinesthesis		P.	relays information on body position and movement
_L_	17. cochlear implant		Q.	receptor sites for these are in large number in the limbic system
			R.	warmth
			S.	subliminal
			T.	hearing aid cannot help
			U.	when absolute threshold is lowered

Can You Apply the Information?

1.   In which of the following locations does transduction take place?
     (a) auditory ossicles   (c) blind spot
     (b) lens   (d) cochlea
     (e) behind closed doors

2.   The fact that a person reports hearing music when the auditory area of the brain is stimulated exemplifies the principle of
     (a) localization of function.   (c) temporal location.
     (b) reduction of sensory information.   (d) sensory gating.

3.   Betty has long had a keen sense of smell. She used to help her mother cook by telling her when it "smelled right." However, since the sudden death of her mother, which left Betty distraught, she seems to have lost her sense of smell for foods. This loss could be explained by the concept of
     (a) absolute thresholds.   (c) subliminal perception.
     (b) perceptual defense.   (d) difference thresholds.

4.   As the president of Knock-M-Dead Exterminators, you have to decide how to spend your advertising dollars most efficiently. Your marketing director is trying to convince you to do some subliminal advertising over radio and television. If you follow that recommendation, you can realistically expect
     (a) between an 18% to 57% increase in extermination jobs.
     (b) only an increase in the number of people calling asking for estimates.
     (c) only that the company name will be recognized easier.
     (d) that you will be making an absolute waste of your money.

5.   You are riding along in your car listening to the radio. You find that the very least you can turn your radio dial is 1/10 of a turn to be able to detect a change in the volume. You are experiencing
     (a) JNDs.   (c) difference thresholds.
     (b) Weber's law   (d) all of these.

6.   If your tattooist was in the middle of doing a tattoo of "Rambo" on your left buttock and he stepped on and broke his glasses, which of the following visual defects would you hope he had?
     (a) hyperopia   (c) presbyopia
     (b) myopia   (d) "Who cares, I'd rather him do it by feel anyway."

7.   You've had a freak accident with a marshmallow and lost the sight in one eye. With your good eye, you are looking at a bright, multicolored object. The light from the object is being projected onto the retina at the point where the optic nerve leaves the eye. It is likely that you will be
     (a) able to see the object as black, white, or a shade of gray.
     (b) able to see the colors of the object, although they may appear dull.
     (c) able to partially focus the object.
     (d) unable to see the object because of a lack of photoreceptors at this point.

8.   If it is true that cones are concentrated in the fovea, why do we see color in images that fall outside the fovea?
     (a) The fovea has no distinct boundaries. It covers a large area of the retina.
     (b) Rods can simulate the illusion of color.
     (c) There are some cones in the periphery of the retina.
     (d) Movement is often experienced as color.

9. Your friend LuAnn claims she was abducted by aliens. While a prisoner, she observed an intergalactic battle between the Goodums and the Evildoers. This battle took place in space outside the orbit of Pluto. She claims the sounds of exploding star cruisers could be heard all over that section of space. You know that she's a little goofy because
    (a) cound waves can't be carried by metal.
    (b) sound waves do not travel in a vacuum.
    (c) the distance from the object producing the sound would be too great.
    (d) compression can't happen in space because there are too many molecules.

10. You are a surgeon and have been asked to insert a prosthesis to replace a portion of a person's auditory system that has become fused and no longer functions properly. This portion was the crucial part that dealt with bone conduction. What portion will you be replacing?
    (a) cochlea   (c) pinna
    (c) eardrum   (d) auditory ossicles

11. Bill likes to work in his shop at night after work. He frequently uses a power saw which is very loud, and afterwards he suffers from tinnitus. It is likely that in the future Bill may suffer from
    (a) conduction deafness.   (c) stimulation deafness.
    (b) nerve deafness.   (d) all of the above.

12. As a young child, Toby suffered many middle ear infections. When Toby turned two, his pediatrician recommended that he consult an otolaryngologist (ear and throat specialist). The specialist would probably be looking for symptoms of what disorder?
    (a) conduction deafness   (c) stimulation deafness
    (b) nerve deafness   (d) tone deafness

13. George has a rare medical problem which will be fatal unless he has immediate surgery. The by-product of the surgery is that he will lose one of his chemical senses. He, however, has a choice as to which one to lose. Which of the following would be appropriate recommendations on your part? (You may choose more than one.)
    (a) Eliminate the sense of smell because his sense of taste will remain intact to help protect him from bad food.
    (b) Eliminate the sense of smell because it has little purpose beside enhancing the flavor of food.
    (c) Eliminate the sense of taste because he would lose his subjective flavor of food if his sense of smell was removed.
    (d) Eliminate the sense of taste because his sense of smell will remain intact to help protect him from bad food.

14. When a person is tested for allergies, a commonly used method is the "scratch test." In this procedure many small, very shallow incisions or "scratches" are made on the back and substances are painted on the scratches to test the body's reaction. Doctors have made a wise choice of the back for this test because
    (a) the pollen-containing substances will have less effect on overall physiological functioning when introduced through the back.
    (b) the back does not scar as easily as other areas of the skin and so there is less permanent disfiguration.
    (c) there are fewer receptors on the back and hence less sensitivity.
    (d) there is less of a problem of sensory adaptation.

15. You walk in the front door from work and detect that your husband has burned the fish dinner. The odor is enough to drive you out of the house. After a while the smell has greatly diminished. At this time you take out the trash. When you re-enter the house you again smell the odor of burned fish. Why did the odor seem less offensive after you had been in the house for a while?
    (a) because of the process known as sensory adaptation
    (b) because you habituated to the smell
    (c) because the degree of sensitivity of the gustatory sense diminished
    (d) because of the process known as counterirritation
    (e) because your husband finally broke down and took a bath

16. If you are asked to think about your hair, you can, but you probably do not usually pay much attention to the way that your hair feels on your head. The reason that you do not is that
    (a) you are selectively attending to only important stimuli.
    (b) you have accommodated to the feel of your hair.
    (c) there are few touch receptors on your head.
    (d) you have been deprived of a sufficient amount of this type of stimulus previously.

Chapter Review

1. Our senses act as a _____ _____ system. Only certain kinds of energy are selected for conversion to nerve impulses because of the _____ of the receptors. Many sensory systems _____ the environment into important features before sending nerve impulses to the brain. Also, sensory systems _____ these important features into usable messages for the brain.

2. Sensory receptors act as biological _____ by converting one form of energy into _____ _____.

3. Localization of function means that the sensation you experience depends upon the specific area of the _____ which receives the message from the sense organs.

4. "Seeing" ultimately takes place in the _____. Thus, the senses do not send back xerox-like pictures of the world, but instead they collect, analyze, and transmit _____ to the _____. This process is called _____.

5. The smallest amount of stimulation necessary for sensation to occur is the _____ _____. A stimulus that causes anxiety or embarrassment may be sensed long before it is perceived because of _____ _____ when the threshold is raised.

6. A threshold or limit is called the _____. Any time information is processed below the normal _____, awareness for it is said to be _____. Studies have shown that such stimuli experienced below the level of conscious awareness are basically _____.

7. The _____ threshold is the amount of change in a stimulus necessary to produce a just noticeable difference. This is also referred to as the study of _____ _____ _____s. According to Weber's Law, the amount of change in a stimulus necessary to produce a JND is a constant _____ of the original stimulus intensity.

8. As a physical property of light, wavelength corresponds to the psychological experience of _____, or the specific color of a stimulus, Colors are narrow bands of the visible spectrum. Colors produced by a very narrow band of wavelengths are said to be pure or _____. Brightness corresponds roughly to the _____ of light waves.

9. The _____ focuses the incoming image on the layer of light-sensitive cells at the back of the eye called the _____. The focusing of the incoming image is called _____. The clear covering on the front of the eye is the _____.

10. If the eye is too short, _____ objects cannot be focused, but _____ objects are clear. This is farsightedness or _____. If the eyeball is too long, _____ objects cannot be focused, and nearsightedness or _____ results. When either the cornea or the lens is misshapen, some of the visual field will be partially focused or fuzzy. This condition is called _____. If the lens becomes less resilient because of age and cannot accommodate as easily, the resulting condition is called _____.

11. The _____ is a colored circular muscle that controls the amount of light that enters the eye through the _____. There are two types of receptors on the retina. The _____ function in bright light and produce _____ sensations and pick up _____ details. By contrast, the _____ are incapable of picking up _____. They are much more sensitive to _____ than the _____. Therefore _____ are mainly responsible for our ability to see in very dim light.

12. Each eye has a place where there are no receptors because the optic nerve exits at the back of the eyeball. This place is called the _____ _____. The cones are concentrated in the _____. This is the place where an image is focused for greatest _____. The number of cones _____ rapidly as we move away from the _____.

13. The _____ reach their greatest numbers about 20 degrees to each side of the _____, so much _____ vision is _____ vision. Since _____ are especially sensitive to dim light, the best night vision occurs when looking slightly to the _____ of an object.

14. Rods and cones have differing maximal color sensitivities. The cones are most sensitive to wavelengths in the _____-_____ region of the spectrum. You may have seen some emergency vehicles this color. Remember, rods do not produce _____, but some colored dim lights will appear brighter than others. At night and under conditions of dim light when rod vision predominates, the brightest-colored light will be _____ or _____-_____. Many emergency vehicles now have _____ emergency lights for nighttime work.

15. The _____ (or three-color) theory of color vision holds that there are three types of cones, each with a heightened sensitivity to a specific color: _____, _____, or _____. Other colors are assumed to result from a combination of these. A basic problem with this theory is that four colors seem to be psychologically primary: the original three and _____.

16. The _____-_____ theory was developed to explain why you can't have a reddish-green or a yellowish-blue. According to this theory the visual system can produce messages for either red or green, yellow or blue, black or white. Coding one color in a pair seems to _____ the opposite message color. Fatigue caused by making one response causes an _____ of the opposite color as the system recovers.

17. In reality, both theories may be correct at a particular level in the visual system. The trichromatic theory seems to apply at the level of the _____ where three types of visual _____ have been found. Also, researchers have recently confirmed that each cone contains only one _____ and that it is controlled by its own gene. The opponent-process theory applies to events recorded in the _____ _____ after information leaves the retina.

18. The person who has total _____ _____ sees the world as if it were a black and white movie.

19. More common than total color blindness is partial color blindness, or _____ _____. Red-green color blindness is a fairly common form of partial color blindness and is usually found in _____. Color blindness is caused by changes in the _____ that control red, green, and blue pigments in the cones.

20. Both of the above conditions (color blindness and color weakness) can be detected by a common test for color blindness called the _____ test.

21. The eyes become more sensitive to light at night due to a process called _____ _____. Most of the eye's increased sensitivity comes from the _____ which contain a pigment called visual purple or _____. Increased concentrations of this pigment correspond directly to improved _____ _____. This process, _____ _____, can be speeded up by being exposed to only _____ light. Night _____ may occur if a person has a _____ _____ deficiency because _____ production declines.

22. Sound travels as invisible waves of _____ and _____ in the air. Basically, any vibrating object will produce wound waves by setting _____ molecules in motion. The _____ of sound waves corresponds to perceived pitch, just as the _____ corresponds to sensed loudness.

23. The external portion of the ear or _____ helps funnel and concentrate sounds. The sound waves set air molecules in motion which collide with the _____ which causes the three bones of the middle ear, called the _____ _____, to vibrate. The third bone is attached to a second membrane called the _____ _____. This membrane moves back and forth and sets up waves in the canals of the _____. When these waves stimulate tiny _____ _____, nerve impulses are sent to the temporal lobes of the brain.

24. The _____ theory of hearing states that as pitch rises, nerve impulses of the same frequency are fed into the auditory nerve. The _____ theory states that pitch is signaled by the area of the cochlea most strongly activated.

25. When the eardrums or auditory ossicles are immobilized by disease or injury, the resulting condition is called _____ deafness. This type of deafness can often be overcome by making sounds _____. _____ deafness is a hearing loss resulting from damage to the auditory nerve. Not much can be done to remedy this type of deafness. Exposure to very loud noise can result in _____ deafness. _____ implants can help overcome deafness by stimulating the auditory nerve directly and bypassing the haircells.

26. The danger of hearing loss depends on both the _____ of sound and the _____ of the exposure. Any activity that causes a temporary loss of hearing (temporary _____ _____) or a whistling or ringing sensation (_____) in the ears may cause _____ deafness.

27. Both gustation and olfaction are _____ in nature. As air enters the nose, it passes over millions of _____ _____ in the lining of the upper nasal passages. This is the point where _____ occurs and nerve signals are sent to the brain.

28. It is currently believed that different odors correspond to different shaped _____ which fit into the "holes" of the odor receptors having the capability of detecting many different types of odors. This is called the _____ and _____ theory. If a person develops a sort of "smell blindness" for one type of odor this is called _____. Approximately 1.2 % of the population cannot smell at all. This can be caused by _____, _____, blows to the _____, or exposure to _____.

29. The four basic taste sensations are _____, _____, _____, and _____. We are most sensitive to the taste of _____ and least sensitive to _____. We experience the sense of taste when food is dissolved and enters the _____ _____ where _____ takes place and a nerve impulse is sent to the brain. The sense of taste is particularly influenced by _____. Part of the reason people seem to have different tastes is based upon _____ differences. Also, as we age, the rate of _____ _____ replacement slows down.

30. The somesthetic senses include the _____ senses (touch, pressure, pain, etc.), the _____ senses (body position and movement), and the _____ senses (balance).

31. The skin receptors produce at least five different sensations: _____ _____, _____, _____, _____, and _____. Some areas of the body are more sensitive than others because they contain a greater concentration of _____. The most frequently found _____ in the skin is for _____.

32. There are two kinds of pain. The _____ system consists of pain (_____ pain) carried by _____ nerve fibers. This pain is sharp and is associated with specific body areas. The _____ system is carried by _____ nerve fibers and is nagging and widespread.

33. Many sensory events never reach conscious awareness. There are three reasons for this. A decrease in sensory response that accompanies a constant or unchanging stimulus is called _____ _____. This does not occur in the eye because of tiny tremors (called _____ _____) in the eye muscles which shift visual images from one receptor to the next.

34. Another reason why some sensory events never reach conscious awareness is because humans have the ability to "tune in on" some incoming information while ignoring others. This is called _____ _____. The ability is probably based on a _____ - centered process of selecting sensory messages.

35. The third reason probably explains why acupuncture works. This process is known as _____ _____ and occurs when the acupuncturist's needles activate small pain fibers which relay through a central biasing system to close the _____ to intense or chronic pain.

36. Both acupuncture and electrical stimulation cause a build up of _____ in the brain. There are a large number of receptors for this chemical in the _____ system and brain areas associated pleasure, pain, and emotion. This chemical is similar to _____ and may explain the "high" or euphoria associated with childbirth, masochism, acupuncture, and other similar painful or stressful events.

37. There are four factors that can be used to influence the amount of pain experienced. These are
     _____, _____, _____, and
     _____. High levels of _____ increase pain so if the
     anxiety can be lowered, less pain will be experienced.

38. If a person can shift _____ away from the pain by being _____, this
     can help alleviate pain. If the painful stimulus can be _____ differently, pain can be
     reduced. Finally, a person might gain some degree of _____ over the painful stimulus by
     being able to terminate it when it gets too intense or by applying another mildly painful stimulus. This last
     process is called _____.

39. The space adaptation syndrome actually refers to space _____. It occurs when sensory
     information from the _____ organs and the _____ canals (both
     of the vestibular system) fails to match the information received from the eyes and the body. This is called the
     _____ _____ theory.

ANSWER KEYS

Do You Know the Information?

Multiple Choice

1. (b) obj. 1, p. 87
2. (d) obj. 2, p. 87
3. (c) obj. 3, p. 88
4. (a) obj. 5, p. 88
5. (d) obj. 6, p. 88
6. (d) obj. 8, p. 89
7. (a) obj. 10, p. 91
8. (b) obj. 11, p. 92
9. (a) obj. 12, p. 92
10. (c) obj. 13, p. 92
11. (a) obj. 14, p. 93
12. (d) obj. 15, p. 94
13. (d) obj. 17, p. 94
14. (b) obj. 18, p. 97
15. (b) obj. 19, p. 98
16. (d) obj. 20, p. 98
17. (b) obj. 22, p. 102
18. (d) obj. 22, p. 102
19. (c) obj. 23, p. 103
20. (d) obj. 24, p. 103
21. (d) obj. 24, p. 104
22. (c) obj. 26, p. 104
23. (b) obj. 27, p. 105
24. (d) obj. 28, p. 106
25. (c) obj. 29, p. 107
26. (a) obj. 32, p. 107
27. (c) obj. 32, p. 109
28. (b) obj. 32, p. 109

29. (c) obj. 33, p. 110
30. (d) obj. 33, p. 110
31. (d) obj. 34, pp. 112-113
32. (a) obj. 36, p. 115

True-False

1. T, obj. 4, p. 88
2. F, obj. 7, p. 89
3. T, obj. 12, p. 92
4. F, obj. 16, p. 94
5. T, obj. 17, p. 94
6. T, obj. 17, p. 96
7. F, obj. 19, p. 98
8. T, obj. 20, p. 100
9. T, obj. 26, p. 105
10. T, obj. 27, pp. 106-107
11. F, obj. 28, p. 107
12. T, obj. 30, p. 108
13. F, obj. 30, p. 107
14. T, obj. 31, p. 108

Matching

1. T, obj. 24, p. 103
2. G, obj. 12, p. 92
3. J, objs. 26-27, p. 105
4. A, obj. 22, p. 101
5. I, obj. 7, p. 89
6. H, obj. 22, p. 102

7. F, obj. 30, p. 107
8. D, obj. 9, p. 90
9. B, obj. 10, p. 91
10. E, obj. 24, p. 103
11. Q, obj. 33, p. 110
12. O, obj. 8, p. 89
13. M, obj. 20, p. 101
14. C, obj. 34, p. 114
15. N, obj. 31, p. 108
16. P, obj. 28, p. 107
17. L, obj. 24, p. 103

Can You Apply the Information?

1. (d) obj. 2, p. 87
2. (a) obj. 3, p. 88
3. (b) obj. 7, p. 89
4. (d) obj. 8, p. 89
5. (d) obj. 9, p. 90
6. (b) obj. 12, p. 92
7. (d) obj. 14, p. 94
8. (c) objs. 14-16, pp. 93-94
9. (b) obj. 21, p. 101
10. (d) obj. 22, p. 102
11. (c) obj. 24, p. 104
12. (a) obj. 24, p. 104
13. (c,d)objs. 26-27, pp. 105-106
14. (c) obj. 30, p. 108
15. (a) obj. 32, p. 109
16. (a) obj. 32, p. 109

Chapter Review

1.   data reduction, sensitivity, analyze, code (p. 87)
2.   transducers, nerve impulses (p. 87)
3.   brain (p. 88)
4.   brain, information, brain, sensation (p. 88)
5.   absolute threshold (p. 88); perceptual defense (p. 89)
6.   limen, limen, subliminal, weak (p. 89)
7.   difference, JND, proportion (p. 90)
8.   hue, saturated, amplitude (p. 91)
9.   lens, retina, accommodation, cornea (p. 92)
10.   nearby, distant, hyperopia, distant, myopia, astigmatism, presbyopia (p. 92)
11.   iris, pupil (p. 92); cones, color, fine, rods, color, light, cones, rods (p. 93)
12.   blind spot, fovea, acuity, decreases, fovea (p. 94)
13.   rods, fovea, peripheral, rod, rods, side (p. 94)
14.   yellowish-green, color, blue, blue-green, blue (p. 96)
15.   trichromatic, red, green, blue, yellow (p. 96)
16.   opponent-process, block, afterimage (p. 97)
17.   retina, pigments, pigment, optic pathways (p. 97)
18.   color blindness (p. 98)
19.   color weakness, males, genes (p. 98)
20.   Ishihara (p. 98)
21.   dark adaptation, rods, rhodopsin, night vision, dark adaptation, red (p. 100); blindness, vitamin A, rhodopsin (p. 101)
22.   compression, rarefaction, air, frequency, amplitude (p. 101)
23.   pinna (p. 101); eardrum, auditory ossicles, oval window, cochlea, hair cells (p. 102)
24.   frequency, place (p. 103)
25.   conduction, louder, Nerve (p. 103); stimulation (p. 104); Cochlear, (p. 103)
26.   loudness, length, threshold shift, tinnitus, stimulation (p. 104)
27.   chemical, nerve fibers, transduction (p. 105)
28.   molecules, lock, key, anosmia (p. 105); infections, allergies, head, chemicals (p. 106)
29.   sweet, salt, sour, bitter, bitter, sweet, taste bud (p. 106); transduction (p. 87); smell, genetic, taste bud (p. 106)
30.   skin, kinesthetic, vestibular (p. 107)
31.   light touch, pressure, pain, cold, warmth, receptors, receptor, pain (p. 107)
32.   warning, somatic, large, reminding, small (p. 108)
33.   sensory adaptation, physiological nystagmus (p. 109)
34.   selective attention (p. 109); brain (p. 110)
35.   sensory gating, gates (p. 110)
36.   endorphins, limbic, morphine (p. 110)
37.   anxiety, attention, control, interpretation, anxiety (p. 112)
38.   attention, distracted (p. 112); interpreted, control, counterirritation (p. 113)
39.   sickness (p. 114); otolith, semicircular, sensory conflict (p. 115)

Chapter 5

Perceiving the World

KEY TERMS AND CONCEPTS

perception
size, shape, and brightness constancy
figure-ground
   reversible figure
perceptual organizing principles
   figure-ground, nearness, similarity,
   continuation, closure, contiguity
perceptual hypothesis
   ambiguous stimulus
depth perception
   visual cliff
monocular and binocular cues
muscular cues
   accommodation vs. convergence
stereoscopic vision
   retinal disparity
pictorial depth cues
   linear perspective, relative size, light
   and shadow, overlap, texture gradient,
   aerial perspective, relative motion
moon illusion
   apparent distance hypothesis
perceptual habit
   inverted vision

adaptation level
   context, frame of reference
illusion versus hallucination
   stoboscopic movement
   Muller-Lyer illusion
    size distance invariance
attention — selective vs. divided
adaptation
habituation
   orientation response
bottom-up and top-down processing
   perceptual expectancy
   mental categories
perceptions as reconstructions
   accuracy of eyewitnesses
    weapon focus
   reality testing
   dishabituation
parapsychology
   clairvoyance, telepathy
   precognition, psychokinesis
coincidence
   Zener cards
   other interpretations of ESP

LEARNING OBJECTIVES

To demonstrate mastery of this chapter you should be able to:
1.   Define perception.

2.   Describe the following constancies:
      a.   size

      b.   shape

      c.   brightness

3.   Give examples of the following as they relate to the organization of perception:
      a.   figure-ground

      b.   nearness

      c.   similarity

      d.   continuity

      e.   closure

      f.   contiguity

4.   Explain what a perceptual hypothesis is.

5.   Define and give an example of an ambiguous stimulus.

6.   Define depth perception and discuss the nativistic and empirical view of it.

7.   Describe the following cues for depth perception and indicate in each case whether the cue is monocular or binocular:
    a.   accommodation

    b.   convergence

    c.   retinal disparity

8.   Describe the visual adaptations found among birds.

9.   Describe the following two-dimensional, monocular, pictorial depth cues:
    a.   linear perspective

    b.   relative size

c.   light and shadow

d.   overlap

e.   texture gradients

f.   aerial perspective

g.   relative motion (motion parallax)

10.   Describe the phenomenon of the moon illusion. Include in your explanation the apparent distance hypothesis.

11.   Define "perceptual habit" and explain how it allows learning to affect perception.

12.   Explain and give an example of context.

13.   Describe and give an example of the concept of adaptation level.

14.   Differentiate between an illusion and a hallucination.

15.   Describe at least one practical use of the stroboscopic movement illusion.

16.   Describe the Muller-Lyer illusion and explain how perceptual habits may account for this illusion.

17.   Define attention and list the factors which affect it. (Include a differentiation between selective attention and divided attention.)

18.   Differentiate habituation from sensory adaptation. Include the concept of the orientation response.

19.   Explain and give experimental evidence of how motives may alter attention and perception.

20.   Explain how perceptual expectancies may influence perception.

* * * * * * * * * *

The following objectives are related to the material in the "Applications" and "Exploration" sections of your text.
21.   Explain why most eyewitness testimony is inaccurate. Include the idea of weapon focus.

22.   Explain what the term "reality testing" means.

23.   Explain Maslow's theory of perceptual awareness.

24.   Discuss how attention affects perception.

25.   Define extrasensory perception.

26.   Define the term parapsychology.

27.   Describe the following psychic abilities:
    a.   clairvoyance

    b.   telepathy

    c.   precognition

    d.   psychokinesis

28.   Explain why most psychologists remain skeptical about psi abilities.

SELF-QUIZZES

Do You Know the Information?

Multiple Choice

1.   Perception is the
    (a)   process of assembling sensations into usable pictures of the world.
    (b)   same as the process of sensation.
    (c)   transducing of physical stimuli into nerve impulses.
    (d)   habituation of attention.

2. Which of the following constancies holds that an object would appear to remain the same even though the retinal image would actually change?
    (a) size
    (b) shape
    (c) brightness
    (d) all of the above

3. The perceptual principle that helps us organize sensations so that incomplete figures are completed and have consistent overall forms is called
    (a) continuation.
    (b) similarity.
    (c) closure.
    (d) figure-ground.

4. An ambiguous stimulus is one in which the
    (a) stimulus is not clearly defined.
    (b) passive nature of perception is revealed.
    (c) stimulus is viewed using only depth cues.
    (d) stimulus allows more than one interpretation.

5. The ability to see three-dimensional space and accurately estimate distances is
    (a) limited to animals (including man) that are capable of learning.
    (b) the definition of the perception of depth.
    (c) facilitated by binocular cues but not by monocular cues.
    (d) described by all of the above.

6. The visual cliff is
    (a) a device used in investigating depth perception.
    (b) the point on the visible spectrum where our vision begins to decline.
    (c) a mechanism in the eyeball that facilitates depth perception.
    (d) a pictorial representation of how the angles of objects determine our perception of distance.

7. Indicate whether each of the following is a monocular (M) depth cue or a binocular (B) cue.
    (a) _____ retinal disparity
    (b) _____ convergence
    (c) _____ accommodation
    (d) _____ overlap

8. The process of the lens in the eye bending or bulging to focus nearby objects and then reporting its activities to the brain is called
    (a) stereoscopic vision.
    (b) convergence.
    (c) accommodation.
    (d) retinal disparity.

9. Retinal disparity provides for the perception of depth because
    (a) the eyes turn in slightly to focus on close objects and this muscle activity is sent to the brain.
    (b) each eye receives a slightly different view of the world and the resulting images are fused into one.
    (c) motion parallax works best in combination with this binocular cue.
    (d) accommodation only works well when objects are beyond 50 feet.

10. Which pictorial depth cue refers to the apparent convergence of parallel lines in the environment?
    (a) relative size
    (b) linear perspective
    (c) aerial perspective
    (d) interposition

11. The moon illusion occurs because of
    (a) the image of the moon being magnified and hence appearing larger on the horizon.
    (b) the distance of the moon being greater when it is directly overhead than when it is on the horizon.
    (c) a greater apparent distance when the moon is on the horizon and seen behind houses and trees.
    (d) the moon casting a larger image on the horizon.

12.   Established patterns of organization and attention are called
 (a) illusions.   (c) adaptation levels.
 (b) categories.   (d) perceptual habits.

13.   The Ames room creates perceptual confusion because
 (a) the person is forced either to perceive the room as square or to refuse to perceive the people changing size.
 (b) the brain has no categories to help analyze the situation.
 (c) most people choose size constancy over shape constancy.
 (d) of the illusion of motion parallax.

14.   Inverted vision experiments with humans have shown that
 (a) with time and active movement, humans can develop new perceptual habits and function normally with completely different visual cues.
 (b) perceptual habits are so ingrained that humans cannot learn to adapt to new visual cues.
 (c) we are like most animals in that we adapt to the differences almost immediately.
 (d) basic physiology can be modified so that when the lens (goggles) are removed, we do not recover.

15.   The fact that you are tall (6 feet 5 inches) but you appear short when compared to a 7 foot 3 inch person demonstrates
 (a) relative size.   (c) context.
 (b) adaptation level.   (d) perceptual prejudice.

16.   In judging size, weight, etc., you have your own personal "medium" point or frame of reference. This is referred to as
 (a) adaptation level.   (c) level of habituation.
 (b) perceptual expectancy. (d) perceptual sensitivity.

17.   The difference between an illusion and a hallucination is
 (a) an illusion is present when a person perceives a stimulus that does not exist, such as a mirage in a desert.
 (b) hallucinations are present when a person distorts an existing stimulus.
 (c) a person who is hallucinating believes a stimulus exists when one does not.
 (d) illusions are additive, hallucinations are subtractive.

18.   Perceptual habits contribute to the effect of the Muller-Lyer illusion because
 (a) people have more experience with the V-tipped line looking farther away than the arrowhead-tipped line.
 (b) a person who has had little or no experience with perceptual habits dealing with this particular illusion is not fooled by it.
 (c) the illusion is based upon years of experience with the edges and corners of rooms and buildings.
 (d) of all of the above.

19.   Which of the following factors does *not directly* affect attention?
 (a) repetition   (c) motivation
 (b) clarity   (d) contrast in stimulation

20.   If a person is said to have habituated to a stimulus
 (a) there is a decrease in the actual number of sensory messages sent to the brain.
 (b) the person is responding automatically to the orientation stimulus.
 (c) there is a decrease in the orientation response.
 (d) the person begins responding more to the stimulus.

21. The study in which males rated a blind date as more attractive after reading a sexually arousing passage demonstrates that
    (a) intense stimuli are attention-getters.
    (b) motives can affect perception.
    (c) perceptual categories do not affect sexual preference.
    (d) an emotional stimulus can shift attention away from relevant information.

22. If information is analyzed starting with small features and building upward into a complete perception, this is called
    (a) perceptual constancy.
    (b) perceptual expectancy.
    (c) bottom-up processing.
    (d) top-down processing.

23. One group of subjects sees a figure and a word that describes it. A second group sees the same figure but with a different descriptive word. Later, both groups are asked to draw what they have seen. Each group tends to conform their drawings to the particular word they have seen. Bruner says that the subjects have built up_____ that have affected their perceptions.
    (a) expectations
    (b) categories
    (c) adaptation levels
    (d) continuations

24. The statement "We see what we believe" refers to the idea that
    (a) perception enables us to objectively test reality.
    (b) our perceptions offer us a way to objectively affirm our existence.
    (c) we are what our beliefs tell us we are.
    (d) perception reflects the needs, expectations, and values of the perceiver.

25. One of the main reasons why eyewitness testimony in a court may be inaccurate is because
    (a) the reconstruction of events may contain the attitudes and subjective beliefs of the eyewitness.
    (b) the person's level of dishabituation may be higher.
    (c) of sensory adaptation.
    (d) of the the lack of all of the necessary cues for accurate perception.

26. Perceptual awareness is marked by
    (a) immersion in the understanding of past experience.
    (b) controlling the experience.
    (c) evaluating the experience as it evolves.
    (d) a lack of self-consciousness.

27. Parapsychology is defined as the study of
    (a) events which seem to defy accepted scientific laws.
    (b) the changes in the pattern of mental functions.
    (c) hypnosis and meditation.
    (d) Zener cards.

28. Zener cards are used to
    (a) help make the study of ESP more objective.
    (b) test for the presence of psychokinesis.
    (c) differentiate psi from psychic phenomena.
    (d) aid the study of hypnosis.

29. Most psychologists remain skeptical about psi abilities because
    (a) the abilities are so inconsistent.
    (b) some subjects who display the abilities have received credit for a run of luck.
    (c) improvements in research methods have usually yielded fewer positive results.
    (d) all of the above are true.

True-False

_____ 1. A newly sighted person's vision is actually fairly good since most of the necessary concepts can be learned before sight is restored.

_____ 2. Infants and new-born animals do not show evidence of depth perception; it is an acquired trait.

_____ 3. The most important source of depth perception is retinal disparity.

_____ 4. Pictorial depth cues strive to give the illusion of three dimensions from a two-dimensional cue.

_____ 5. If an artist wishes to depict two objects of the same size at different distances, she should make the more distant object smaller.

_____ 6. People who have lost one eye depend less on motion parallax for depth perception because it is primarily a binocular cue.

_____ 7. The moon appears larger on the horizon because extra cues there cause the eyes to focus on a more distant point than they do when you look overhead. This causes changes in accommodation.

_____ 8. Learning helps to build perceptual habits that may force us to perceive our world in incorrect or stereotyped ways.

_____ 9. The Muller-Lyer illusion is responsible for the illusion of motion in a motion picture.

_____10. Past experience, motives, context, or suggestions may create a perceptual expectancy that sets a person to perceive in a certain way.

_____11. Reality testing may involve using a different sensory modality to serve as a check on perceptions.

_____12. By paying close attention, a person can dishabituate to a stimulus and bring renewed freshness to perception.

_____13. The author of your text says that an open but skeptical mind is probably the best attitude to maintain toward psychic phenomena.

Can You Apply the Information?

1. An old joke — Two men are in an airplane. First man, "Boy, we sure are high up. Those cars on the ground look like ants." Second man, "You fool! Those *are* ants. We're still on the ground!" The problem here is obviously a failure of
   (a) dishabituation.
   (b) shape constancy.
   (c) size constancy.
   (d) brightness constancy.
   (e) intelligence.

2. Anyone who is learning to read must be able to distinguish that "p," "b," and "d" are three different letters with entirely different sounds. This means that someone learning to read must disregard (or unlearn) _____ with regards to those letters.
   (a) size constancy
   (b) shape constancy
   (c) native perception
   (d) figure-ground

3. In a grocery store, if the apples and oranges are all mixed together in a bin but the oranges tend to stand out more than the apples, this demonstrates the principle of
   (a) contiguity.
   (b) continuation.
   (c) nearness.
   (d) similarity.

4. When a ventriloquist appears to make sound come out of a dummy's mouth, he or she is using which perceptual organizing cue?
   (a) nearness
   (b) continuity
   (c) similarity
   (d) contiguity

5. Soldiers on the ground always wear camouflage uniforms with the pattern of the camouflage similar to the surrounding environment. The purpose is simply to
   (a) break up similarity organization.
   (b) break up figure-ground organization.
   (c) break up contiguity organization.
   (d) break up nearness organization.

6. A common scenario in detective novels is the point in time when the sleuth puts the available evidence together and comes up with, what he or she believes to be, the identity and motive(s) of the culprit. This does not stop the collection of further evidence even if the initial judgements are overturned. What the sleuth does is develop
   (a) a perceptual hypothesis.
   (b) a perceptual habit.
   (c) a perceptual expectancy.
   (d) a reversible figure.

7. An inkblot from the Rorschach Inkblot personality test is a good example of an ambiguous stimulus.
   (a) True
   (b) False

8. If you hold your index fingers approximately four inches in front of your eyes, four inches apart, pointed toward each other, and slowly bring them together, a small finger will "appear" in the middle with a fingernail at each end. This appearance demonstrates which bodily cue for depth perception?
   (a) convergence
   (b) accommodation
   (c) a monocular one
   (d) retinal disparity

9. You observe a car going 55 mph in a shopping center parking lot. You are instantly alarmed. The same car, driver, and speed on an interstate highway would not even slightly arouse your attention. The difference in the two perceptions is a good example of how _____ affects perceptions.
   (a) nearness
   (b) motion parallax
   (c) ambiguous stimuli
   (d) context

10. You have a friend who is a long-distance runner (a 13 mile race is nothing for him) who consents to run with you in a 10,000 meter (6.2 miles) race. He describes the race as "short" or "a breeze," whereas you do well just to finish because you are used to 3 mile races. It is obvious that you and your friend have different
   (a) accommodation levels.
   (b) adaptation levels.
   (c) contexts.
   (d) averages.

11. You are driving your car down a long flat stretch of highway on a hot summer day and the heat waves coming from the asphalt one-half mile ahead appear to be chickens running across the road. What is this phenomenon?
   (a) an illusion
   (b) stroboscopic movement
   (c) a hallucination
   (d) brightness constancy

12. You are very tired because you stayed up all night studying for exams. When you finally get to bed the following night and turn off the lights, you see what appears to be little green Martians dancing around your bed. What is this phenomenon?
   (a) an example of relative size
   (b) a hallucination
   (c) an illusion
   (d) a delusion

13.   Having both the radio and the television on at the same time usually causes a problem for most people because of
      (a) selective attention.
      (b) divided attention.
      (c) contrast.
      (d) incongruity.

14.   Which of the following is an example of habituation?
      (a) A person can see better in the dark after being in a dimly lit room for 30 minutes.
      (b) Your hand is fatigued after carrying a heavy book for six hours.
      (c) Because of a shot of novacaine a person feels less pain in a sore tooth while having it filled.
      (d) While taking a test Sally does not think about how the shoes feel on her feet.

15.   Bill usually gets mad when his wife Laura comes home even 15 minutes late. On this particular night Laura is one hour late. As Bill waits for his wife, his anger turns into concern. He is genuinely worried about her. When she finally comes in the door Bill says, "Laura, where have you been? I've been worried about you." Accustomed to Bill's usual nasty remarks she snaps back, "What do you mean yelling at me like that? I'm a grown woman!" A fight begins. Laura's unjustified retort is due to
      (a) context.
      (b) her adaptation level .
      (c) perceptual expectancy.
      (d) categories.

16.   You are still seeing those little green Martians. You reach out to try to grab one. This is an example of
      (a) an illusion.
      (b) an ambiguous stimulus.
      (c) reality testing.
      (d) nearness.

17.   You're taking a test and the air conditioning blower goes off in the room. You didn't notice how loud the blower was, but now the silence is "deafening." Noticing the silence is an example of
      (a) habituation.
      (b) overlap.
      (c) illusion.
      (d) dishabituation.

18.   You are playing poker. Even when your mind is blank, one of the other players is able to become aware of your "hand." Your friend is
      (a) clairvoyant.
      (b) telepathic.
      (c) psychokinetic.
      (d) precognitive.

19.   Another friend in the same poker game can perceive the kinds of cards you're holding only when you're concentrating on them. This friend is displaying
      (a) clairvoyance.
      (b) telepathy.
      (c) precognition.
      (d) psychokinesis.

20.   Minerva Mrytle, the famous psychic, makes predictions for the coming new year every December. She predicts bumper world food crops and a new breakthrough in nuclear arms control. Which skill is she using?
      (a) clairvoyance
      (b) telepathy
      (c) precognition
      (d) psychokinesis

21.   A researcher who is investigating a person's ability to make a desk float in the air is studying
      (a) clairvoyance.
      (b) precognition.
      (c) psychokinesis.
      (d) suggestibility.

Chapter Review

1.   The process of assembling sensations into a usable picture of the world is called
_____.

2.   A newly sighted person does not immediately recognize his environment, but rather must
_____ to identify objects, to read clocks, numbers and letters, and to judge size and
distances.

3.   The fact that the perceived size of an object remains the same even though the size of its retinal image
changes is called _____ _____. _____
_____ refers to the idea that objects are perceived as having the same shape even
though the retinal image of the object changes depending on the angle from which the object is viewed. Even
though under changing lighting conditions objects reflect different proportions of light, we still perceive the
apparent brightness of an object as the same. This is known as _____
_____.

4.   The simplest organization of sensations is to group them so that an object stands out against some plainer
background. This process is called _____ - _____ organi-
zation.

5.   There are also other ways to organize perceptions such as when stimuli close together are grouped together.
This is called _____. When stimuli are closely related in size, shape, color, or
form, they are grouped on the basis of _____.

6.   Stimuli may also be perceived together or in a certain way because we tend toward simplicity. This organiza-
tional principle is called _____. If an incomplete figure is seen as complete so that it
will have a consistent overall form, _____ is influencing perception. When
two events appear close together in space and time, then _____ may explain
why one event seems to be caused by the other.

7.   A "guess" about a phenomenon held until evidence contradicts it is called a _____
_____. A stimulus which allows for more than one interpretation is called
_____.

8.   The ability to see three-dimensional space and to estimate distances is known as _____
_____. If you believe this ability is learned then you are a(n) _____, but if
you believe that it is an innate ability you are a(n) _____. Research indicates that this ability
consistently emerges in humans at about _____ months of age. The nearly universal emergence at this time
suggests that it depends more on _____ development than it does on individual _____.
This ability has been investigated by using the _____ _____.

9.   Cues that require the use of only one eye for the perception of depth are called
_____. Depth cues that require the use of both eyes are called
_____ cues.

10.   A number of depth cues combine to produce the experience of three-dimensional space. One such cue is
_____ which refers to the ability of the lens in each eye to bend more to focus
objects close to the eye than at a distance. This cue is a _____ cue.

11. A second bodily cue for depth occurs when the eyes must turn in to focus on an object which is 50 feet or less away. This second bodily source of depth is _____, a _____ cue.

12. _____ _____ is based upon the fact that the eyes are about two and one-half inches apart so each eye receives a slightly different view of an object. When the two images are _____ into one overall visual image, _____ vision occurs. _____ _____ is the most important source of depth perception and is a _____ cue.

13. Pictorial depth cues give the sensation of depth or three-dimensionality from _____ dimensions. All of the pictorial depth cues are _____. One such pictorial depth cue is _____ _____, which refers to the apparent convergence of parallel lines in the environment.

14. If an artist wishes to depict two objects of the same size at different distances, the artist makes the more distant object _____. This is the process of using _____ _____ to produce the sensation of depth.

15. Most objects in the environment are lighted in such a way as to create definite patterns of _____ and _____. The perception of depth is experienced when one object partially _____ the view of another. This monocular cue for depth is also called _____.

16. If you are standing in the middle of a cobblestone street, the street looks coarse near your feet, but the _____ of the stones gets smaller and finer as you look off into the distance. This gradual decrease in fine detail refers to _____ _____.

17. Smog, fog, dust, and haze also add to the apparent distance of an object. Objects seen at a great distance tend to be hazy, light in color, and lacking in detail due to _____ _____.

18. The last monocular pictorial depth cue occurs when looking out of a car window or moving your head. Objects near to you appear to move _____ than objects in the distance. This cue is known as _____ _____ or _____ _____.

19. The moon illusion refers to the fact that the moon appears _____ when it is low in the sky than when it is overhead. This is because the _____ _____ of the moon is greater when it is on the horizon and seen behind houses, trees and other environmental cues. Since the moon casts the same size image on the horizon, but seems farther away than when it is overhead, you compensate by perceiving it as _____ on the horizon.

20. Learning may affect perception by establishing patterns of organization and attention referred to as _____ _____. These may become so ingrained that they lead us to misperceive a stimulus. A lopsided room that is carefully constructed can be made to appear square. This is the case with the _____ _____, named after the man who designed it. In this room the perceiver is faced with maintaining _____ constancy or _____ constancy. Most people choose to maintain _____ constancy, thus objects can be made to appear to shrink or grow merely by placing them at various points in the room.

21. Perceptual habits are just that — habits. This is supported by experiments in which a person's vision is _____. These experiments indicate that humans can learn to _____ to a radically different perception of the world, but the key is _____ _____.

22. An important factor affecting perception is the _____ in which a stimulus is judged. For example, someone who is five feet tall would look tall in a room full of midgets. Standards by which stimuli are judged are called _____ _____ _____. Lifting a ten pound weight would feel easy if you carry around fifty pound sacks of seed all day. This depends on your _____ _____.

23. A stimulus that exists but is distorted by the perceiver is called a(n) _____. This is different from a(n) _____ in which the stimulus actually does not exist. A(n) _____ is responsible for putting the "motion" in motion pictures. It is called _____ _____.

24. The famous Muller-Lyer illusion illustrates how perceptual habits and past experience combine to produce illusions. In this illusion, a horizontal line with "arrowheads" appears _____ than the horizontal line with "Vs" on each end. People who have not _____ lots of straight lines, sharp edges, and corners are not fooled as much by the Muller-Lyer illusion.

25. The first stage of perception is _____, the selection of incoming messages. When some messages are given priority and some are put on hold, this is known as _____ _____. _____ _____ often arises from our limited capacity to process information. It can be affected by stimuli which are _____, _____, or related to _____, _____, or _____.

26. A decrease in the actual number of sensory messages sent to the brain is called _____. After messages are sent to the brain the body makes an _____ _____. When a stimulus is repeated without change, the _____ _____ decreases or _____.

27. Attention can be affected by _____. They may also alter what is _____. For example, subjects rated a picture of a blind date as more attractive after reading an _____ passage.

28. In _____ - _____ processing we analyze information starting with small units or features and build into a complete perception. In _____ - _____ processing preexisting knowledge is used to rapidly organize features into a meaningful whole.

29. Past experience, motives, context, or suggestion may set you to perceive in a certain way. This set pattern of perceiving is called _____ _____. Many times this set way of perceiving may be created by _____. Perceptual learning may build up a set of mental _____ which then help to "pigeonhole" or sort experiences.

30. _____ reflects the needs, expectations, attitudes, values, and beliefs of the perceiver. In this light not only do we "believe what we see," but we "_____ what we _____."

31. Although eyewitness testimony can be a key element in establishing guilt or innocence, such testimony frequently is _____. The perceptions of an emotionally distraught eyewitness may frequently be very _____, but our everyday perceptions may be just as _____. For instance, many fall prey to _____ _____ where they fix their entire attention on the knife or gun and do not attend to other details. In any situation having an element of doubt or uncertainty, _____ _____ involves obtaining additional information as a check on the accuracy of perceptions.

32. Some people perceive things more _____ than others. Maslow characterized people with especially accurate perceptions of themselves and others as _____, _____, and _____. He found their perceptual styles were marked by immersion in the _____ and a lack of _____ - _____. Zen masters pay _____ to bring about a _____ of perception.

33. _____ is the study of events which lie outside normal experiences and seem to defy accepted scientific laws. Such events are called _____ phenomena.

34. Four areas of psi phenomena are under investigation. One such area deals with the ability to perceive events or gain information in ways that appear unaffected by distance or normal physical barriers. This area is known as _____. Another area of study is _____, the ability to read another person's thoughts.

35. Two other areas are _____ and _____. The first is the ability to predict future events accurately. The second is the ability to exert influence over inanimate objects by will power.

36. Many people doubt the existence of psychic phenomena because of many problems. One of these is _____ which can at least partially be avoided by making the study of ESP more _____. One way of doing this is to use _____ cards.

37. Psychologists are also skeptical about psi abilities because of _____, _____, and _____. Psi abilities seem to be very _____. Many subjects receive credit for a _____ _____ _____.

38. Another problem is that most of the spectacular findings in parapsychology cannot be _____. Many believers in psychic phenomena _____ negative experimental results in their favor. Your author stresses that the best attitude toward ESP is to maintain an _____ mind while being carefully _____ of evidence reported in the popular press or by researchers who are "true believers."

ANSWER KEYS

Do You Know the Information?

Multiple Choice

1. (a) obj. 1, p. 120
2. (d) obj. 2, pp. 120-121
3. (c) obj. 3, p. 122
4. (d) obj. 5, p. 123
5. (b) obj. 6, p. 125
6. (a) obj. 6, p. 125
7. (a) B, (b) B, (c) M, (d) M,
    obj.7,9 pp. 126-129
8. (c) obj. 7, p. 126
9. (b) obj. 7, p. 126
10. (b) obj. 9, p. 128
11. (c) obj. 10, p. 131
12. (d) obj. 11, p. 131
13. (a) obj. 11, p. 132
14. (a) obj. 11, p. 133
15. (c) obj. 12, p. 134
16. (a) obj. 13, p. 134
17. (c) obj. 14, p. 134
18. (d) obj. 16, pp. 135-136
19. (b) obj. 17, pp. 136-137
20. (c) obj. 18, p. 137
21. (b) obj. 19, p. 137

22. (c) obj. 20, p. 138
23. (b) obj. 20, p. 139
24. (d) obj. 21, p. 140
25. (a) obj. 21, pp. 140-141
26. (d) obj. 23, p. 142
27. (a) obj. 26, p. 143
28. (a) obj. 27, p. 144
29. (d) obj. 28, pp. 145-146

True-False

1. F, obj. 2, p. 120
2. F, obj. 6, p. 126
3. T, obj. 7, p. 126
4. T, obj. 9, p. 128
5. T, obj. 9, p. 129
6. F, obj. 9, p. 130
7. T, obj. 10, p. 131
8. T, obj. 11, pp. 131-132
9. F, obj. 15, p. 134
10. T, obj. 20, p. 138
11. T, obj. 22, p. 142
12. T, obj. 24, p. 142
13. T, obj. 28, p. 146

Can You Apply the Information?

1. (c) obj. 2, p. 121
2. (b) obj. 2, p. 121
3. (d) obj. 3, p. 122
4. (d) obj. 3, p. 122
5. (b) obj. 3, p. 122
6. (a) obj. 4, p. 123
7. (a) obj. 5, p. 123
8. (d) obj. 7, p. 126
9. (d) obj. 12, p. 134
10. (b) obj. 13, p. 134
11. (a) obj. 14, p. 134
12. (b) obj. 14, p. 134
13. (a) obj. 17, p. 136
14. (d) obj. 18, p. 137
15. (c) obj. 20, pp. 138-139
16. (c) obj. 22, p. 142
17. (d) obj. 24, p. 142
18. (a) obj. 27, p. 143
19. (b) obj. 27, p. 144
20. (c) obj. 27, p. 144
21. (c) obj. 27, p. 144

Chapter Review

1. perception (p. 119)
2. learn (p. 120)
3. size constancy (p. 120); Shape constancy, brightness constancy (p. 121)
4. figure-ground (p. 122)
5. nearness, similarity (p. 122)
6. continuation(continuity), closure, contiguity (p. 122)
7. perceptual hypothesis, ambiguous (p. 123)
8. depth perception, empiricist, nativist (p. 125); four, brain, learning (p. 126); visual cliff (p. 125)
9. monocular, binocular (p. 126)
10. accommodation, monocular (p. 126)
11. convergence, binocular (p. 126)
12. Retinal disparity, fused, stereoscopic, Retinal disparity, binocular (p. 126)
13. two, monocular, linear perspective (p. 128)
14. smaller, relative size (p. 129)
15. light, shadow, overlaps, interposition (p. 129)
16. texture, texture gradient (p. 129)
17. aerial perspective (p. 129)
18. faster (more), relative motion (motion parallax), motion parallax (relative motion) (p. 130)
19. larger, apparent distance (p. 130); larger (p. 131)

20.   perceptual habits (p. 131); Ames room, shape (size), size (shape), shape (p. 132)
21.   distorted (changed, inverted), adapt (adjust) (p. 133); active movement (p. 134)
22.   context, frames of reference, adaptation level (p. 134)
23.   illusion, hallucination, illusion, stroboscopic movement (p. 134)
24.   shorter, experienced (p. 135)
25.   attention, selective attention, Divided attention (p. 136); intense, repetitious, contrast, change, incongruity (p. 137)
26.   adaptation, orientation response, orientation response, habituates (p. 137)
27.   motives, perceived, arousing (p. 137)
28.   bottom-up, top-down (p. 138)
29.   perceptual expectancy (p. 138); suggestion, categories (p. 139)
30.   Perception, see, believe (p. 140)
31.   wrong, inaccurate (wrong) (p. 140); inaccurate (wrong), weapon focus (p. 141); reality testing (p. 142)
32.   accurately, alive, open, aware, present, self-consciousness, attention, dishabituation (p. 142)
33.   Parapsychology, psi (p. 143)
34.   clairvoyance, telepathy (p. 143)
35.   precognition, psychokinesis (p. 144)
36.   coincidence, objective, Zener (p. 144)
37.   fraud, statistics, chance, inconsistent, run of luck (p. 145)
38.   replicated, reinterpret (p. 145); open, skeptical (p. 146)

Chapter 6

States of Consciousness

KEY TERMS, CONCEPTS, AND INDIVIDUALS

consciousness
altered state of consciousness
   sweat lodge ritual
sleep — the gentle tyrant
   innate biological rhythm
   microsleep
sleep deprivation
   sleep deprivation psychosis
sleep needs and patterns
   long and short sleepers
stages of sleep
   electroencephalogram
   brain waves
      beta, alpha
      sleep spindles, delta
   hypnic jerks, myoclonus
   REM and NREM sleep
      somnambulism, sleeptalking
      night terrors versus nightmares
      narcolepsy, cataplexy
insomnia
   drug dependency insomnia
   temporary insomnia
   chronic insomnia
sleep apnea, SIDS
dreams
   frequency, duration
   REM rebound, REM myth
   purpose of REM sleep
dream interpretation
   wish fulfillment
   activation-synthesis hypothesis
hypnosis
   Franz Mesmer & James Braid
   Stanford Hypnotic Susceptibility Scale
hypnosis — common factors
   basic suggestion effect

what hypnosis can do
stage hypnosis
sensory deprivation (D. O. Hebb)
   hypnogogic images
   benefits of sensory deprivation
   REST
psychoactive drug
   physical dependence (addiction)
      withdrawal symptoms
      drug tolerance
   psychological dependence
patterns of abuse
uppers
   amphetamine
      amphetamine psychosis
   cocaine
      signs of abuse
   caffeine
      caffeinism
   nicotine
downers
   barbiturates
      drug interaction
   alcohol
      depressant
      stages of alcoholism
      alcohol treatment
   marijuana
interpreting your dreams
   Sigmund Freud, Calvin Hall
   Rosalind Cartwright, Ann Faraday
how to catch a dream
meaning of dreams
dreams as problem solvers
lucid dreaming
why people abuse drugs
   Thomas Szasz

LEARNING OBJECTIVES

To demonstrate mastery of this chapter you should be able to:

1. Define consciousness according to William James.

   Consciousness is an ever-changing "stream" or flow of awareness.

2. Define "altered state of consciousness."

   A distinct change in the quality and pattern of mental activity

3. Explain how sleep is defined by Webb.

   "gentle tyrant"
   Sleep is an innate biological rhythm that can never be entirely sidestepped. But if flexibility is needed, sleep will give way temporarily, especially at times of great danger.

4. Define the term microsleep.

   A brief shift in brain activity to patterns normally recorded during sleep.

5. Describe the general effects of 48 hours of sleep deprivation.

6. Name and describe the condition that occurs when a person is deprived of sleep for a longer period of time.

   Sleep deprivation psychosis brings about confusion and disorientation, delusions, and hallucinations.
   - Most common reactions to this are inattention, staring, trembling hands, drooping eyelids, increased pain sensitivity, and a reduced sense of well being.

7. Describe the characteristics of long and short sleepers.

   Short sleepers average 5 hours of sleep per night. or less.
   Long sleepers are people that tend to worry a lot during the day.

8. Explain the relationship between age and sleep needs.

   As people age they tend to sleep less.

9. **Name the important brain structures which generate sleep.**
    Sleep is actively produced by several structures in the brain: the hypothalamus, the reticular formation, and a "sleep center" in the brainstem.

10. **Explain the stages of sleep.**

    a. **Stage 1** - Begin to lose consciousness and enter light sleep, heart rate slows even more.
        ↳ reflex muscle contractions (hypnic jerk)
        → muscle spasms in legs (myoclonus)

    dozy asleep

    b. **Stage 2** - Sleep deepens, short bursts of activity, sleep spindles, begin, and body temperature drops further. Sleep spindles mark true boundary of sleep. (4 minutes)

    admit asleep

    c. **Stage 3**
        Brain wave called Delta begins, which are very large and slow. Signal deeper sleep and further loss of consciousness

    d. **Stage 4** → Deep sleep is reached after one hour of sleep. brainwave pattern becomes almost pure delta waves, and sleeper is in oblivion.

11. **Differentiate between the two basic states of sleep: REM and NREM.**
    REM sleep - Sleep marked by rapid eye movements, a return to stage 1 patterns. Usually associated with dreaming.

    NREM Sleep - Non-Rapid eye movement sleep characteristic of stages 2,3 and 4, and largely dream-free.

12. **Explain the relationship between REM sleep and dreaming.**

13. **State how many times per night most people dream and how long the dreams usually last. (See page 160.)**
    Most people dream 4 or 5 times a night. The first dream lasts only about 10 minutes; the last averages 30 minutes and may run as long as 50.

14. **Describe and differentiate the sleep disturbances nightmares vs. night terrors, and sleepwalking vs. sleeptalking.**

    → Both Sleepwalking and sleeptalking take place during NREM. A link with the deeper stages of sleep seems to explain why sleeptalking makes little sense and why sleepwalkers are confused and remember little when awakened.
    → A nightmare is simply a bad dream that takes place during REM sleep. Usually brief and remembered in detail. Night Terrors is when a person suffers total panic and may hallucinate frightening images into the room. Occurs during NREM.

15. Describe narcolepsy and cataplexy.

Narcolepsy is sudden, irresistible, daytime sleep attacks that may last anywhere from a few minutes to a half hour. Victims may fall asleep while standing, talking, or even driving.

Cataplexy is a sudden temporary paralysis of the muscles, leading to complete body collapse.

16. Define insomnia. (Include a list and description of the characteristics and treatments of the three types of insomnia.)

Insomnia is difficulty in going to sleep, frequent nightmare awakenings, waking too early, or any combination of these problems.

a. Drug-dependency → People who take sleeping pills consistently to try to sleep. They begin to need an ever greater number of pills to get to sleep. They must be painstakingly withdrawn

b. Temporary Insomnia → caused by worry, stress, or excitement usually sets up a cycle in which heightened physical arousal blocks sleep. Then, frustration and anger cause more arousal, which further delays sleep. Delayed sleep causes more frustration, and so on. A way to beat this is to get up and do something satisfying.

c. Chronic Insomnia → said to exist if sleeping problems last for more than three weeks.

17. Describe the effects of prescription and nonprescription drugs on insomnia.

18. List and describe five behavioral interventions for insomnia. (Highlight 6-2)

a. Stimulants — Avoid stimulants such as coffee, and cigarettes.

b. Worries — schedule time in the early evening to write down worries or concerns and what you will do about them the next day.

c. Relaxation — Learn a physical or mental strategy for relaxing, such as progressive muscle relaxation, meditation, or blotting out worries with calming images.

d. Stimulus control — ① Go to bed only when you feel sleepy. ② Avoid Naps ③ Awaken at the same time each morning. ④ Avoid non-sleep activities in bed. ⑤ Always leave bed if sleep hasn't occurred in 10 min. ⑥ Do something else when upset about not being able to sleep.

e. Paradoxical Intention — To remove the pressures of trying to get to sleep, try instead to keep your eyes open (in the dark) and stay awake as long as possible.

19. Describe the sleep disorder known as sleep apnea and its relationship to SIDS. A person who snores loudly, with short silences and loud gasps or snorts

Sleep apnea is suspected to be one of the causes of SIDS.

20. Describe the functions of REM sleep and the consequences of deprivation of REM sleep.

21. **Explain how Freud viewed dreams, and present the evidence against his view.**

Freud concluded that many dreams represent wish fulfillment. Dreams represent thoughts expressed in images or pictures, rather than in words.
↳ A study of the effects of prolonged starvation showed no particular increase in dreams about food and eating.

22. **Describe the activation-synthesis hypothesis concerning dreaming.** During REM sleep, certain brain cells are activated that normally control eye movements, balance, and actions. However, messages from the cells are blocked from actually reaching the body, so no movement occurs. But the cells continue to tell higher brain areas of their activities. Struggling to interpret this information, the brain searches through stored memories and manufactures a dream.

23. **Define hypnosis. (Include a history of hypnosis from Mesmer through its use today.)**

Hypnosis is an altered state of consciousness, characterized by narrowed attention and an increased ~~open~~ openness to suggestion. * Began in 1700's with Franz Mesmer, Austrian physician, believed that he could cure diseases by passing magnets over the body. Made heavy use of the power of suggestion. Mesmer's theories of "animal magnetism" were rejected. Word coined later by English surgeon named James Braid. Greek word hypnos means "sleep" used it to describe hypnotic state. It is not sleep, EEG records are similar to those awake.

24. **Explain how a person's hypnotic susceptibility can be determined.**

Hypnotic susceptibility can be measured by making a series of suggestions and counting the number to which a person responds.

25. **List the four common factors in all hypnotic techniques.**

a. to focus attention on what is being said

b. to relax and feel tired

c. to "let go" and accept suggestions easily

d. to use vivid imagination

26. **Explain what the basic suggestion effect is.**

Hypnotized persons feel that suggested actions or experiences are automatic — they seem to just "happen" without effort.

27. **Describe the dissociation in awareness caused by hypnosis.**

To illustrate, researcher Ernest Hilgard asks hypnotized subjects to plunge one hand into a painful bath of ice water. Subjects told to feel no pain say they feel none. The same subjects are then asked if there is any part of their mind that does feel pain. With free hand, many ~~ne~~ write, "It hurts," or "stop it "your hurting me." while continuing to act pain-free.

28.   Explain how hypnosis may affect a person's acting in a way that he or she would not normally act.

29.   Explain what can and cannot be achieved with hypnosis.

30.   Explain what sensory deprivation is and describe its positive and negative effects.

Sensory deprivation refers to any major reduction in external stimulation.

* After emerging from sensory deprivation, some experience color distortions, heightensed visual illusions, slower reactions, and a brief warping of visual lines and spaces.
* Beneficial: Sensory Enhancement, Relaxation, changing Habits (REST → restricted environmental stimulation therapy)   ↳ can allow one to quit smoking or even lose weight

31.   Define the term psychoactive drug.

A psychoactive drug is a substance capable of altering attention, memory, judgement, time sense, self-control, emotion, or perception.

32.   Differentiate physical dependence from psychological dependence.

* When a person compulsively uses a drug to maintain bodily comfort, a _physical dependence exists_. (addiction)

* When a person develops _a psychological dependence_, he or she feels that a drug is necessary to maintain emotional or psychological well-being.

33.   List and describe five different types of drug-taking behaviors.

a. _experimental_ → short term based on curiosity

b. _social-recreational_ → occasional social use for pleasure or relaxation.

c. _Situational_ → use to cope with a specific problem such as boredom or staying awake for night work

d. Intensive → daily use with elements of dependence

e. Compulsive → intense use and extreme of dependence.

34. Describe the following frequently abused drugs in terms of their effects, possible medical uses, side effects or long term symptoms, organic damage potential, and potential for physical and/or psychological dependence.

a. **amphetamines** → once prescribed to aid weight loss or to combat mild depression. ❷ Now frowned on because becoming too dependant on. Only legitimate use is to treat narcolepsy and overdoses of depressant drugs. Rapidly produce a drug tolerance. Higher doses can cause nausea, vomiting, high blood pressure, fatal heart arrhythmias, and crippling strokes. Speed the use of bodily resources. Possible after-effects: fatigue, depression, terrifying nightmares, confusion, uncontrolled irritability, and aggression.

b. **cocaine (include the three signs of abuse)** → effects are feelings of alertness, euphoria, well-being, power, boundless energy, and pleasure! Can cause convulsions, heart attack, or a stroke. "Crack babies" - by the time they start school, they often suffer from tremors, hyperactivity, listlessness, slowed language learning, and disorganized thinking. The brain adapts to cocaine abuse in ways that upset its chemical balance, causing depression when cocaine is withdrawn. SIGNS OF ABUSE = Compulsive Use, Loss of Control, Disregarding consequences.

c. **caffeine** → stimulates the brain by blocking chemicals that normally inhibit or slow nerve activity. Suppresses fatigue or drowsiness and increases feelings of alertness. Non-Prescription drugs contain it such as stay awake pills, cold remedies, and many name-brand aspirin. Caffeinism = Insomnia, irritability, loss of appetite, chills, racing heart, and elevated body temperature. Encourages dev. of breast cysts, bladder cancer, heart problems, high blood

d. **nicotine** → So toxic that it is sometimes used as an insecticide. pressure. causes stomach pain, vomiting and diarrhea, cold sweats, dizziness, confusion, and tremors. Convulsions, Respiratory failure, and death. Build a tolerance for nicotine. Addicting. Withdrawal causes headaches, sweating, cramps, insomnia, digestive upset, irritability, and craving for cigarettes. Cancer causing (Lung)

e. **barbiturates** depress activity in the brain. medically they are used to calm patients or to induce sleep. Repeated use can cause a physical dependence and emotional depression
   mixing with alcohol can be very fatal

f. **alcohol** → not a stimulant. a central nervous system depressant. Reduce inhibition and produce feelings of relaxation and euphoria. Usually impairs sexual performance thinking and perception become dulled and/or shortsighted = <u>alcohol myopia</u>. Reduces anxiety and temporarily makes people feel better about themselves

g. **marijuana** → alters sensory impressions, psychological dependency, sense of euphoria or well-being, relaxation, altered time sense and perceptual distortions. Impairs short-term memory and slows learning.

35. **List and explain the three phases in the development of a drinking problem.**
a. _Initial phase_ : begins to turn to alcohol to relieve tension or to feel good more often. (①Increasing Consumption, ②Morning Drinking, ③Regretted behavior, ④Blackouts)

b. Crucial phase: Person begins to lose control over drinking. One drink starts a chain reaction leading to a pattern.

c. Chronic phase: alcoholics drink compulsively and continuously rarely eat ; become intoxicated from far less alcohol than before; crave alcohol when deprived of it. Social ties deteriorate.
Addicted!

36. **Generally describe the treatment process for alcoholism. Name the form of therapy that has probably been the most successful.** ①Begin by sobering up the person and cutting of their supply "detoxification" ②Try to restore the alcoholic's health. When alcoholics have "dried out" and health has been restored, they may be treated with tranquilizers, antidepressants, or psychotherapy. ③ Alcoholics Anonymous (AA)

AA has probably been the most successful!

* * * * * * * * * *

The following objectives are related to the material in the "Applications" and "Explorations" sections of your text.

37. **List and describe the four processes identified by Freud which disguise the hidden meaning of dreams.**
a. Condensation – a single character in a dream may represent several people at once.

b. Displacement – may cause the most important emotions or actions of a dream to be redirected toward safe or seemingly unimportant images.

c. Symbolization - dreams are often expressed in images that are symbolic rather than literal in their meaning. To uncover the meaning of dreams it helps to ask what feelings or ideas a dream image might symbolize
d. Secondary Elaboration – the tendency to make a dream more logical, and to add details when remembering it.

38. **Describe the dream theories of Freud, Hall and Cartwright. (See pages 161-162 and 179-180.)**
Freud- many dreams represent wish. fulfillment. Dreams represent thoughts expressed in images or pictures, rather than in words. Believed that the conscience relaxes during sleep, allowing dreams to express unconscious desires and conflicts in disguised dream symbols.

Hall- dreams as plays and the dreamer as a playwright.

Cartwright – dreams are primarily "feeling statements."

39. Outline procedures for using dreams to improve creativity.

Before going to bed, try to think intently about a problem you wish to solve. Steep yourself in the problem by stating it clearly and reviewing all relevant information.

40. Define lucid dreams and describe methods for increasing their frequency.

In lucid dreams, the dreamer "wakes" within an ordinary dream and feels capable of normal thought and action. They know they are dreaming, but feel fully conscious within the dream world.
① When you wake from a dream (spontaneously) take a few minutes to try to memorize it. ② Engage in 10-15 minutes of reading or any other activity requiring awakefulness. ③ While lying in bed and returning to sleep say to yourself "Next time I'm dreaming, I want to remember I'm dreaming." ④ Visualize yourself lying in bed asleep while in the dream you just rehearsed.

41. List the predictors of adolescent drug abuse.

peer drug use
parental drug use
delinquency
parental maladjustment
poor self-esteem
social nonconformity
stressful life changes

42. Discuss the social and psychological factors involved in drug abuse.

43. Describe both traditional and contemporary approaches to the prevention of drug abuse.

Traditional approaches have emphasized limiting drug supplies, strict law enforcement, and legal penalties.

SELF-QUIZZES

Do You Know the Information?

Multiple Choice

1. Consciousness refers to
   (a) a state of awareness best characterized by the absence of sleep.
   (b) a stream or an everchanging flow of awareness.
   (c) the state during which rational decisions are made.
   (d) all the sensations, perceptions, etc. that you are aware of at any instant.

2. The idea that sleep is a "gentle tyrant" — an innate biological rhythm that can never be entirely side-stepped — is supported by the idea that
   (a) animals that have had brain operations which prevent sleep fall into a coma and die.
   (b) animals cannot be taught to do without sleep.
   (c) tryptophan is a sleep-inducing agent.
   (d) a and b express above.

3. Microsleep is
   (a) the time required for the onset of sleep in an individual who has been deprived of 24 hours or more of sleep.
   (b) a momentary shift in brain activity to the pattern characteristic of sleep.
   (c) very similar to a nap that lasts 30 minutes or less.
   (d) the shift from NREM to REM sleep.

4. Which of the following statements regarding the effects of losing 48 hours of sleep is *false*?
   (a) Most subjects displayed irritability.
   (b) The ability to pay attention and remain vigilant declined.
   (c) Performance on complex tasks declined.
   (d) The ability to follow a simple routine was impaired.

5. The condition caused by long periods without sleep and characterized by body tremors, hallucinations, and staring is called
   (a) hallucinosis.
   (b) sleep-deprivation psychosis.
   (c) dream deficit psychosis.
   (d) Korsakoff's psychosis.

6. What is the length of the average sleep-waking cycle?
   (a) 23 hours
   (b) 24 hours
   (c) 25 hours
   (d) it depends upon the length of the class

7. What is the average ratio of time awake to time asleep?
   (a) 3 to 2
   (b) 4 to 1
   (c) 2 to 1
   (d) 1 to 3
   (e) Ohio 3, Ohio State 0

8. Circle the structures that actively generate sleep.
   (a) temporal lobes
   (b) reticular formation
   (c) hippocampus
   (d) spinal cord
   (e) hypothalamus
   (f) brainstem

For questions 9-11, match one of the letters of the correct brain waves to each question.

   (a) alpha   (c) delta

   (b) beta   (d) theta

_____ 9. the brain wave pattern recorded during deep sleep

_____ 10. the brain wave observed just prior to sleep

_____ 11. the brain wave usually observed during waking hours

12. Dreaming usually appears in
    (a) REM sleep.
    (b) Stage 4 REM.
    (c) Stage 1 NREM.
    (d) NREM sleep.

13. The amount of REM sleep usually is increased by
    (a) an increased amount of stress.
    (b) daytime fatigue.
    (c) unusual amounts of exercise or physical exertion.
    (d) sleep-deprivation psychosis.

14. Circle all of the following which occur during REM sleep.
    (a) muscle paralysis
    (b) sexual arousal
    (c) blood pressure fluctuations
    (d) irregular heartbeat
    (e) movement of the eyes
    (f) acting out of dreams
    (g) delta waves
    (h) sleep spindles

15. Which of the following statements about somnambulism is *incorrect?*
    (a) Somnambulists may commit dangerous acts while sleepwalking.
    (b) Sleepwalking generally occurs during dreaming or REM sleep.
    (c) The somnambulist's eyes are generally open.
    (d) Sleepwalkers can generally respond to questions or commands.

16. A night terror is different from a nightmare because
    (a) night terrors occur during Stage 4, whereas nightmares occur during REM sleep.
    (b) nightmares usually last longer than night terrors and involve more physiological arousal than night terrors.
    (c) nightmares are simply bad dreams and the dreamer cannot remember the dream when awakened.
    (d) of none of the above.

17. The sleep disorder characterized by sudden, repeated "sleep attacks" is known as
    (a) cataplexy.
    (b) insomnia.
    (c) hypnogogic hallucinations.
    (d) narcolepsy.

18. Temporary insomnia is caused by
    (a) drugs that decrease Stage 4 and REM sleep.
    (b) stress which causes heightened physical arousal.
    (c) barbiturates.
    (d) tryptophan.

19. Treatment for chronic insomnia usually begins with
    (a) sedatives.
    (b) urging insomniacs to eat a snack before sleeping.
    (c) a careful analysis of the person's sleep history.
    (d) a mild nonprescription sleeping aid such as Sominex.

20. Prescription sedatives (usually barbiturates)
    (a) can produce a drug-dependency insomnia.
    (b) when taken to combat insomnia, can result in a drug tolerance so that the initial dosage becomes ineffective.
    (c) decrease Stage 4 and REM sleep.
    (d) have all of the above characteristics.

21. Sleep apnea
    (a) is thought to be one cause of SIDS.
    (b) may cause a person to awaken hundreds of times per night to breathe.
    (c) becomes more common after age 60 and should be suspected any time loud snoring is present.
    (d) is described by all of the above.

22. How many times per night do most people dream?
    (a) 1-2   (c) 7-8
    (b) 4-5   (d) 3-4

23. REM rebound refers to
    (a) the increase in total sleep time that occurs when a person is deprived of sleep.
    (b) a person's ability to recover cognitive abilities such as attention and concentration when deprived of REM sleep.
    (c) an increased need to dream because of a deprivation of dream sleep.
    (d) the ability of REM sleep to compensate for a lack of NREM sleep.

24. REM sleep is apparently important for
    (a) sorting and integration of memories formed during the day.
    (b) stimulating the developing brain.
    (c) restoring brain chemicals needed for learning and memory.
    (d) all of the above functions.

25. Freud viewed dreams as
    (a) reflections of our waking personalities.   (c) a message about what is missing in our life.
    (b) an opportunity for wish fulfillment.   (d) an expression of conscious urges.

26. The activation-synthesis hypothesis concerning dreams holds that
    (a) people activate or "create" dreams based on unconsciously repressed urges.
    (b) dreams are created based on psychological processes.
    (c) dreams are brought about by areas of the brain trying to come up with a logical explanation of the activity in lower brain areas.
    (d) all of the above are true.

27. Hypnosis is
    (a) *not* a form of sleep.   (c) a state of increased openness to suggestion.
    (b) characterized by narrowed attention.   (d) all of the above.

28. Interest in hypnosis began in the 1700's with Mesmer. Mesmer believed that
    (a) he could cure diseases by passing magnets over the afflicted person's body.
    (b) hypnosis was a stage of sleep.
    (c) the power of hypnosis releases superhuman strength.
    (d) James Braid, the English surgeon, was a quack and a fraud.

29. Hypnotic susceptibility can be measured by
     (a) recording the length of time it takes to hypnotize the person.
     (b) investigating whether or not the subject is capable of self-hypnosis.
     (c) assessing the increase in a person's strength.
     (d) recording the number of suggestions to which a person responds.

30. Which of the following is *not* one of the four common factors in all hypnotic techniques?
     (a) to relax and feel tired   (c) to accept suggestions easily
     (b) to focus attention on what is being said   (d) to feel the sensation of gently falling or floating

31. A hypnotized person is told to feel no pain and says he feels none when a painful stimulus is applied. At the same time the person reports that there is a part of his mind that feels the pain. This indicates that
     (a) hypnosis really can relieve pain.
     (b) it takes increased motivation to actually experience reduced pain.
     (c) hypnosis can cause a dissociation in awareness.
     (d) the "hidden observer" does not remain in the background .

32. Hypnosis can *definitely* be used to accomplish which of the following?
     (a) carry out age regression   (c) produce amnesia
     (b) help induce relaxation   (d) significantly improve a person's strength

33. To get people to do what they do in front of audiences most stage hypnotists
     (a) use trickery and deception.
     (b) select responsive subjects.
     (c) take advantage of the fact that the hypnosis label can be disinhibiting.
     (d) do all of the above.

34. Hypnogogic images are
     (a) like real objects in the environment.
     (b) the same as hallucinations.
     (c) dreamlike and vivid, similar to those experienced just before falling asleep.
     (d) linked to an increase in alpha waves produced by the brain.

35. Sensory deprivation has been found to
     (a) help people quit smoking and break other bad habits.
     (b) be stressful and aversive, even for brief periods of time.
     (c) dull the acuity of senses such as hearing and touch.
     (d) have few benefits.

36. A substance capable of altering attention, memory, judgment, time sense, self-control, emotion, or perception is called a(n) _____ drug.
     (a) addictive   (c) psychoactive
     (b) depressant   (d) sedative

37. The difference between physical dependence and psychological dependence is
     (a) the latter may involve a drug tolerance.
     (b) there may be agonizing withdrawal symptoms when a drug is withheld from a person with a physical dependence.
     (c) there is usually a physiological craving for the drug in cases of psychological dependence.
     (d) not described by any of the above.

38.   The one charasteristic that alcohol, caffeine, nicotine, and marijuana all share is (see Table 6-4)
    (a) they are all physically addictive.   (c) they all produce the same effects.
    (b) they are all psychologically addictive.   (d) they all have the same medical uses.

For questions 39-47, put the appropriate letter or letters of the drugs which apply to the statements. More than one letter may be used for each of the following questions.
    (a) amphetamines   (e) barbiturates
    (b) cocaine   (f) alcohol
    (c) caffeine   (g) marijuana
    (d) nicotine

_____39. can lead to psychological dependence

_____40. acts as stimulant

_____41. most commonly used psychoactive drug in U.S.

_____42. encourages breast cysts, may contribute to insomnia, stomach & heart problems, and high blood pressure

_____43. can cause physical dependence

_____44. when combined with alcohol can produce dangerous drug interaction

_____45. physiologically depressing

_____46. lowers sperm production and may cause abnormal menstrual cycles and problems with ovulation

_____47. hallucinogenic

48.   Amphetamines can cause a loss of contact with reality known as
    (a) speed delusions.   (c) euphoric neurosis.
    (b) hallucinations.   (d) amphetamine psychosis.

49.   When one drug enhances the effect of another this is known as a
    (a) dosage excess.   (c) drug intolerance.
    (b) drug interaction.   (d) drug narcosis.

50.   During the crucial phase in the development of a drinking problem
    (a) the person begins to lose control over drinking habits.
    (b) the person begins to drink more and may begin to worry about drinking.
    (c) blackouts usually begin to occur.
    (d) the person drinks compulsively and feels a powerful need for alcohol when deprived of it.

51.   The usual first step in the treatment of alcoholism is
    (a) family therapy.   (c) detoxification.
    (b) vitamin therapy.   (d) tranquilization.

52.   The approach that has generally had the most success in dealing with alcoholism is
    (a) restoration of the alcoholic's physical health.   (c) psychotherapy.
    (b) A.A.   (d) behavior modification.

53. Which of the following is *not* one of the four processes identified by Freud that helps disguise the meaning of dreams?
   (a) symbolization
   (b) documentation
   (c) displacement
   (d) condensation

54. Calvin Hall sees dreams as
   (a) usually more pleasant than unpleasant.
   (b) predominantly filled with sexual themes.
   (c) extensions of a person's everyday experiences.
   (d) messages from the unconscious.

55. Which of the following dream theorists assumes the meaning of a dream can be found in the overall emotional tone of the dream?
   (a) Sigmund Freud
   (b) Calvin Hall
   (c) Rosalind Cartwright
   (d) Ann Faraday

56. If you go to bed drunk every night you are likely to
   (a) have less REM sleep.
   (b) have more REM sleep.
   (c) decrease your NREM sleep.
   (d) have less Stage 4 sleep, your deepest stage of sleep.
   (e) drool all over your peewa.

57. Dreams are a way of filling in gaps in personal experience. To understand the dream you should play the part of each of the principal characters and objects in the dream. This is the point of view of
   (a) Jung.
   (b) Faraday.
   (c) Hall.
   (d) Perls.

58. Thomas Szasz believes that
   (a) the government should not attempt to try to influence morality by regulating what drugs a person puts into his or her body.
   (b) drug use is high because usage is a deeply ingrained pattern in our society.
   (c) there should be stricter enforcement of drug control laws to try to control the flow of nonprescription drugs.
   (d) only extremely small towns still report low rates of drug use.

True-False

_____ 1. An altered state of consciousness represents a distinct change in the quantity of mental functioning.

_____ 2. The sweat lodge ritual of the Sioux Indians is regarded as a way of attaining an altered state of consciousness as a pathway to enlightenment.

_____ 3. The average sleep-waking cycle is about 25 hours, but we keep it on a 24 hour schedule by being tied to external time markers like light and darkness.

_____ 4. Most individuals average six to seven hours of sleep per night.

_____ 5. Short sleepers tend to be worriers and thus they do not sleep as long as non-worriers.

_____ 6. Although people find that their sleep habits may change in many ways during old age, the general trend is for older people to sleep more than average.

_____ 7. Sleep is caused by fatigue which causes a buildup of a sleep-inducing chemical in the blood.

_____ 8. In Stage 1 sleep, as the muscles relax, sometimes a reflex muscle contraction occurs which is called myoclonus.

_____ 9. A person moves from Stage 1 sleep through Stage 4 and then begins the cycle again with Stage 1.

_____10. The two states of sleep are REM and NREM.

_____11. REM sleep averages only about one and one-half hours per night.

_____12. The first dream in the night lasts about ten minutes. Each succeeding dream lasts a little longer.

_____13. The narcoleptic's sleep attacks and muscle paralysis probably result from an intrusion of NREM into the waking state.

_____14. Narcolepsy appears to be a hereditary sleep disorder.

_____15. The belief that a person would go crazy if permanently kept from dreaming is called the "REM myth."

_____16. Evidence against Freud's view of dreams includes a study that showed volunteers subjected to the effects of prolonged starvation exhibited no particular decrease in dreams about sex.

_____17. James Braid is most closely associated with "animal magnetism."

_____18. Out of every ten people only about four can be hypnotized.

_____19. Amphetamines do not supply energy to the body. They speed the expenditure of bodily resources.

_____20. According to Schachter, "The heavy smoker gets nothing out of smoking. He smokes only to prevent withdrawal."

_____21. Using lucid dreamers who can signal while they are dreaming may make it possible to get firsthand data from dreams.

_____22. Consumer Reports magazine recommends that drugs such as alcohol and tobacco be reclassified to reflect actual scientific knowledge of the drug.

Matching *(Use the letters on the right only once.)*

_____ 1. altered state of consciousness
_____ 2. hypnosis
_____ 3. key element of hypnosis
_____ 4. to combat insomnia
_____ 5. Faraday's approach to dreams
_____ 6. occur in Stages 3 & 4
_____ 7. sleep deprivation psychosis
_____ 8. effects last only 15-30 min.
_____ 9. can impair sexual performance
_____ 10. best way to quit smoking
_____ 11. hypnogogic images
_____ 12. experimental use
_____ 13. situational use
_____ 14. intensive use
_____ 15. REST

A. try to stay awake as long as possible
B. daily use having elements of dependence
C. cold turkey
D. fanciful, dreamlike images during sensory deprivation
E. cocaine
F. disorientation, delusions, hallucinations
G. characterized by decreased motivation, loss of energy, lethargy
H. used to cope with a specific problem
I. amphetamines
J. a message from yourself to yourself
K. alcohol
L. term coined by James Braid
M. somnambulism & sleeptalking
N. basic suggestion effect
O. can significantly increase strength
P. marijuana
Q. defined as change in quality and pattern of mental activity
R. muscle paralysis and sexual arousal
S. short-term use motivated by curiosity
T. can stimulate creative thinking

Can You Apply the Information?

1. You are a sleepy quality control inspector at a local bottling company. While inspecting a continuously moving line of bottles for 30 minutes you notice that you have not been consciously aware of the bottles for several seconds. You have most likely suffered
    (a) a symptom of sleep-deprivation psychosis.
    (b) a cataplectic attack.
    (c) paradoxical sleep.
    (d) microsleep.
    (e) myoclonus.

2. If Ralph consistently sleeps 6 hours a night, how would you describe his sleep patterns?
    (a) below average
    (b) average
    (c) above average
    (d) decidedly abnormal

3. You are a neurologist and your patient says to you that she feels funny. You notice that the EEG is showing almost pure delta waves. You surmise that
    (a) the EEG has a loose wire.
    (b) you must be hallucinating.
    (c) she is obviously in REM sleep.
    (d) she is in Stage 2.
    (e) she is sleeptalking in NREM sleep.

4. If your doctor tells you that she wants to increase your NREM sleep, which of the following will be *most* likely to do it?
   (a) Drink a small glass of wine to relax before bedtime.
   (b) Walk briskly around a city block once a day.
   (c) Take on added responsibility at work.
   (d) Jog in a 10,000 meter race.

5. Ruth has decided to add a new dimension to her sexual relationship with her husband. What she intends to do is wake him during the night and then "make love." For her plan to succeed, which stage of sleep would be best to wake her husband from?
   (a) any REM period
   (b) stage 2
   (c) stage 3
   (d) stage 4
   (e) It makes no difference, he won't wake up anyway.

6. During a lecture on sleeping and dreaming you hear someone in the audience say, "I'm 65 years old and I've never had a dream in my life." Since you are now knowledgeable on the topic, you think to yourself:
   (a) he is one of those people who never dreams.
   (b) he probably drinks 8-10 cups of coffee per day.
   (c) he probably just doesn't remember his dreams.
   (d) maybe he is is schizophrenic.

7. A child is plagued by nights when he wakes in a panic, screams and thrashes about, but remembers nothing in the morning. This child is probably suffering from
   (a) night terrors.
   (b) horribly scary REM nightmares.
   (c) sleep deprivation psychosis.
   (d) insomnia.

8. Probably the worst thing a person can do to help cure insomnia is
   (a) to take prescription sedatives.
   (b) avoid beds for everything but sleeping.
   (c) take a nonprescription, heal-yourself drug such as Nytol.
   (d) have a regular time to go to bed.
   (e) once in bed, try to stay awake as long as possible.

9. It's Saturday night and you have had too much to drink. In fact, you've had way too much to drink. You fall asleep. It is very likely
   (a) you'll dream about riding in a boat on a rolling ocean.
   (b) you will have an above average number of dreams and many of them will be bizarre.
   (c) the next night you will spend more time in REM sleep.
   (d) that you will get more Stage 4 sleep than any other stage.

10. In which situation would hypnosis probably be most effective?
    (a) childbirth
    (b) World Weightlifting Championships
    (c) a college instructor learning the names of 100 students
    (d) a psychotherapist using hypnosis to take you back to a trauma that you experienced at three years of age

11. A doctor has prescribed a sleeping pill for your insomnia, but after a couple of weeks you have to increase your dosage because one pill a night no longer helps you get to sleep. This occurs because
    (a) the drugs are now stimulating the central nervous system.
    (b) you have developed a physical addiction.
    (c) you have built up a drug tolerance.
    (d) you have a psychological condition rather than a physical one.

12. If you know someone who wakes up in the morning and feels as if he or she has to take Drug X to have a good day, then this person is probably
    (a) psychologically dependent upon the drug.
    (b) experiencing severe withdrawal symptoms.
    (c) very tolerant physically to Drug X.
    (d) physically addicted to the drug.

13. You are the doctor on duty in the emergency room of a local hospital when an 18 year old female is brought in. She is unconscious with a very slow, irregular heartbeat and shallow respiration. The friend who accompanied the girl says she's not sure what the unconscious patient took. They were both at a party and there were many drugs being taken. If the friend gave you the following list, which would be the most likely candidate?
    (a) marijuana
    (b) amphetamines
    (c) cocaine
    (d) barbiturates

14. Your wife gets up in the morning after a party the previous night at which she had been drinking. At the party she had a loud argument with another woman. She has a Bloody Mary for breakfast. According to your text, in which phase in the development of a drinking problem is she?
    (a) initial
    (b) crucial
    (c) critical
    (d) chronic

15. "I love to get stoned on grass because it makes me dream more, and I have a lot of bizarre dreams, too. I guess this is due to more REM sleep." The person who made this statement
    (a) obviously understands the effects of marijuana on dreaming.
    (b) would probably also agree with Freud's view of dreams.
    (c) had a "high" dream.
    (d) is mistaken about marijuana's effect.

Chapter Review

1. Consciousness consists of all the _____, _____, _____, and _____ that you are aware of at any given moment. Most of each day is spent in _____ consciousness which is perceived as real with a familiar sense of _____ and _____. An altered state of consciousness (ASC) is a distinct change in the _____ and _____ of mental functioning. An example is the _____ _____ ritual of the Sioux Indians. Although some people seek an ASC primarily for _____, the Sioux use this ritual to acquire an altered state as a pathway to _____ or as a source of _____ experience. _____ conditioning affects the altered states a person considers _____.

2. Webb describes sleep as a "gentle _____" because it is an _____ rhythm that can never be entirely side-stepped. Animals cannot be taught to do without _____, and animals who are prevented from sleeping fall into a _____ and _____. Animals and humans deprived of sleep will engage in _____, a brief shift in brain activity to patterns normally found in _____.

3. Volunteers who are kept awake for 48 hours show _____ _____ on complex mental tasks. Performance on tasks which were _____ was found to decline most. Longer periods of sleep deprivation may bring about _____-_____ _____ which is characterized by confusion, disorientation, _____, and _____.

4.   The sleep-waking cycle is actually _____ hours long, but external time markers like light and dark help us to reset our biological clocks daily. Only 8 percent of the population averages _____ hours sleep or less. Most people sleep _____ to _____ hours per night. People who are long sleepers are described as _____. Increasing age usually brings a(n) _____ in sleep time, whereas infants spend up to _____ hours a day sleeping. Most studies of sleep patterns show a consistent ratio of _____ to _____ between time awake and time asleep.

5.   Sleep is actively produced by several structures in the brain: the _____, _____ _____, and a sleep center in the _____.

6.   When a person is awake the brain waves are usually small fast ones called _____ waves. Immediately before sleep the EEG patterns shift to larger, slower waves called _____ which continues into Stage 1 with other small, irregular waves. Sometimes in this stage reflex muscle contractions occur called _____ _____. Muscle spasms which may later occur in the legs are called _____. In Stage 2, sleep deepens and the EEG begins to show short bursts of activity called "_____ _____" which seem to mark the boundary of true sleep. In Stage 3 a different brain wave called _____ begins to appear. These waves signal deeper sleep. In Stage 4, the brain wave pattern is almost pure _____, and this stage is called _____ sleep.

7.   Sleeping is a cyclical phenomenon. The sleeper first moves into Stage _____, then through Stages _____ and _____, and finally to Stage _____. After this, the sleeper returns (through Stages _____ and _____) to Stage _____.

8.   The two basic states of sleep are _____ and another state during which we usually dream called _____. We generally spend about _____ hours per night in the latter state. Exercise and physical exertion generally increase the amount of _____ sleep we get while _____ sleep increases with added _____.

9.   During REM sleep the heart beats _____ while _____ _____ and _____ fluctuate. Both sexes appear to be _____ aroused. The muscles are usually _____; however, a pattern of violent thrashing occurs when REM paralysis fails (termed REM _____ disorder).

10.   Both sleepwalking and sleeptalking occur during _____ sleep. This probably accounts for why most sleeptalking makes little _____ and for why most sleepwalkers wake up rather _____.

11.   Another Stage 4 disorder is _____ _____. These are severely frightening experiences that can be distinguished from normal _____ which are simply bad dreams that occur during _____ sleep.

12.   One of the most dramatic sleep disorders is characterized by sudden attacks of sleepiness. This disorder is known as _____. Many victims also suffer from sudden temporary paralysis of their muscles called_____. It is thought that this disorder has _____ origins because it tends to run in families.

13. If a person has difficulty going to sleep, wakes up frequently at night, and/or wakes up too early this person has _____.

14. As remedies for insomnia, nonprescription drugs have almost no effect. Even worse are prescription drugs or sedatives (usually _____) which decrease both Stage _____ and _____ sleep. An additional problem with prescription sedatives is that a drug _____' rapidly builds so that the initial dosage becomes ineffective. A greater number of pills is then required to produce sleep. This can lead to a serious type of insomnia known as _____-_____ insomnia.

15. There are two other types of insomnia. Worry, stress, or excitement can cause _____ insomnia. This sets up a cycle in which the inability to sleep causes more arousal, which causes more insomnia, etc. This cycle suggests that one of the best ways to beat the cycle is to avoid _____ it. The other type of insomnia is termed _____. Treatment for this type usually begins with an analysis of a person's sleep _____. It is also very helpful to adopt a _____ _____. It may also be helpful to avoid _____, to link only _____ with your bed, _____ down your worries, and to use _____ intention which takes the _____ away from trying to get to sleep.

16. If a person stops breathing for 20 seconds to two minutes while sleeping and then must wake up to breathe, the person probably has _____ _____. People with this sleep disorder complain of _____. This disorder is thought to be one cause of _____ due to immaturity of the breathing centers in the _____.

17. Most people dream _____ to _____ times per night. Dreams are usually on a _____ minute cycle. The first dream generally lasts about _____ minutes with each succeeding dream lasting a little longer. The last dream of the night generally lasts about _____ minutes. Dreams do not occur in a _____; they occur in _____ time.

18. People prevented from dreaming for several nights in a row exhibit what is known as _____ _____ when allowed to dream without interruption. Although people may complain of difficulty in concentrating while being deprived of _____ sleep, it is not true that a person will go _____ if permanently kept from _____. This is now known as the _____ - _____.

19. During infancy, REM sleep may sreve the purpose of _____ the developing brain. Later, REM sleep may serve the purpose of restoring the brain's _____ needed for learning and memory, helping integrate and store _____ learned during the day, preventing _____ deprivation during sleep, and processing _____ events.

20. Calvin Hall sees dreams as merely extensions of everyday _____. He has collected and analyzed over 10,000 dreams and finds that the favorite dream setting is familiar _____ in a _____.

21. Freud viewed dreams as a vehicle for _____ _____. Some studies do not support Freud. In one study on the effects of starvation, volunteers showed no _____ in dreams about food and eating.

22. The _____-_____ hypothesis is a radically different view of dreaming. According to this view, during _____ sleep certain brain cells are activated that normally control eye movements, balance and actions. However, messages from these cells are blocked, so no movement occurs. These cells continue to tell higher _____ _____ of their activities. In order to come up with a reasonable _____ of all of this activity, the _____ manufactures a _____.

23. _____ is an altered state of consciousness, characterized by narrowed _____ and an increased openness to _____. Interest in this area began in the 1700's with _____. He believed that he could cure disease by passing _____ over a person's body.

24. The term hypnotism was coined by _____. Today we recognize that hypnosis is not _____. Approximately _____ out of ten people can be hypnotized. A typical hypnotic test is the _____ _____ _____ Scale.

25. There are many different hypnotic routines. Common factors in all hypnotic techniques encourage a person to: (1) focus _____ on what is being said; (2) _____ and feel tired; (3) "let go" and accept _____ easily; and (4) use vivid _____. A key element in hypnosis is the _____ _____ effect. Hypnosis may cause a split or _____ in awareness.

26. Hypnosis does not seem to have a significant effect on _____, however, _____ can be enhanced through hypnosis. Hypnosis can relieve _____ and has been used to _____ subjects to childhood, although this has been debated. Hypnotic suggestions concerning _____ seem to be among the most effective.

27. Hypnosis seems to have its greatest value as a tool for inducing _____, as a means of controlling _____ (in dentistry and childbirth, for example), and as an adjunct to other forms of psychological _____ and counseling.

28. Little or no _____ is necessary to do a good stage hypnosis act. On stage, people are unusually _____ because they don't want to "ruin the act." Also, the stage hypnotist usually selects volunteers who are quite _____, and the label "hypnotized" acts as a _____. The subjects begin to feel like stars, and all the hypnotist need do is _____ the action. In addition, most stage hypnotists use _____ to put on a good show.

29 Any major reduction in external stimulation is referred to as _____ _____. The results may include misjudging _____ and trouble _____. Many people also report _____ images which are similar to those experienced just before falling asleep. On the positive side, many people experience increased sensory _____, _____, and help in changing _____.

30. A substance capable of altering attention, memory, judgement, time sense, self-control, emotion, or perception is called a _____ drug.

31. When a person uses a drug to maintain bodily comfort, a _____ dependence exists. This is commonly referred to as _____ and occurs with drugs that cause _____symptoms. This state is often accompanied by a drug _____ in which the user must use larger and larger doses to achieve the desired effect. When a person feels a need for a drug to maintain emotional well-being, a _____ dependence exists.

32. If drug use is motivated by curiosity, it is classified as _____. Other classifications are _____ _____, — occasional drug use, _____, — used to cope with a specific problem, _____ — daily use having elements of dependence, _____ — intensive use and extreme dependence.

33. Amphetamines are _____ and are used medically to treat _____. Amphetamines are used illicitly to help a person stay _____ or temporarily improve mental or physical _____. Amphetamines rapidly produce a drug _____. They also speed the expenditure of bodily _____. Possible effects include _____, _____, nightmares, confusion, and _____. Amphetamines (speed) may kill because they can cause a loss of contact with reality known as _____ _____.

34. Cocaine is a powerful central nervous system _____ derived from the leaves of the coca plant. While cocaine does not fit the classical pattern of physical _____, it shows much evidence for its potential for _____ use. It produces sensations of _____, _____, and boundless energy. Cocaine is very much like _____ in its effect on the central nervous system, but its effects are much more _____-acting. Serious signs of cocaine abuse include _____ use, loss of _____, and disregarding _____.

35. _____ is the most frequently used psychoactive drug in the U.S. It _____ the brain and increases feelings of _____. It is found in _____, _____, _____ _____, _____, and _____. This drug can lead to an unhealthy dependence called _____. This condition may result in _____, _____, loss of _____, racing _____, and elevated _____. Even in the absence of this condition there are some risks including _____, _____ problems, high _____ _____, and the development of _____ _____ in women. Pregnant women are now urged to avoid this drug entirely because of its suspected link with _____ _____.

36. _____ is a natural _____ found in tobacco. In large doses it causes stomach _____, _____ and _____, cold _____, _____, _____, and _____. The Surgeon General reports that it is _____. Smoking is responsible for about 97% of all of the _____ cancer deaths in the U.S. Schachter believes that smokers only smoke to avoid _____, and that it is best to quit smoking _____ _____.

37.   Barbiturates are _____ drugs that _____ activity in the brain. They are used medically to calm patients or to induce sleep. In mild doses, barbiturates have an effect similar to _____, but an overdose can cause coma or _____. When combined with alcohol, barbiturates are particularly dangerous. When they are mixed, one drug may enhance the effect of another. This is known as _____ _____. Barbiturates are capable of causing a physical _____ and an emotional _____.

38.   Alcohol is a _____. In small amounts alcohol reduces _____ and produces feelings of _____ and _____. Greater amounts of alcohol cause progressively more dangerous impairment of brain function until the drinker loses _____. However, long before that, thinking and perception become _____, a condition called alcohol _____.

39.   Progression from a "social drinker" to a problem drinker to an alcoholic is often subtle. In the initial phase, the drinker begins to turn more frequently to alcohol to relieve _____. Four danger signals in this period are _____ consumption, drinking in the _____, behavior that is _____, and _____.

40.   After the initial phase comes the _____ phase in which a person begins to lose _____ over his or her drinking. The last phase is called the _____ phase in which the person begins to drink _____ and _____.

41.   Treatment for alcoholism begins by sobering the person up and cutting off the supply of alcohol. The procedure is referred to as _____ and frequently produces all the symptoms of drug withdrawal. The next step is to try to restore the alcoholic's _____. After he has dried out and his health has been restored, the alcoholic may be treated with _____, _____, or _____. Probably the method which has been the most effective in treating alcoholism is _____.

42.   The active ingredient in marijuana is ____ ____ ____. It is a mild _____, and it also accumulates in the body's _____ tissue — particularly the _____ and the _____ organs. The evidence is conflicting as to whether marijuana produces _____ _____, but its danger lies in its _____ _____.

43.   Marijuana generally causes _____, _____, altered _____ sense, and _____ distortions. It is dangerous to _____ under the influence of marijuana or any other intoxicating drug.

44.   Marijuana is quite irritating to the _____. It also lowers _____ production in males or makes what _____ he has _____. THC has also been found to cause abnormal _____ cycles and disrupt _____ in female monkeys. It also suppresses the _____ system, and causes _____ damage in animals.

45.   To help discover the meaning of dreams, Freud identified four dream processes. When a single character in a dream represents several people at once, this is known as _____. If the most important emotions of a dream are redirected toward safe images, this is known as _____. Freud believed that the meaning in dreams is _____ rather than literal. The last process is the tendency to reorganize a dream to make it more logical when remembering it. This is known as _____ _____.

46. Dream theorist Calvin Hall thinks of dreams as _____ and the dreamer as a _____, yet the images of dreams are more _____ than those experienced while awake. Rosalind Cartwright, on the other hand, prefers to look at the overall _____ _____ of the dream as a major clue to its meaning.

47. Ann Faraday considers dreams a message from _____ to yourself. She suggests the following techniques for catching a dream:
    (a) Before retiring, plan to _____ your dreams.
    (b) If possible, arrange to awaken _____.
    (c) If you rarely remember your dreams, you may want to set your alarm clock to go off _____ hour(s) before you usually awaken.
    (d) Upon awakening, lie still and review the dream images with your _____ _____.
    (e) Make your first dream record with your _____ _____.
    (f) _____ the dream again and record as many additional details as possible.
    (g) Put your dreams into a permanent _____ _____.
    (h) Remember that a number of drugs _____ dreaming.

48. Two such drugs that may have an effect on REM sleep are alcohol and marijuana. Alcohol is known to _____ REM sleep. Marijuana either slightly _____ REM sleep or has no effect at all on it.

49. Fritz Perls, the originator of gestalt therapy, considered dreams a message about what is _____ in our lives. Perls felt that dreams are a way of filling in gaps in _____ _____. He recommended that to understand a dream a person should "take the part of" each of the _____ and _____ in the dream.

50. History is full of cases where dreams have been a pathway to creativity and discovery. Dr. Otto Loewi won a Nobel Prize for his research on the chemical transmission of nerve impulses. He was baffled at one point in his research but had a tremendous breakthrough based on a _____.

51. During a _____ dream the dreamer "wakes" and feels capable of normal thought and action. In order to show that these dreams are real, subjects have been able to make a _____ _____ during the dream. This is particularly exciting because researchers now appear to be able to explore dreams with _____ _____ from the dreamer's world itself.

52. There are many reasons why people use drugs. Some people use drugs out of _____ or the desire to _____ to a group. Others use drugs to search for _____ or to escape feelings of _____. Many abusers turn to drugs to _____ with life or to produce immediate feelings of _____. Some observers believe that we use drugs because drug use is so deeply _____ in modern society and because well-meaning but misguided physicians _____ too much drug use. In addition, it is obvious that our our society is the target of large, expensive _____ campaigns.

53. Thomas Szasz believes that it is futile for the government to try to legislate _____ by regulating the drugs that a person chooses to put in his or her body. *Consumer Reports* supports Szasz's view and recommends that we stop _____ the horrors of drugs because this only serves to popularize drugs. Also *CR* recommends that two very harmful but popular drugs, _____ and _____, be reclassified based upon _____ evidence.

ANSWER KEYS

Do You Know the Information?

Multiple Choice

1. (d) obj. 1, p. 150
2. (d) obj. 3, p. 151
3. (b) obj. 4, p. 151
4. (c) obj. 5, p. 152
5. (b) obj. 6, p. 152
6. (c) obj. 7, p. 152
7. (c) obj. 8, p. 153
8. (b,e,f) obj.9, p. 154
9. (c) obj. 10, p. 155
10. (a) obj. 10, p. 154
11. (b) obj. 10, p. 154
12. (a) obj. 11, p. 155
13. (a) obj. 11, p. 155
14. (a-e) obj.12, pp. 155-156
15. (b) obj. 13, p. 160
16. (a) obj. 14, p. 156
17. (d) obj. 14, p. 156
18. (b) obj. 15, p. 157
19. (c) obj. 16, p. 158
20. (d) obj. 16, p. 158
21. (d) obj. 17, p. 158
22. (c) obj. 19, p. 159
23. (c) obj. 20, p. 160
24. (d) obj. 20, p. 160
25. (b) obj. 21, p. 161
26. (c) obj. 22, p. 162
27. (d) obj. 23, p. 163
28. (a) obj. 23, p. 163
29. (d) obj. 24, p. 163
30. (d) obj. 25, p. 163
31. (c) obj. 27, p. 164
32. (b) obj. 29, p. 164
33. (d) obj. 29, p. 165
34. (c) obj. 30, p. 166
35. (a) obj. 30, p. 166
36. (c) obj. 31, p. 167
37. (b) obj. 32, p. 167
38. (b) obj. 32, pp. 168-169
39. (a-g) obj.32, p. 169

40. (a-d) obj.34, pp. 170-173
41. (c) obj. 34, p. 172
42. (c) obj. 34, pp. 172-173
43. (a,b,d,e,f)obj. 34, p. 169
44. (e) obj. 34, p. 174
45. (e,f) obj.34, p. 174
46. (g) obj. 34, p. 178
47. (g) obj. 34, p. 178
48. (d) obj. 34, p. 171
49. (b) obj. 34, p. 174
50. (a) obj. 35, p. 176
51. (c) obj. 36, p. 176
52. (b) obj. 36, p. 177
53. (b) obj. 37, pp. 179-180
54. (c) obj. 38, p. 161
55. (c) obj. 38, p. 180
56. (a) obj. 39, p. 181
57. (d) obj. 39, p. 181
58. (a) obj. 43, p. 184

True-False

1. F, obj. 2, p. 150
2. T, obj. 2, p. 151
3. T, obj. 7, p. 152
4. F, obj. 7, p. 153
5. F, obj. 7, p. 153
6. F, obj. 8, p. 153
7. F, obj. 9, p. 154
8. F, obj. 10, p. 155
9. F, obj. 10, p. 155
10. T, obj. 11, p. 155
11. T, obj. 11, p. 155
12. T, obj. 13, p. 160
13. F, obj. 15, p. 157
14. T, obj. 15, p. 157
15. T, obj. 20, p. 160
16. F, obj. 21, p. 161
17. F, obj. 23, p. 163
18. F, obj.24, p. 163

19. T, obj. 34, p. 171
20. T, obj. 34, p. 174
21. T, obj. 40, p. 182
22. T, obj. 43, p. 184

Matching

1. Q, obj. 1, p. 150
2. L, obj. 23, p. 163
3. N, obj. 26, p. 164
4. A, obj. 18, p. 159
5. J, obj. 39, p. 180
6. M, obj. 14, p. 156
7. F, obj. 6, p. 152
8. E, obj. 34, p. 171
9. K, obj. 34, p. 174
10. C, obj. 34, p. 174
11. D, obj. 30, p. 166
12. S, obj. 33, p. 170
13. H, obj. 33, p. 170
14. B, obj. 33, p. 170
15. T, obj. 30, p. 167

Can You Apply the Information?

1. (d) obj. 4, p. 151
2. (a) obj. 7, p. 153
3. (e) objs. 10,11,14, pp. 154-156
4. (d) obj. 11, p. 155
5. (a) obj. 12, p. 155
7. (a) obj. 14, p. 156
8. (a) objs. 17-18, p. 158
6. (c) obj. 13, p. 160
9. (c) objs. 20,39, pp. 160, 181
10. (a) obj. 29, p. 164
11. (c) obj. 32, p. 167
12. (a) obj. 32, p. 167
13. (d) obj. 34, p. 174
14. (a) obj. 35, p. 176
15. (d) obj. 39, p. 181

Chapter Review

1. sensations, perceptions, memories, feelings, waking, time, place, quality, pattern, sweat lodge (p. 150); pleasure, enlightenment, mystical, Cultural, normal (p. 151)
2. tyrant, innate biological, sleep, coma, die, microsleep, sleep (p. 151)
3. little impairment, boring (low-level, self-motivated), sleep-deprivation psychosis, delusions, hallucinations (p. 152)
4. 25 (p. 152); five, seven, eight, worriers, reduction, 20, 2, 1 (p. 153)
5. hypothalamus, reticular formation, brainstem (p. 154)
6. beta, alpha, hypnic jerks, myoclonus (p. 154); sleep spindles, delta, delta, deep (p. 155)
7. one, two, three, four, three, two, one (p. 155)
8. NREM, REM, one and one-half, NREM, REM, stress (p. 155)
9. irregularly, blood pressure, breathing, sexually (p. 155); paralyzed, behavior (p. 156)
10. deep, sense, confused (p. 156)
11. night terrors, nightmares, REM (p. 156)
12. narcolepsy, cataplexy, hereditary (p. 157)
13. insomnia (p. 158)
14. barbiturates, four, REM, tolerance, drug-dependency (p. 158)
15. temporary, fighting, chronic, history, regular schedule, stimulants (p. 158); sleep (p. 159); write (p. 158); paradoxical, pressure (p. 159)
16. sleep apnea, hypersomnia, SIDS, brainstem (p. 159)
17. four, five, 90, 10, 30, flash, real (p. 160)
18. REM rebound, REM, crazy, dreaming, REM myth (p. 160)
19. stimulating, chemicals, information, sensory, emotional (p. 14860)
20. experiences, rooms, house (p. 161)
21. wish fulfillment, increase (p. 161)
22. activation-synthesis, REM, brain areas, interpretation, brain, dream (p. 162)
23. Hypnosis, attention, suggestion, Mesmer, magnets (p. 163)
24. Braid, sleep, eight, Stanford Hypnotic Susceptibility (p. 163)
25. attention, relax, suggestions, imagination (p. 163); basic suggestion, dissociation (p. 164)
26. strength, memory, pain, regress, sensations (p. 164)
27. relaxation, pain (p. 164); therapy (p. 165)
28. hypnosis, suggestible, responsive, disinhibitor, direct, deception (p. 165)
29. sensory deprivation (p. 165); time, concentrating, hypnogogic, acuity, relaxation, habits (p. 166)
30. psychoactive (p. 167)
31. physical, addiction, withdrawal, tolerance, psychological (p. 167)
32. experimental, social-recreational, situational, intensive, compulsive (p. 170)
33. stimulants, narcolepsy, awake, performance, tolerance (p. 170); resources, fatigue, depression, aggression, amphetamine psychosis (p. 171)
34. stimulant (p. 171); addiction, compulsive (p. 172); alertness, euphoria, amphetamines, short (p. 171); compulsive, control, consequences (p. 172)
35. Caffeine, stimulates, alertness, coffee, tea, soft drinks, chocolate, cocoa, caffeinism, insomnia, irritability, appetite, heart, temperature, insomnia (p. 172); heart, blood pressure (p. 173); breast cysts (p. 172); birth defects (p. 173)
36. Nicotine, stimulant, pain, vomiting, diarrhea, sweats, dizziness, confusion, tremors, addicting, lung (p. 173); withdrawal, cold turkey (p. 174)
37. sedative, depress, alcohol, death, drug interaction, dependence (addiction), depression (p. 174)
38. depressant, inhibitions, relaxation, euphoria, consciousness, dull (shortsighted), myopia (p. 174)
39. tension, increasing, morning, regretted, blackouts (p. 176)
40. crucial, control, chronic, compulsively, continuously (p. 176)
41. detoxification, health (p. 176); tranquilizers, antidepressants, psychotherapy, AA (p. 177)
42. THC, hallucinogen, fatty, brain, reproductive, physical dependence, psychological dependence (p. 177)

43. euphoria, relaxation, time, perceptual, drive (p. 177)
44. lungs, sperm, sperm, abnormal, menstrual, ovulation, immune, genetic (p. 178)
45. condensation, displacement (p. 179); symbolic, secondary elaboration (p. 180)
46. play, playwright, primitive, emotional tone (p. 180)
47. yourself, remember, gradually (naturally), one, eyes closed, eyes closed, Review, dream diary (p. 180); suppress (p. 181)
48. decrease, decreases (p. 181)
49. missing, personal experience, characters, objects (p. 181)
50. dream (p. 181)
51. lucid, prearranged signal, firsthand data (p. 182)
52. curiosity, belong, meaning, inadequacy, cope, pleasure, ingrained, encourage, advertising (p. 183)
53. morality, publicizing, alcohol, tobacco, scientific (p. 184)

Chapter 7

Conditioning and Learning I

KEY TERMS, CONCEPTS, AND INDIVIDUALS

classical (respondent) conditioning
operant conditioning
learning defined
   reinforcement
   antecedents
   consequences
Pavlov
   unconditioned stimulus
   conditioned stimulus
   unconditioned response
   conditioned response
higher order conditioning
extinction
   spontaneous recovery
stimulus generalization
stimulus discrimination
conditioned emotional response
vicarious conditioning
E.L. Thorndike
classical and operant conditioning compared
B.F. Skinner
response contingent
   shaping
negative attention seeking
positive reinforcement

negative reinforcement
punishment
   response cost
primary and secondary reinforcement
generalized reinforcer
Premack principle
delay of reinforcement
response chaining
superstitious behavior
continuous reinforcement
partial reinforcement
   fixed ratio
   variable ratio
   fixed interval
   variable interval
stimulus control
discriminative stimulus
behavioral self-management
innate behaviors
   fixed action pattern
   reflex
   instinct
biological constraint
prepared fear theory
instinctive drift

LEARNING OBJECTIVES

To demonstrate mastery of this chapter you should be able to:

1. Define learning. A relatively permanent change in behavior that can be attributed to experience.

2.   Define reinforcement and explain its role in conditioning. (See also Figure 7-1.)
     Reinforcement is any procedure that strengthens learning and
makes a particular response more probable.

3.   Differentiate between antecedents and consequences and explain how they are related to classical and operant
     conditioning. (See also Figure 7-1.)
     Events that occur before a response is an antecedent. Those that
     follow a response are called consequences.
     → In classical conditioning, antecedent events become associated with
     on another. A stimulus that does not produce a response is linked with
     one that does.
     → Operant conditioning involves learning that is affected by consequences.
     Each time a response is made, it may be followed by a reinforcer,
     by punishment, or by nothing.

4.   Give a brief history of classical conditioning.
     20th century - Pavlov, Russian physiologist, was studying digestion.
     To observe salivation, he placed meat powder or some tidbit on a
     dog's tonge. After many times, Pavlov noticed the dogs salivated before the
     food reached their mouth. Later, the dogs began to salivate at the
     sight of Pavlov. Salivation is normally a reflex response. In order
     for dogs to do what they did, they had to have been learning something

5.   Describe the following terms as they apply to classical conditioning:
     a.   unconditioned stimulus (US) → A stimulus innately capable of eliciting
          a response

     b.   unconditioned response (UR) An innate reflex response elicited by an
          unconditioned stimulus

     c.   conditioned stimulus (CS) → stimulus that was neutral that acquires the
          capacity to evoke a response by being paired with an (UR)

     d.   conditioned response (CR) → A reflex response that has become associated
     with a new stimulus.

6.   Describe and give an example of classical conditioning using the abbreviations US, UR, CS, and CR.
     Before Conditioning   Example
     US ⟶ UR   Puff of air → eye blink
     NS ⟶ no effect   Horn → No effect
     After Conditioning   Example
     CS ⟶ CR   Horn → Eye blink

7.   Explain how reinforcement occurs during the acquisition of a classically conditioned response.
     In classical conditioning, reinforcement occurs whenever
     the CS is followed by, or paired with, an unconditioned
     stimulus.

8.   Explain what higher order conditioning is and give a practical example of it.
     In higher-order conditioning, a well-learned CS is used to reinforce
     further learning. In other words, the CS has become strong enough to be
     used like an unconditioned stimulus.

          Example: Salivating child first use clapping of hands and lemon juice
          then take away juice. She will still salivate at the clap of hands.

          ring of bell + clapping of hands

9.   Describe and give examples of the following concepts as they relate to classical conditioning:

a. extinction → by removing reinforcement. If the (US) never again follows the (CS).

(Example) if bell is rung many times and not followed by lemon juice, the child's tendency to salivate to the ringing of the bell will be inhibited.

b. spontaneous recovery

↳ The first time the bell is rung until the child quits responding, we might assume that extinction is complete. However if the bell is rung the next day, the child might respond again at first.

c. stimulus generalization → once a person or an animal has learned to respond to a conditioned stimulus, other stimuli similar to the CS may also trigger a response.

(example) child salivates to sound of ringing phone or doorbell

d. stimulus discrimination → child is conditioned with a bell. At first, the buzzer produces salivation. But after hearing the buzzer several times more, the child stops responding to it. Child has now learned to discriminate, or respond differently to, the bell and the buzzer.

10.   Describe the relationship between classical conditioning and reflex responses. In its simplest form, classical conditioning depends on reflex responses.
-Reflex is a dependable, inborn stimulus-and-response connection.

(example) pain causes reflex withdrawal of various parts of the body.

11.   Explain what a conditioned emotional response (CER) is and how it is acquired. A person with some type of fear. They can often trace their fear back to a time when they were exposed to the feared object or stimulus in the past.

* often broadened into phobias by stimulus generalization

12.   Explain the concept and the importance of vicarious classical conditioning.
occurs when we observe another person's emotional reactions to a stimulus and learn to respond emotionally to the same stimulus

13.   State the basic principle of operant conditioning and give its name according to E.L. Thorndike.
Acts that are reinforced tend to be repeated.

* law of effect → learning is strengthened each time a response is followed by a satisfying state of affairs.

14.   Contrast operant conditioning with classical conditioning.
Classical conditioning tends to be passive and involuntary. It simply "happens to" the learner when a CS is closely followed by a US.

Operant conditioning refers mainly to learning voluntary responses

15.   Explain what response contingent reinforcement is. what is reinforcing for one person may not be for another.

* Any event that follows a response and increases its probability.

16.   Explain how shaping occurs.

17.   Explain how extinction and spontaneous recovery occur in operant conditioning.

18.   Explain how negative attention-seeking behavior can be diminished.

19.   Compare and contrast positive reinforcement, negative reinforcement, and punishment and give an example of each. Include the concept of response cost.

20.   Differentiate primary reinforcers from secondary reinforcers and list four of each kind.

21.   Discuss two ways in which a secondary reinforcer becomes reinforcing.
      a.

      b.

22. Discuss the major advantages and disadvantages of primary reinforcers and secondary reinforcers (tokens, for instance), and describe how tokens have been used to help "special" groups of people.

23. Explain how a secondary reinforcer can become a generalized reinforcer.

24. Explain how the Premack principle (involving prepotent responses) can be used as reinforcement.

25. Describe how the delay of reinforcement can influence the effectiveness of the reinforcement.

26. Describe response chaining and explain how it can counteract the effects of delaying reinforcement.

27. Explain why superstitious behavior develops and why it persists.

28. Compare and contrast the effects of continuous and partial reinforcement.

29.   Describe, give an example of, and explain the effects of the following schedules of partial reinforcement:
       a.   Fixed Ratio (FR)

       b.   Variable Ratio (VR)

       c.   Fixed Interval (FI)

       d.   Variable Interval (VI)

30.   Explain the concept of stimulus control.

31.   Describe the processes of generalization and discrimination as they relate to operant conditioning.

* * * * * * * * * *

The following objectives are related to the material in the "Applications" and "Explorations" sections of your text.
32.   Explain how learning principles can be used to change your behavior. Include the concepts of self-recording and
       behavioral contracting.

33. List and explain the six techniques given on how to break bad habits. Using these, describe how one of your bad habits could be broken.

   a.

   b.

   c.

   d.

   e.

   f.

   Description:

34. Describe and give an example of a fixed action pattern.

35. Define instinct and explain why most psychologists reject the idea that humans have any.

36. Discuss the concept of biological constraints.

37. Explain why some fears are easier to acquire than others and name the explanatory theory.

38. Discuss the concept of instinctive drift.

SELF-QUIZZES

Do You Know the Information?

Multiple Choice

1. A relatively permanent change in behavior due to reinforcement is called
    (a) species specific behavior.
    (b) reflex.
    (c) learning.
    (d) reinforcement.
    (e) FAP.

2. Reinforcement refers to
    (a) any procedure which alters the chances that a response will be made.
    (b) learning which occurs because of practice.
    (c) repeating a response to produce learning.
    (d) any event which increases the probability that a response will occur again.

3. The person most closely associated with the development and refinement of classical conditioning was
    (a) B. F. Skinner.
    (b) Breland.
    (c) Pavlov.
    (d) Maslow.

4. In classical conditioning, the US
    (a) usually produces a reflexive response.
    (b) is the stimulus that elicits the CR.
    (c) produces a learned response.
    (d) is the same as the CS.

5. In classical conditioning the CR produces
    (a) the UR.
    (b) the CS.
    (c) the US.
    (d) the BS.
    (e) none of these.

6. In classical conditioning, reinforcement occurs when
    (a) the CS is followed by the CR.
    (b) the CS is paired with or followed by the US.
    (c) the CR is followed by the US.
    (d) the UR is paired with the US.

7. In higher order conditioning
    (a) the US is used to learn to new, but related responses.
    (b) there are more cognitive processes involved than in regular conditioning.
    (c) there are new responses learned.
    (d) a well-learned CS is used to reinforce further learning.

8. If the US never follows the CS, what will occur?
    (a) reinforcement
    (b) extinction
    (c) discrimination
    (d) spontaneous recovery

9. An extinguished response that reappears following a period of separation from the training situation is called
    (a) stimulus generalization.
    (b) stimulus control.
    (c) spontaneous recovery.
    (d) acquisition.

10. Conditioned emotional responses are learned when
    (a) a person is emotionally traumatized in the presence of the stimulus.
    (b) a fearful response is reinforced.
    (c) the response to the stimulus discriminates to related responses.
    (d) associated fearful responses are desensitized.

11. CERs can play an important role in our daily psychological functioning through the development of
    (a) phobias.
    (b) reflexes.
    (c) instincts.
    (d) discriminations.

12. When CERs are learned by observing others this is called
    (a) generalization.
    (b) vicarious classical conditioning.
    (c) operant conditioning.
    (d) nonreward.

13. What is the basic principle of operant conditioning?
    (a) Acts followed by reinforcement tend to be repeated.
    (b) The US will not consistently produce the CR unless the CR is rewarding.
    (c) Reward is more effective than reinforcement.
    (d) Punishment is more effective than reinforcement.

14. Unlike classical conditioning, in operant conditioning
    (a) reinforcement is necessary.
    (b) the relevant responses are reflexive.
    (c) combined learning trials are used.
    (d) the response is emitted rather than elicited.

15. If a reinforcement is response contingent then the reinforcement
    (a) depends upon making a response.
    (b) is effective.
    (c) affects the performance of responses already learned.
    (d) is all of the above.

16. Shaping occurs when
    (a) reinforcement is given for any response as long as the organism actively behaves.
    (b) only the first response is reinforced.
    (c) successive approximations to the desired response are reinforced.
    (d) reinforcement is only given for every other response.

17. Negative reinforcement
    (a) is the same as punishment.
    (b) is a pleasant stimulus just like positive reinforcement.
    (c) decreases or suppresses behavior.
    (d) has the same effect on a response as positive reinforcement.

18. Negative reinforcement and punishment are different in that
    (a) negative reinforcement decreases responding.
    (b) one is a pleasant stimulus and the other is unpleasant.
    (c) negative reinforcement increases responding and punishment decreases responding.
    (d) punishment ends discomfort.

19. Praise, affection, and attention are all examples of _____ reinforcers.
    (a) latent
    (b) secondary
    (c) negative
    (d) primary

20.   Secondary reinforcers gain their rewarding value by being
    (a) exchanged for primary reinforcers.   (c) learned.
    (b) associated with primary reinforcers.   (d) all of these.

21.   A major disadvantage of primary reinforcers is that they
    (a) may produce satiation too rapidly.
    (b) may begin producing a reduction in responding like punishment.
    (c) cannot be given immediately.
    (d) function like tokens.

22.   If a secondary reinforcer becomes independent of its connection with a primary reinforcer, it becomes
    (a) a learned reinforcer.   (c) a generalized reinforcer.
    (b) more effective.   (d) the basis for operant conditioning.

23.   If there is a delay between the behavior and the reinforcement
    (a) the two will be paired for a longer period of time and hence, more reinforcement will occur.
    (b) the effectiveness of the reinforcement will be diminished.
    (c) latent learning will occur.
    (d) the reinforcer will be more effective if it is primary.

24.   When a series of behaviors or responses is maintained by one reinforcer _____ has occurred.
    (a) feedback   (c) cognitive learning
    (b) response chaining   (d) successive approximation

25.   Schedules of partial reinforcement, as contrasted with continuous reinforcement, produce
    (a) equally fast learning.   (c) more reinforcements per response.
    (b) more rapid shaping.   (d) slower extinction.

26.   Which schedule of reinforcement would produce the highest rate of responding?
    (a) variable interval   (c) fixed interval
    (b) variable ratio   (d) fixed ratio

27.   The stimulus control principle of operant conditioning states that
    (a) responses reinforced in a particular situation tend to come under the control of stimuli present in that situation.
    (b) a response following a stimulus will tend to occur again.
    (c) a response not followed by reinforcement may be strengthened.
    (d) stimuli following a response alter the chances of its being repeated.

28.   Which factors produce discrimination?
    (a) reinforcement and stimulus control   (c) shaping and extinction
    (b) generalization and extinction   (d) stimulus control and partial reinforcement

29.   In order to break a bad habit a person should
    (a) find out what is reinforcing the habit and remove, avoid, or delay the reinforcement.
    (b) avoid the cues that elicit the habit.
    (c) make an incompatible response in the presence of the stimuli that usually precede the habit.
    (d) do all of the above.

30.   When a person attempts to break a bad habit by deliberately repeating the habit until it becomes boring, painful, or produces fatigue, the technique is called
    (a) habit reversal.   (c) modified punishment.
    (b) negative practice.   (d) negative repetition.

31. Which of the following are considered characteristics of an instinct? Circle one or more.
     (a) involves a cognitive element   (c) involves only the spinal cord
     (b) species specific   (d) inborn

32. Most psychologists reject the idea of human instincts because
     (a) the majority of our activities are affected by learning.
     (b) instincts cannot be positively reinforced.
     (c) humans tend to have a sufficient number of fixed action patterns.
     (d) humans have no innate behavior patterns.

33. The prepared fear theory holds that
     (a) some fears are instinctive and naturally occur in all of us.
     (b) certain stimuli in our early history posed danger and have become highly effective conditioning stimuli.
     (c) some people are just naturally easier to condition than others.
     (d) we are more easily conditioned by watching others in certain cases than by experiencing the conditioning ourselves.

34. Instinctive drift refers to
     (a) the use of partial schedules of reinforcement to produce long chains of behavior.
     (b) the inability of one stimulus to consistently elicit an instinctive response.
     (c) learned responses "drifting" toward innate ones.
     (d) the classical conditioning of instinctive or innate responses.

True-False

_____ 1. Operant conditioning deals with antecedents, whereas classical conditioning deals with consequences.

_____ 2. The US typically produces a UR.

_____ 3. Classical conditioning depends heavily on voluntary behavior.

_____ 4. Extinction occurs in operant conditioning when a learned response is reinforced excessively.

_____ 5. Positive reinforcement takes place when a pleasant event follows an action and increases the probability of the recurrence of the action.

_____ 6. A primary reinforcer is unlearned whereas a secondary reinforcer is learned.

_____ 7. The Premack principle holds that a low probability behavior can be made a high probability behavior by proper reinforcement.

_____ 8. A reward reinforces only the last response preceding it. This is the principle of superstitious behavior.

_____ 9. The effect of a partial schedule of reinforcement is to make the organism slow down and quit responding faster than continuous reinforcement would.

_____ 10. Stimulus control refers to the fact that stimuli present when a response is rewarded tend to control that response on future occasions.

_____ 11. A fixed action pattern is an instinctual chain of movements found in all members of a species which prepares them to meet major needs in their lives.

Matching *(Use the letters on the right only once.)*

_____ 1. CS
_____ 2. stimulus generalization
_____ 3. vicarious
_____ 4. law of effect
_____ 5. paid by amount of work done
_____ 6. develops a great sense of time
_____ 7. produces greatest resistance to extinction
_____ 8. instinctual chain of movements
_____ 9. biological constraint

A. dependent upon continuous reinforcement
B. secondhand
C. credits given for tasks and rent reduction given if minimum earned
D. limit to learning
E. reflex
F. after conditioning, produces a CR
G. FI
H. involves multiple stimuli
I. FR
J. behavior rewarded is behavior repeated
K. VI
L. FAP

Can You Apply the Information?

For questions 1-3 use the following example:

Barbara is running down the street. As she opens the gate to her friend's yard, a big dog jumps out and bites her. She is terribly startled and cries out in pain. She now cries whenever she sees a dog.

1. Which is the US?
    (a) the dog
    (b) pain
    (c) crying out
    (d) touching the gate

2. Identify the CS.
    (a) the dog
    (b) pain
    (c) crying out
    (d) being startled

3. What is the CR?
    (a) running down the street
    (b) touching the gate
    (c) pain
    (d) crying

4. You have conditioned Ronald to blink to the sound of a bell. You begin sneezing every time right before you ring the bell. After a brief period of time, Ronald begins blinking not to the bell, but to your sneeze. What is this called?

    (a) secondhand conditioning
    (b) secondary reinforcement
    (c) higher order conditioning
    (d) stimulus acquisition
    (e) shower therapy

5. If a dog never bites or makes a menacing move toward Barbara again it is possible that _____ may occur.
    (a) reinforcement
    (b) conditioning
    (c) stimulus generalization
    (d) extinction

6. As a result of her experience Barbara becomes afraid and cries when she sees any four-legged furry animal. What has occurred?
    (a) spontaneous recovery
    (b) vicarious conditioning
    (c) stimulus generalization
    (d) extinction

7. In this example, Barbara has developed a(n)
   (a) propensity for vicarious conditioning.
   (b) conditioned emotional response.
   (c) fixed ratio schedule of reinforcement.
   (d) delayed reinforcement behavior.

8. Mary learns not to play around a hot stove because she saw her brother burned severely while doing so. Mary's avoidance of the stove is a result of
   (a) vicarious conditioning.
   (b) stimulus generalization.
   (c) partial reinforcement.
   (d) US-CR pairing.

9. You are trying to teach Jose to eat with a spoon. First you praise him for picking it up. Then you reinforce him for lifting it closer to his mouth. Next you reward him for putting food in the spoon. You are teaching Jose using
   (a) generalization.
   (b) successive discrimination.
   (c) shaping.
   (d) all of these.

10. Bryan, three years old, is especially obnoxious whenever his mother is talking on the telephone. In order to decrease this behavior, his mother should
    (a) promise him a treat if he'll be good for the duration of her 15 minute phone calls.
    (b) ignore him when he is being obnoxious and reward him the moment he is quiet.
    (c) give him a good spanking when she gets off the phone.
    (d) threaten him while she tries to continue her conversation.

11. If a child regularly throws temper tantrums
    (a) he or she has had some positive reinforcement in the past for doing so.
    (b) extinction will probably not work now.
    (c) there has to have been some primary reinforcement for such behavior in the past.
    (d) the child has strong instincts.
    (e) you can bet the parents probably flunked their psych class.

12. Oxygen is a good
    (a) negative reinforcer.
    (b) primary reinforcer.
    (c) secondary reinforcer.
    (d) generalized reinforcer.
    (e) thing to have.

13. Your daughter isn't wild about eating her peas. You get her to eat them by telling her she can have some ice cream when she is finished with the peas. You are utilizing
    (a) a generalized reinforcer.
    (b) the Premack principle.
    (c) a secondary reinforcer.
    (d) delay of reinforcement.

14. "Step on a crack and you'll break your mother's back." If this is an actual superstition and not just a rhyme, you can bet that a long time ago
    (a) stimulus generalization occurred for some child.
    (b) there were successive approximations made which paid off.
    (c) some child came home and found his mother laid out with a broken back.
    (d) a child suffered vicarious classical conditioning.

15. You drive a cab for a living and get paid 40 cents for every passenger mile driven. Sometimes traffic is light and you can drive 50 miles an hour. What schedule of reinforcement are you on?
    (a) VI
    (b) FI
    (c) VR
    (d) FR

16. You work for the federal government and your reinforcement is money. You are salaried and get paid on the 1st and the 16th of each month. You have found that the huge bureaucracy covers up your lazy tendencies. You can get by with almost no work. Which schedule of reinforcement are you on?
    (a) VI
    (b) FI
    (c) VR
    (d) FR

17. Your camera has a built-in flash. A tiny light comes on to signal that the flash is ready. If you push the button before the light comes on, you ruin a picture. If you wait for the light signal, you get a good picture. You very quickly learn when to respond and when not to. A psychologist might say that
    (a) this is a good example of a conditioned response (CR).
    (b) stimulus generalization has occurred.
    (c) you have been shaped.
    (d) the tiny light now exerts stimulus control.

18. While walking along a sidewalk you look ahead and see what appears to be a Kennedy half dollar. You reach down and pick it up. It turns out to be a flattened bottle cap. You are embarrassed and hope nobody saw you. What has caused your error?
    (a) shaping
    (b) spontaneous recovery
    (c) stimulus discrimination
    (d) stimulus generalization

19. At first a child calls all men "Dada." When most men do not reinforce her for her efforts but her father does, she limits her use of "Dada" to her father alone. Learning has occurred through
    (a) continuous reinforcement.
    (b) shaping.
    (c) discrimination.
    (d) generalization.

20. Bertha is a heavy smoker and wants to reduce the habit and eventually quit. According to what you learned in the chapter, if she simply records the number of times she smokes in a day, you would expect her
    (a) smoking to decrease.
    (b) smoking to increase.
    (c) smoking to remain the same.
    (d) to wear out lots and lots of pencils.

21. The circling ritual dogs go through in settling down to sleep is an example of
    (a) a reflex.
    (b) a FAP.
    (c) an instinct.
    (d) none of these.

Chapter Review

1. _____ is a relatively permanent change in behavior due to _____.
   Any event which _____ the chances that a _____ will occur again is called _____.

2. Events before a response are called _____. Those that follow a response are called _____. Classical conditioning involves learning to associate _____ events with one another. Operant conditioning involves learning affected by _____.

3. The Russian physiologist _____ first investigated classical conditioning. He taught dogs to salivate to the sound of a bell rung before meat powder was given to the dogs. In this example the meat powder is considered to be the _____ stimulus, and the bell is the _____ stimulus.

4. A dog naturally salivates when food is placed in its mouth. Such "built-in" automatic, unlearned responses are called _____. Pavlov called these unlearned responses _____, whereas salivation to the sound of a bell alone is called a _____ response.

5. In classical conditioning the connection between a conditioned stimulus and conditioned response is reinforced when the _____ _____ is followed by a(n) _____ _____.

6. In _____ _____ conditioning a well-learned CS is used to reinforce further learning.

7. In classical conditioning if the US does not follow the CS, the CR will be _____. After a rest period, the presentation of the CS may elicit the CR. This is called _____ _____.

8. Once a subject is conditioned to respond to a particular stimulus, other stimuli similar to the CS may elicit a response. This is called _____ _____. In the opposite process, the subjects learn to respond to one stimulus, but not to others. This is called _____.

9. Classical conditioning depends upon _____ responses. Fears such as phobias may be learned through classical conditioning and are called _____ _____ _____.

10. The importance of CERs is extended by the fact that they can be learned _____. Learning to react emotionally to the experiences of others is called _____ classical conditioning.

11. The basic principle of operant conditioning is that acts followed by _____ tend to be _____. Thorndike called this the law of _____. Classical conditioning is _____ and _____. Operant conditioning concentrates on _____ responses.

12. To be effective, reinforcement should be _____ _____. In other words, getting a reinforcer depends on making a desired _____.

13. When we gradually mold responses to a final desired pattern, the process is called _____. The basic principle of this process is that gradual or _____ _____ to the desired responses are rewarded.

14. Just as in classical conditioning, if a response learned through operant conditioning is not reinforced, it gradually ceases to be a part of an organism's behavior. This process is called _____. If the organism is removed from the testing apparatus and given a rest period, he is likely to resume making the learned response when returned to the testing situation. This is known as _____ _____.

15. _____ and _____ from parents are very powerful reinforcers for most children. If children are engaging in negative _____ _____ behavior, a good way to decrease it is to _____ it, assuming the parent is in control of the reinforcers.

16. When a pleasant event follows an action, the event is called a _____ reinforcer. _____ reinforcement occurs when a response causes the _____ of an unpleasant event. Both of these reinforcers _____ behavior. _____ is any event which follows a response and _____ the likelihood of it occurring again. This event can either be the _____ of an aversive event or the _____ of a positive event. When the latter is used, it is called _____ cost.

17. Reinforcers that are unlearned and biological in nature are called _____ reinforcers. _____ reinforcers are learned.

18. A secondary reinforcer may become reinforcing by being _____ with a primary reinforcer. They may also become rewards when they can be _____ for primary reinforcers. One problem with primary reinforcers is that people and animals receiving them may _____ quickly. When a secondary reinforcer has value which appears independent of its connection with a primary reinforcer, the secondary reinforcer has become a _____ reinforcer.

19. When any _____ (high-frequency) response is used to _____ a low-frequency response, this is called the _____ principle.

20. Reinforcement usually has its greatest effect on learning when the time lapse between a response and the reward is _____. Experiments show that when reward is _____, learning is retarded or does not occur at all.

21. It is often possible for single reinforcement to maintain a long _____ of responses such as the sequence of events necessary to prepare a meal.

22. When behaviors develop as a result of _____ but actually have nothing to do with bringing about the _____, the behaviors are called _____. These acts appear to pay off to the person or animal. The existence of such behaviors points to the fact that a reinforcement will reinforce not only the last _____ that precedes it, but also other _____ occurring shortly before the reinforcement is given.

23. When reinforcement follows every response this is known as _____ reinforcement. Reinforcement which does not follow every response is termed _____ reinforcement. This latter type of reward makes a response very resistant to _____.

24. If every 3rd, 4th, 5th, or Nth response is followed by reinforcement, this is a _____ _____ schedule of reinforcement. This type of schedule produces an extremely _____ rate of response. In contrast to this, variable _____ schedules produce slightly _____ rates of responding. Since reward is less predictable, this type of schedule produces greater _____ to extinction than the former type of schedule.

25. If a subject has to wait a set amount of time between one reward and the next, the schedule of reinforcement is called _____ _____. This schedule produces _____ response rates including periods of _____. When subjects are rewarded for the first response made after a variable amount of time has passed, the schedule is called _____ _____. This type of schedule produces _____, _____ responding and tremendous resistance to _____.

26. Responses which are reinforced in a particular situation tend to come under the control of _____ present in that situation. This is the principle of _____ _____.

27. Stimuli similar to those which precede a rewarded response also tend to produce a response because of _____ _____. When an organism responds differently to different stimuli, this is known as _____ .

28. Reinforcement can be used to change one's behavior. Start by choosing a _____ behavior; that is, identify what you want to change. Then record a _____ so you'll know how much time you already spend performing the behavior. Next, establish _____ and make them realistic.

29. You also need to choose _____ for reaching your daily goals. Be sure to _____ your progress. _____ your successes and _____ your plan as you learn more about your behavior.

30. You may find that merely _____ how often a certain behavior is performed is enough to modify it to your satisfaction. This is called _____-_____. If you have trouble modifying your behavior, you may find that _____ _____ will help increase your motivation.

31. There are several techniques which you can use to help you break a bad habit.
    (1) Try to discover what is _____ a habit and remove, avoid, or delay the _____.
    (2) Try to get the same _____ with new responses.
    (3) Try to _____ or _____ _____ cues that elicit the bad habit.
    (4) Try to scramble the _____ of events that leads up to the undesired response.
    (5) Make an _____ response in the presence of stimuli that usually precede the bad habit.
    (6) Use _____ _____ to associate the habit with discomfort.
    (7) Utilize _____ to change the habit. For instance, keep a daily _____ of how often a behavior occurs.

32. A _____ _____ _____ is an instinctual chain of movements found in all members of a species. A more complex behavior is an _____. To qualify as _____, a behavior must be _____, and _____ _____. Most psychologists feel that humans do not have _____ because of our _____ capacity.

33. There are a number of _____ _____ or limits to animal learning.

34. Seligman believes that we are prepared by evolution to readily develop fears to certain stimuli such as spiders. He believes that such stimuli posed dangers earlier in human history. Through natural selection, they have become highly effective conditioning stimuli. This is called the _____ _____ theory.

35. Teaching animals using operant conditioning is sometimes difficult. Sometimes the behavior being conditioned may be intruded upon by innate behavior patterns. Two noted psychologists and animal trainers Keller and Marion Breland called this phenomenon _____ _____.

ANSWER KEYS

Do You Know the Information?

Multiple Choice

1. (c) obj. 1, p. 189
2. (d) obj. 2, p. 189
3. (c) obj. 4, p. 190
4. (a) obj. 5, p. 191
5. (e) obj. 5, p. 191
6. (b) obj. 7, p. 192
7. (d) obj. 8, p. 192
8. (b) obj. 9, p. 193
9. (c) obj. 9, p. 193
10. (a) obj. 11, p. 194
11. (a) obj. 11, p. 194
12. (b) obj. 12, p. 195
13. (a) obj. 13, p. 195
14. (d) obj. 14, p. 196
15. (d) obj. 15, p. 197
16. (c) obj. 16, p. 198
17. (d) obj. 19, p. 199
18. (c) obj. 19, p. 199
19. (b) obj. 20, p. 200
20. (d) obj. 21, p. 201
21. (a) obj. 22, p. 201
22. (c) obj. 23, p. 202
23. (b) obj. 25, p. 203
24. (b) obj. 26, p. 203
25. (d) obj. 28, p. 204
26. (d) obj. 29, p. 205
27. (a) obj. 30, p. 206

28. (b) obj. 31, p. 207
29. (d) obj. 33, pp. 210-211
30. (b) obj. 33, p. 211
31. (b,d) obj. 35, p. 213
32. (a) obj. 35, p. 213
33. (b) obj. 37, p. 213
34. (c) obj. 38, p. 214

True-False

1. F, obj. 3, p. 190
2. T, obj. 5, p. 191
3. F, obj. 10, p. 191
4. F, obj. 17, p. 199
5. T, obj. 19, p. 199
6. T, obj. 20, p. 200
7. F, obj. 24, p. 202
8. F, obj. 27, p. 203
9. F, obj. 28, p. 204
10. T, obj. 30, p. 206
11. T, obj. 34, p. 212

Matching

1. F, obj. 5, p. 191
2. H, obj. 9, p. 193
3. B, obj. 12, p. 195
4. J, obj. 13, p. 195
5. I, obj. 29, p. 205

6. G, obj. 29, p. 206
7. K, obj. 29, p. 206
8. L, obj. 34, p. 212
9. D, obj. 36, p. 213

Can You Apply the Information?

1. (b) obj. 6, p. 191
2. (a) obj. 6, p. 191
3. (d) obj. 6, p. 191
4. (c) obj. 8, p. 192
5. (d) obj. 9, p. 193
6. (c) obj. 9, p. 193
7. (b) obj. 11, p. 194
8. (a) obj. 12, p. 195
9. (c) obj. 16, p. 198
10. (b) obj. 18, p. 199
11. (a) obj. 19, p. 199
12. (b) obj. 20, p. 200
13. (b) obj. 24, p. 202
14. (c) obj. 27, p. 203
15. (d) obj. 29, p. 205
16. (b) obj. 29, p. 206
17. (d) obj. 30, p. 206
18. (d) obj. 31, p. 207
19. (c) obj. 31, p. 207
20. (a) obj. 32, p. 210
21. (b) obj. 34, p. 212

Chapter Review

1. Learning, reinforcement, increases, response, reinforcement (p. 189)
2. antecedents, consequences, antecedent, consequences (p. 189)
3. Pavlov (p. 190); unconditioned, conditioned (p. 191)
4. reflexes, unconditioned, conditioned (p. 191)
5. conditioned stimulus, unconditioned stimulus (p. 191)
6. higher order (p. 192)
7. extinguished, spontaneous recovery (p. 193)
8. stimulus generalization, discrimination (p. 193)
9. reflex, conditioned emotional responses (p. 194)
10. indirectly, vicarious (p. 195)
11. reinforcement, repeated, effect, passive, involuntary, voluntary, (p. 196)
12. response contingent, response (p. 197)

13. shaping, successive approximations (p. 198)
14. extinction, spontaneous recovery (p. 198)
15. Attention, approval, attention seeking, ignore (p. 199)
16. positive, negative, removal, increase, Punishment, decrease, application, removal, response (p. 199)
17. primary, Secondary (p. 200)
18. associated, exchanged, satiate, generalized (p. 201)
19. prepotent, reinforce, Premack (p. 202)
20. brief (short, minimal), delayed (p. 203)
21. chain (p. 203)
22. reinforcement, reinforcement, superstitious, response, responses (p. 203)
23. continuous, partial, extinction (p. 204)
24. fixed ratio, high, ratio, lower, resistance (p. 205)
25. fixed interval, moderate, inactivity, variable interval, slow, steady, extinction (p. 206)
26. stimuli, stimulus control (p. 206)
27. stimulus generalization, discrimination (p. 207)
28. target, baseline, goals (p. 209)
29. reinforcers, record, Reward, adjust (p. 210)
30. recording, self-recording, behavioral contracting (p. 210)
31. reinforcing, reinforcement, reinforcement, avoid, narrow down, chain, incompatible, negative practice, feedback, record (p. 211)
32. fixed action pattern, instinct, instinctual, complex, species specific, instincts, learning (p. 213)
33. biological constraints (p. 213)
34. prepared fear (p. 213)
35. instinctive drift (p. 214)

Chapter 8

Conditioning and Learning II

LEARNING OBJECTIVES

To demonstrate mastery of this chapter you should be able to:
1. Explain what two-factor learning is.

2. Explain classical and operant conditioning in terms of the informational view.

3.   Define feedback and explain its importance in learning.

4.   Describe programmed instruction and computer-assisted instruction and discuss their application in learning and teaching.

5.   List and discuss three factors which influence the effectiveness of punishment.
      a.

      b.

      c.

6.   Differentiate the effects of severe punishment from mild punishment.

7.   Explain how the undesirable side effects of punishment can be lessened.

8.   Explain how escape and avoidance learning relate to punishment.

9.   Define cognitive learning.

10.   Describe the following concepts:
      a.   cognitive map

      b.   latent learning

11.   Explain the difference between discovery learning and rote learning.

12.   Discuss the factors which determine whether or not modeling or observational learning will occur.

13.   Describe the experiment with children and the Bo-Bo doll that demonstrates the powerful effect of modeling on behavior.

14.   Explain how television may serve as a disinhibiting factor.

15.   Discuss biofeedback in terms of the process involved, its possible applications, and the contradictory evidence as to its value.

16.   Define the terms motor skill and motor program, and explain how a motor program guides movement.

17.   List and explain six rules that can aid skill learning.
       a.

       b.

       c.

       d.

       e.

       f.

18.   Explain how mental practice can help the learning of skills.

19.   Describe the following concepts as they relate to motor skill learning:
       a.   spaced practice

       b.   massed practice (Is this generally better or worse than spaced practice?)

20.   Define and give an example of positive and negative transfer.

* * * * * * * * * *

The following objectives are related to the material in the "Applications" and "Explorations" sections of your text.

21.   List and explain the seven techniques involved in self-regulated learning.

a.

b.

c.

d.

e.

f.

g.

22.   Present evidence to support the viewpoint that watching violence on television can cause a desensitization to violence.

23.   Explain how it is known that watching TV can increase prosocial behavior.

SELF-QUIZZES

Do You Know the Information?

Multiple Choice

1. Two-factor learning refers to the idea that learning involves both
   (a) primary and secondary reinforcers.
   (b) positive and negative reinforcement.
   (c) classical and operant conditioning.
   (d) reinforcers and punishment.

2. According to the informational view of conditioning,
   (a) CS's and operant reinforcers both predict US's.
   (b) CS's and operant reinforcers both create expectancies.
   (c) CS's predict US's and operant reinforcers predict CS's.
   (d) all of the above are correct.

3. In order to make feedback effective it should be _____, _____, and _____.
   (a) positive, accurate, consistent
   (b) frequent, immediate, detailed
   (c) frequent, immediate, constructive
   (d) timely, consistent, humane

4. Programmed instruction and computer-assisted instruction are examples of new applications of
   (a) KR.
   (b) negative reinforcement.
   (c) latent learning.
   (d) primary reinforcement.

5. For punishment to be effective it should
   (a) be severe, but humane.
   (b) immediately follow the response.
   (c) be consistent.
   (d) be all of the above.

6. As opposed to mild punishment, more severe punishment
   (a) is not as effective at suppressing behavior.
   (b) abolishes the unwanted behavior.
   (c) more effectively stops behavior.
   (d) actually encourages the behavior to reappear later.

7. Which of the following is *not* one of the basic tools available to control simple learning?
   (a) Negative reinforcement strengthens a response by removing an unpleasant stimulus.
   (b) Nonreinforcement causes a response to extinguish.
   (c) Reinforcement strengthens a response.
   (d) Punishment suppresses a response.

8. Which of the following is *not* one of the six guidelines which should be followed when using punishment?
   (a) Use the minimum necessary to suppress the behavior.
   (b) Expect aggression from the punished person.
   (c) Punish with kindness and respect.
   (d) Don't use punishment if you could ignore the behavior and make it go away.

9. Frequent punishment may make a child
   (a) unhappy.
   (b) aggressive.
   (c) fearful of the source of punishment.
   (d) all of the above.

10. Punishment can increase
    (a) avoidance.
    (b) escape.
    (c) aggression.
    (d) all of the above.

11. Escape learning is to _____ as avoidance learning is to _____.
    (a) positive reinforcement; punishment
    (b) punishment; non-reinforcement
    (c) classical conditioning; operant conditioning
    (d) negative reinforcement; two-factor learning

12. Learning that involves understanding, knowing, and other higher mental processes is termed
    (a) latent learning.
    (b) cognitive learning.
    (c) modeling.
    (d) motor learning.

13. _____ learning occurs with no obvious reinforcement of the correct response.
    (a) Latent
    (b) Cognitive
    (c) Verbal
    (d) Motor

14. As opposed to rote learning, discovery learning involves
    (a) memorization and repetition of facts.
    (b) a useful solution to the problem.
    (c) understanding and insight.
    (d) reinforcement.

15. Which of the following factors affects whether modeling (observational learning) will occur?
    (a) perceived size of the model
    (b) whether the model is live or on TV
    (c) if the model is successful or was rewarded
    (d) whether or not the learner has imitated before

16. In the experiment on observational learning using the Bo-Bo doll
    (a) most children imitated the attack they had seen an adult perform.
    (b) the live model inspired the most modeling.
    (c) the children seemed to perform only the acts they had previously seen performed.
    (d) the cartoon was actually slightly more effective in encouraging aggression than the live model.

17. With regards to the influences that television violence may have on people who view television, it is probably safe to say that television
    (a) may actually teach new antisocial actions.
    (b) may disinhibit dangerous impulses that viewers already have.
    (c) may promote observational learning of aggression.
    (d) may do all of the above.

18. Which of the following was *not* one of the findings from William's study of the effects of TV on children of a small Canadian town?
    (a) reading development increased
    (b) creativity test scores decreased
    (c) stereotyping of sex roles increased
    (d) verbal and physical aggression increased

19. Which of the following have been changed using biofeedback?
    (a) brain waves
    (b) blood pressure
    (c) memory
    (d) epileptic seizures
    (e) visual accuracy
    (f) muscle tension
    (g) blood flow
    (h) hand temperature
    (i) heart rhythms

20. As motor _____ develop, motor _____ become automated.
    (a) programs; skills
    (b) skills; programs
    (c) brain centers; programs
    (d) brain centers; skills

21. According to the rules to aid skill learning
(a) spaced practice hinders learning by increasing fatigue over a period of time.
(b) an experienced person should direct attention to areas that need improvement.
(c) learn verbal rules to back up motor learning.
(d) practice should continue even if the practice is not exactly like what will be required of the final skill.

22. When the mastery of one task adversely affects the acquisition of a new task, _____ occurs.
(a) negative practice   (c) relearning
(b) positive transfer   (d) negative transfer

23. Which of the following is *not* a characteristic that is consistent with self-regulated learning?
(a) rating your own progress over time   (c) reinforcing yourself for meeting your goals
(b) being inherently bright to start with   (d) doing whatever is necessary to master a topic or skill

24. Which of the following statements *best* describes the effects of TV on children?
(a) Violence on TV makes children more sensitive to aggressive acts in the real world.
(b) Children who watch a great deal of televised violence will be more prone to behave aggressively.
(c) TV has been shown to cause aggression in children.
(d) Although found to be a tremendous source of entertainment, TV has not been found to have a definite positive or negative effect on children.

25. Cline (1972) investigated the physiological arousal and sensitivity to violence of heavy TV viewers as opposed to boys who watched little or no TV. He found that
(a) boys who were heavy TV viewers showed much less arousal (emotion).
(b) boys who watched little or no TV were not sensitive to the violence because of their lack of exposure to it.
(c) both groups reacted about the same because of the severity of the violence.
(d) the greatest physiological arousal was found after the second hour of TV viewing.

True-False

_____ 1. According to the informational view, conditioning creates expectancies which alter behavior.

_____ 2. More frequent feedback in a learning situation generally means faster learning or improved performance.

_____ 3. Punishers are determined to be different than reinforcers based on their effects on behavior.

_____ 4. Punishment is most effective when everyone has had a chance to cool down and review the situation.

_____ 5. If a person chooses to use punishment, an alternate, desirable behavior should be rewarded.

_____ 6. Punishment which attacks a person's self-esteem will be most effective in suppressing unwanted behavior.

_____ 7. The overall emotional adjustment of a child disciplined mainly by reward is usually superior to one disciplined mainly by punishment.

_____ 8. Using punishment on a child to stop an unwanted behavior can be negatively reinforcing for the adult if the behavior stops.

_____ 9. Rote learning is the first stage of discovery learning.

_____10.   A cartoon version of aggressive adults attacking a Bo-Bo doll was only slightly less effective in encouraging aggression in children than a live adult model attacking a Bo-Bo doll.

_____11.   Television may disinhibit dangerous impulses that viewers already have.

_____12.   Many of the reported benefits of biofeedback may simply reflect general relaxation.

_____13.   Mental practice (thinking about a performance) can aid learning.

_____14.   Massed practice facilitates motor learning since less is forgotten between trials.

_____15.   Self-instruction appears to be the most important aspect of effective learning.

_____16.   Children who were exposed to a TV program emphasizing helping were more willing than others to model this prosocial behavior.

Do you understand the concepts of positive reinforcement, negative reinforcement, and punishment? Using the following code, place the correct symbol in each box.

+	pleasant event	↑ increases responding
−	unpleasant event	↓ decreases responding

	Nature of Event	Effect on Responding
Positive reinforcement		
Negative reinforcement		
Punishment		

Can You Apply the Information?

1.   Alan's library has a new anti-theft device. If a person walks through it with a book that is not properly checked out, an alarm sounds. Many people (Alan included) have "absentmindedly" walked through after browsing in the library. After a few such experiences, Alan can feel the tension rising as he approaches the device. Circle all of the following statements which are *correct*.
(a)   The CR is the buzzer.
(b)   Alan would probably like to use a door without the alarm system.
(c)   This example is probably two-factor learning.
(d)   As Alan approaches the detection system, a mental expectancy is created. This is in agreement with the informational view.

2. Bobby, a third-grader, has been having ever increasing difficulty with his mathematics school work. Because of this he has become more self-conscious during classtime and it is beginning to affect his work in other subjects. After consultation with the school counselor, his parents decide to enroll Bobby in a CAI mathematics program. Should they expect his math ability to improve?
   (a) *Yes*, because even though it will take longer and require more effort on his part the individual nature of the program is sufficient to give him the needed feedback to learn the material without distraction.
   (b) *Yes*, because Bobby will not feel like he is being watched and evaluated by his teacher.
   (c) *No*, because the feedback is often not frequent enough to keep him from practicing errors.
   (d) *No*, because the drill and practice routines in printed workbooks is still superior to CAI drill and practice based programs.

3. You're getting your first kiss. From the sound (a nice, long "Ummm") that your date makes you are encouraged to continue. Your date's sound is a(n)
   (a) punisher.
   (b) reinforcer.
   (c) expectancy.
   (d) non-reinforcer.

4. Same situation as above except in this case your date vomits on you during the kiss. (Pretty gross, huh?) The next time this person calls to invite you out, you respectfully decline because
   (a) of positive reinforcement.
   (b) of negative reinforcement.
   (c) of punishment.
   (d) you can't "stomach" the person.

5. If you control your son's behavior by using large amounts of punishment, your son will be likely to
   (a) play very roughly with his friends.
   (b) try to avoid you.
   (c) have a poorer emotional adjustment than the boy next door who is controlled mainly through rewards.
   (d) have all of the above characteristics.

6. Both of Mary's parents work long days so that Mary does not get as much attention from them as she would like. She has been misbehaving with increasing frequency when they are home to the point that severe punishment appears to be the only way to temporarily stop her behavior. Which of the following could explain the deteriorating conditions in Mary's household? (You may choose more than one.)
   (a) The "punisher" is perceived by Mary as a "reinforcer" because it gives her the attention that she desires.
   (b) The severe punishment routine used by the parents has become a habit because it is negatively reinforced, i.e., the punishment temporarily stops Mary's behavior thus reinforcing the use of punishment again.
   (c) Mary is not receiving any positive reinforcement (attention) for her good behavior.
   (d) Through repeated use of punishment Mary is learning to be more frustrated and aggressive towards her parents.

7. The lights go out in your house. It is so dark that you can't see your hand in front of your face. You have to find the flashlight that is in your bedroom. No problem! You can easily walk around your house in the dark. It is likely that
   (a) you know your way around because of discovery learning.
   (b) you have a cognitive map of your house.
   (c) darkness has become a generalized reinforcer.
   (d) you'll be in the local Emergency Room in an hour with swollen toes.

8. Which of the following would *not* be an effective technique to help you learn to water ski?
   (a) Alternate short practice sessions with rest periods.
   (b) Begin with learning to get up, then progress to other individual skills.
   (c) Repeat the important rule to yourself, "Lean back."
   (d) Learn to snow ski first. Even though most of the rules are opposite, you would still get used to the feeling of wearing skis.

9. Okay, you have gone through seven chapters in this textbook, are now completing the eighth and you still are not quite getting the material. You have been doing only what was minimally required in this psychology course. However, you have just decided to pull yourself up by the proverbial "bootstraps" and learn this stuff. Which of the following recommendations may be *most* influential in meeting this goal?
   (a) Rent a video only when you meet your performance criteria.
   (b) Attack this as though you will learn everything you will ever need to know about human behavior.
   (c) Use this study guide and the learning checks in the textbook as a way of keeping a record of your progress.
   (d) Establish a clear set of learning goals for the course.

Chapter Review

1. Many real world situations involve a combination of classical and operant conditioning and are analyzed using _____-_____ learning.

2. According to the _____ view, conditioning creates _____ which alter response patterns. In classical conditioning the _____creates an _____ that the _____ will be presented. Learning in operant conditioning is based on the _____ that a _____ will have a particular _____.

3. Particularly important to human learning is _____, information about what effect a response has had. To be most effective, _____ should be _____, _____, and _____.

4. Recently, new applications of feedback have been developed. One of these is _____ _____ which gives information to students in a format that requires precise answers about information as it is presented. In _____-_____ instruction (abbreviated ____ ____ ____), an individual _____ _____ transmits lessons to a display screen while the student responds by typing answers or by touching the display screen with an electronic pencil. People often do better with this type os instruction because they don't feel like they are being _____ or _____ by a teacher.

5. The simplest computerized instruction consists of self-paced _____ and _____, a method similar to that found in printed _____.

6. _____, like reinforcers, are best defined by observing their effects on behavior. Usually, they can either be the _____ of an aversive event or the _____ of a positive event. When the latter is used it is called _____ cost. To be most effective, punishment should occur _____ a response is being made or _____ thereafter. It should also occur_____ _____ a response occurs, and it should be _____, but humane. It other words, the effectiveness of punishment depends upon its _____, _____, and _____.

7. Punishment that is effective in stopping behavior is usually _____. More often, however, punishment only temporarily _____ a response. Responses _____ by _____ punishment usually reappear later.

8. There are three basic tools available to control simple learning: (1) _____ strengthens a response; (2) _____ causes a response to be extinguished; (3) _____ (when mild) suppresses a response but does not remove it. The three basic tools work best in _____ .

9. If you choose to use mild punishment, it is best to also _____ an alternate, desirable response. Do not use punishment if you can _____ behavior in any other way. Punishment should be applied _____ and one should use the _____ necessary. Be _____ , expect _____ from the person being punished, and punish with _____ and _____ .

10. There are three basic problems with punishment. One is that punishment is _____ , and as a result situations and people associated with punishment also tend to be perceived as _____ . Second, unpleasant stimuli usually encourage _____ learning and _____ learning. Third, punishment can greatly increase _____ .

11. The overall emotional adjustment of a child disciplined mainly by reward is usually _____ to one disciplined mainly by punishment. Frequent punishment makes a person _____ , _____ , _____ , _____ , and _____ of the source of the punishment.

12. _____ _____ refers to understanding, knowing, anticipating, or otherwise making use of higher mental processes. It extends into the realms of memory, thinking, problem-solving, and the use of concepts and language. A _____ _____ is an internal representation of relationships that acts as a guide in gaining an overall mental picture of some stimulus complex.

13. Cognitive learning is closely related to _____ learning where learning sometimes occurs with no obvious reinforcement at all.

14. In contrast to _____ learning where skills are acquired by repetition and memorization, _____ learning skills are acquired by using insight and understanding.

15. For modeling (observational learning) to occur several things must take place. The learner must pay _____ to the model and _____ what was done. Then the learner must be able to _____ the learned behavior. If a model is _____ or _____ the learner is more likely to imitate the behavior. This is also the case for models who are _____ , _____ , or high in _____ . Once a new response is tried, normal _____ determines if it will be repeated thereafter.

16. The phenomenon of modeling was demonstrated in a classic experiment where children either saw a live model, a filmed model, or a cartoon version of a model displaying _____ toward a blow-up "Bo-Bo" doll. When later frustrated and allowed to play with the Bo-Bo doll, most _____ the _____ . The cartoon was only slightly less effective in encouraging _____ than the live model.

17. Television may _____ dangerous impulses that viewers may already have. For example, many TV programs give the message that violence is _____ , acceptable behavior.

18.   The process whereby bodily activities are monitored and converted into a signal that provides the person with information about what the body is doing is called _____. This process has been useful for helping people control things such as _____ _____. Many questions remain about the value of this process. Many of the reported benefits may simply reflect _____ _____. The procedure may simply act as a "_____" to help a person accomplish tasks involving _____-_____.

19.   A _____ _____ is a series of actions molded into a smooth and efficient performance. As these actions improve, we develop _____ _____ (mental plans or models of what a _____ action should be like) for them.

20.   There are six points which aid skill learning.
       (1) Begin by observing and imitating a _____ _____.
       (2) Learn _____ _____ to back up motor learning.
       (3) Practice should be as _____ as possible.
       (4) Get _____. Whenever possible, someone experienced in the skill should direct attention to _____ _____ when they occur.
       (5) Try to practice _____ _____ rather than break the task into artificial parts.
       (6) Learn to _____ and _____ your own performance. Research has also shown that _____ _____ (thinking about a skill) can aid learning.

21.   Motor learning proceeds most efficiently when short practice sessions are alternated with rest periods. This is called _____ practice. It may be contrasted with _____ practice in which one practice period follows the next in quick succession.

22.   _____ transfer is said to result when mastery of one task aids mastery of a second task. In _____ transfer, skills developed in one situation conflict with those required for mastery of a new task.

23.   _____-_____ learners see learning as a process they can control hence they are not _____. There are several techniques which you can use to enhance learning:
       (1) Try to begin each learning session with specific _____ in mind.
       (2) Plan a _____ strategy by taking _____ for initiating activities which promote learning.
       (3) Engage in self-instruction, that is in effect become your own _____.
       (4) Keep records of your progress toward your learning goals, i.e., _____ yourself.
       (5) Use _____-_____ when you meet your performance standards.
       (6) Frequently _____ your performance records and goals.
       (7) Take _____ _____ in order to make adjustments if you are not meeting your goals.

24.   Hundreds of studies involving over 10,000 children all point to the conclusion that if children watch a great deal of televised violence, they will be more prone to behave _____.

25.   Not only does TV encourage violence, it may also lower _____ to violent acts. Victor Cline found that among groups of boys shown a brutal and bloody fight scene, those boys who averaged 42 hours per week of TV viewing showed _____ emotion than those boys who watched little or no TV.

26.   Although TV can be a negative influence on children, it can also be positive. After watching TV programs that emphasize helping, children have been found to be willing to exhibit _____ behavior.

ANSWER KEYS

Do You Know the Information?

Multiple Choice

1. (c) obj. 1, p. 218
2. (b) obj. 2, pp. 218-219
3. (b) obj. 4, p. 219
4. (a) obj. 4, p. 219
5. (d) obj. 5, p. 221
6. (c) obj. 6, p. 221
7. (a) obj. 7, p. 222
8. (b) obj. 7, p. 223
9. (d) obj. 7, p. 224
10. (d) objs.7-8, pp. 223-224
11. (d) obj. 8, p. 223
12. (b) obj. 9, p. 225
13. (a) obj. 10, p. 225
14. (c) obj. 11, p. 226
15. (c) obj. 12, p. 227
16. (a) obj. 13, p. 227
17. (d) obj. 14, pp. 228-229
18. (a) obj. 14, p. 229
19. (b,d,f,g,h,i)obj. 15, p. 231
20. (a) obj. 16, p. 232
21. (c) obj. 17, p. 232
22. (d) obj. 20, p. 233
23. (b) obj. 24, p. 234
24. (b) obj. 22, pp. 237-238
25. (a) obj. 22, p. 237

True-False

1. T, obj. 2, p. 218
2. T, obj. 3, p. 219
3. T, obj. 5, p. 221
4. F, obj. 5, p. 221
5. T, obj. 7, p. 222
6. F, obj. 7, p. 223
7. T, obj. 7, p. 224
8. T, obj. 7, p. 224
9. F, obj. 11, p. 226
10. T, obj. 13, p. 227
11. T, obj. 14, p. 228
12. T, obj. 15, p. 231
13. T, obj. 18, p. 232
14. F, obj. 19, p. 233
15. F, obj. 21, p. 235
16. T, obj. 23, p. 238

	Event	Effect
Pos. reinf.	+	↑
Neg. reinf.	−	↑
Punishment	−	↓

Can You Apply the Information?

1. (b,c,d)objs. 1-2, pp. 218-219
2. (b) objs.3-4, p. 219
3. (b) obj. 5, p. 221
4. (c) obj. 7, p. 222
5. (d) objs. 7-8, pp. 223-224
6. (a-d) objs. 5-7, pp. 221-224
7. (b) obj. 10, p. 225
8. (d) objs.17-20, pp. 232-233
9. (c) obj. 21, p. 235

Chapter Review

1.   two-factor (p. 218)
2.   informational, expectancies, CS, expectancy (prediction) (p. 218);, US, expectancy, response, effect (p. 219)
3.   feedback, feedback, frequent, immediate, detailed (p. 219)
4.   programmed instruction, computer-assisted, CAI, computer terminal, watched, evaluated (p. 219)
5.   drill, practice, workbooks (p. 219)
6.   Punishers, onset, removal, response, while, immediately, each time, severe, timing, consistency, intensity (p. 221)
7.   severe, suppresses, suppressed, mild (p. 221)
8.   reinforcement, nonreinforcement, punishment, combination (p. 222)
9.   reinforce (p. 222); discourage, immediately, minimum, consistent, anger, kindness, respect (p. 223)
10.   aversive, aversive, escape, avoidance (p. 223); aggression (p. 224)

11.   superior, unhappy, confused, anxious, aggressive, fearful (p. 224)
12.   Cognitive learning, cognitive map (p. 225)
13.   latent (p. 225)
14.   rote, discovery (p. 226)
15.   attention, remember, reproduce, successful, rewarded, attractive, admired, status, reinforcement (p. 227)
16.   aggression, imitated, attack, aggression (p. 227)
17.   disinhibit, normal (p. 228)
18.   biofeedback (p. 230); migraine headaches (brain waves, blood pressure, heart rhythms), general relaxation, mirror, self-regulation (p. 231)
19.   motor skill, motor programs, skilled (p. 231)
20.   skilled model, verbal rules, lifelike, feedback, correct responses, natural units, evaluate, analyze, mental practice (p. 232)
21.   spaced, massed (p. 233)
22.   positive, negative (p. 233)
23.   Self-regulated, passive (p. 234); goals, learning, responsibility, teacher, monitor, self-reinforcement (p. 235); evaluate, corrective action (p. 236)
24.   aggressively (p. 237)
25.   sensitivity, less (p. 237)
26.   prosocial (p. 238)

Chapter 9

Memory

LEARNING OBJECTIVES

To demonstrate mastery of this chapter you should be able to:

1. Explain the three functions of memory.

   a.

   b.

   c.

2. List the three interrelated memory systems.

   a.

   b.

   c.

3. Explain sensory memory. (Include an explanation of how icons and echoes function in this memory system.)

4. Explain how information is transferred from sensory memory to short-term memory.

5. Describe short-term memory in terms of capacity, how information is encoded, permanence, and susceptibility to interference.

6. Describe long-term memory in terms of permanence, capacity, and the basis of how information is stored. (Include a brief description of dual memory.)

7. Describe chunking and rehearsal and explain how they help memory.

8. Discuss the permanence of memory including the work of Penfield and the Loftuses.

9. Explain how memories are constructed. (Include the concepts of constructive processing and pseudo-memories).

10. Discuss the effects of hypnosis on memory. (See Highlight 9-1.)

11. Briefly describe how long-term memories are organized including the network model and redintegration.

12.   Explain the tip-of-the-tongue state (including the feeling of knowing).

13.   Describe and give an example of each of the following ways of measuring memory:
       a.   recall

       b.   recognition (compare to recall and include the idea of distractors)

       c.   relearning (include the concept of savings)

14.   Distinguish between explicit and implicit memories.

15.   Describe eidetic imagery and its effects on long-term memory.

16.   Describe the concept of internal imagery and explain how it differs from eidetic imagery and exceptional memory.

17.   Explain Ebbinghaus' curve of forgetting.

18.   Discuss the effects of cramming versus spaced review on memory.

19.   Discuss the following explanations of forgetting:
a.   encoding failure

b.   decay of memory traces

c.   disuse (also giving three reasons to question this explanation)

d.   cue-dependent forgetting

e.   state-dependent learning

f.   interference (also list and explain the two types of interference as well as how they are investigated in the laboratory)

g.   repression (and differentiate it from suppression)

h.   retrograde amnesia

20.   Describe the role of consolidation in memory.

21.   Describe the effects of stimulants and alcohol on memory.

22.   Name the structure in the brain which is responsible for switching information from STM to LTM. (Include a discussion of the relationship between learning and transmitter chemicals, brain circuits and receptor sites.)

23.   Describe each of the following in terms of how it can improve memory:
   a.   knowledge of results

   b.   recitation

   c.   rehearsal

   d.   selection

   e.   organization

   f.   whole versus part learning

g.   serial position effect

h.   cues

i.   overlearning

j.   spaced practice

k.   sleep

l.   review

m.   strategy

* * * * * * * * *

The following objectives are related to the material in the "Applications" and "Exploration" sections of your text.

24.   Define and explain the role of mnemonic systems in storing and retrieving information.

25.   Differentiate procedural (skill) memory from fact memory.

26.   Differentiate the two kinds of fact memory — semantic memory and episodic memory.

SELF QUIZZES

Do You Know the Information?

Multiple Choice

1. Memory functions like a computer because
   - (a) information is encoded.
   - (b) information is stored.
   - (c) memories must be retrieved to be useful.
   - (d) of all of the above.

2. Memory that holds an exact copy for about a second of what is seen or heard is called
   - (a) eidetic imagery.
   - (b) LTM.
   - (c) sensory memory.
   - (d) short-term memory.

3. Which of the following statements about short-term memory is *incorrect*?
   - (a) It is severely affected by interference.
   - (b) Most of its memories are encoded as images.
   - (c) Information removed from STM is lost.
   - (d) Selective attention determines what information moves from sensory memory to STM.

4. Which of the following statements about long-term memory is *incorrect*?
   - (a) It has a limited (although large) capacity to store information.
   - (b) Information is stored on the basis of meaning and importance.
   - (c) It acts as a permanent storehouse for information.
   - (d) It contains everything you know about the world.

5. Which of the following statements concerning STM and LTM is *correct*?
   - (a) LTM is more subject to the effects of interference than is STM.
   - (b) Selective attention screens the memories going directly into LTM.
   - (c) The permanent loss of information once it is removed from STM keeps some useless trivia from cluttering up our brains.
   - (d) Even if rehearsal is prevented, STM can still hold information for long periods of time.

6. Humans can normally retain about how many bits of information in STM?
   - (a) 2
   - (b) 4
   - (c) 7
   - (d) 10

7. Which of the following statements concerning LTM is (are) *true*?
   - (a) Brain stimulation produces memorylike experiences in most people.
   - (b) Most long-term memories are only relatively permanent.
   - (c) Hypnosis can significantly improve memory.
   - (d) Memories are frequently updated in a process called constructive processing.

8. The information in long-term memory is organized in terms of
   - (a) networks of linked ideas.
   - (b) formal or personal meaning.
   - (c) rules, images, categories, symbols, similarity.
   - (d) all of the above.

9. The tip-of-the-tongue state occurs when
   - (a) a memory is in STM but is not consolidated to LTM.
   - (b) the amount of memory saved exceeds the amount relearned.
   - (c) a person can tell if he or she will remember something.
   - (d) an answer or memory is just out of reach.

10. Remembering or reproducing important facts and information without explicit cues or stimuli is called
    (a) redintegration.
    (b) recall.
    (c) relearning.
    (d) recognition.

11. A test involving matching and multiple choice items measures memory using
    (a) redintegration.
    (b) recall.
    (c) relearning.
    (d) recognition.

12. The importance of savings lies in its
    (a) ability to make relearning at a later date easier.
    (b) ability to make recall easier.
    (c) beneficial effect on short-term memory.
    (d) organizational and coding effects.

13. _____ memories are to awareness as _____ memories are to experience without awareness.
    (a) Explicit; long-term
    (b) Explicit; implicit
    (c) Implicit; short-term
    (d) Redintegrative; recall

14. Which of the following statements regarding eidetic imagery and internal images is *incorrect*?
    (a) Most eidetic imagery disappears during adolescence and is quite rare in adulthood.
    (b) Eidetic images are projected out in front of a person.
    (c) Most eidetic memorizers have a better than average long-term memory.
    (d) Internal images occur when a person can "visualize" a memory in his or her head.

15. Ebbinghaus' curve of forgetting demonstrates that
    (a) forgetting is slow at first but increases dramatically as time increases.
    (b) meaningful words are forgotten more rapidly than shorter nonsense syllables.
    (c) intense review (cramming) before a test is an ineffective study technique.
    (d) forgetting is rapid at first and then levels off to a slow decline.

16. One of the most probable explanations of STM forgetting centers around
    (a) the decay of memory traces.
    (b) too much overlearning which may cause confusion.
    (c) cue-dependent forgetting.
    (d) disuse.

17. If a memory is not used, it may be forgotten through disuse. One problem with this explanation is
    (a) that some memories that are used are unable to be retrieved.
    (b) disuse fails to explain why some unused memories fade and others do not.
    (c) sometimes an elderly person has fantastic memory for recent events but can't remember the long-forgotten, trivial incidents.
    (d) all of the above.

18. You're trying to remember something. The memory is available but not accessible because the stimuli present at the time of learning are now absent. This is called
    (a) repression.
    (b) interference.
    (c) decay.
    (d) cue-dependent forgetting.

19. The tendency for new memories to interfere with old memories is called
    (a) retroactive interference.
    (b) repression.
    (c) retrograde forgetting.
    (d) proactive interference.

20. To investigate proactive interference the experimental group learns A, learns B, and then is tested on B. What happens with the control group?
    (a) They rest, then learn B and are tested on B.
    (b) They are the same as the experimental group except they rest during B.
    (c) They do nothing but test A to measure the effects of relaxation.
    (d) They learn A, learn B, and then are tested on B.

21. When you cannot recall a memory that is unpleasant or disturbing, you may be experiencing which of the following?
    (a) repression   (c) suppression
    (b) depression   (d) regression

22. The difference between suppression and repression is
    (a) suppression is an active attempt not to think of something.
    (b) true repression is an unconscious event.
    (c) when we use repression we are unaware that forgetting has even occurred.
    (d) all of the above.

23. Most flashbulb memories are
    (a) negative.
    (b) positive.
    (c) probably of important, surprising, or emotional events.
    (d) the result of increased levels of growth hormone secreted during emotion or stress.

24. The process of consolidation refers to how information
    (a) gets into STM.   (c) is recalled from STM.
    (b) is retrieved from LTM.   (d) is formed into a long-term memory.

25. Which of the following can prevent a memory from being consolidated?
    (a) lack of rehearsal   (c) a head injury
    (b) electroconvulsive shock   (d) all of these can prevent consolidation

26. Recent studies have shown that learning may occur because
    (a) there may be an increase in the number of receptor sites for transmitter chemicals.
    (b) nerve cells in a circuit may alter the amount of transmitter chemicals they release.
    (c) certain circuits may be strengthened or weakened.
    (d) of all of the above.

27. Circle any of the following which will tend to increase your ability to retain information in memory.
    (a) boil the information in paragraphs down to several key ideas
    (b) using massed instead of spaced practice
    (c) rehearsing the items or concepts
    (d) learning in a novel environment to heighten your attention
    (e) using sleep learning devices
    (f) learning the information in a place where there is little distraction or interference
    (g) drinking a few beers while studying

28. The serial position effect indicates the last material to be learned in a sequence and the most difficult to recall is
    (a) the last part.   (c) the middle part.
    (b) the first part.   (d) all are learned equally well.

29.   Which of the following is *not* a search strategy for finding a "lost" memory?
      (a) Mentally re-create the learning environment.
      (b) Recall from a single viewpoint to avoid the inherent confusion factor.
      (c) Recall events in different orders.
      (d) Write down everything you can remember.

30.   Which of the following statements regarding memory is *true*?
      (a) procedural memory is involved in recalling who was the first president of the United States
      (b) episodic memories are more easily forgotten than semantic memories
      (c) our basic factual knowledge of the world is stored in episodic memory
      (d) semantic memories record life events

True-False

_____   1.   The three memory systems are sensory memory, short-term memory, and long-term memory.

_____   2.   The process of selective attention is responsible for what information travels from short-term to long-term memory.

_____   3.   One might accurately say that long-term memories are relatively permanent.

_____   4.   Memories for things which never happened but which nevertheless are firmly believed by people are called pseudo-memories.

_____   5.   Redintegration is the process that connects short-term memories for recoding.

_____   6.   The feeling of knowing is when a person has the answer to a question just out of reach.

_____   7.   Recognition as a measure of memory is usually superior to recall.

_____   8.   A savings score is determined by the number or false positives..

_____   9.   The incidence of eidetic imagery is much greater among adults than among children.

_____10.   According to Ebbinghaus' curve of forgetting, most forgetting occurs at first.

_____11.   The less time there is between reviewing for a test and the taking of the test, the more forgetting that will occur.

_____12.   An obvious reason for forgetting is that a memory was never formed in the first place.

_____13.   Information learned in one particular emotional or physiological state is best remembered in that same state. This is state-dependent learning.

_____14.   Stimulants like nicotine and caffeine in controlled dosages have been shown to enhance memory.

_____15.   The hypothalamus plays an important role in the formation of long-term memories.

_____16.   Learning something beyond bare mastery is called overlearning. It improves learning.

_____17. In the progressive part method of memorizing, the learner learns part A, then part B, then part C, and then puts them all together.

_____18. A mnemonic is a kind of memory system or aid.

Matching *(Use the letter on the right only once.)*

_____ 1.   image
_____ 2.   most memory chores handled by
_____ 3.   putting smaller units together into larger ones
_____ 4.   STM prolonged by
_____ 5.   updating memories
_____ 6.   prior learning interferes with later learning
_____ 7.   a head injury may cause it
_____ 8.   particularly important brain structure for memory
_____ 9.   Karl Lashley looked for this
_____10.   middle of the list harder to learn
_____11.   relies heavily on mental pictures
_____12.   basic factual knowledge about world

A.   semantic memory
B.   hypothalamus
C.   proactive inhibition
D.   rehearsal
E.   echo
F.   dual memory
G.   episodic memory
H.   mnemonics
I.   chunking
J.   retrograde amnesia
K.   retroactive inhibition
L.   constructive processing
M.   icon
N.   hippocampus
O.   STM
P.   engram
Q.   serial position effect

Can You Apply the Information?

1.   Which of the following would require only the use of STM?
     (a) remembering the measured height of a cabinet as you write the number down
     (b) remembering your name as you write it on a job application
     (c) remembering the letters of the alphabet
     (d) remembering your mother's name

2.   If you smell a perfume that reminds you of what happened on a date 20 years ago at a drive-in movie, you are experiencing
     (a) recognition.   (c) relearning.
     (b) recall.   (d) redintegration.

3.   Gloria is a vice-president at IBM and must travel to France on business. She decides to take a refresher course in French. She finds that the language is easier to master the second time around. She has experienced
     (a) internal images.   (c) savings.
     (b) recall.   (d) recognition.

4.   One of your classmates always does well on psychology exams. One day after class you get the opportunity to corner her to find out her secret. She reports that during a test she can actually see her notes on the desk in front of her. You surmise that she probably has
     (a) eidetic imagery.   (d) internal images.
     (b) fantastic relearning skills.   (e) pulled a little whoopee in class.
     (c) efficient organizing skills for LTM.

5. According to Ebbinghaus' curve of forgetting, if a person is studying for a test he or she should
   (a) use spaced practice for review and not get anxious and cram shortly before a test.
   (b) study for a week to 10 days before the test but put the books away a day before the test.
   (c) avoid interference by studying only a couple of hours before the test with an hour or so of cramming.
   (d) use spaced practice with short, daily study sessions and cram right before the test.

6. You're out shopping and someone gives you a phone number to remember. You say it over and over many times but can't find a pencil to write it down. You forget the number. Your forgetting is probably due to
   (a) repression.
   (b) disuse.
   (c) decay.
   (d) lack of relevant cues.

7. You have a psychology test scheduled for 11 a.m. You studied for it last night and again this morning. It is now 10 a.m. and you decide to take a break and study anthropology. It is likely that
   (a) you will suffer retroactive interference for the psychology material.
   (b) consolidation of the psychology will not occur.
   (c) proactive interference will occur for the psychology material.
   (d) your hippocampus will not be allowed to function properly.

8. Last year while ice skating you fell in front of a group of people and made a fool of yourself. When reminded of the incident this year you cannot remember it at all. This forgetting is probably a result of
   (a) interference.
   (b) suppression.
   (c) repression.
   (d) electroconvulsive shock.

9. You are embarrassed when you think of how you acted at the party, so you try not to remember it. This is an example of
   (a) repression.
   (b) suppression.
   (c) lack of consolidation.
   (d) a disorder of the hippocampus.

10. John is 42 years old and can vividly remember his first day in school when he was only 6. He remembers being excited and scared at the same time. This memory is most likely a(n)
   (a) eidetic image.
   (b) pseudo-memory.
   (c) short-term memory.
   (d) flashbulb memory.

11. Herman can easily learn his multiplication tables but can't remember what he was doing on the ladder before he fell and hit his head. Herman is suffering from
   (a) retrograde amnesia.
   (b) suppression.
   (c) anterograde amnesia.
   (d) decay of engrams.

12. Erin is suffering from intractable depression. Psychotherapy and psychopharmacotherapy have not worked, so her psychiatrists decide to use electroconvulsive therapy on her. It seems to work well, but she has trouble remembering what happens in the two hours after the treatment. She is suffering from
   (a) retrograde amnesia.
   (b) short-term memory decay.
   (c) anterograde amnesia.
   (d) repression.

13. You are plotting to overthrow a government. You want to develop a technique to keep people from remembering what you are planning to do, but you don't want to permanently affect their memories or their ability to remember. Which of the following should you do?
   (a) destroy the hippocampus
   (b) wipe out their LTM systems
   (c) interrupt the consolidation process
   (d) all of the above

14.   Remembering the 12 cranial nerves by learning a rhyme to go with them is an example of
(a) chaining.
(b) using a mnemonic system.
(c) memory transfer.
(d) chunking.

15.   Remembering that the funny-looking things at the end of your feet are called toes is an example of
(a) sensory memory.
(b) semantic memory.
(c) procedural memory.
(d) episodic memory.

Chapter Review

1.   In some ways memory acts like a _____ because information is first _____.
Then the information is _____, and finally it is _____.

2.   There are several steps in placing information in permanent memory. First, incoming information enters
_____ memory. If the information is seen, an _____ (image) persists. If
the information is heard, an _____ is held.

3.   _____ _____ determines what information goes from _____
memory to _____ - _____ memory. In this second system, memories are
usually stored as _____. This memory system is not _____ and is
severely affected by _____ or _____.

4.   The third stage of memory is called _____ - _____ memory and is
relatively _____ with almost limitless _____. Information is generally stored
on the basis of _____. Most of our daily memory chores are handled by _____
memory, a combination of ___ ___ ___ and ___ ___ ___ .

5.   STM can only hold about _____ (___ or ____ two) bits of information. If separate bits of information can
be combined or _____, more information can be handled. STM can be prolonged if
it is _____.

6.   It is probably most accurate to say that long-term memories are _____
_____. As new memories are formed, older memories are often
_____. This process is called _____ processing.
Gaps in memory may be filled in by _____ , _____ , or _____
_____. Such memories are then called _____-
_____.

7.   Research shows that a _____ person is more likely than normal to use
_____ to fill in gaps in memory. It can be concluded that _____
does not greatly improve memory.

8.   The information in LTM is usually organized around _____ , _____ ,
_____ , _____ , _____ meaning, or
_____ meaning. Some researchers believe that LTM is organized as a network of linked
_____, hence the term _____ model.
_____ memories demonstrate the "branches" of memory networks.

9.   The experience of having an answer or a memory just out of reach is known as the _____ - _____ -
_____ - _____ state. If people can tell beforehand that they are likely to remember something, this is called the _____ of _____.

10. There are some common techniques for retrieving information. To _____ means to remember or reproduce important facts and information without explicit cues. A multiple-choice examination is based on the retrieval mechanism known as _____. This is a more sensitive testing procedure than _____, but this depends greatly on the kind of _____used.

11. Testing memory by _____ shows that it takes less time and effort to master previously learned material. This difference in time is known as _____.

12. When dealing with _____ memories one works with past experiences that they are _____ of or have brought to mind. _____ memories on the other hand lie outside the realm of awareness.

13. _____ _____ occurs when a person has visual images clear enough to be scanned or retained for at least 30 seconds after viewing a picture. Such memory is usually only observed in _____. The majority of _____ memorizers have no better _____-_____ memory than the average person.

14. Although most adults do not exhibit _____ memory, some adults have extremely vivid _____ _____ which can result in very accurate memories.

15. In Ebbinghaus' famous experiment involving memory and the _____ of _____, he found that _____ was _____ at first and then _____ declined. Students who _____ periodically and then intensely right before an exam have been found to remember much more than students who do not.

16. Probably the most obvious reason for forgetting is that a _____ was never formed in the first place. Another view of forgetting is that _____ _____ (changes in nerve cells or brain activity) fade or _____ over a period of time. Such fading applies to _____ memory and ___ ___ ___.

17. The decay of memory traces also has appeal as an explanation for long-term forgetting. Perhaps long-term memory traces fade from _____. There are reasons to question this idea. One is the recovery of seemingly forgotten memories through _____. Another is that _____ fails to explain why some unused memories _____ and others are carried for life. A third contradiction deals with the apparent fading of _____ memories in elderly people while they can remember trivial events from 30 years ago.

18. There are other explanations of LTM forgetting. One of them emphasizes that many memories appear to be _____ but not _____ because _____ present at the time of learning are no longer present when the memory needs to be retrieved. This is called _____-_____ forgetting. This is similar to _____-_____learning in which information learned under one internal state is best recalled when in a similar _____.

19. Another possibility is that much forgetting can be attributed to _____ of memories with one another. When recent learning interferes with memory of prior learning, _____ _____ has occurred. The opposite is when old learning interferes with new learning. This is called _____ _____.

20. When memories which are painful or threatening are held out of consciousness by forces within one's personality, this is called _____. This can be distinguished from _____, an active attempt to put something out of mind. Some memories (_____ memories), however, are not forgotten but are frozen in time because of major personal experiences.

21. The forming of a long-term memory is called _____. One part of the brain (the _____) is especially important for this purpose. Memory is especially susceptible to _____ during the time that it takes for it to be transferred from temporary storage to long-term storage.

22. If a person suffers a head injury, a gap in memory may be formed . If the gap occurs for information before the injury, this is called _____ amnesia. If the gap is for information after the injury, this is called _____ amnesia. Another way to wipe out a memory that is being formed is to apply a mild electrical shock to the brain. This is called _____ _____.

23. Common drugs such as _____ interfere with _____. In controlled dosages, _____ drugs such as nicotine or caffeine have been shown to enhance memory.

24. Researchers have found that learning may be related to the amount of _____ chemicals released by certain nerve cells in a circuit. Such changes essentially determine which circuits get _____ and which become _____. Other researchers have shown that an increase in _____ sites for _____ chemicals occurs during learning.

25. Several suggestions have been made for improving memory. One of these emphasizes the importance of _____ or knowledge of results. This method can help you identify material that needs extra practice. A good way to provide knowledge of results is through _____, repeating to yourself what you have learned.

26. Numerous studies have shown that memory is greatly improved by _____, that is, study continued beyond bare mastery. Another suggestion is to boil down paragraphs to one or two important terms or ideas. This is the process of _____. In addition, the more you _____ as you read, the better you will remember.

27. _____ practice is generally superior to _____ practice. By scheduling your time into brief study sessions, you maximize your study skills.

28. Students may find it helpful to _____ class notes and the important ideas or concepts in a class. Also, it is generally better to study _____ units of information rather than small parts. Try to study the largest _____ amount of information possible at one time.

29. For very long or complex material, try the _____ _____ method. In this approach, you study part "A" until it is mastered. Next you study parts "____" and "____"; then "____", "____", and "____", and so forth.

30. Whenever you must learn something in order, be aware of the _____ effect. This is the tendency to make the most errors in remembering the _____ of the list, so you should give those items the most attention.

31.   Remember that _____ after study produces the least interference. It is wise to _____ shortly before an exam to cut down the time during which you must remember details. The best _____ for remembering are those that were present during encoding. Successful recall is usually the result of a planned search of memory using a _____.

32.   Memory systems or aids are called _____ techniques. By using these techniques, _____ learning (learning by simple repetition) can be avoided. The superiority of _____ learning over rote learning has been demonstrated many times.

33.   The basic principles of mnemonics are as follows:
      (1) Use _____ pictures as they are generally easier to remember than _____.
      (2) Make the things you are attempting to remember _____.
      (3) Connect new information to what you already know, thereby making it _____.
      (4) Form _____, unusual, or _____ mental associations because they can make stored images more _____.

34.   LTM tends to fall into two categories. _____ memory includes actions like typing or playing tennis. Specific information which is learned is placed in _____ memory. This kind of memory is further divided into two other types. Most of our factual knowledge about the world is almost totally immune to forgetting and is called _____ memory. _____ memory records life events day after day and is more easily forgotten than _____ memories.

ANSWER KEYS

Do You Know the Information?

Multiple Choice

1. (d) obj. 1, p. 242
2. (c) obj. 3, p. 242
3. (b) obj. 5, pp. 242-243
4. (a) obj. 6, p. 243
5. (c) objs. 5,6,7, pp. 243-245
6. (c) obj. 7, p. 245
7. (b,d)objs. 8,9,10, pp. 245-247
8. (d) obj. 11, p. 247
9. (d) obj. 12, p. 248
10. (b) obj. 13, p. 248
11. (d) obj. 13, p. 249
12. (a) obj. 13, p. 250
13. (b) obj. 14, p. 250
14. (c) objs.15-16, pp. 251-252
15. (d) obj. 17, p. 253
16. (a) obj. 19, p. 254
17. (b) obj. 19, p. 254
18. (d) obj. 19, p. 255
19. (a) obj. 19, p. 256
20. (a) obj. 19, p. 257
21. (a) obj. 19, p. 258

22. (d) obj. 19, p. 258
23. (c) obj. 19, p. 258
24. (d) obj. 20, p. 258
25. (d) objs.7, 20, pp. 245, 258
26. (d) obj. 22, p. 260
27. (a,c,f)objs. 19, 23, pp. 256-261
28. (c) obj. 23, p. 261
29. (b) obj. 23, pp. 262-263
30. (b) obj. 26, p. 268

True-False

1. T, obj. 2, pp. 242-243
2. F, obj. 4, p. 242
3. T, obj. 8, p. 246
4. T, obj. 9, p. 246
5. F, obj. 11, p. 248
6. F, obj. 12, p. 248
7. T, obj. 13, p. 249
8. F, obj. 13, p. 250
9. F, obj. 15, p. 251
10. T, obj. 17, p. 253

11. F, obj. 18, p. 253
12. T, obj. 19, p. 254
13. T, obj. 19, p. 255
14. T, obj. 21, p. 259
15. F, obj. 22, p. 259
16. T, obj. 23, p. 262
17. F, obj. 23, p. 261
18. T, obj. 24, p. 264

Matching

1. M, obj. 3, p. 242
2. F, obj. 6, p. 244
3. I, obj. 7, p. 245
4. D, obj. 7, p. 245
5. L, obj. 9, p. 246
6. C, obj. 19, p. 257
7. J, obj. 19, p. 258
8. N, obj. 22, p. 259
9. P, obj. 22, p. 260
10. Q, obj. 23, p. 261
11. H, obj. 24, p. 264
12. A, obj. 26, p. 267

Can You Apply the Information?

1. (a) objs.5,6,26, pp. 242-243, 267
2. (d) obj. 11, p. 248
3. (c) obj. 13, p. 250
4. (a) objs.15,16, pp. 251-252
5. (d) obj. 18, p. 253
6. (c) obj. 19, p. 254
7. (a) obj. 19, pp. 256-257
8. (c) obj. 19, p. 258
9. (b) obj. 19, p. 258
10. (d) obj. 19, p. 258
11. (a) obj. 19, p. 258
12. (c) obj. 19, p. 258
13. (c) obj. 20, p. 258
14. (b) obj. 24, p. 264
15. (b) obj. 26, p. 267

Chapter Review

1. computer, encoded, stored, retrieved (p. 242)
2. sensory, icon, echo (p. 242)
3. Selective attention, sensory, short-term (p. 242); sounds, permanent, interruption, interference (p. 243)
4. long-term, permanent, capacity, meaning (p. 243); dual, STM, LTM (p. 244)
5. seven, plus, minus, chunked, rehearsed (p. 245)
6. relatively permanent, updated (changed, revised, lost), constructive, logic, guesses, new information, pseudo-memories (p. 246)
7. hypnotized, imagination (p. 246); hypnosis (p. 247)
8. rules, images, categories, symbols, similarity, formal, personal, ideas, network (p. 247); Redintegrative (p. 248)
9. tip-of-the-tongue, feeling, knowing (p. 248)
10. recall (p. 248); recognition, recall (p. 249); distractors (p. 250)
11. relearning, savings (p. 250)
12. Explicit, aware, Implicit (p. 250)
13. Eidetic imagery, children, eidetic, long-term (p. 251)
14. eidetic, internal images (p. 251)
15. curve, forgetting, forgetting, rapid, slowly, review (p. 253)
16. memory, memory traces, decay, sensory, STM (p. 254)
17. disuse, redintegration, disuse, fade, recent (p. 254)
18. available, accessible, cues, cue-dependent, state-dependent, state (p. 255)
19. interference, retroactive interference (p. 256); proactive interference (p. 257)
20. repression, suppression, flashbulb (p. 258)
21. consolidation (p. 258); hippocampus (p. 259); interference (p. 258)
22. retrograde, anterograde (p. 258); electroconvulsive shock (p. 259)
23. alcohol, consolidation, stimulating (p. 259)
24. transmitter, stronger, weaker, receptor, transmitter (p. 260)
25. feedback, recitation (p. 261)
26. overlearning (p 262); selection, rehearse (p. 261)
27. Spaced, massed (p. 262)
28. organize, whole (large), meaningful (p. 261)
29. progressive part, A, B, A, B, C (p. 261)
30. serial position, middle (p. 261)
31. sleep, review, cues, strategy (p. 262)
32. mnemonic, rote, mnemonic (p. 264)
33. visual, words, meaningful, familiar, bizarre, exaggerated, distinctive (p. 264)
34. Procedural (skill), fact, semantic (p. 268); Episodic, semantic (p. 269)

Chapter 10

Cognition and Creativity

LEARNING OBJECTIVES

To demonstrate mastery of this chapter you should be able to:

1. Define the term "thinking." (cognition) mental manipulation of images, concepts, words, rules, and symbols.

2. Describe thinking in animals as exemplified by delayed response problems and insight.

    <u>delayed response problem</u> – example → A dog is locked up and watches a person put food under one of three boxes, shuffles them around as the dog watches. the shorter the delay the better possibility thec dog will know where the food is.

    <u>Insight</u> – a sudden mental reorganization of the elements of a problem that makes the solution obvious. example → multiple - stick problem. Several sticks of increasing length were arranged btwn. the cage and a banana. Chimp had to use 1st stick to get 2nd stick → to get 3rd → to get banana.

3. Give two examples of apparently intelligent thought by an animal.

    a. Monkeys can learn to select, from among three objects, the one that differs from the other two.

    b. When a container of sugar water is moved a set distance farther from a beehive each day, the bees begin to go to the new location before the water is moved.

4. List the four basic units of thought.
    a. Images
    b. muscular responses
    c. Concepts
    d. language or symbols

5. Describe mental imagery and synesthesia. Explain how both stored and created images may be used to solve problems (including how the size of a mental image may be important).

    <u>Synesthesia</u> – images cross normal sensory barriers Experiencing one sense in terms normally associated with another sense

6. Explain how muscular imagery aids thinking.

7. **Define the terms "concept" and "concept formation," explain how they aid thought processes, and describe how they are learned.** Concept is an idea that represents a class of objects or events. → They allow us to think more abstractly, free from distracting details.

Concept formation is the process of classifying information into meaningful categories.
↳ based on experience with positive and negative instances of the concept.

8. **Define the terms conjunctive concept, disjunctive concept, and relational concept.**
conjunctive concept → a class of objects having more than one feature in common. Sometimes called "and" concepts.

disjunctive concepts → refer to objects that have at least one of several possible features. "either-or concepts"

relational concepts → classify objects on the basis of their relationship to something else or by the relationship btwn. features of an object. Larger, above, left, north, upside down.

9. **Explain the difference between the denotative and the connotative meaning of a word or concept, and describe how the connotative meaning of a word is measured.** The denotative meaning of a word or concept is its exact definition. The connotative meaning is its emotional or personal meaning.
Osgood uses a method called the semantic differential to measure connotative meaning.
↳ Words or concepts are rated on a series of scales, most of their connotative meaning boils down to the dimensions good-bad, strong-weak, and active-passive

10. **Explain how language aids thought.** Most thinking leans heavily on language, because it allows the world to be encoded into symbols that are easy to manipulate.

11. **Define semantics.** study of the meaning of words and language

12. **Briefly describe the following three requirements of a language and their related concepts:**
   a. **symbols** – stand for objects and ideas

      1. **phonemes** – basic speech sounds

      2. **morphemes** – speech sounds collected into meaningful units, such as syllables

    b.   grammar

        1.   syntax

        2.   transformation rules

    c.   productivity

13.   Explain why forms of language other than speech are believed possible.

14.   Explain the extent to which primates have been taught to use language.

15.   Describe the criticisms and practical value of attempts to teach language to primates.

16.   Differentiate between mechanical problem solving and problem solving through understanding.

17.   Define heuristics and explain how they aid problem solving.

18.   Tell how each of the following contribute to insight:
      a.   selective encoding

      b.   selective combination

      c.   selective comparison

19.   Explain how fixation and functional fixedness block problem solving, and give an example of each.

20.   List and explain four common barriers to creative thinking.
      a.

      b.

      c.

      d.

21.   Describe the following four kinds of thought:
      a.   inductive

      b.   deductive

      c.   logical

      d.   illogical

22.   Describe the following characteristics of creative thinking:
      a.   fluency

      b.   flexibility

      c.   originality

23.   Describe the two most common daydream themes and discuss how fantasy (daydreams) relates to creativity.

24.   Explain the relationship of creativity to divergent and convergent thinking.

25.   Describe how the ability to think divergently can be measured.

26.   List and describe the five stages of creative thinking.
      a.

      b.

      c.

      d.

      e.

27.   Discuss the five qualities which characterize creative persons.
       a.

       b.

       c.

       d.

       e.

28.   Explain the following three common intuitive thinking errors:
       a.   representativeness

       b.   base rate

       c.   framing

* * * * * * * * * *

The following objectives are related to the material in the "Applications" and "Exploration" sections of your text.
29.   List and explain three common problems which cause difficulties in thinking and problem solving.
       a.

       b.

       c.

30.   Describe six practical steps for encouraging creativity.
       a.

       b.

c.

d.

e.

f.

31. Describe the process of brainstorming, and explain how it can be used to solve problems.

32. Define the term artificial intelligence (include a description of what it is based upon).

33. Describe both the potential uses and drawbacks of artificial intelligence.

SELF-QUIZZES

Do You Know the Information?

Multiple Choice

1. Thinking is
   (a) the mental manipulation of images, concepts, words, rules, symbols, and precepts.
   (b) a uniquely human acitivity.
   (c) dependent upon tiny, sometimes unobservable muscular responses.
   (d) all of the above.

2. Which of the following has demonstrated that animals are able to think?
   (a) an animal choosing the correct goal box after a brief delay
   (b) a pigeon selecting the photograph of a human from photos of other objects
   (c) a multiple stick problem in which several sticks had to be used to gain a reward
   (d) all of the above

3. Which of the following is *not* one of the basic units of thought?
   (a) language
   (b) muscular responses
   (c) conditional relationships
   (d) images

4. Stored images can be used to solve problems by
   (a) using ideas already stored in memory to generate more original solutions.
   (b) translating kinesthetic sensations into phonemes.
   (c) bringing prior experience to bear on the problem.
   (d) allowing language to help solve the problem.

5. The larger the size of the mental image, the
   (a) more confusing the image will be to existing precepts.
   (b) easier it is to see details.
   (c) fewer muscular responses that will be needed to solve the problem.
   (d) smaller the created image necessary to solve the problem.

6. People who "talk" with their hands thereby using gestures to help themselves think are demonstrating
   (a) implicit actions.
   (b) micromovements.
   (c) kinesthetic sensations.
   (d) none of the above.

7. Concepts aid the thought process by
   (a) allowing us to function on an abstract level.
   (b) helping us understand ideas so we can better apply transformation rules.
   (c) preventing us from overlooking the minute details of a particular situation.
   (d) allowing us to break down experiences into integral component parts.

8. Disjunctive concepts
   (a) classify objects on the basis of their relationship to something else.
   (b) include classes of objects that have one or more features in common.
   (c) include things such as "large," "above," and "left."
   (d) refer to objects that have at least one of several possible features.

9. The explicit definition of a word or concept is its
   (a) semantic definition.
   (b) denotative meaning.
   (c) functional meaning.
   (d) connotative meaning.

10. The semantic differential measures the _____ meaning of a word or concept.
    (a) inductive
    (b) connotative
    (c) functional
    (d) denotative

11. Semantic problems usually occur when
    (a) the world is encoded into symbols.
    (b) we study the meaning of words.
    (c) a word has an unclear meaning.
    (d) the link between language and thought become evident.

12. Which of the following is *not* one of the requirements of a language?
    (a) must carry meaning
    (b) must have a set of rules
    (c) must be regenerative
    (d) must be productive

13. Phonemes are
    (a) the basic speech sounds.
    (b) the set of rules used to form sounds into words.
    (c) speech sounds which have been collected into meaningful units.
    (d) rules pertaining to word order in sentences.

14. ASL can be characterized as
    (a) a type of code.
    (b) being universally understood.
    (c) having a spatial grammar.
    (d) being based on French sign.

15. Which of the following statements about teaching language to primates is *incorrect?*
    (a) Conversations between chimps when not prompted by humans have been recorded.
    (b) One chimp even learned to state conditional relationships, that is, if...then statements.
    (c) Kanzi the chimp appears to have the grammar understanding of a 2-year-old child.
    (d) Viki the chimp learned to vocalize about 150 words.

16. Mechanical problem solving involves
    (a) a high level of thinking based on understanding.
    (b) trial and error or rote solutions.
    (c) the sudden appearance of the answer after a period of unsuccessful thought.
    (d) the use of transformation rules.
    (e) for example, a mechanic trying to figure out how to get his zipper down in an emergency.

17. Which of the following is *not* a heuristic strategy?
    (a) Identify how the current state of affairs differs from the desired goal.
    (b) Work in a step-by-step fashion from the starting point toward the desired goal.
    (c) If you can't reach the goal directly, try to identify an intermediate goal.
    (d) Try representing the problem in other ways.
    (e) Generate a possible solution and then test it.

18. The *ideal* problem solving strategy occurs when
    (a) all possibilities are tried.
    (b) possible solutions are mulled over unconsciously.
    (c) a general thinking strategy is employed.
    (d) the requirements for success are stated but not in sufficient detail for further action.

19. Bringing together seemingly unrelated bits of useful information to solve a problem is called
    (a) selective encoding.
    (b) selective combination.
    (c) selective comparison.
    (d) selective representation.
    (e) doing your taxes.

20. The inability to see new uses for familiar objects or objects that have been used in a particular way is called
    (a) illogical problem solving.
    (b) perceptual rigidity.
    (c) functional fixedness.
    (d) simplicity.

21. If you have values which block creative thinking because you believe that fantasy is a waste of time, then you are suffering from _____ barriers.
    (a) learned
    (b) perceptual
    (c) emotional
    (d) cultural

22. Thinking which goes from general principles to specific situations is termed
    (a) deductive.
    (b) logical .
    (c) inductive.
    (d) illogical .

23. Which of the following is *not* an aspect of creative thinking?
    (a) flexibility
    (b) fluency
    (c) originality
    (d) convergency

24. Which of the following are the two most common daydreaming themes?
    (a) sex and aggression
    (b) sex and the suffering martyr
    (c) suffering martyr and conquering hero
    (d) conquering hero and sex

25. What is the one factor that the Unusual Uses, Consequences, and Anagrams tests have in common?
    (a) They are all tests of divergent thinking.
    (b) They are all tests of convergent thinking.
    (c) They are all tests of logical thinking.
    (d) They are all tests of illogical thinking.

26. Indicate which of the following are characteristics of creative individuals.
    (a) highly intelligent
    (b) an openness to experience
    (c) a preference for complexity
    (d) introverted
    (e) neurotic
    (f) a willingness to take risks
    (g) intuitive

27. When people give different answers to the same problem when it is posed in a slightly different way, this is known as
    (a) ignoring the base rate.
    (b) rigid mental set.
    (c) representativeness.
    (d) framing.
    (e) fibbing.

28. Indicate which of the following are difficulties in thinking and problem solving.
    (a) overcomprehension.
    (b) problems with logic.
    (c) disjunctive conceptual thinking.
    (d) rigid mental set.
    (e) divergent thinking.
    (f) oversimplification.

29. Which of the following are suggestions for enhancing creativity?
    (a) Be a convergent thinker.
    (b) Allow time for incubation.
    (c) Develop a narrow but consistent chain of thought.
    (d) Create the right atmosphere by spending time with creative individuals.
    (e) Look for analogies.

30. The idea of brainstorming is to
    (a) produce as many ideas as possible.
    (b) encourage ideas that seem to be workable.
    (c) critically evaluate each proposed idea before moving on to the next idea.
    (d) allow for selective encoding.

31. Artificial intelligence is based upon
    (a) the fact that many tasks can be reduced to a set of rules applied to a body of knowledge.
    (b) organized knowledge and acquired strategies.
    (c) programs used to simulate human behavior.
    (d) the speed of computers when it comes to doing things like mathematical computations.

32. Computer programs which have advanced knowledge of a specific topic by virtue of having converted complex skills into rules which a computer can follow are called
    (a) computer simulations.   (c) automatic processors.
    (b) cognitive programs   (d) expert systems.

Matching *(Use the letters on the right only once.)*

_____ 1. synesthesia
_____ 2. mental imagery
_____ 3. concept
_____ 4. prototype
_____ 5. semantics
_____ 6. morphemes
_____ 7. syntax
_____ 8. mechanical solutions
_____ 9. heuristic
_____ 10. selective encoding
_____ 11. inductive
_____ 12. illumination
_____ 13. base rate
_____ 14. expert system

A. clearly stated rules that a computer can follow
B. rules pertaining to word order
C. going from specific facts to general principles
D. images cross normal sensory barriers
E. answer suddenly appears
F. problem-solving strategy
G. selecting information relevant to a problem
H. study of meaning of words
I. mental sensory representation
J. ends with insight
K. going from general principles to specific situations
L. achieved by rote or trial and error
M. solving on unconscious level
N. sounds collected into meaningful units
O. represents class of objects or events
P. an ideal model
Q. underlying probability of an event

True-False

_____ 1. Thinking is accompanied by muscular tension and micromovements throughout the body.

_____ 2. Concept formation is the process whereby we classify information into meaningful categories.

_____ 3. Adults are likely to acquire concepts by learning or formulating rules.

_____ 4. Identifying concepts is difficult even when we come up with a prototype relevant to what we see.

_____ 5. Conjunctive concepts refer to objects that have at least one of a number of features.

_____ 6. We create sentences by using transformation rules.

_____ 7. A language that is productive can generate new ideas.

_____ 8. Solutions based on understanding use habitual modes of thought.

_____ 9. Insight is said to have occurred when an answer appears after a period of logical divergent thought.

_____10. The point at which a useful idea or insight becomes set in one's mind is known as fixation.

_____11. According to work on daydreaming, most people find that their daydreams distract them and make concentrating difficult.

_____12. Perhaps the greatest value of fantasy and daydreaming lies in their contribution to creativity.

_____13. A person who thinks creatively thinks divergently.

_____14. Creative individuals tend to be uncomfortable with rules and limits imposed by others.

_____15. The way a problem is presented appears to have no affect on how it is solved.

_____16. A syllogism is evaluated solely by the validity of its conclusion.

_____17. Artificial intelligence refers to computer programs which do things that humans are incapable of doing.

_____18. Computer programs which are expert systems are very good but only within a very narrow range of problem solving.

Can You Apply the Information?

1. Letisha is listening to the New York Philharmonic and is experiencing bursts of color as well as the sound sensations. She is just experiencing
    (a) physiological nystagmus.
    (d) micromovements.
    (b) synesthesia.
    (e) something she should see a psychologist about.
    (c) saccades.

2. Mark is trapped in a burning room. There are three objects in the room. He can use one of the objects to help him get out of the room, but he's never seen any of them before. Mark had better rely on
    (a) Superman.
    (c) created images.
    (b) muscular imagery .
    (d) stored images.

3. In order to be a bird, an organism must have feathers and wings. This is an example of a
    (a) disjunctive concept.
    (c) conjunctive concept.
    (b) relational concept.
    (d) mental imagery.

4. Whenever anyone talks about dogs, Rita always thinks of her favorite German shepherd, Huck. She rates the qualities, attributes, and behaviors of other dogs by whether Huck has those same characteristics. It is likely that Huck serves as
    (a) an example of Rita's relational concept of dogs.
    (b) an example of Rita's disjunctive concept of dogs.
    (c) an example of Rita's conjunctive concept of dogs.
    (d) a prototype of Rita's general dog concept.

5. Amy says the word "vomit" at the dinner table. Her mother doesn't like the word at all. They both know what the word means. The word doesn't bother Amy, but her mother is disgusted. It is likely that her mother is reacting to the word's _____ meaning.
    (a) connotative
    (b) relational
    (c) denotative
    (d) encoded

6. A three-month-old baby makes all sorts of sounds and noises. Most of these sounds are probably
    (a) grammar.
    (b) morphemes.
    (c) phonemes.
    (d) following transformation rules.

7. Tom doesn't really know much about cars, but he loves to work on them. To fix a car he takes out parts and replaces them until the car runs better. He is solving a problem using
    (a) insight.
    (b) understanding.
    (c) a mechanical solution.
    (d) functional fixedness.

8. You are a mathematician and have been trying to solve a perplexing problem for two weeks. One evening while walking in the garden you suddenly realize you've been trying to solve the problem in the wrong way. How stupid! You merely have to move two variables and the equation makes sense. This is an example of
    (a) rote problem solving.
    (b) insight.
    (c) trial and error learning.
    (d) a delayed response problem.

9. Tom is still working on his car. He figures that since the oil filter is on the lower part of the engine, he should crawl under the car to change it. He does so but finds all sorts of stuff between him and the filter. He works for 45 minutes trying to get to the filter to unscrew it. All he really needs to do is unscrew the filter while standing up looking down at the engine. Tom is experiencing
    (a) functional fixedness.
    (b) internal misrepresentations.
    (c) fixation.
    (d) consummate stupidity.

10. Benjamin is studying and a gnat keeps buzzing around his ears bugging him. He uses his psychology book as a weapon to smash the little bugger between the pages. It is obvious that Benjamin is *not* suffering from
    (a) functional fixedness.
    (b) problems with general properties.
    (c) negative oversimplification.
    (d) images.
    (e) ungnatural fears.

11. Your professor asks a really "off the wall" question in class. You can't come up with a creative solution because you're worried about making a fool of yourself. Your barrier to creative thinking is called a(n) _____ barrier.
    (a) perceptual
    (b) learned
    (c) cultural
    (d) emotional

12. You are asked to think of as many uses for a paper clip as you can. It is likely that you are taking a test for
    (a) solutions through understanding.
    (b) divergent thinking.
    (c) inductive reasoning.
    (d) convergent thinking.

Chapter Review

1. Thinking refers to the _____ _____ of images, concepts, words, rules, symbols, and precepts. At its most basic, it is the _____ _____ of a problem or situation. Many animals are capable of choosing the correct solution to a problem a brief time after being shown the correct solution. This is called a _____ _____ problem.

2. In addition, chimps have been shown to be able to solve problems by using _____.
    In _____ , the elements of a problem are reorganized and the solution suddenly appears.

3. There are many basic units of thought. Four basic units that serve as internal representations include _____, _____ responses, _____, and _____.

4. If you use mental pictures to help you solve problems, this is called _____. A person who senses a stimulus in more than one modality is experiencing _____. Problem solving can be aided by using _____ _____ to bring prior experience to bear on the problem. To generate more original solutions _____ _____ may be used. The larger the _____, the _____ it is to see the _____ in it. When working with three dimensional images it is easiest to locate objects in the image _____ or _____ the viewer.

5. Jerome Bruner believes that we often represent things in a kind of _____ imagery created by actions or implicit actions.

6. A _____ is a word or idea that represents a class of objects or events. _____ allow us to function on an _____ level. _____ _____ is the process whereby we classify information into meaningful _____. Concepts are formed based on positive or negative _____ of the concept or by specific _____.

7. Several general types of concepts have been identified. A _____ concept embraces a class of objects that have one or more features in common. _____ concepts classify objects on the basis of their relationship to something else or by the relationship between features of an object. _____ concepts refer to objects that have at least one of a number of features.

8. Concepts have two types of meaning. The _____ meaning of a word or concept is its explicit definition. The _____ meaning of a word is its emotional or personal meaning. The latter type of meaning has been measured using Osgood's _____ _____.

9. The study of word meaning and language is called _____.

10. A language must provide _____ that can be used to stand for objects and ideas. The symbols we call words are built out of _____ (basic speech sounds) and _____ (speech sounds collected into meaningful units).

11. Language must also have a _____ or set of rules for making sounds into words and words into sentences. _____ refers to the rules pertaining to word order in sentences. The rules used to change core ideas into sentences are called _____ rules. However, the biological tendency to learn a language does not specify whether it should be _____ or _____.

12. Language must be able to be used to produce new possibilities or to generate new ideas. In other words, it must be _____.

13.   Some of the most revealing research on thinking and problem solving capacities has centered on attempts to
       teach _____ to chimpanzees and other primates. The first major breakthrough occurred
       with a female chimp named Washoe. She was taught to use _____ _____
       _____ a set of hand gestures used by the deaf in which each gesture stands for a word.
       Washoe now has a vocabulary of about 240 signs and can construct _____-word sentences.

14.   Another female chimp named Sarah has been taught to use 130 words consisting of _____
       _____ arranged on a magnetic board. Sarah has been required to use proper
       _____ _____. She has learned to answer _____,
       to label things as the same or different, to classify objects, and to construct _____
       sentences. One of her most outstanding achievements is the use of sentences involving
       _____ _____.

15.   Kanzi, a _____ chimp, creates sentences which follow correct _____ order and his
       _____ is good for new word combinations. In addition, his _____ is on
       a par with a 2-year-old.

16.   A number of different approaches to thinking and problem solving can be identified.
       _____ solutions may be achieved by trial and error or by rote.

17.   Many problems are unsolvable by mechanical means. In this case a higher level of thinking based on
       _____ is necessary. This is usually done in two phases: initially, one is interested in the
       _____ _____ of a correct solution, and then a functional (or
       _____) solution is usually selected. A third approach to problem solving occurs when
       an answer suddenly appears after a period of unsuccessful thought. This is called
       _____.

18.   A problem solving strategy can also be called a _____. When solving problems,
       a trial-and-error strategy in which all possibilities are tried is called a _____
       _____ strategy. The ideal strategy is a general thinking strategy in which one
       must _____, _____, _____,
       _____, _____, and _____.

19.   Insight apparently involves three abilities. The ability to select information which is relevant to a problem is
       called selective _____. Selective _____ brings
       together seemingly unrelated bits of information. The ability to compare new problems to old information or
       to problems already solved is termed selective _____.

20.   A barrier to problem solving occurs when a person gets "hung up" on wrong solutions or becomes blind to
       other alternatives. This is called _____. _____ _____
       occurs when a person cannot see a new use for a familiar object or for objects that have previously been used
       in a particular way. This is an example of _____.

21.   There are four common barriers to creative thinking. Fear of making a fool of oneself leads to
       _____ barriers. _____ barriers are a result of values
       which portray fantasy as a waste of time. Conventions about uses may lead to
       _____ barriers, and _____ barriers result
       from habits which lead to a failure to identify important elements of a problem.

22. Going from specific facts or observations to general principles is _____ thinking. Going from general principles to specific situations is _____ thinking. Thinking which is _____ proceeds from given information to new conclusions on the basis of _____. Thinking which is intuitive, associative, or personal is _____.

23. Creative thinking is characterized by _____ (the total number of ideas), _____ (the number of times thought shifts from one class of possibilities to another), and _____ (the degree of novelty of ideas).

24. Creative thinking requires _____ thought, not _____ thought, which occurs when the lines of thought converge on a correct thought. The former type of thought is generally measured by tests requiring that _____ possibilities be generated from one starting point.

25. The two most common daydreaming themes deal with the _____ _____, and the _____ _____. Daydreams and fantasy often fill a need for _____. Perhaps the greatest value of fantasy is its contribution to _____.

26. The best summary of the sequence of events in thinking proposes five stages. The first step is _____, where the problem must be defined and important dimensions identified. _____ is next, where the persons saturate themselves with as much information as possible pertaining to the problem.

27. The third stage, _____, involves a period during which all attempted solutions have proven futile, and the person leaves the problem "cooking" in the background. This stage is often ended by a rapid insight or series of insights which mark the fourth stage referred to as _____. The final step, _____, involves testing and critically evaluating the solution obtained during the stage of illumination If the solution proves faulty, the thinker reverts to the stage of _____.

28. Researcher David MacKinnon has discovered several important factors about creative people. First, there is little correlation between creativity and _____.

29. Creative people usually have a greater than average range of _____ and _____. They also have an _____ to experience.

30. Creative people enjoy _____ thought, ideas, concepts, and possibilities. They value _____ and have a preference for _____.

31. There are many errors that we can make when using intuition. A choice that seems to be _____ of what we already know may be erroneously given greater weight. One might also ignore the _____ _____ or underlying probability of an event. Also the way a problem is stated or _____ can make a difference.

32. There are several factors which can contribute to difficulties in thinking and problem solving. One of these difficulties is a rigid _____ _____. Another major thinking difficulty centers on the process of _____ _____. It is entirely possible to draw true conclusions using faulty _____ or to draw false conclusions using valid _____. Another basic source of thinking errors is the process of _____ - _____.

33. Several suggestions have been offered as to how to begin increasing creativity. One of these is to define the problem _____. A variety of experiments show that people make more original, spontane- ous, and imaginative responses when exposed to others (models) doing the same thing, so you should create the right _____.

34. Trying to hurry or force a problem's solution may simply encourage fixation on a dead end, so always allow time for _____. Creativity requires divergent thinking, so remember to seek varied _____. Representing a problem in a variety of ways is often the key to solution. One way to do this is to look for _____. Finally, delay _____ so that creativity is not inhibited.

35. _____ is an alternative approach to enhancing creativity. It involves encour- aging participants to produce as many ideas as possible while absolutely prohibiting _____ of the ideas. This technique helps people solve problems by allowing them to consider many possible solutions before negatively rejecting them.

36. Artificial intelligence refers to computer programs capable of doing things that require _____ when done by people. It is based on the fact that many tasks can be reduced to a set of _____ applied to a body of _____.

37. In computer simulations, programs are used to simulate human _____. Programs that display advanced knowledge of specific topic or skill are called _____ _____. These programs are limited in that they are very adept only within a _____ _____ of problem solving.

ANSWER KEYS

Do You Know the Information?

Multiple Choice

1. (a) obj. 1, p. 272
2. (d) obj. 2-3, pp. 272-273
3. (c) obj. 4, p. 274
4. (c) obj. 5, p. 275
5. (b) obj. 5, p. 275
6. (c) obj. 6, p. 275
7. (a) obj. 7, p. 276
8. (d) obj. 8, p. 277
9. (b) obj. 9, p. 277
10. (b) obj. 9, p. 277
11. (c) obj. 11, p. 278
12. (c) obj. 12, p. 279
13. (a) obj. 12, p. 279
14. (c) obj. 13, p. 279
15. (d) objs. 14-15, pp. 280-281
16. (b) obj. 16, p. 282
17. (b) obj. 17, p. 283
18. (c) obj. 17, p. 283
19. (b) obj. 18, p. 284

20. (c) obj. 19, p. 284
21. (d) obj. 20, p. 285
22. (a) obj. 21, p. 285
23. (d) obj. 22, p. 285
24. (c) obj. 23, p. 286
25. (a) obj. 25, p. 286
26. (b,c,f,g) obj. 27, p. 289
27. (d) obj. 28, p. 290
28. (b,d,f) obj. 29, pp. 291-293
29. (b,d,e) obj. 30, pp. 293-294
30. (a) obj. 31, p. 295
31. (a) obj. 32, p. 296
32. (d) obj. 33, p. 296

Matching

1. D, obj. 5, p. 274
2. I, obj. 6, p. 275
3. O, obj. 7, p. 276
4. P, obj. 8, p. 276
5. H, obj. 11, p. 278

6. N, obj. 12, p. 279
7. B, obj. 12, p. 279
8. L, obj. 16, p. 282
9. F, obj. 17, p. 283
10. G, obj. 18, p. 283
11. C, obj. 21, p. 285
12. J, obj. 26, p. 287
13. Q, obj. 28, p. 290
14. A, obj. 33, p. 296

True-False

1. T, obj. 6, p. 276
2. T, obj. 7, p. 276
3. T, obj. 7, p. 276
4. F, obj. 8, p. 277
5. F, obj. 8, p. 276
6. T, obj. 12, p. 279
7. T, obj. 12, p. 280
8. F, obj. 16, p. 282
9. F, obj. 18, p. 283

True-False (continued)

10. F, obj. 19, p. 284
11. F, obj. 23, p. 286
12. T, obj. 23, p. 286
13. T, obj. 24, p. 286
14. T, obj. 27, p. 289
15. F, obj. 28, p. 290
16. F, obj. 29, p. 292
17. F, obj. 32, p. 296
18. T, obj. 33, p. 297

Can You Apply the Information?

1. (b) obj. 5, p. 274
2. (c) obj. 5, p. 275
3. (c) obj. 8, p. 276
4. (d) obj. 8, p. 276
5. (a) obj. 9, p. 277
6. (c) obj. 12, p. 279

7. (c) obj. 16, p. 282
8. (b) objs.16,18, pp. 282-283
9. (c) obj. 19, p. 284
10. (a) obj. 19, p. 284
11. (d) obj. 20, p. 285
12. (b) obj. 24, p. 286

Chapter Review

1.   mental manipulation, internal representation, delayed response (p. 272)
2.   insight, insight (p. 272)
3.   images, muscular, concepts, language (symbols) (p. 274)
4.   imagery, synesthesia (p. 274); stored images, created images, image, easier, detail, above, below (p. 275)
5.   muscular (p. 275)
6.   concept, Concepts, abstract, Concept formation, categories, instances, rules (p. 276)
7.   conjunctive, Relational, Disjunctive (p. 276)
8.   denotative, connotative, semantic differential (p. 277)
9.   semantics (p. 278)
10.   symbols, phonemes, morphemes (p. 279)
11.   grammar, Syntax, transformation, spoken, gestural (p. 279)
12.   productive (p. 280)
13.   language, American Sign Language, six, plastic chips (p. 280)
14.   word order, questions, compound, conditional relationships (p. 280)
15.   pygmy, word, syntax (p. 281); grammar (p. 282)
16.   Mechanical (p. 282)
17.   understanding, general properties, workable (p. 282); insight (p. 283)
18.   heuristic, random search, identify, define, explore, act, look, learn (p. 283)
19.   encoding (p. 283); combination, comparison (p. 284)
20.   fixation, Functional fixedness, fixation (p. 284)
21.   emotional, Cultural, learned, perceptual (p. 285)
22.   inductive, deductive, logical, rules, illogical (p. 285)
23.   fluency, flexibility, originality (p. 285)
24.   divergent, convergent, many (p. 286)
25.   conquering hero, suffering martyr, stimulation, creativity (p. 286)
26.   orientation, Preparation (p. 287)
27.   incubation, illumination, verification, incubation (p. 287)
28.   intelligence (p. 288)
29.   knowledge, interests, openness (p. 289)
30.   symbolic, independence, complexity (p. 289)
31.   representative, base rate, framed (p. 290)
32.   mental set (p. 291); logical reasoning, logic, logic (p. 292); over-simplification (p. 293)
33.   broadly, atmosphere (p. 293)
34.   incubation, input, analogies, evaluation (p. 294)
35.   Brainstorming, criticism (p. 295)
36.   intelligence, rules, information (p. 296)
37.   behavior, expert systems (p. 296); narrow range (p. 297)

Chapter 11

Motivation

motivation defined
need model of motivation
incentive value
types of motivation
    primary
    stimulus
    secondary (learned)
homeostasis
factors in hunger
    stomach
    blood sugar level
    liver
    hypothalamus
        feeding vs. satiety systems
    external cues
    set point
    cultural factors
    taste
factors in obesity
    external eating cues
    emotions
taste aversion
    bait shyness
self-selection feeding
thirst

extracellular vs. intracellular
pain — an episodic drive
sex — a nonhomeostatic drive
how sex and pain are different from
        other primary drives
stimulus needs:
        exploration, manipulation, curiosity
arousal theory
        inverted U function
        Yerkes-Dodson law
circadian rhythms
        shift work and jet lag
        preadaptation
biorhythm theory
opponent process theory
need for achievement vs. need for power
        characteristics of achievers
fear of success
Maslow's hierarchy of motives
        prepotent
        needs — basic, growth, and meta
intrinsic vs. extrinsic motivation
behavioral dieting
eating disorders — causes and treatment
        anorexia and bulimia

LEARNING OBJECTIVES

To demonstrate mastery of this chapter you should be able to:
1. Define motivation. "the dynamics of behavior, the process of initiating, sustaining, and directing activities of the organism.

2.   Describe or analyze a motivational sequence using the "need reduction" model.

Motivated activities begin with a <u>need</u>.
Need causes a psychological state or feeling called a <u>drive</u>
Drives activate a <u>response</u> (or a series of actions)
to attain a <u>goal</u> that will satisfy a need.

3.   Explain how the incentive value of a goal can affect motivation, and describe how incentive value is related to internal need.

4.   List and describe the three types of motives and give an example of each.
a. <u>Primary Motives</u>- based on biological needs that must be met for survival. Innate.   (Examples) hunger, thirst, pain avoidance, need
for air, sleep, elimination of wastes
b. <u>Stimulus Motives</u>- Innate. Not necessary for survival of organism
Purpose is to provide the nervous system with useful information
and stimulation.   (examples) activity, curiosity, exploration, manipulation
physical contact.
c. <u>Learned Motives</u>- account for the great diversity of human
activities   (examples) acquired needs for power, affiliation, approval
status, security and achievement.
5.   Define homeostasis.   body equilibrium

"standing steady" or "steady state"

6.   Discuss why hunger cannot be fully explained by the contractions of an empty stomach.
Many people experience hunger as an overall
feeling of weakness or shakiness that does
not seem to be associated with the stomach.
* Also, people have had their stomachs removed
and they still become hungry.

7.   Describe the relationship of each of the following to hunger:
a. blood sugar   → low blood sugar stimulates feelings of
hunger

b. liver → Responds to a lack of bodily "fuel" by
sending nerve impulses to the brain, triggering
a desire to eat.

c. hypothalamus → near base of a brain
receives messages from the liver and stomach
sensitive to ~~low~~ level of sugar in blood.

feeding system (lateral hypothalamus) → if activated electrically, will begin eating. If area is destroyed, refuses to eat and will die if not force fed.

satiety system (ventromedial hypothalamus) - "stop system" if destroyed, dramatic overeating results.

d. external cues → signs and/or signals linked with food most likely to eat when food is attractive, highly visible, and easy to obtain.

e. diet → In general sweetness, high fat content, and variety tend to encourage overeating. Once excess weight is gained, it can be maintained with a normal diet.

f. cultural factors → learning to think of some foods as desirable and others as revolting obviously has much to do with eating habits. whats good in one culture may be gross to others.

g. taste → Even tastes for various foods may differ.
    An experiment showed that the hungrier a person is, the more pleasant a sweet food tastes

8. **Explain how a person's set point is related to genetics and to obesity in childhood and adulthood.**
    - Childrens parents who are overweight are much likely to be overweight themselves.

    - The set point may be lastingly altered when a child is overfed. If a weight problem begins in childhood, the person

9. **Explain the relationship between how much a person overeats and the person's obesity.**
    Overeating occurs mainly when a person is gaining weight. Once excess weight is gained, it can be maintained with a normal diet. An added problem is that as people gain weight, many reduce their activity level and burn fewer calories. As a result, some overweight persons may continue to gain weight while consuming fewer calories than "skinnier"

10. **Describe the relationship between emotionality and overeating.** → People with weight problems
    - are just as likely to eat when they are anxious, angry, or sad, as when hungry.

    - Unhappiness often accompanies obesity in our fat-conscious culture.
    - Result is a pattern of overeating that leads to emotional distress, and still more overeating, making weight control difficult.

11. **Explain the paradox of yo-yo dieting.** → repeated weight loss and gain. Frequent weight cycling caused by dieting tends to slow the body's metabolic rate. This makes it harder to lose weight each time a person diets and easier to regain weight when the diet ends.

12. **Explain how a taste aversion is acquired, and give a practical example of the process.**
    A taste aversion can be easily learned if a food causes sickness or if it is eaten just before nausea is caused by something else.

13.   Discuss the effects of weight cycling on metabolic rate.

14.   Name the brain structure that appears to control thirst (as well as hunger).

In the hypothalamus

15.   Define and differentiate between extracellular and intracellular thirst.

extracellular thirst – occurs when water is lost from the fluids surrounding the cells of your body.
Intracellular thirst – occurs when fluid is drawn out of cells due to an increased concentration of salts and minerals outside of the cell.

16.   Explain and give examples of the following types of primary drives:

a.   episodic Pain avoidance. It occurs in distinct episodes, since it is aroused only when damage to the tissues of the body takes place.

(example) dogs grew up not knowing pain and when confronted with it they didn't know better.

b.   non-homeostatic – the sex drive can be aroused at virtually any time by almost anything.

(example) an animal copulates until it seems to have no further interest in sexual behavior. A new sexual partner is provided. Immediately the animal starts up again.

17.   Describe the evidence for the existence of drives for exploration, manipulation, curiosity, and stimulation.

18.   Explain the arousal theory of motivation and relate it to the Yerkes-Dodson law. Give an example of the Yerkes-Dodson law. Assumes that there is an ideal level of arousal for various activities and that individuals behave in ways that keep arousal near this ideal level. Assumes that an individual becomes uncomfortable when arousal is too low.

- If a task is relatively simple, the optimal level of arousal will be high. When a task is more complex, the best performances occur at low levels of arousal.

(example) at a track meet it is almost impossible for a sprinter to get too aroused for a race.
Task is direct: Run as fast as you can for a short distance.

19. Explain how circadian rhythms affect energy levels, motivation and performance. (Include an explanation of how and why shift work and jet lag may adversely affect a person and how to minimize the effects of shifting one's rhythms.) Most people are more energetic and alert at the high point of their circadian rhythms.

→ Often make errors or perform poorly when their body rhythms are disturbed by jet lag.

→ Shift work has the same effect, causing lower efficiency, as well as fatigue, irritability, upset stomach, nervousness, depression, and a decline in mental agility.

→ to minimize the effects of shifting one's rhythms, preadapt yourself to your new schedule beforehand.

20. Use the ideas of Solomon's opponent-process theory to explain how a person might learn to like hazardous, painful, or frightening pursuits. If a stimulus causes strong emotion, such as fear or pleasure, an opposite emotion tends to occur when the stimulus ends.

→ With repeating a hazardous, painful, or frightening pursuit, an individual starts to get used to it.

21. Define need for achievement (nAch) and differentiate it from the need for power.
→ The need for achievement can be defined as a desire to meet some internalized standard of excellence. Strives to do well in any situation in which evaluation takes place.

→ The need for power is a desire to have impact or control over others. People with strong needs for power want their importance to be visible.

22. Describe the characteristics of people who are achievers, and relate nAch to risk taking.
→ Those high in nAch are moderate risk takers. When faced with a problem or challenge, persons high in nAch avoid goals that are too easy because they offer no sense of satisfaction. They also avoid long shots because there is no hope of success or because if success occurs, it will be due to luck rather than skill. Persons low in nAch select either sure things or impossible goals.

23. List three reasons why people might avoid success.
a. Success can require a stressful shift in self-concept.

b. Many people fear rejection when they stand out in a group

c. Some people fear the extra demands of being a "successful person"

24. Explain why women may have extra reasons to fear success. (Include an explanation of the sex differences or similarities in the fear of success as well as parental influences which encourage success.)

By adulthood, many men and women have learned to consider it "unfeminine" for a woman to excel.

For women it is a conflict btwn. achievement and social acceptance.

25. List (in order from lowest to highest) the needs found in Maslow's hierarchy of motives.

highest to lowest: ① Psychological needs ② Safety and security ③ Love and belonging ④ Esteem and self-esteem ⑤ Self-actualization

26. Explain why Maslow's lower (physiological) needs are considered prepotent.

Since they are necessary for survival, they tend to be prepotent, or dominant over the higher needs.

27. Discuss the meaning of meta-need. → less powerful but humanly important

expressions of tendencies for self-actualization, the full development of personal potential.

28. Distinguish between intrinsic and extrinsic motivation, and explain how each type of motivation may affect a person's interest in work and leisure activities.

Intrinsic motivation - occurs when there is no obvious external award or ulterior purpose behind your actions.

Extrinsic motivation stems from obvious external factors, such as pay, grades, rewards, obligations, and approval.

* People are more likely to be creative when they are intrinsically motivated than when extrinsic rewards are stressed.

* * * * * * * * * * *

The following objectives are related to the material in the "Applications" and Exploration" sections of your text.

29. Explain what is meant by behavioral dieting, and describe the techniques which can enable a person to control his/her weight.

30.   Define and describe the essential features of anorexia nervosa and bulimia nervosa. Describe some of their effects on health. (Include an explanation of what causes them and what treatments are available for them.)

31.   Explain how normal dieting may lead to binging and purging.

SELF-QUIZZES

Do You Know the Information?

Multiple Choice

1.   Needs cause a psychological state or feeling to develop called a
   (a) response.   (c) drive.
   (b) motive.   (d) incentive.

2.   The pull exerted by a goal is called its
   (a) incentive value.   (c) drive reduction effect.
   (b) intrinsic motivation.   (d) stimulus factor.

3.   Motives which appear to be innate but which are not necessary for the survival of the organism are called
   (a) learned.   (c) primary.
   (b) secondary.   (d) stimulus.

4.   Circle the secondary motives.
   (a) need for air   (f) need to avoid pain
   (b) need for affiliation   (g) need to explore
   (c) need for sleep   (h) need to manipulate
   (d) exploration   (i) need for security
   (e) need for status   (j) regulation of body temperature

5. Within the body there are ideal levels for temperatures, concentration of blood chemicals, etc. When the body deviates from these ideal levels, automatic reactions restore equilibrium. This process is known as
   (a) the Yerkes-Dodson law.
   (c) biothermoregulation.
   (b) homeostasis.
   (d) primary motivation.

6. The stomach can't be the main regulator of hunger because
   (a) there is no correlation between hunger pangs and stomach contractions.
   (b) when the stomach can no longer send sensory messages about its fullness, hunger is still present.
   (c) if blood from a starving dog is transferred into another dog, the second dog will no longer eat.
   (d) of all of the above.

7. Hunger and thirst appear to be primarily controlled by
   (a) blood content.
   (c) cultural factors.
   (b) stomach contractions.
   (d) the hypothalamus.

8. The hypothalamus receives information about hunger from
   (a) the level of sugar in the blood.
   (c) the liver.
   (b) the stomach.
   (d) all of these.

9. If the feeding center in an animal is destroyed the animal will
   (a) overeat and die.
   (b) begin eating only if its stomach is empty.
   (c) eat until it is full and the hunger motive is gone, then it will cease eating and die.
   (d) refuse to eat and will die.

10. Which of the following statements regarding hunger is *false*?
    (a) Cultural values greatly affect the incentive value of various foods.
    (b) Overeating occurs mainly while a person is gaining weight.
    (c) The satiety center in the hypothalamus tells a person when to stop eating.
    (d) Obese people are thought to be externally cued eaters.

11. Experiments concerning sensitivity to external cues and body weight reveal that
    (a) people of all weights can be found who are unusually sensitive to external cues.
    (b) obese subjects tend to eat more when they are falsely led to believe that it is close to mealtime.
    (c) normal-weight subjects eat less when they are falsely led to believe that it is close to mealtime.
    (d) all of the above occur.

12. Which of the following statements regarding set-point is *incorrect*?
    (a) Your personal set point is the weight you maintain when you are making no effort to gain or lose weight.
    (b) The set-point appears to be partially inherited and partially determined by early feeding patterns.
    (c) It would be better (in terms of fat cells) to be overweight as a child instead of overweight as an adult.
    (d) When an overweight person loses weight, the body goes below the set point, and the person feels hungry most of the time.

13. Which of the following statements about emotionality and obesity is *incorret*?
    (a) Overweight people are generally unaffected by emotions.
    (b) Obesity is frequently accompanied by unhappiness.
    (c) People with weight problems are just as likely to eat when they are anxious or angry as when hungry.
    (d) The overweight person may develop a pattern of overeating which produces distress, and, in turn, leads to more overeating.

14. "Yo-yo" dieting is a name given to the process of frequent weight cycling and its effect on metabolic rate whereby a person finds it _____ to lose weight with each new diet and _____ to regain weight when the diet ends.
   (a) harder; harder
   (b) harder; easier
   (c) easier; harder
   (d) easier; easier

15. If a food causes sickness or if it precedes sickness caused by something else a(n) _____ _____ may be acquired.
   (a) taste aversion
   (b) specfic hunger
   (c) physiological hypoglycemia
   (d) episodic drive

16. When fluid is drawn out of cells and the cells shrink, this thirst is called
   (a) extracellular.
   (b) intracellular.
   (c) hypothalamic.
   (d) Miller Time.

17. The sex drive is different from most other primary drives in that it
   (a) increases as deprivation increases.
   (b) is necessary for individual survival.
   (c) is nonhomeostatic.
   (d) is described by all of the above.

18. The Yerkes-Dodson law relates _____ to _____.
   (a) fear of success; need for achievement
   (b) task difficulty; need for achievement
   (c) drive level; homeostasis
   (d) arousal level; task difficulty

19. According to the Yerkes-Dodson law, if a task is relatively simple, the optimal level of arousal will be
   (a) high.
   (b) moderate.
   (c) low.
   (d) it really doesn't matter.

20. Circadian rhythms refer to the
   (a) complex daily cycle of changes in the body.
   (b) body's fluctuating blood sugar level.
   (c) changes in the body as compared to the changes in the moon.
   (d) physical, emotional, and intellectual changes in the body.

21. The effects of disrupting sleep-waking cycles or circadian rhythms
   (a) are worse for shift work than for jet lag.
   (b) may take up to a month for amelioration by resynchronization.
   (c) may include upset stomach, nervousness, and depression.
   (d) may be minimized by rotating shifts backward.
   (e) are prevented by consuming purgatives such as sheep's dung and wine.

22. According to the opponent-process theory
   (a) if people do not want to be highly aroused, they desire low arousal.
   (b) a stimulus that causes a strong emotion is often followed by an opposite emotion when the stimulus ends.
   (c) the need for achievement is strongest in people with lower status.
   (d) the motive to avoid success is strongest in women with the highest IQ.

23. Which of the following statements regarding the need for achievement is *incorrect*?
   (a) People high in nAch are moderate risk-takers.
   (b) College students high in nAch tend to blame their failure on someone else.
   (c) The need for achievement can be defined as a desire to meet some internalized standard of excellence.
   (d) The need for achievement differs from the need for power in that the latter is more concerned with the desire to have impact or control over others.

24.   People avoid success because
      (a)   they fear the extra demands of being successful.
      (b)   they fear rejection when they stand out in a group.
      (c)   success can require a shift in the self-concept.
      (d)   of all of the above.

25.   According to Bloom, which of the following conditions is necessary for the achievement of extraordinary success by high achievers? (You may choose more than one.)
      (a)   natural talent   (c)   intensive practice
      (b)   whole hearted parental support   (d)   innate ability

26.   The needs in Maslow's hierarchy are ranked in which of the following ways?
      (a)   physiological, safety and security, love and belonging, esteem, self-esteem, self-actualization
      (b)   safety and security, physiological, love and belonging, esteem, self-actualization
      (c)   physiological, love and belonging, safety and security, esteem, self-actualization
      (d)   self-actualization, esteem, love and belonging, physiological, safety and security.

27.   Maslow's physiological needs are considered to be prepotent over the higher needs because
      (a)   the higher needs can be more easily met.
      (b)   the physiological needs are necessary for survival.
      (c)   self-actualization is not a universal drive.
      (d)   a person must always satisfy the physiological and actuation needs before dealing with the higher needs.

28.   Motivation that makes an activity an end in itself is called
      (a)   internal.   (c)   ulterior.
      (b)   extrinsic.   (d)   intrinsic.

29.   When talking about work output, the quantity of work is usually tied to _____ factors while the quality of work is usually tied to _____ factors.
      (a)   intrinsic; extrinsic   (c)   meta-need; prepotent
      (b)   extrinsic; intrinsic   (d)   growth-need; biological

30.   Indicate by circling which of the following are behavioral dieting techniques.
      (a)   Avoid exercise—it increases appetite.
      (b)   Weaken personal eating cues.
      (c)   Focus on the amount of food not the calories.
      (d)   Keep a diet diary.
      (e)   Involve other people in your diet program.
      (f)   Eat small snacks in between light meals to keep your appetite down.

31.   People generally become bulimic because
      (a)   of a desire for perfection.
      (b)   of a very distorted body image.
      (c)   they have a need to maintain control over things around them.
      (d)   they are generally overweight in the first place.

32.   Which of the following statements regarding eating disorders is *false*?
      (a)   Anorexics have a distorted body image.
      (b)   Many people with eating disorders actually resist help.
      (c)   Treatment of eating disorders involves therapy to explore the personal conflicts and family issues which are involved in the disorder.
      (d)   Anorexia, but not bulimia, is far more prevalent in females than males.

True-False

_____ 1. Motivation is defined as the process of balancing needs against goals.

_____ 2. Adopted children whose birth parents are overweight are still more likely to have a weight similar to that of their adoptive parents.

_____ 3. Obese people generally eat normal amounts of food after they have gained their weight.

_____ 4. Human infants are capable of selecting a balanced diet over several months when they are given a daily "cafeteria" choice of nutritious foods.

_____ 5. Avoiding pain is an unlearned motive basic to the survival of humans and animals.

_____ 6. The Coolidge Effect is the phenomenon observed when an organism resumes sexual activity with a new partner after showing no further interest in sexual activity with the same partner.

_____ 7. As evidence for the existence of drives such as curiosity and exploration, it has been noted that monkeys will learn to perform a simple task to open a window that allowed them to view the outside world.

_____ 8. According to the arousal theory of motivation there is an ideal level of arousal for activities, and individuals behave in ways that keep arousal near this ideal level.

_____ 9. Circadian rhythms control things such as urine output and liver function.

_____10. The biological effects of shifting one's circadian rhythms can be minimized by preadapting as much as possible beforehand to the new schedule.

_____11. People low in nAch will seek out goals that require more luck than skill to achieve.

_____12. Women seem to act as if they fear success because they see a conflict between success and femininity.

_____13. The meta-needs are self-actualization motives.

_____14. The complexity and challenge of a task are barriers to reaching a goal when intrinsic motivation is stressed.

_____15. Studies of people with anorexia nervosa demonstrate that a considerable weight loss results in a loss of appetite.

Can You Apply the Information?

1. If you're in an airplane crash and left without food for 3 weeks, you may find yourself eating roots, insects, and leaves. In this case it can be said that
    (a) the internal need was low but the incentive value high.
    (b) the internal need and the incentive value were both low.
    (c) the pull of the goal was high but its push was low.
    (d) the pull of the goal was low but the internal need was strong.

2. Coming into a warm room and taking off your sweater is an example of
    (a) the motivation of homeostasis.   (c) intrinsic motivation.
    (b) a learned motive.   (d) none of these.

3. Unfortunately you find out that you have a cancerous tumor in your stomach and your stomach must be removed. What will likely happen to you?
   (a) You will have trouble deciding when you are hungry.
   (b) You will probably overeat because you won't know when you're full.
   (c) You will probably feel hunger and eat regularly.
   (d) You will lose weight due to the absence of hunger pangs.

4. You are going to redecorate your Italian restaurant with soft lights, background music, pleasant colors, candles, etc. In short, you want to make the atmosphere conducive to eating. You will probably make
   (a) some obese people eat more.
   (b) some normal-weight people eat more.
   (c) some thin people eat more.
   (d) all of the above.

5. A weight problem that begins in adulthood is more serious than a weight problem beginning in childhood because fat cells are more easily added to adults.
   (a) True
   (b) False

6. Bob has tried to lose weight by going on six different diets in the last six months. By now, he has discovered that
   (a) he loses weight quickly and has no trouble keeping it off.
   (b) he loses about one pound per week during the diet and regains one pound per day when the diet is over.
   (c) he loses about one pound per week during the diet and can not keep it off for months.
   (d) pounds drop off him quickly but he regains the weight just as fast when the diet is over.

7. Martha has been dieting and gaining weight and dieting again for years. Now when she diets, she has much more trouble losing the weight and then keeping it off. She should consider that
   (a) her frequent weight cycling has resulted in more fat cells which will make it harder in the future to lose weight.
   (b) her body's metabolic rate has been slowed by the frequent weight cycling.
   (c) she may have developed certain taste aversions that are causing her weight to maintain a steady state.
   (d) her external eating cues are stronger now.

8. You go out for a good time on Saturday night and eat too much pizza and drink too much cheap wine. Your stomach can't take anymore and after your 8th piece of pizza you get very sick. It is likely that
   (a) you will acquire a taste aversion through classical conditioning, and you won't want to eat pizza for a while.
   (b) you will develop specific hungers for the nutrients in pizza.
   (c) your appetite for pizza will now become episodic.
   (d) the incentive value of pizza will increase.

9. Gladys is a neurosurgeon and has decided not to operate on her mother's hypothalamus. According to the Yerkes-Dodson law Gladys
   (a) made a wise choice because her arousal would probably have been too low for a complex task.
   (b) should have operated anyway.
   (c) would have had too much arousal for a complex task, and her performance (and her mother) would have suffered.
   (d) would have done fine since her arousal would have been high for a simple task.

10. Fred works the graveyard shift (11p.m. to 7a.m.). According to circadian rhythms, if Fred has to change shifts, it would be best if
    (a) he rotates forward (7a.m. to 4p.m.).
    (b) he could change shifts every two weeks.
    (c) his shift started 4 hours earlier.
    (d) he naps during the day rather than sleep for extended periods.
    (e) he sleeps only during leap years.

11.   For which of the following does a "scientist" need your date of birth?
      (a) circadian rhythm theory   (d) dream interpretation theory
      (b) logarithm theory   (e) rhythm method theory
      (c) biorhythm theory

12.   A person who has a high need for achievement is gambling. The casino has a $100 limit on bets. Our high nAch person will be most likely to
      (a) bet all he has on one roll.
      (b) avoid all risk.
      (c) make many bets of very small amounts.
      (d) take a moderate amount of risk if there seems to be a chance of winning.

13.   Rick cooks because he loves it (and he can cook one heck of a TV dinner). Tom cooks because his family has to eat. What can be said of this situation?
      (a) Rick's cooking motives are extrinsic.
      (b) Rick's primary reason for cooking is to strive for self-actualization.
      (c) The incentive value of cooking is primarily external.
      (d) The motive to cook by Rick is intrinsic.

14.   Ed and Terri enjoy doing ceramics as a hobby. To make some money they decide to open up a ceramics shop. Their love of ceramics has decreased dramatically because
      (a) their motivation went from intrinsic to extrinsic.
      (b) there was no longer any incentive value to the ceramics.
      (c) intrinsic value overtook extrinsic value.
      (d) their motivation was prepotent.

15.   Felice is a 14-year-old female who has conflict in her family. There is discord between the parents. Her brother who is two years older is constantly in trouble at home and at school. Because of her brother, Felice feels that she must try to be the "perfect" daughter — helpful, considerate, obedient. She is 5'6" tall and weighs 90 pounds, but she decides to go on a diet. Which of the following statements is *least* appropriate in her situation?
      (a) She is more likely to become anorexic than bulimic.
      (b) The probability is considerable that unless her problem is avoided or brought under control quickly that she will die.
      (c) She may eventually need to be hospitalized and started on a strictly controlled diet.
      (d) She has some major problems with the idea of control.

Chapter Review

1.   _____ refers to the dynamics of behavior, the process of initiating, sustaining, and directing activities of the organism. Many motivated behaviors begin with a _____.

2.   In the need reduction model of motivation, a need causes a psychological state called a _____ to develop. This in turn activates a _____ (or a series of actions) designed to attain a _____. Relieving the need temporarily ends the motivational chain of events. After achieving the _____ a person experiences _____ _____.

3. Motivated behavior can be energized by _____ stimuli as well as by the "push" of _____ needs. The "pull" exerted by a goal or _____ stimulus is called its _____ _____.

4. Motives can be divided into three major categories. The first, referred to as _____ motives, are based on _____ needs which are _____ and must be met for _____. _____ motives also appear to be _____, but they are not necessary for the _____ of the organism. The last category, called _____ motives, are _____ and they account for the great diversity of human activity.

5. While it is certainly true that eating is limited when the stomach is _____, it can be shown that the stomach is not essential for experiencing _____. For one thing, cutting the _____ from the stomach does not abolish _____. Also people who have had their stomachs _____ continue to feel _____ and eat regularly.

6. One important factor involved in hunger appears to be the level of _____ in the blood. Another important factor is the _____ which responds to a lack of bodily fuel by sending nerve impulses to the _____ in the brain.

7. If the _____ system of the hypothalamus is stimulated, even a well-fed animal will begin eating. If it is destroyed the animal will die of _____. The hypothalamus also has an area that seems to operate as a _____ system (or "stop center") for eating. If this area is destroyed, dramatic _____ results.

8. Recent evidence suggests that fat stored in the body also influences hunger. The body acts as if there is a _____-_____ for the proportion of body fat that is maintained. This point appears to be partially _____ and partially determined by early _____ patterns.

9. The _____-_____ may be lastingly altered when a child is overfed. If a weight problem begins in childhood, the person as an adult will have _____ fat cells and _____ fat cells in the body. If the person does not have a weight problem until adulthood, his or her fat cells will be _____, but there will not be an _____ in the number.

10. At one time the overweight were thought to be especially sensitive to _____ cues for food. It is now known that people of all weights can be found who are especially sensitive to _____ cues. Obese people generally eat _____ amounts of food. Once excess weight is gained, it can be maintained with a _____ diet.

11. People with weight problems are just as likely to eat when _____ _____ as when _____. Another problem is that their additional weight causes them _____ distress. If people with weight problems diet and have frequent weight cyclings, this tends to slow the body's _____ rate and make it harder to lose weight and easier to gain weight.

12. In some countries people eat what Americans would find disgusting and vice versa. This demonstrates that eating is partially controlled by _____ factors. It has also been shown that _____ may affect hunger because the hungrier a person is, the more pleasant a sweet food tastes.

13.   If a food causes sickness or if it simply precedes sickness caused by something else, we may develop a
       _____ _____ which is a special case of _____
       conditioning. Using this method coyotes have been trained to develop _____
       _____ to lamb.

14.   Infants given a free choice of foods such as fresh, unsweetened, unseasoned foods were found to eat a
       balanced diet. This is called _____-_____ feeding.

15.   Like hunger, thirst appears to be controlled by the _____, where separate
       thirst and thirst satiety centers are found. Thirst caused by a loss of water from the fluids surrounding your
       body's cells is termed _____. When fluid is drawn out of cells because of an
       increase in salt this is called _____ thirst.

16.   Two primary drives, _____ and the avoidance of _____, are unlike the rest. The
       avoidance of _____ is different because it is _____ in nature,
       because we _____ the other primary motives, and because the drive is partially
       _____.

17.   Compared to the other primary drives, the _____ drive is unusual because it is not necessary for the
       _____ of an individual, it is _____, and its
       _____ is sought as actively as its _____.

18.   The drives for exploration, manipulation, and curiosity are examples of _____ needs.
       These drives were demonstrated in experiments showing that monkeys would learn tasks for no
       _____ except exploration and manipulation.

19.   The _____ theory of motivation assumes that there is an ideal level of
       _____ for various activities and that individuals behave in ways to keep themselves near
       this ideal level. The relationship of a person's _____ to the _____ of
       the task is referred to as the _____-_____ law. If a task is
       _____, the optimal level of _____ will be
       _____.

20.   Internal biological clocks which guide the body through many complex cycles of change every 24 hours are
       called _____ - _____. During their high point in these
       cycles, people are more _____.

21.   Both shift work and jet lag can cause problems because the rhythms get out of _____ with
       the sun and clocks. This can cause a loss of _____ as well as
       _____. Resynchronization can take from _____
       day(s) to _____ weeks and is aided by getting _____ and by
       _____ as much as possible. Traveling from _____ to
       _____ appears to be most disruptive to a person's circadian rhythms.

22.   _____ theory states that we are all subject to three separate cycles that begin at
       birth: a _____ cycle, an _____ cycle, and an
       _____ cycle. By plotting positive and negative phases, it is supposedly
       possible to predict "good" and "bad" days. Why should the three cycles begin at _____?
       Accident studies have shown no _____ between cycles and job performance or
       anything else.

23. According to Solomon's _____-_____ theory, a stimulus that causes strong emotion is often followed by an _____ emotion when the stimulus ends.

24. The desire to meet some internalized standard of excellence is called need for _____. It is different from a need for _____ which is a desire to have _____ or _____ over others.

25. People who are high in nAch tend to be _____ risk-takers. College students high in nAch tend to attribute success to their own _____ and failure to insufficient _____.

26. People who fear success generally do so for any of three reasons. (1) Success can require a stressful shift in the _____-_____. (2) Many people fear _____ when they stand out in a group. (3) Some people fear the extra _____ of being a successful person.

27. Studies of achievement motivation in women reveal that many fear success because they (and men) feel that there is a conflict between _____ and success.

28. Maslow has proposed a _____ (or ordering) of human needs. The first of the needs are the _____ ones. They are considered _____ because generally the higher needs are not expressed until the lower needs are met and the lower needs are necessary for _____.

29. After the physiological needs come the needs for _____ and _____, then _____ and _____, _____ and _____-_____, and last, _____-_____. More generally the needs are ordered _____, _____, and _____.

30. _____ motivation occurs when there is no external reward for your actions while _____ motivation stems from obvious external factors. For some behaviors external incentives may be required to get a person's skills to the level where _____ motivation can take over.

31. Increasing external incentives does not always strengthen motivation. Apparently, "play" can be turned into "work" by _____ a person to do something he or she would otherwise enjoy. People are more _____ when they are intrinsically motivated. The _____ of work may be increased by salary and bonuses, but the _____ of work is tied more to intrinsic factors.

32. What is really needed to control weight is a complete overhaul of _____ _____ and control of the _____ for eating. This approach has been called _____ _____ and has repeatedly proved superior to simple dieting for weight control.

33. Behavioral dieting involves several steps. Keeping a diet _____ can be useful as a means of learning your eating habits. Along with this, count _____. Also, develop techniques to control the act of eating like taking _____ portions and _____ your mouthfuls.

34. You should also learn to _____ your personal eating cues by avoiding situations that stimulate your eating behavior. You should avoid _____ and be sure to get regular _____. It helps to make a list of _____ you will receive if you change your eating habits and _____ that will occur if you don't. _____ your progress daily, beware of _____, and set a "_____" for weight control.

35. The problem which is characterized as a relentless pursuit of excessive thinness is called _____ nervosa. The binge-purge syndrome is known as _____ nervosa. Both disorders seem to occur more in _____.

36. Both disorders are related to an exaggerated fear of becoming _____. Anorexics are usually described as _____ daughters. Both anorexics and bulimics are concerned with trying to achieve _____ over some area of their life. Anorexics usually need hospitalization and _____ to explore _____ conflicts and _____ issues. Bulimics will usually not seek treatment until their eating habits are _____.

ANSWER KEYS

Do You Know the Information?

Multiple Choice

1. (c) obj. 2, p. 301
2. (a) obj. 3, p. 302
3. (d) obj. 4, p. 302
4. (b,e,i) obj.4, p. 303
5. (b) obj. 5, p. 303
6. (b) obj. 7, p. 304
7. (d) objs. 7,14, pp. 304, 308
8. (d) obj. 7, p. 304
9. (d) obj. 7, p. 304
10. (d) objs.7,9, pp. 305-307
11. (d) obj. 7, p. 306
12. (c) obj. 8, p. 305
13. (a) obj. 10, p. 306
14. (b) obj. 11, p. 306
15. (a) obj. 12, p. 307
16. (b) obj. 15, p. 308
17. (c) obj. 16, p. 309
18. (d) obj. 18, p. 311
19. (a) obj. 18, p. 311
20. (a) obj. 19, p. 312
21. (c) obj. 19, p. 313

22. (b) obj. 20, p. 314
23. (b) objs.21-22, p. 315
24. (d) obj. 23, p. 316
25. (b) obj. 24, p. 317
26. (a) obj. 25, p. 318
27. (b) obj. 26, p. 317
28. (d) obj. 28, p. 319
29. (b) obj. 28, p. 319
30. (b,d,e) obj.29, pp. 320-321
31. (c) obj. 31, pp. 323-324
32. (d) objs. 30-31, pp. 322-324

True-False

1. F, obj. 1, p. 301
2. F, obj. 8, p. 305
3. T, obj. 9, p. 306
4. T, obj. 12, pp. 307-308
5. F, obj. 16, p. 308
6. T, obj. 16, p. 309
7. T, obj. 17, p. 310
8. T, obj. 18, p. 310
9. T, obj. 19, p. 312

10. T, obj. 19, p. 313
11. T, obj. 22, p. 315
12. T, obj. 24, p. 317
13. T, obj. 27, p. 318
14. F, obj. 28, p. 319
15. F, obj. 30, p. 322

Can You Apply the Information?

1. (d) obj. 3, p. 302
2. (a) obj. 5, p. 303
3. (c) obj. 7, p. 304
4. (d) obj. 7, p. 306
5. (b) obj. 8, p. 305
6. (b) obj. 11, pp. 306-307
7. (b) obj. 13, p. 306
8. (a) obj. 12, p. 307
9. (c) obj. 18, pp. 311-312
10. (a) obj. 19, p. 313
11. (c) obj. 19, p. 314
12. (d) obj. 22, p. 315
13. (d) obj. 28, p. 319
14. (a) obj. 28, p. 319
15. (b) objs. 30-31, pp. 322-324

Chapter Review

1. Motivation, need (p. 301)
2. drive, response, goal, goal, need reduction (p. 301)
3. external, internal, external, incentive value (p. 302)
4. primary, biological, innate, survival, Stimulus, innate, survival (p. 302); secondary, learned (p. 303)
5. full (distended), hunger, nerves, hunger, removed, hunger (p. 304)
6. sugar, liver, hypothalamus (p. 304)
7. feeding, starvation, satiety (p. 304); overeating (p. 305)
8. set-point, inherited, feeding (p. 305)
9. set-point, more, larger, larger, increase (p. 305)
10. external, external, normal, normal (p. 306)
11. emotionally upset, hungry, emotional, metabolic (p. 306)
12. cultural, taste (p. 307)
13. taste aversion, classical, bait shyness (p. 307)
14. self-selection (p. 307)
15. hypothalamus, extracellular, intracellular (p. 308)
16. sex, pain, pain, episodic, seek, learned (p. 308)
17. sex, survival (p. 308); nonhomeostatic, arousal, reduction (p. 309)
18. stimulus (p. 309); reward (p. 310)
19. arousal, arousal (p. 310); arousal, complexity, Yerkes-Dodson, simple (complex), arousal, high (low) (p. 311)
20. circadian rhythms, energetic (alert) (p. 312)
21. phase, efficiency, fatigue (irritability, nervousness, depression, nausea, etc.), several, two, outside, preadapting, west, east (p. 313)
22. Biorhythm, physical, emotional, intellectual, birth, correlation (relationship) (p. 314)
23. opponent-process, opposite (p. 314)
24. achievement, power, impact, control (p. 315)
25. moderate, ability, effort (p. 315)
26. self-concept, rejection, demands (p. 316)
27. femininity (p. 317)
28. hierarchy, physiological, prepotent, survival (p. 317)
29. safety, security, love, belonging, esteem, self-esteem, self-actualization, basic, growth, meta (p. 318)
30. Intrinsic, extrinsic, intrinsic (p. 319)
31. requiring, creative, quantity, quality (p. 319)
32. eating habits, cues, behavioral dieting (p. 320)
33. diary, calories, smaller, counting (p. 321)
34. weaken, snacks, exercise, rewards, punishment, Chart, relapse, threshold (p. 321)
35. anorexia, bulimia, females (p. 322)
36. fat, perfect, control (p. 323); counseling, personal, family, intolerable (p. 324)

Chapter 12

Emotion

KEY TERMS, CONCEPTS, AND INDIVIDUALS

voodoo death
  parasympathetic rebound
elements of emotion
  adaptive behaviors, physiological changes,
  emotional expressions, emotional feelings
primary emotions
  mood
  mixing primary emotions
autonomic nervous system
  sympathetic & parasympathetic branches
pupil dilation
lie detector (polygraph)
  general emotional arousal
  relevant, irrelevant & control questions
basic emotional reactions and development
emotions and evolution
  similarity of emotional expression
kinesics
  body language and emotional tone
  facial blends
lying — illustrators and emblems
theories of emotion
  James-Lange, Cannon-Bard,

Schachter's cognitive theory,
  Valin's attribution addition
  contemporary model
effect of facial expressions on emotions
  (facial feedback hypothesis)
primary and secondary appraisal
coping with threat
  problem-focused coping
  emotion-focused coping
test anxiety
psychological defense mechanisms
  denial, repression,
  reaction formation, regression,
  projection, rationalization,
  compensation, sublimation
learned helplessness
  and depression
  how to combat it
  hope
depression
  recognizing it
  coping with it
triangular theory of love

LEARNING OBJECTIVES

To demonstrate mastery of this chapter you should be able to:

1. Explain how the body's reaction to strong emotion such as fear could cause death (voodoo death). (Also see p. 331.)

    Death occurs by the body's delayed reaction to death.

208

2. **Explain the relationship between emotions and adaptive behavior.**
    Emotions are linked to such basic adaptive behaviors as attacking, retreating, seeking comfort, helping others, reproducing, and the like.

3. **List and describe the four elements of emotion.**
    a. <u>Adaptive behaviors</u> → actions that aid humans and animals in their attempts to survive and adapt to changing condition
    b. <u>Physiological changes in emotion</u> → changes in bodily activities and general arousal that accompany emotional states
    c. <u>Emotional Expression</u> → Any behavior that gives an outward sign that an emotion is occuring, especially those signs that communicate the presence of emotion to others,
    d. <u>Emotional Feelings</u> → the private, subjective experience of having an emotion.

4. **List the eight primary emotions proposed by Plutchik and explain his concept of mixing them. Describe what a mood is.**
    a. fear
    b. surprise
    c. sadness
    d. disgust
    e. anger
    f. anticipation
    g. joy
    h. acceptance
    → Mildest forms of various emotions are called moods. Moods act as a subtle emotional undercurrent that affects much day-to-day behavior.
    → Emotions can be mixed to yield a third, more complex emotion.

5. **Describe the most typical reactions to unpleasant emotions.**
    Muscle tension, a pounding heart, irritability, dryness of the throat and mouth, sweating, butterflies in the stomach, frequent urination, trembling restlessness, sensitivity to loud noises, and a large number of internal reactions.

6. **Briefly describe the changes brought about by the sympathetic branch of the autonomic nervous system and the functions they serve.** Prepares the body for emergency action — "for fighting or fleeing" — by arousing a number of bodily systems and inhibiting others.
    → Sugar released into blood stream for quick energy, heart beats faster to distribute blood to muscles, digestion is temporarily inhibited, blood flow in the skin is restricted to reduce bleeding.

7. **Name the system that restores the body to its normal calm state (include an explanation of how that is accomplished).** The parasypathetic branch → the heart is slowed down, the pupils return to normal size, blood pressure drops, . Helps build up and conserve bodily energy.

8. Describe the relationship between pupil dilation and emotion.

    → Arousal, interest, or attention can activate the
    sympathetic nervous system and cause the pupils
    to dilate.

    large pupils → pleasant feelings
    small pupils → negative feelings

9. Explain how the polygraph detects lying. → Draws a record of changes
    in heart rate, blood pressure, breathing rate, and
    the galvanic skin response.

10. Discuss the limitations and/or accuracy of lie detector devices. The machine only
    records general emotional arousal — it can't tell
    the difference between lying and fear, anxiety

    or excitement.

11. Identify the three unlearned basic reactions, and describe, in general, the course of emotional development
    according to Bridges. (Include an explanation of the interplay between the emotions of infants and adults.)

    anger, fear, joy

12. Describe the evidence that supports the conclusion that most emotional expressions are universal. (Include a brief
    description of Darwin's view of human emotion.) The most basic expressions appear
    * to be fairly universal

    * Despite cultural differences, facial expressions of fear,
        surprise, sadness, disgust, anger, happiness, and contempt
        are recognized by people of all cultures.

    * Smile is most universal expression

13. Define kinesics. List and describe the emotional messages conveyed by facial expressions and body language. (Include an explanation of how overall posture indicates one's emotional state.) The study of communication through body movement, posture, gesture and facial expressions informally referred to as body language.

    pleasantness — unpleasantness
    attention — rejection
    activation
    relaxation / tension
    liking / disliking

14. Discuss the behavioral clues to lying including a differentiation of illustrators from emblems. Explain how they and the ANS reveal lying. Illustrators, tend to decrease when lying. A person who usually talks with their hands may be much less animated when lying.

    Emblems are gestures that have clear meanings within a particular culture.

    → Signs of strong emotion produced by the ANS. They reveal emotions

15. Briefly describe the James-Lange theory of emotion (including its positive and negative points). Emotional feelings follow bodily arousal

16. Briefly describe the Cannon-Bard theory of emotion. Emotional feelings and bodily arousal are both organized in the brain

17. Briefly describe Schachter's cognitive theory of emotion and include experimental evidence supporting his theory. Emotion occurs when a particular label is applied to general physical arousal.

    ex.) Subjects watched a slapstick movie. before the movie 1/3 of the subjects received an injection of adrenaline. 1/3 with placebo injection. Remaining subjects got a tranquilizer

    adrenaliners → rated the movie the funniest and showed most amusement watching it

    tranquilizers → least amused

    placeboers → in between

18.   Describe and give an example of the effects of attribution on emotion.

alters   perceptions   of   emotion

*male college students were shown slides of nude
women. Each guy heard an amplified heart beat
each slide that he thought was his own.
- when asked to say which slide he found most
attractive, he consistently rated slides paired with
a "pounding heart".
He attributed his "emotion" to the slide

19.   Explain the facial feedback hypothesis.

Emotional activity causes innately programmed
changes in facial expression. The face then provides
cues to the brain that help us determine what
emotion we are feeling.

20.   Explain the contemporary model of emotion.

21.   Name and explain the two steps in coping with a threatening situation. (Include an example that illustrates how
these two aspects can be used.)

a.   Primary Appraisal → You decide if a situation is relevant or
irrelevant, positive or threatening.
"Am I ok, or in trouble?"

b.   Secondary Appraisal → assess your resources and choose a
way to meet the threat or challenge.

22.   Differentiate problem-focused coping from emotion-focused coping including an explanation of how they may
help or hinder each other.   Problem - focused coping is aimed at managing
or altering the distressing situation itself.
Emotion - focused coping the person tries instead to
control his or her emotional reaction.

23.   Describe the two major components of test anxiety and describe four ways to reduce it.

components

a.   Psychological arousal

b.   excessive worry

reducing techniques

a.   Preparation

b.   Relaxation

c.   Rehearsal

d.   Restructuring Thoughts

24.   Define the term psychological defense mechanism. Explain how they reduce anxiety and discuss the positive and negative aspects of using them. (See also p. 345 for positive and negative points.)

Any technique used to avoid, deny, or distort sources of threat, anxiety, or unpleasant emotion. Also used to maintain an idealized self-image so that we can comfortably live with ourselves.

25.   Describe the following defense mechanisms and give an example of each:
a.   denial

b.   repression

c.   reaction formation

d.   regression

e.   projection

    f.   rationalization

    g.   compensation

    h.   sublimation

26.   Describe the development of learned helplessness.

27.   Tell how learned helplessness relates to depression and how it is affected by attributions.

28.   Explain how helplessness may be unlearned.

* * * * * * * * * *

The following objectives are related to the material in the "Applications" and "Exploration" sections of your text.

29.   Distinguish mild depression from severe depression, and describe how depression can be combatted. (Include a description of the problems which typically contribute to depression among college students.)

30. Explain Sternberg's triangular theory of love (including the three "ingredients").

31. Describe the emotional states resulting from the various combinations of Sternberg's factors.

<hr>

SELF-QUIZZES

Do You Know the Information?

Multiple Choice

1. Voodoo deaths are thought to be caused by
    (a) overreaction of the parasympathetic branch of the ANS.
    (b) sympathetic nervous system arousal.
    (c) the fear of impending death.
    (d) unexplained supernatural powers.

2. Emotions appear to aid which of the following?
    (a) the meaning of life
    (b) depth of caring in our relationships
    (c) motivation
    (d) survival
    (e) all of the above

3. Which of the four elements of emotion is exemplified when a person has intense trembling of the hands?
    (a) emotional expressions
    (b) physiological changes
    (c) emotional feelings
    (d) adaptive behaviors

4. Which of the following is a *correct* match?
    (a) emotional expressions — "butterflies" in the stomach
    (b) physiological changes — trembling hands
    (c) emotional feelings — your private experience
    (d) none of the above is a correct match

5. Circle the following emotions that Plutchik considers primary.
    (a) love
    (b) hate
    (c) disgust
    (d) fear
    (e) disappointment
    (f) joy
    (g) anticipation
    (h) acceptance
    (i) awe
    (j) aggression
    (k) terror
    (l) surprise
    (m) sadness
    (n) anger

6. The sympathetic branch of the ANS
    (a) calms a person after emotional arousal.
    (b) arouses some bodily systems and inhibits others.
    (c) helps build up and conserve bodily energy.
    (d) is none of the above.

7. Parasympathetic rebound refers to
    (a) overreaction of the parasympathetic system to any intense emotion.
    (b) overreaction of the parasympathetic system to fear.
    (c) the cause of all unexplained cases of sudden death.
    (d) the trauma caused by disruption of a close relationship.

8. Lie detection devices
    (a) measure the difference between the physiological and the psychological responses to a question.
    (b) are accurate indicators of when a person is not telling the truth.
    (c) measure the difference between the baseline and the increased levels of physiological arousal in response to questions.
    (d) are regulated by federal law.

9. Which of the following statements about lie detectors is *incorrect?*
    (a) Studies of the accuracy of lie detector devices show them only at or slightly above the chance level.
    (b) Bodily changes caused by the ANS are good indicators of emotion.
    (c) Lie detector devices only record general emotional arousal.
    (d) The machines' most common error is to label a guilty person innocent, rather than vice versa.

10. The only emotional response newborn infants clearly express is
    (a) fear, joy, and sadness.
    (b) rage.
    (c) general excitement.
    (d) some of the complex adult emotions.

11. According to Charles Darwin humans have emotions because
    (a) they are learned.
    (b) in the evolutionary chain animals did not use them.
    (c) of genetic mutations.
    (d) they are an aid to survival.

12. Emotional expressions appear to be the same for all people because
    (a) the grimace is the most recognizable facial expression of emotion.
    (b) children who are blind and deaf at birth use the same facial expressions as more "normal" children.
    (c) everybody expresses emotions.
    (d) the physiological arousal for different emotions is the same for all people.

13.   Which of the following is *not* a dimension of emotion conveyed by facial expression?
      (a)   arousal   (c)   hope-disappointment
      (b)   attention-rejection   (d)   pleasantness-unpleasantness

14.   Which of the following are communicated by the body (as opposed to strictly the face)?
      (a)   liking or disliking   (c)   relaxation or tension
      (b)   deception or fibbing   (d)   all of these

15.   Which of the following statements about lying is *true*?
      (a)   Illustrators tend to increase when a person is telling a lie.
      (b)   Good clues about lying come from the ANS which make the body blush, perspire, etc.
      (c)   Emblems are gestures like talking with your hands.
      (d)   Speech errors and a higher-pitched voice are illustrators.

16.   Which theory first stressed that emotion follows bodily arousal?
      (a)   Cannon-Bard   (c)   James-Lange
      (b)   commonsense   (d)   Schachter

17.   One criticism of the James-Lange theory of emotion is
      (a)   all children tend to develop emotions in the same sequence.
      (b)   that it ignores the cognitive factors in emotion.
      (c)   people tend to label an emotion according to the situation.
      (d)   all of the above are criticisms of the James-Lange theory.

18.   The theory of emotion that says emotion and bodily changes occur simultaneously is the _____ theory.
      (a)   cognitive   (c)   Cannon-Bard
      (b)   commonsense   (d)   James-Lange

19.   Schachter's theory of emotion puts emphasis on
      (a)   bodily arousal.
      (b)   the reversal of parasympathetic and sympathetic cues.
      (c)   the simultaneous perception of emotional feelings and their bodily expressions.
      (d)   the labels or interpretations of bodily arousal.

20.   Which of the following statements is *false*?
      (a)   Arousal, interest, or attention constricts the pupils.
      (b)   Making faces may bring about changes in the autonomic nervous system.
      (c)   The physiological reactions parents feel when hearing a baby cry encourage the parents to tend to his/her
            needs, thus increasing its chances for survival.
      (d)   Important to emotions are our attributions or our tendency to associate bodily arousal with a particular per-
            son, object, or situation.

21.   The facial feedback hypothesis appears to demonstrate that
      (a)   facial expressions may determine emotions.
      (b)   emotions may determine facial expressions.
      (c)   physiological changes are reflected in facial expression.
      (d)   the face is a "physiological billboard."

22.   Which view of emotion puts emphasis on cognitive appraisals of situations while also recognizing the importance
      of the role of other parts of emotion like facial expressions?
      (a)   contemporary model   (c)   James-Lange theory
      (b)   Cannon-Bard   (d)   Schachter's cognitive theory

23.   Appraisal of a situation or stimulus would mean different things to different people because
       (a) feedback from arousal adds to emotional experience.
       (b) of the facial feedback hypothesis as it applies to each individual.
       (c) the personal meaning for each individual would be different.
       (d) each person would use different adaptive behaviors.

24.   The two major components of test anxiety are
       (a) worry plus physiological arousal.
       (b) sweating and self-doubt.
       (c) upsetting thoughts and feelings.
       (d) underpreparation plus fear.
       (e) stupidity plus not knowing where your class is.

25.   Which of the following is *not* a good way to reduce test anxiety?
       (a) Overprepare for tests
       (b) Get physiologically "up" for the test
       (c) Diminish your self-defeating thoughts
       (d) Rehearse how to cope with upsetting events

26.   Psychological defense mechanisms
       (a) are conscious acts designed to display a more favorable external personality to the world.
       (b) have no adaptive value because they use great amounts of emotional energy to control anxiety.
       (c) distort sources of anxiety to maintain an idealized self-image.
       (d) are rarely self-deceptive.

27.   When you protect yourself from something unpleasant by refusing to perceive it, _____ has occurred.
       (a) suppression
       (b) denial
       (c) regression
       (d) compensation

28.   When painful thoughts are prevented from entering consciousness, _____ has occurred.
       (a) repression
       (b) compensation
       (c) sublimation
       (d) suppression

29.   When dangerous impulses are avoided by exaggerating opposite behavior, _____ has occurred.
       (a) sublimation
       (b) compensation
       (c) repression
       (d) reaction formation

30.   _____ is justifying one's own behavior by making an unobtainable goal seem less appealing.
       (a) sublimation
       (b) rationalization
       (c) denial
       (d) compensation

31.   The defense mechanism which is used to rechannel frustrated energy and desires into productive and socially acceptable behaviors is called _____.
       (a) projection
       (b) substitution
       (c) sublimation
       (d) compensation

32.   The condition in which people give up because they perceive a situation to be hopeless is called
       (a) learned helplessness.
       (b) lowered internal aggression.
       (c) anxiety.
       (d) the avoidance reaction.

33.   Which of the following is *not* one of the common problems which causes depression among college students?
       (a) problems with studying and grades
       (b) money and sex worries
       (c) isolation and loneliness
       (d) the breakup of an intimate relationship

34. Which of the following are included in the National Association for Mental Health's list of depression danger signals?
    (a) withdrawal from others
    (b) decreased dependency on others
    (c) difficulty in handling most feelings
    (d) hypersensitivity to words and actions of others
    (e) racing thoughts and reduced reaction times
    (f) decreased physical complaints

35. The three ingredients of Sternberg's triangular theory of love are
    (a) passion, commitment, and intimacy.
    (b) arousal, balance, and sharing.
    (c) affection, sharing, and communication.
    (d) respect, shared interests, and friendship.

True-False

_____ 1. Adaptive behavior is one element of emotion. Examples of this would be attack, helping others, and reproduction.

_____ 2. According to Plutchik, adjacent primary emotions can be mixed to yield a third, simpler emotion.

_____ 3. The actions of the parasympathetic branch generally calm and relax the body.

_____ 4. Most people tend to interpret large pupil size as a sign of pleasant feelings and small pupil size as a sign of negative feelings.

_____ 5. The three basic unlearned reactions are surprise, disgust, and joy.

_____ 6. Because children who are born deaf and blind have little opportunity to learn emotional expression from others, they have very different facial gestures for joy and sadness than other hearing and sighted children.

_____ 7. The study of kinesics reveals that body language usually just communicates a person's overall emotional tone.

_____ 8. Shifty eyes and squirming are examples of illustrators which increase in number when a person is telling a lie.

_____ 9. Emblems like the thumbs-up or A-Okay sign increase when a person is lying.

_____ 10. James (of the James-Lange theory of emotion) pointed out that we often do not experience an emotion until after we react.

_____ 11. According to Schacter, emotional arousal, behavior, and experience are controlled by the thalamus and are nearly simultaneous.

_____ 12. According to the attribution theory, the perception of emotion in any situation depends on the intensity of the bodily arousal.

_____ 13. The contemporary model of emotion puts emphasis on appraisal as well as other aspects of other theories.

_____ 14. A primary appraisal of a situation is when one chooses a means of meeting the challenge.

_____ 15. The symptoms that occur in depression are unlike those of learned helplessness in which there is frenzied but ineffective activity.

_____16.   Learned helplessness may be unlearned by giving a person a chance to succeed.

_____17.   Fatuous love is based on an intense sense of intimacy with another.

Can You Apply the Information?

1.   Over the last two weeks, most of your co-workers have been laid off. You're worried that you might be next but you don't want to upset your spouse. When you got home from work today all of the following indicators of emotional distress were present. Which one told your spouse you were upset?
     (a) increased heart rate   (c) perspiration
     (b) increased blood pressure   (d) trembling hands

2.   You are confronted by a large, menacing person on a dark street. Which physiological mechanism will probably take over?
     (a) parasympathetic branch of the ANS   (c) sympathetic branch of the ANS
     (b) central nervous system   (d) peripheral nervous system

3.   You're a private detective investigating embezzlement at a large department store. Which of the following would probably give you the *best* results?
     (a) Interview each employee where you can get a videotape of their lower body without them knowing it.
     (b) Test each employee with a polygraph.
     (c) Watch for facial expressions indicating tension.
     (d) Use a polygraph with an experienced tester.

4.   You're an insurance investigator examining the theft of some valuable artworks. You believe it is an "inside job" after talking with the four family members who claimed to have been home during the robbery but heard nothing. Which one was probably lying?
     (a) Bob, the retired accountant, who squirmed in his chair during the questioning.
     (b) Nelda, the sign language teacher, who sat with her arms folded during the questioning.
     (c) Billy, the graduate student, who played with his beard during most of the questions.
     (d) Mary, the little rich girl, who bit her lips during the interrogation.

5.   You're in your car driving on an icy road when all of a sudden you lose control and your car begins spinning around and around. You remain calm and manage to regain control after skidding about 75 yards. You pull over to the side of the road and begin to shake almost uncontrollably. You realize you're scared to death. This situation best supports which theory of emotion?
     (a) commonsense   (c) Cannon-Bard
     (b) James-Lange   (d) Schachter's cognitive

6.   According to the attribution theory which of the following statements is *correct*?
     (a) Bill and Jane will love each other more if their feelings are accurately attributed to their physiological arousal.
     (b) Jane is more likely to respond to Bill's kiss after riding a gigantic roller coaster than after riding on the merry-go-round.
     (c) The intensification of feelings between two people is most often due to frustration.
     (d) None of these is correct.

7. You are preparing for your final exam in psychology and it is not going well. Which of the following steps would best keep you from feeling depressed?
   (a) a brief period of intense exercise
   (b) reviewing the key points of the covered material
   (c) make a "happy face" for ten minutes
   (d) going ahead and letting yourself feel bad for ten minutes

8. In the situation described in question 1, your first step in coping will be
   (a) primary appraisal in which you decide if the situation is threatening or not
   (b) to instinctively shout or scream
   (c) to choose a means to meet the threat
   (d) secondary appraisal

9. It's 11:30 p.m. and Brenda has a test tomorrow. She has procrastinated up until now and hasn't studied more than 15 minutes. She's really getting into a panic. She's wringing her hands, she's nervous, she's shaking. The wise thing to do at this point would be to
   (a) engage in primary appraisal.
   (b) try to beat the effects of learned helplessness.
   (c) attribute the situation to a surplus of arousal.
   (d) try some emotion-focused coping.
   (e) call out for that fourth pizza.

10. Bill is taking the final exam in his psychology class. All of a sudden he finds that he is drawing a blank on five of the last six essay questions. Twenty minutes later he looks at the clock and realizes that he has only ten minutes remaining. He begins to panic. Which of the methods used to reduce test anxiety should Bill have concentrated on *before* the test? Pick two.
   (a) be prepared
   (b) learn to relax
   (c) rehearse how to cope
   (d) change self-defeating thinking

11. In your class your professor says, "Tell me about the defense mechanisms that you use." Which of the following statements about this situation is *true*?
   (a) Most of the students will report using denial.
   (b) Students will enjoy discussing repressed events since it is the most primitive defense mechanism.
   (c) According to Freud, since the defense mechanisms are unconscious, we can't really meaningfully talk about the mechanisms which may be of the most value to us.
   (d) All of the above are true.

12. A man who is upset because he thinks other men are "making eyes" at him may unconsciously be transferring his own sexual interests to them. This would be a case of the defense mechanism
   (a) reaction formation.
   (b) projection.
   (c) sublimation.
   (d) denial.

13. Teaching yourself chess because you are missing a leg and cannot play football is an example of
   (a) reaction formation.
   (b) rationalization.
   (c) compensation.
   (d) sublimation.

14. Gladys and Bill are secretaries at a large law firm. They both intensely dislike each other, but they are so sugary, syrupy sweet to each other that it makes everyone in the office want to barf. They are probably both exhibiting the defense mechanism known as
   (a) reaction formation.
   (b) compensation.
   (c) sublimation.
   (d) regression.

15. Bill was abused as a young child. Now as a teenager his parents act as if they do not love him and they call him stupid. He would like to move away from home, but he has no money, no job, no skills to get a job, and he flunked out of school. It is very likely that Bill
   (a) will not use primary appraisal again.   (c) will avoid love relationships for fear of attribution.
   (b) is experiencing learned helplessness.   (d) would flunk a polygraph test if it were given now.

16. Linda has been feeling blue the last couple of days. She should probably go see a therapist about her depression.
   (a) True   (b) False

17. George and Barbara are each other's best friend and tell each other everything. They have been together for 43 years and seem to get closer every year. Although popular stereotypes contradict it, they also still have a passion which is unmatched by many younger couples. Which of the following statements about them is *true*?
   (a) They exhibit fatuous love.
   (b) They probably have more passion than commitment.
   (c) They exhibit companionate love.
   (d) They are a good example of consummate love.

Chapter Review

1. There is evidence that voodoo deaths actually occur. The probable cause is the person's intense and prolonged _____ response which triggers an overactivity of the _____ nervous system.

2. The four elements of emotion are _____ behaviors like attack or helping others, _____ changes like an increase in blood pressure, emotional _____ like trembling hands, and emotional _____ or a person's private emotional experience. The mildest forms of emotions are called _____.

3. Plutchik believes that there are eight _____ _____ and that adjacent ones can be mixed to yield a third more complex _____.

4. The consistency of the physical reactions to emotion is due to the activity of the _____ nervous system. The _____ branch is primarily responsible for _____ the body to prepare for action. In contrast, the _____ branch _____ the body.

5. Arousal, interest, or attention can activate the _____ nervous system and cause the pupils to _____. This can occur during _____ or _____ emotions.

6. Devices called "lie detectors" record general _____ _____. Such devices appear to be rather _____, performing at about the _____ level. Their most common error is to label an _____ person _____.

7. There are three reactions which are considered unlearned. These are _____, _____, and _____. According to Bridges, there is a consistent _____ in which emotions appear and the first split is between _____ and _____ emotions.

8. Development of the ability to express emotion is probably related to _____ of the _____ since children of all cultures show a _____ pattern.

9. According to _____, emotional expressions were retained during the course of human evolution because communicating feelings to others was an aid to _____.

10. There is evidence to support the contention that there is a universality of emotional expressions. Children born _____ and _____ use the same facial expressions as other children to display many emotions. It is nice to note that the most universal and easily recognizable facial expression of emotion is the _____.

11. The study of communication through body movement, posture, gestures, and facial expressions is called _____. It is generally agreed that body language does not communicate specific emotional messages but just the overall _____ _____.

12. Facial expressions are capable of accurately portraying three feelings: _____- _____, _____- _____, and _____. The most general emotional feelings communicated by the body are _____ or _____ and _____ or _____. Overall _____ can also indicate a person's emotional state. In addition, it has been shown that _____ is best revealed by the _____ body.

13. People tend to exhibit certain behaviors when they lie. They tend to decrease certain gestures (called _____) like animated handmoving. Conversely, they increase movements called _____ like the thumbs-up or A-Okay sign. Among the best clues as to when a person is lying are the signs of strong emotion produced by the _____ nervous system.

14. The James-Lange theory of emotion says that emotional _____ follow _____ _____. James pointed out that often we do not experience an emotion until _____ reacting.

15. The Cannon-Bard theory of emotion states that emotional feelings and bodily arousal occur _____ and that the emotions are organized in the _____.

16. Schachter's cognitive theory of emotion emphasizes the importance of _____ applied to feelings of bodily arousal. Support for this theory comes from studies that show subjects who experience _____ rated a slapstick movie as much funnier than subjects who received a tranquilizer before the movie.

17. Closely related to the cognitive theory of emotion is the process of _____ which refers to the emotional effects of associating bodily _____ with a particular person, object, or situation. This theory predicts that adding fear, anger, frustration, etc., to a relationship tends to _____ a couple's love for each other.

18. According to some psychologists, emotional activity causes innately programmed changes in
_____ expression. This then helps us to figure out what _____ we are
feeling. This is known as the _____ feedback hypothesis. Some go further and actually say
that making _____ can actually cause emotions by creating changes in the
_____ nervous system.

19. The _____ model of emotion asserts the importance of
_____ and also parts of other theories such as _____ expressions.

20. The appraisal of a situation greatly affects the emotional reaction to it. _____
appraisal is when a person makes a decision about the nature of a situation. When the person makes a
decision about how to meet a threatening or challenging situation, this is called
_____ appraisal.

21. _____ - _____ coping is aimed at managing or altering the
distressing situation itself. In _____ - _____ coping, the
person tries instead to control his/her emotional reaction.

22. Test anxiety involves the combination of heightened _____ and excessive
_____. To reduce this anxiety it is best to be fully _____
for the test and one must be able to _____. It also helps to
_____ how to cope with upsetting events. Changing _____-
_____ thinking can be the best solution of all.

23. A defense mechanism is any technique used to distort sources of _____ or to maintain an
idealized _____-_____. Defense mechanisms operate
_____.

24. When defense mechanisms are overused, a person becomes less _____ because
great amounts of emotional energy are used to control _____. The value of
defense mechanisms lies in their ability to help prevent a person from being overwhelmed by a temporary
threat. Defense mechanisms may also provide time to learn to _____.

25. One of the most primitive defense mechanisms is _____, or protecting oneself from an
unpleasant reality by refusing to accept it. Another defense mechanism occurs when a person can't recall a
very unpleasant memory. This is called _____.

26. _____ _____ is a defense mechanism in which impulses are not
only repressed, but they are also held in check by exaggerated, opposite behavior. A person who escapes into
the past is using the defense mechanism _____. Another defense mechanism
known as _____ is the unconscious transference of a person's own shortcom-
ings or unacceptable impulses to others.

27. The defense mechanism which unconsciously provides us with convincing reasons for behavior which we
ourselves find somewhat questionable is called _____.

28. _____ is a form of behavior whereby a person tries to make up for some
personal defect or fault. The defense mechanism which is defined as working off frustrated desires in constructive substitute activities is called _____.

29. _____ _____ may develop when an organism has little or no control over his or her destiny. In humans, it is usually accompanied by feelings of hopelessness, powerlessness, and decreased activity. These are the same symptoms that generally accompany _____. These conditions may be eliminated if the person experiences _____.

30. Four problems which typically cause depression in college students are _____, _____ and loneliness, problems with _____ and _____, and the _____ of an intimate relationship.

31. In order to distinguish normal from severe depression the National Association for Mental Health lists ten danger signals. The first of these is a general and lasting feeling of _____ and _____ or an inability to _____.

32. Other signs of severe depression include changes in _____ _____ such as eating, sleeping, and sex, loss of _____-_____, _____ from others, threats or attempts to commit _____, _____ to the words or actions of others, difficulty in handling most _____, feelings of _____, and extreme _____ on others.

33. One way depression can be combatted is to make a daily _____. It is also recommended that one write down _____-_____ or _____ thoughts. It is wise to remember that a case of the "blues" is normal.

34. Robert Sternberg has a _____ theory of love. He believes that love is made up of closeness (_____), physiological arousal (_____), and one's decision to love another person only (_____).

ANSWER KEYS

Do You Know the Information?

Multiple Choice

1. (a) obj. 1, p. 328	13. (c) obj. 13, p. 336	26. (c) obj. 24, p. 344
2. (e) obj. 2, p. 328	14. (d) obj. 13, p. 336	27. (b) obj. 25, p. 344
3. (a) obj. 3, p. 329	15. (b) obj. 14, p. 337	28. (a) obj. 25, p. 344
4. (c) obj. 3, p. 329	16. (c) obj. 15, p. 337	29. (d) obj. 25, p. 344
5. (c,d,f,g,h,l,m,n) obj. 4, p. 329	17. (b) obj. 15, p. 337	30. (b) obj. 25, p. 345
6. (b) obj. 6, p. 330	18. (c) obj. 16, p. 337	31. (c) obj. 25, p. 345
7. (b) obj. 7, p. 331	19. (d) obj. 17, p. 337	32. (a) obj. 26, p. 346
8. (c) obj. 9, p. 332	20. (a) objs. 8,11,18,19, pp. 330,334,338-339	33. (b) obj. 29, p. 349
9. (d) obj. 10, p. 333	21. (a) obj. 19, p. 339	34. (a,c,d) obj. 29, p. 349
10. (c) obj. 11, p. 334	22. (a) obj. 20, p. 341	35. (a) obj. 30, p. 350
11. (d) obj. 12, p. 334	23. (c) obj. 20, p. 341	
12. (b) obj. 12, p. 335	24. (a) obj. 23, p. 343	
	25. (b) obj. 23, p. 343	

True-False

1. T, obj. 2, p. 329
2. F, obj. 4, p. 329
3. T, obj. 5, p. 330
4. T, obj. 8, p. 330
5. F, obj. 11, p. 334
6. F, obj. 12, p. 335
7. T, obj. 13, p. 335
8. F, obj. 14, p. 337
9. T, obj. 14, p. 337
10. T, obj. 15, p. 337
11. F, obj. 17, p. 337
12. F, obj. 18, p. 338

13. T, obj. 20, p. 341
14. F, obj. 21, p. 342
15. F, obj. 27, p. 347
16. T, obj. 28, p. 347
17. F, obj. 31, p. 350

Can You Apply the Information?

1. (d) objs. 2-3, pp. 328-329
2. (c) obj. 6, p. 330
3. (a) objs. 9,10,13, pp. 332-333, 335-337
4. (b) obj. 14, p. 337
5. (b) obj. 15, p. 337

6. (b) obj. 18, p. 338
7. (c) obj. 19, p. 339
8. (a) obj. 21, p. 342
9. (d) obj. 22, p. 342
10. (a,c) obj.23, p. 343
11. (c) obj. 24, p. 344
12. (b) obj. 25, p. 345
13. (c) obj. 25, p. 345
14. (a) obj. 25, p. 344
15. (b) obj. 26, p. 346
16. (b) obj. 29, p. 349
17. (d) obj. 31, p. 352

Chapter Review

1. emotional, parasympathetic (p. 328)
2. adaptive, physiological, expressions, feelings, moods (p. 329)
3. primary emotions, emotion (p. 329)
4. autonomic (p. 329); sympathetic, arousing, parasympathetic, calms (relaxes) (p. 330)
5. sympathetic, dilate, pleasant, unpleasant (p. 330)
6. emotional arousal, inaccurate, chance (p. 332); innocent, guilty (p. 333)
7. anger, fear, joy, order, pleasant, unpleasant (p. 334)
8. maturation, brain, similar (p. 334)
9. Darwin, survival (p. 334)
10. deaf, blind, smile (p. 335)
11. kinesics, emotional tone (p. 335)
12. pleasantness-unpleasantness, attention-rejection, activation, relaxation, tension, liking, disliking, posture, deception, lower (p. 336)
13. illustrators, emblems, autonomic (p. 337)
14. feelings, bodily arousal, after (p. 337)
15. simultaneously, brain (p. 337)
16. labels, arousal (p. 337)
17. attribution, arousal, increase (intensify) (p. 338)
18. facial, emotion, facial, faces, autonomic (p. 339)
19. contemporary, appraisal, facial (p. 341)
20. Primary, secondary (p. 342)
21. Problem-focused, emotion-focused (p. 342)
22. arousal, worry, prepared, relax, rehearse, self-defeating (p. 343)
23. anxiety, self-image, unconsciously (p. 344)
24. adaptable, anxiety, cope (p. 345)
25. denial, repression (p. 344)
26. Reaction formation (p. 344); regression, projection (p. 345)
27. rationalization (p. 345)
28. compensation, sublimation (p. 345)
29. Learned helplessness (p. 346); depression, success (p. 347)
30. stress, isolation, studying, grades, breakup (p. 349)
31. hopelessness, despair, concentrate (p. 349)
32. physical activities, self-esteem, withdrawal, suicide, hypersensitivity, feelings, guilt, dependency (p. 350)
33. schedule, self-critical, negative (p. 349)
34. triangular, intimacy, passion, commitment (p. 350)

Chapter 13

Health, Stress, and Coping

LEARNING OBJECTIVES

To demonstrate mastery of this chapter you should be able to:

1. **Define stress.** A condition that occurs anytime we must adjust or adapt to the environment.

2. **Describe the causes of stress.** Naturally, unpleasant events such as work
   *pressures, marital problems, or financial troubles produce stress.
   * So do travel, sports, a new job, mountain climbing, dating, and other pleasant activities.

3. **Explain the factors which determine the severity of stress.**
   * Pressure, a lack of control, unpredictability of the stressor, and intense or repeated emotional shocks.
   * When it is a threat and when a person does not feel competent to cope with it.

227

4. **Explain how stress is affected by one's perception of a situation.**

Some people are stressed by events that others view as a thrill or challenge. To know if a person is stressed, we must know what meaning the person places on events.

5. **Discuss the factors involved in "burnout."** → A condition that exists when physically, mentally, and emotionally drained. Three aspects:

① emotional exhaustion → fatigued, tense, and apathetic, suffer from various physical complaints.

② depersonalization, or detachment from others → treat clients as if they were objects and find it difficult to care about them.

③ feeling of reduced personal accomplishment → do poor work and feel helpless, hopeless, or angry.

6. **Identify and describe the two different kinds of frustration.**

a. External → based on conditions outside of the individual that impede progress toward a goal. Based on delay, failure, rejection, loss, and other direct blocking of motives. Either social (slow drivers) or non-social (stuck doors).

b. Personal → based on personal characteristics
   ex. (4ft. tall want to be a pro-basketball player)

7. **List four factors which increase frustration.**

a. Strength
b. Urgency
c. importance of a blocked motive increases
d. repetition

8. **Describe the common reactions to frustration (see Figure 13-2).**

Aggression
Persistance → characterized by vigorous efforts
Displayed Aggression →
Escape, or withdrawal

9. **Explain how scapegoating is a special form of displaced aggression.**

10. **Define the term conflict.**

11.   Describe and give an example of each of the following four types of conflict:
       a.   approach-approach

       b.   avoidance-avoidance

       c.   approach-avoidance (Include the terms ambivalence and partial approach in your response.)

       d.   double approach-avoidance (Include the term vacillate in your response.)

12.   Discuss the relationship between stress and health.

13.   Discuss the relationship between life changes and health.

14.   Explain how microstressors (hassles) affect emotional and physical health. (Include a description of the problem
       of acculturative stress.)

15.   Distinguish between psychosomatic disorders and hypochondria.

16.   List the causes of psychosomatic disorders and name several of the most common types of psychosomatic problems.

17.   Describe the Type A personality (including an explanation of how hardiness influences the typical Type A traits).

18.   Briefly discuss the twelve strategies for reducing hostility.
       a.

       b.

       c.

       d.

       e.

       f.

       g.

       h.

       i.

       j.

       k.

       l.

19.   Explain the concept of the General Adaptation Syndrome.

20.   List and describe the three stages of the General Adaptation Syndrome..
      a.

      b.

      c.

21.   Explain how stress can affect the immune system.

22.   Define the terms health psychology and behavioral medicine.

23.   List eight behavioral risk factors that can adversely affect one's health.
      a.
      b.
      c.
      d.
      e.
      f.
      g.
      h.

24.   Explain how health psychologists work to lessen behavioral risks to health.

The following objectives are related to the material in the "Applications" and "Exploration" sections of your text.

25.   List the three categories of responses that are triggered by stress.

a.

b.

c.

26.   Discuss the stress management techniques that can be used to diminish or break the cycle of stress responses. (Include a discussion of the effective ways to avoid frustration.).

27.   Discuss four strategies for coping with conflict.

a.

b.

c.

d.

28.   Distinguish between concentrative and receptive meditation.

29.   Discuss how concentrative meditation can be used as a self-control technique in reducing stress.

SELF-QUIZZES

Do You Know the Information?

Multiple Choice

1. _____ occurs whenever a challenge or threat forces a person to adjust or adapt.
   (a) conflict   (c) frustration
   (b) stress   (d) defense

2. Circle the five aspects of stress which make it more intense.
   (a) related to family   (f) when it makes demands on body
   (b) linked to pressure   (g) when person believes he or she
   (c) personal   lacks competence
   (d) uncontrollable   (h) intense or repeated
   (e) unpredictable

3. The aspect of burnout called depersonalization refers to
   (a) workers doing poor work and feeling helpless, hopeless, or angry.
   (b) a detached feeling toward other people.
   (c) workers feeling fatigued, tense, and apathetic.
   (d) a chronic feeling of not caring about anything.

4. Jethro has aspirations of being a brain surgeon but has the IQ of a chicken. It is likely that he will encounter
   (a) external frustration.   (c) internal frustration.
   (b) personal frustration.   (d) Type B behavior.

5. Frustration usually increases as the _____ of a blocked motive increases.
   (a) urgency   (c) delay
   (b) loss   (d) rejection

6. Circle the five common reactions to frustration listed by your author.
   (a) crying   (f) variability
   (b) withdrawal, escape   (g) depression
   (c) disgust   (h) direct aggression
   (d) displaced aggression   (i) anger
   (e) cursing   (j) persistence

7. When aggression is habitually redirected toward a person or group, _____ has occurred.
   (a) scapegoating   (c) stereotyping
   (b) prejudice   (d) escape

8. When a person is being simultaneously attracted to and repelled by the same goal or activity, the conflict is called
   (a) approach-avoidance.   (c) approach-approach.
   (b) avoidance-avoidance.   (d) double approach-avoidance.

9. The SRRS scale seems to be *most* appropriate for
   (a) military personnel.
   (b) young adults whose lives are constantly changing.
   (c) single, college-age students.
   (d) older, more established adults.

10. Hypochondriacal disorders are those in which
    (a) people imagine they suffer from disease.
    (b) physiological damage is caused by psychological stress.
    (c) the symptoms are vague and diffuse.
    (d) individuals have physiological symptoms but no underlying physiological cause.

11. Causes of psychosomatic diseases include
    (a) personality traits.
    (b) specific organ weaknesses.
    (c) hereditary differences.
    (d) all of the above.

12. As opposed to Type B personalities, Type A personalities
    (a) have a higher rate of heart disease.
    (b) have a chronic sense of time urgency.
    (c) have chronic anger or hostility.
    (d) include all of the above.

13. The hardy personality is one who
    (a) is able to suffer frustration without getting upset.
    (b) seems to be unusually resistant to stress.
    (c) suffers as much stress as the average person but tends to have a low endocrine response to it .
    (d) has control over his/her life and work.

14. Which of the following is *not* an effective strategy for reducing hostility?
    (a) Learn to be assertive.
    (b) Learn to laugh at other people.
    (c) Pratice trusting others more.
    (d) Try to put yourself mentally in the other person's shoes.

15. The _____ is a consistent series of stages of physical reaction to stress.
    (a) stress management response
    (b) resistance pattern
    (c) autonomic response system
    (d) general adaptation syndrome

16. In which stage of the general adaptation syndrome is the body better able to cope with the original source of stress but less resistant to other stresses?
    (a) alarm reaction
    (b) stage of exhaustion
    (c) stage of resistance
    (d) stage of preparation

17. The immune system
    (a) appears to be less affected by stress when a person feels less responsibility for or control over a situation.
    (b) is adversely affected by stress and illness may be the result.
    (c) is regulated by the endocrine system.
    (d) is not described by any of the above statements.

18. Which of the following statements is *incorrect*?
    (a) Behavioral medicine applies psychological principles to mental disorders.
    (b) The core of health psychology is to use psychological principles to promote health and prevent illness.
    (c) Most causes of poor health are under our control.
    (d) Engaging in health-promoting practices can double the remaining life expectancy of a middle-aged man.

19. Which of the following statements is *incorrect*?
    (a) Control over a situation, even if it is only perceived control, lessens a person's stress reaction.
    (b) Positive life events have less effect on a person's susceptibility to illness than unhappy events.
    (c) Stress triggers ineffective behavior, upsetting thoughts, and bodily effects.
    (d) Microstressors may be better predictors of daily emotional and physical health than major stressors.

20. Which of the following ways of handling conflict is *ineffective*?
    (a) When all else fails, make a decision and stick with it.
    (b) Look for workable compromises.
    (c) Try out important decisions partially when possible.
    (d) Persistence at a response will probably pay off eventually.

Can You Apply the Information?

1. Beulah really wants to put on a size 6 dress but she weights 185 pounds. Her frustration is probably
    (a) internal.
    (b) external.
    (c) personal
    (d) situational.
    (e) due to a Twinkie overdose.

2. If you are in a hurry to get to a meeting and someone stops you to talk about the weather, you will probably experience _____ frustration.
    (a) internal
    (b) external
    (c) personal conflict
    (d) conflict

3. When you get an "F" on a test and then go home and yell at your children, you are displaying
    (a) compensation.
    (b) scapegoating.
    (c) aggression.
    (d) displaced aggression.
    (e) an American tradition.

4. You love to swim. Should you buy a house on a lake or on the ocean? This is an example of
    (a) approach-avoidance conflict.
    (b) avoidance-avoidance conflict.
    (c) approach-approach conflict.
    (d) double approach-avoidance.

5. Take a flu shot or get the flu. This is an _____ conflict.
    (a) avoidance-avoidance
    (b) approach-avoidance
    (c) approach-approach conflict
    (d) double approach-avoidance

6. You are trying to lose weight and are hungry. When you look into the refrigerator you see a bunch of celery and a piece of pie. This is an example of a(n) _____ conflict.
    (a) avoidance-avoidance
    (b) approach-approach
    (c) double approach-avoidance
    (d) approach-avoidance

7. Bob is hard-driving. He is constantly in a hurry and he has an explosive temper. He has trouble developing relationships because he alienates people with his anger. Bob could be described as
    (a) manic.
    (b) oppositional.
    (c) a hardy Type B.
    (d) Type A.

8. Lucy is in a high stress position but seems to thrive. When she and her colleagues are confronted with new demands, others see the demands as threats but Lucy sees them as a challenge. Lucy usually perceives herself as in control of her life. It can be said with some assurance about Lucy that
    (a) she is a Type A personality.
    (b) she is a Type B personality.
    (c) she is usually in the G. A. S. resistance stage.
    (d) she has a hardy personality.

9. Bill has learned to relax himself by focusing on his breathing. The type of meditation he is using is called
    (a) intrinsic.
    (b) concentrative.
    (c) receptive.
    (d) transcendental.

10.   Your friend Kathy has come to you for some help. She has been offered a new job with a substantial pay increase, but she will have to move to Europe, leaving her fiance (who can't go with her) and family behind. The job has tremendous potential for the future, but she has to commit to three years overseas before she can return home. Your advice is to

   (a)   take a two week vacation to the place in Europe where she will have her job in order to "try it out."

   (b)   reject the offer because it is obviously so demanding that a compromise would be unlikely.

   (c)   take the job and stick it out for the three years even if after two months it turns out that that was obviously wrong.

   (d)   avoid making a comparison of the pros and cons and go with her intuition.

Chapter Review

1.   Stress occurs when we must _____ or _____ to the environment. Generally, people suffer less stress in situations over which they feel they have some _____.

2.   When emotional "shocks" are _____ or _____, _____, _____, or linked to _____, the stress will be magnified and damage is likely to occur. The stress is also intensified when the "shocks" happen to a person who believes he or she lacks _____ to meet a particular demand.

3.   The condition in which an employee is physically, mentally, and emotionally drained is called _____. It involves emotional _____, _____ (a detachment from others), and a feeling of reduced personal _____. This problem is especially prevalent for those in the _____ professions. It may help to _____ jobs, build a stronger social _____ system at work, or use _____ groups.

4.   There are two different types of frustration. If an individual cannot get his or her money or merchandise out of a candy machine, this person will probably experience _____ frustration. Wanting to be a jockey but weighing 300 pounds would lead to _____ frustration.

5.   Frustration usually increases as the _____, _____ or _____ of a blocked motive increases. Also, frustrations which are _____ are more frustrating.

6.   Although _____ is one of the most persistent and frequent responses to frustration, there are several other responses. Frustration is often met with _____, characterized by more vigorous efforts and more variable responses. When a person uses a new or variable response to try to get around the frustration, this is called variability or _____.

7.   Since aggression in response to frustration is disruptive and generally discouraged, the aggression is frequently _____ or redirected. Another major reaction to frustration is _____ or withdrawal, either physically or psychologically leaving the frustrating situation.

8.   _____ is a form of displaced aggression. The aggression is not aimed directly at the frustrating event or person but is _____ directed at another person or group of people.

9. There are four types of conflict. The simplest conflict comes from having to choose between two desirable alternatives and is called an _____-_____ conflict.

10. When forced to choose between two undesirable alternatives an _____-_____ conflict develops. In an _____-_____ conflict a person is simultaneously attracted to and repelled by the same activity or goal.

11. The last type of conflict is the most typical of the choices we must usually make. In _____ _____-_____ conflicts a person is forced to choose between two alternatives, each of which has positive and negative qualities.

12. Dr. Thomas Holmes has found that stressful events reduce the body's natural defenses against disease and increase the likelihood of _____. More surprising is the finding that almost any major life _____, whether positive or negative, requires adjustment and increases susceptibility to _____ and _____. Lazarus believes that daily _____ are related to immediate _____.

13. A _____ disorder is one in which _____ and _____ factors are associated with actual _____ to tissues of the body. _____ imagine that they suffer from disease. The most common examples of the former disorders are _____ and _____.

14. _____ is not the only cause of psychosomatic troubles. Usually several factors are combined to produce damage. The factors may include _____ differences, _____ traits, specific _____ weaknesses, and _____ tendencies to focus stress on a particular part of the body.

15. Researchers have studied the personality characteristics of people who are especially prone to suffer heart attacks. People who run a high risk of heart attack are classified _____ _____. This type of person is _____, highly _____, _____-oriented and has a chronic sense of _____ _____ and _____. This person runs a high risk of _____ _____.

16. Several suggestions for reducing hostility are: become _____ of hostile thoughts by _____ them down in a notebook; _____ that you have a problem with anger; _____ these thoughts when they occur; look for the ways in which these thoughts are _____; try to put yourself in the other person's shoes; learn to _____ at yourself to defuse your anger; learn ways to _____; practice _____ others more; make a better effort at _____; learn to be _____ rather than aggressive; put life in perspective by pretending that today is the _____ day of your life; try to _____ people.

17. People who seem to be unusually resistant to stress are said to possess a _____ personality. These people possess a sense of personal _____, they perceive _____ over their life and work, and they have a tendency to see life as a series of _____.

18. The answer to how stress causes physical damage seems to lie in the body's defenses against stress, a pattern of reactions known as the _____ _____ _____, or the _____. _____. _____.

19. The first stage of G.A.S. is the _____ reaction. During this stage the body mobilizes its defenses aginst stress. If stress continues, the second stage, called the stage of _____, begins. At this point the body's defenses are stabilized. If the stress does not cease, the stage of _____ may be reached. In this stage the body's resources are _____ and the stress hormones are _____.

20. The immune system is regulated at least in part by the _____. Stress, upsetting thoughts, and emotions may affect the immune system in ways that increase susceptibility to _____. If a person perceives himself/herself to be in _____ of a situation, this susceptibility is diminished.

21. The approach of _____ psychology is to use psychological principles to promote _____ and prevent _____. The field of _____ medicine applies psychological knowledge to medical problems. Eight major behavioral risk factors have been identified which can be controlled and which increase the chances of accident, disease and early death: high _____ _____, _____, abuse of _____, over_____, un-der_____, Type _____ behavior, and driving too _____.

22. Health psychologists try to _____ behavioral risk factors. They also try to _____ behaviors that promote health.

23. Stress triggers _____ effects, _____ behavior, and upsetting _____. To combat each of these problems, _____ _____ may be of some help.

24. To lessen the effects on the body, _____, _____, and progressive _____ may help. To make your ineffective behavior more effective, it may be helpful to _____ _____, get _____, be _____ in your problem solving, strike a _____ among all of your interests and demands, recognize and accept your _____, and seek _____ support.

25. To diminish upsetting thoughts, it may be helpful to make _____ statements instead of _____ self-statements. _____ statements are used to block out or _____ self-talk in stressful situations.

26. There are several suggestions to help avoid needless frustration:
    (a) Try to identify the _____ of your frustration.
    (b) If possible try to _____ the source of frustration.
    (c) Ask yourself whether or not the efforts are worth changing the source of your frustration.
    (d) Try to distinguish between barriers which are _____ or _____.

27. To handle conflicts more effectively one should not be _____ when making an important decision. Try out important decisions _____ when possible. Look for workable _____. When all else fails, make a decision and live with it.

28. There are two major forms of meditation. The first is when attention is given to a single point and is called _____ meditation. The second is open or expansive and is called _____ meditation. It is not necessary to have a customized _____ to do meditation.

ANSWER KEYS

Do You Know the Information?

Multiple Choice

1. (b) obj. 1, p. 356
2. (b,d,e,g,h)objs. 3-4, pp. 356-357
3. (b) obj. 5, p. 357
4. (b) obj. 6, p. 358
5. (a) obj. 7, p. 358
6. (b,d,f,h,j)obj.8, p. 359
7. (a) obj. 9, p. 359
8. (a) obj. 11, p. 361
9. (d) obj. 13, p. 363

10. (a) obj. 15, p. 365
11. (d) obj. 16, p. 365
12. (d) obj. 17, p. 365
13. (b) obj. 17, p. 367
14. (b) obj. 18, pp. 366-367
15. (d) obj. 19, p. 367
16. (c) obj. 20, p. 367
17. (b) obj. 21, p. 368
18. (a) obj.22-24, pp. 369-370
19. (b) objs.4,13,25, p. 362
20. (d) obj. 27, p. 375

Can You Apply the Information?

1. (c) obj. 6, p. 358
2. (b) obj. 6, p. 358
3. (d) objs.8-9, p. 359
4. (c) obj. 11, p. 359
5. (a) obj. 11, p. 360
6. (c) obj. 11, p. 361
7. (d) obj. 17, pp. 365-366
8. (d) obj. 17, p. 367
9. (d) objs.28, p. 376
10. (a) obj. 27, p. 375

Chapter Review

1. adjust, adapt, control (p. 356)
2. intense, repeated, unpredictable, uncontrollable, pressure, competence (p. 357)
3. burnout, exhaustion, depersonalization, accomplishment (p. 356); helping (p. 357); redesign, support, support (p. 358)
4. external, personal (p. 358)
5. strength, urgency, importance, repeated (p. 358)
6. aggression, persistence, circumvention (p. 358)
7. displaced, escape (p. 359)
8. Scapegoating, habitually (p. 359)
9. approach-approach (p. 359)
10. avoidance-avoidance (p. 360); approach-avoidance (p. 361)
11. double approach-avoidance (p. 361)
12. illness, change, accident, illness (p. 362); microstressors (hassles), health (p. 363)
13. psychosomatic, psychological, emotional, damage, Hypochondriacs, gastrointestinal (ulcers), respiratory (asthma) (p. 365)
14. Stress, hereditary, personality, organ, learned (p. 365)
15. Type A, ambitious, competitive, achievement, time urgency, anger (hostility), heart attack (p. 365)
16. aware, writing, admit, interrupt (p. 366); irrational (unreasonable), laugh, relax, trusting, listening, assertive, last, forgive (p. 367)
17. hardy, commitment, control, challenges (p. 367)

18.   General Adaptation Syndrome, G.A.S. (p. 367)
19.   alarm, resistance (p. 367); exhaustion, exhausted, depleted (p. 368)
20.   brain, disease, control (p. 368)
21.   health, health, illness, behavioral, blood pressure, smoking, drugs (alcohol), eating, exercising, A, fast (p. 369)
22.   remove, increase (p. 370)
23.   bodily, ineffective, thoughts, stress management (p. 372)
24.   exercise, meditation, relaxation, slow down, organized, systematic, balance (p. 372); limits, social (p. 374)
25.   coping, negative, Coping, counteract, (p. 374)
26.   source, change, real (imagined), imagined (real) (p. 375)
27.   hasty, partially, compromise (p. 375)
28.   concentrative, receptive, mantra (p. 376)

Chapter 14

Child Development

KEY TERMS, CONCEPTS, AND INDIVIDUALS

developmental psychology defined
neonate
    adaptive reflexes
        Moro, grasping,
        rooting, sucking
    infant intelligence
    sensory preference
maturation
    principle of motor primacy
    effects of practice
nature-nurture controversy
    chromosome
    genes — dominant & recessive
    human growth sequence
childhood temperament
developmental level
intrauterine environment
    congenital vs. genetic problems
    effects of drugs on fetus
        alcohol — fetal alcohol syndrome
        tobacco
conventional vs. prepared childbirth
    Lamaze/Leboyer method
    father's participation in birth
maternal influences
    super mother
    zoo-keeper mother
    proactive maternal involvement
paternal influences
social development
    self-awareness, social referencing
    critical period
        imprinting
emotional attachment — separation anxiety

types of attachment
effects of day-care
    mother-infant bonding
    Klaus and Kennel
stages of language acquisition
    "language dance"
biological predisposition for language
psycholinguist
effects of learning on language
    signals/turn taking
cognitive development
    differences in child and adult thinking
        transformations
    Jean Piaget
    assimilation, accommodation
    stages in cognitive development
        sensorimotor, preoperational,
        concrete operational, formal operations
evaluating Piaget
    infant cognition
levels of moral development
    preconventional, conventional,
    postconventional
effects of early isolation/deprivation
    deprivation dwarfism, hospitalism,
    perceptual stimulation
effects of enrichment
    visually directed reaching
facilitating early development
    White"s three goals for healthy development
    statistical vs. particular child
    responsiveness
    ways to enrich a child's environment
methods of biological engineering

LEARNING OBJECTIVES

To demonstrate mastery of this chapter you should be able to:

1. Define developmental psychology.

2. Name and describe four adaptive reflexes of a neonate.

   a.

   b.

   c.

   d.

3. Describe the intellectual capabilities and the sensory preferences of a neonate.

4. Discuss the concepts of maturation, readiness (principle of motor primacy), and practice (training).

5. Explain what is meant by the nature-nurture controversy and give supporting evidence for each position. Discuss the outcome of this debate.

6. Explain the basic mechanisms of the transmission of heredity.

7. Define or describe each of the following terms:
   a. chromosome

   b. DNA

   c. gene

   d. polygenetic

   e. dominant trait (gene)

   f. recessive trait (gene)

   g. sex-linked trait

8. Explain how sex is determined.

9. Characterize the three types of children according to temperament .
   a.

   b.

   c.

10. List the three factors which combine to determine a person's developmental level.
    a.
    b.
    c.

11. Distinguish between congenital and genetic problems.

12.   Discuss the effects of environmental influences (including drugs and tobacco) on an unborn child. Include a description of the relationship between the blood supplies of the mother and her developing child.

13.   Describe the fetal alcohol syndrome.

14.   Explain how prepared childbirth differs from conventional deliveries and discuss the advantages and disadvantages of each.. Include an evaluation of how important it is for the father to be present at the time of birth.

15.   Briefly describe the Leboyer method of childbirth including the possible advantages and disadvantages.

16.   Describe the range of effects of the maternal caregiving styles.

17.   Discuss the importance of paternal influences in child development.

18.   Explain the importance of social awareness and social referencing in development.

19.   Discuss the concepts of critical periods, imprinting and emotional attachment (including the concept of separation anxiety).

20.   Differentiate between the three types of attachment identified by Mary Ainsworth.

21.   Discuss the effects of daycare on children's sense of security and whether or not extended early contact is essential for mother/infant bonding.

22.   Describe Harlow's "motherless monkey" research and its outcomes. Relate these findings to the importance of meeting a baby's affectional needs and to the incidence of child abuse.

23.   List five stages of language acquisition.
       a.
       b.
       c.
       d.
       e.

24. Discuss pre-language communication between parents and children including
    a. a description of the "language dance" and an explanation as to why children probably do it.

    b. a description of the role of learning in the acquisition of language.

    c. an explanation of how parents can communicate (especially with signals and turn-taking) with infants before the infants can talk.

25. Explain how a child's intelligence and thinking differ from an adult's. Explain the concept of transformation.

26. With regards to Piaget's stages of cognitive development,
    a. explain the concepts of assimilation and accommodation.

    b. list (in order) and briefly describe each stage
       1.

       2.

       3.

       4.

c.   evaluate the usefulness of Piaget's theory including a review of current research on infant cognition.

27.   With regards to moral development in humans,
a.   list (in order) and briefly describe each of Kohlberg's three levels (six stages) of moral development.
Preconventional

stage 1.

stage 2.

Conventional

stage 3.

stage 4.

Post conventional

stage 5.

stage 6.

b.   describe how Kohlberg's moral development levels are distributed among the population

c.   explain Gilligan's argument against Kohlberg's system and describe the current status of the argument

28.   Compare, contrast, and give examples of the effects of enrichment and deprivation on development. Include a description of the two factors or elements in early deprivation.

29.   Describe Harlow's experiment dealing with contact comfort, and state the results of the experiment. Relate his findings to the merits of breast and bottle feeding.

30.   Discuss the effects of deliberate enrichment of the environment in infancy.

31.   Describe the benefits of early childhood education programs (e.g., Headstart).

* * * * * * * * * *

The following objectives are related to the material in the "Applications" and "Exploration" sections of your text.
32.   Describe White's practical advice on effective parenting for each of the following areas:
        a.   attachment

b. overindulgence

c. the outside world

d. respecting individual variation (include a differentiation between the statistical child and the particular child)

e. enrichment

f. responsiveness

g. forced teaching

33. Describe the methods of encouraging intellectual development in children at each of Piaget's cognitive stages.

32. Define, describe and discuss the social implications of each of the following terms:
a. artificial insemination

b. in vitro fertilization

c. sex selection

  d.   genetic counseling

  e.   amniocentesis

  f.   eugenics

  g.   genetic engineering

SELF-QUIZZES

Do You Know the Information?

Multiple Choice

1.   Developmental psychology is the study of
     (a) the role of maturation in the unfolding of human potential.
     (b) the stages of life and the important tasks of each.
     (c) the language, personality, and emotions of children and adolescents.
     (d) progressive changes in behavior and abilities from conception to death.

2.   When startled by a loud sound, an infant makes movements similar to an embrace. This is called a_____ reflex.
     (a) Moro   (c) grasping
     (b) rooting   (d) sucking

3.   If you touch an infant's cheek, he or she will turn toward you. This reflex is known as the _____ reflex.
     (a) Moro   (c) grasping
     (b) rooting   (d) sucking

4.   Which of the following statements is *false*?
     (a) The easiest way to describe an infant is as a bundle of reflexes.
     (b) Children as young as 3- to 8-weeks-old show signs of understanding that a person's voice and body are
          connected.
     (c) Infants as young as 20-days-old can imitate adult facial features.
     (d) Infants as young as 3-days-old demonstrate a preference for complex visual patterns, such as checkerboards,
          over simple colored rectangles.

5.   Which of the following *most* accurately describes the course of human development?
     (a) The sequence of development differs from culture to culture.
     (b) It is totally unlike the development of nonhumans.
     (c) Each individual displays a unique order of development.
     (d) It follows an identifiable order but can vary in rate.

6. "Until the necessary physical structures are mature, no amount of practice will be sufficient to establish a skill." This is a statement of the principle of
   (a) motor primacy.
   (b) maturation.
   (c) accommodation.
   (d) motor learning.

7. Which of the following statements concerning the nature/nurture controversy is *false*?
   (a) A person's chromosomes affect the sequence of growth, the timing of puberty, and the course of aging.
   (b) The outcome of the controversy is that there is a constant interaction between the forces of nature and nurture.
   (c) The broad outlines of the human growth sequence are greatly influenced by the environment and are therefore universal.
   (d) The differences in environment are largely responsible for children making greater use of their native capacities today than they did 30,000 years ago.

8. Which of the following statements is *false*?
   (a) Chromosomes are smaller areas on genes.
   (b) Each sperm cell and each ovum contain the same number of chromosomes.
   (c) Recessive traits are only expressed when two recessive genes are paired.
   (d) A polygenetic trait is determined by many genes working in combination.

9. Sex is determined by
   (a) the interaction of two recessive genes.
   (b) the X or Y chromosomes found in male sperm.
   (c) specific genes for primary and secondary sex characteristics.
   (d) none of the above mechanisms.

10. "Difficult" infants
    (a) tend to under-react to stimulation.
    (b) are not prone to tantrums.
    (c) will try most new foods easily.
    (d) are moody and easily angered.

11. Congenital problems
    (a) may be caused by poor maternal nutrition.
    (b) are sometimes called "birth defects."
    (c) are different from genetic problems.
    (d) are all of the above.

12. The placenta provides a connection between the bloodstreams of the mother and the developing child. Which of the following statements accurately describes the nature of this connection?
    (a) The blood supplies intermingle freely.
    (b) In the sixth month, some of the mother's blood flows into the fetus as the first installment of its blood supply.
    (c) The placenta lets nutrients pass to the embryo but all harmful entities are prevented from passing through.
    (d) The mother's blood never mixes with that of the unborn child.

13. Babies can be born addicted to drugs. This is possible because
    (a) the fetal blood has a high degree of affinity for narcotizers.
    (b) there are critical periods in development.
    (c) there is an exchange of materials between the two bloodstreams.
    (d) narcotics affect the mother's genes.

14. Characteristics of children who suffer from fetal alcohol syndrome include
    (a) prematurity.
    (b) low birth weight.
    (c) bodily defects and deformities .
    (d) all of the above.

15. Which of the following statements about childbirth is *false*?
    (a) Some form of painkiller is used in almost all deliveries in the United States.
    (b) Prepared childbirth typically shortens labor but results in more pain for the mother.
    (c) Fathers who want to be present at the birth of their children are more likely to help care for them later.
    (d) After the first 15 or 20 minutes after birth, there are no significant differences between Leboyer babies and more conventionally birthed babies.

16. With regard to maternal influences, research has demonstrated that
    (a) proactive maternal involvement is related to a lack of behavioral problems in 4-year-olds.
    (b) the "super mother" caregiving style produces unusually competent, or "C" type, children.
    (c) the "zoo-keeper mother" caregiving style produces unusually incompetent, or "A" type, children.
    (d) a mother's responsiveness loses its influence on a child's intellectual abilities after the age of 4.

17. Whereas mothers typically emphasize _____ functions with children, fathers tend to have an important role as a _____ for the infant.
    (a) comforting, model
    (b) caregiver, disciplinarian
    (c) emotional, model
    (d) caregiver, playmate

18. Which of the following statements regarding social development is *incorrect*?
    (a) Self-awareness depends upon maturation of the nervous system.
    (b) Realizing that a red spot was on his or her nose was the experiment used to demonstrate self-awareness.
    (c) Social referencing occurs when babies glance at their caregiver.
    (d) The real core of social development is found in how fast the child begins social referencing.

19. The period of time during which environmental influences have their greatest impact is called the
    (a) deterministic period.
    (b) critical period.
    (c) imprinting period.
    (d) period of maximal impact.

20. Which of the following statements regarding emotional attachment in humans is *incorrect*?
    (a) The occurrence of separation anxiety signals the formation of an emotional bond between infants and their caregivers.
    (b) A mother's acceptance and sensitivity to her baby's signals and rhythms is a key ingredient for secure attachment.
    (c) Babies born by cesarean section have a harder time developing affectionate bonds with their mothers.
    (d) Signs of insecurity in children's relationships with their mothers may occur if daycare exceeds 20 or more hours per week.

21. Baby monkeys separated from their mothers at birth and raised in isolation
    (a) become troubled adult animals.
    (b) demonstrate the importance of meeting affectional needs.
    (c) show a pattern of behavior similar to humans who have been neglected and abused during childhood.
    (d) show all of the above.

22. Telegraphic speech refers to
    (a) simple two-word sentences characteristic of early speech.
    (b) the continuous outpouring of repeated language sounds.
    (c) the seemingly meaningless babble of young infants.
    (d) children using one word to express an entire thought.

23. Language dance refers to
    (a) the early communication pattern between parent and child where the baby smiles and the parent smiles back.
    (b) infants moving their arms and legs in synchrony to the rhythms of human speech.
    (c) the biological predisposition to form vowels before consonants.
    (d) a funky new wave dance from San Francisco.

24. One possible reason why all children do the language dance and why they use a limited number of patterns in their first sentences is that
    (a) children learn language from adults.
    (b) language recognition is innate.
    (c) infants have a readiness to interact socially with parents.
    (d) all of the above.

25. Which of the following statements about language development is *incorrect?*
    (a) Imitation and reinforcement play important roles in language learning.
    (b) A psycholinguist is a specialist in the psychology of word meanings.
    (c) Parents and children create a system of shared signals which helps establish future turn taking.
    (d) Parents and children begin to communicate long before the child can speak.

26. Which of the following statements concerning cognitive development is *incorrect?*
    (a) During the preoperational stage a child begins to think symbolically.
    (b) Transformations appear unable to be made before the "age of reason."
    (c) As compared to adults, children use fewer generalizations, categories, and principles.
    (d) Generally speaking, a child's thinking is more abstract than that of an adult.

27. Assimilation refers to
    (a) passing through a series of stages in intellectual growth.
    (b) using existing patterns in new situations.
    (c) modifying existing ideas to fit new requirements.
    (d) the nonverbal use of objects.

28. According to Piaget, the development of the concept of object permanence takes place during the
    (a) sensorimotor stage.   (c) concrete operational stage.
    (b) preoperational stage.   (d) formal operations stage.

29. Mastery of the concept of conservation usually occurs during the
    (a) sensorimotor stage.   (c) concrete operational stage.
    (b) preoperational stage.   (d) formal operations stage.

30. During the formal operations stage, children begin to
    (a) accurately use concepts of time, space, and number.
    (b) think in terms of abstract principles and hypothetical possibilities.
    (c) make more purposeful movements.
    (d) think primarily about concrete objects or situations.

31. At present
    (a) researchers have found cycles of brain growth that correspond to the times of Piaget's stages.
    (b) some research indicates that Piaget may have mistaken babies' limited physical skills for mental incompetence.
    (c) Piaget's findings run counter to the findings of learning theorists.
    (d) all of the above statements are true.

32.   Morality based on trying to please others is typical of which level of moral development?
(a) postconventional   (c) preconventional
(b) conventional   (d) none of these

33.   According to Gilligan and her critique of Kohlberg's system of moral development,
(a) women's concerns with relationships appears to be a moral weakness rather than a strength.
(b) stage 5 postconventional morality only applies to women.
(c) the moral maturity of women needs to be judged on the basis of justice and autonomy.
(d) there is no difference in the moral reasoning abilities of men and women.

34.   A pattern of depression marked by weeping, sadness, and long periods of immobility in institutionalized infants
is termed
(a) perceptual understimulation.   (c) perceptual hunger.
(b) hospitalism.   (d) anaclitic depression.

35.   The two major elements in early deprivation are
(a) lack of attachment and lack of perceptual stimulation.
(b) lack of exercise and lack of correct diet.
(c) hospitalism and poor maturational timetable.
(d) lack of stimulation and poor diet.

36.   Harlow found that infant monkeys separated from their mothers at birth
(a) spent more time clinging to the terry cloth mother.
(b) spent more time with the wire mother because she was the source of food.
(c) roamed freely and only ran to the terry cloth mother when frightened.
(d) suffered from perceptual problems as adults.

37.   Harlow's contact comfort experiments suggest that
(a) all mothers should breast feed their children.
(b) children will benefit more from being breast fed than bottle fed.
(c) touching and cuddling are the important factors in feeding and can be provided with any type of feeding.
(d) bottle feeding can provide the best combination of the right nutrients for maximum development of the child.

38.   Among the things that parents can do to provide varied sensory experiences during infancy include
(a) spending increased time interacting with an infant to help develop language and thinking abilities.
(b) surrounding the infant with things to see, smell, taste, and touch.
(c) rearranging the infant's room occasionally.
(d) all of the above.

39.   According to Piaget the experiences most likely to encourage intellectual development are those which are
(a) very different from the child's present level of ability.
(b) mildly frustrating so as to challenge the child.
(c) related to visual or motor stimulation.
(d) slightly novel or unusual.

40.   Selective breeding for desirable characteristics is called
(a) genetic counseling.   (c) gene carding.
(b) eugenics.   (d) genetic engineering.

41.   Amniocentesis is a test that
(a) is conducted during genetic counseling.   (c) can detect many genetic defects.
(b) involves taking a sample of maternal blood. (d) cannot identify fetal sex.

True-False

_____ 1. Infants will spend more time looking at a human face than at a scrambled face or a same-size oval.

_____ 2. Maturation refers to the growth and development of the body.

_____ 3. It is not possible for brown-eyed parents to have blue-eyed children because brown genes are always dominant over blue genes.

_____ 4. The temperament of an infant can affect his or her behavior which in turn affects the types of responses that the parent gives.

_____ 5. The factors which determine a person's developmental level are heredity, environment, and the person's own behavior.

_____ 6. Congenital problems are those which result from the transmission of abnormal genes at conception.

_____ 7. A mother who smokes heavily is more likely to miscarry than non-smokers.

_____ 8. The Lamaze method of natural childbirth is partly designed to reduce the fears and anxiety concerning childbirth.

_____ 9. A child's sex role development is significantly influenced by his or her maternal and paternal caregiving styles.

_____10. Imprinting is an instinctive, innate ability that can take place at any time.

_____11. Extended contact (for about three hours) immediately after birth is necessary for the mother-infant bond.

_____12. Children who are in day-care, even high-quality day-care, more than 20 hours per week, may have problems with their maternal attachment, intellectual development, socio-emotional development, or physical health.

_____13. Conversational "turn-taking" refers to how children learn the "language dance."

_____14. Kohlberg found that preconventional stages of morality are most typical of young children and delinquents.

_____15. Rats raised in a stimulus-enriched environment out-performed other rats in maze tests and had heavier, larger brains with a thicker cortex.

_____16. In most cases a child can be considered abnormal if he or she has not demonstrated a certain ability during the developmental norm for this ability.

Can You Apply the Information?

1. Lindsey is holding her two-month-old son when her 5-year-old daughter comes in the back door. Slam! goes the door. Her son jumps and throws his arms out in an embrace. Which reflex has her son just exhibited?
   (a) rooting
   (b) grasping
   (c) Moro
   (d) Babinski

2. Olaf and Sven are both 2 years old. When their mothers take them to an art museum, Olaf is interested in looking at abstract pictures where facial features and body parts are out of place. Sven, on the other hand, spends more time looking at very traditional paintings where all body parts are where they should be. This apparent difference between the two children is probably because
    (a) Olaf is maturing at a faster rate than Sven.
    (b) the order of maturation for the two children is different.
    (c) Olaf has had more experience with three-dimensional objects.
    (d) Sven was never exposed to complex patterns as he was growing up.

3. Practice will
    (a) accelerate a child's locomotor abilities.
    (b) accelerate a child's developmental rate for the skill being practiced but slow down other skills.
    (c) have little effect on the child's ability if the ability is maturationally controlled.
    (d) will have a demonstrable effect on the skill before it develops but will have little effect on the skill as it is being perfected.

4. Most experts now conclude that
    (a) heredity is most important during infancy and childhood, and environment is most important during adolescence and adulthood.
    (b) heredity and enviromnent are inseparable, interacting factors in development.
    (c) environment is the most important factor in development since it can override the effects of heredity.
    (d) heredity is important for only a few psychological traits such as intelligence and temperament.

5. At her son's birthday party Jennifer observes a child who does not interact with the other children and appears rather unexpressive. How would this child probably be classified according to temperament?
    (a) slow-to-warm-up   (c) easy
    (b) difficult   (d) doesn't fit into one category

6. Hemophilia is a blood clotting disorder which can be passed through generations of a family. It is a congenital disorder that can therefore be quite serious for a neonate.
    (a) True   (b) False

7. Murray and Rebecca were about to have a baby when Murray, who is in the Navy, was deployed on a six-month cruise to the Mediterranean. He had taken Lamaze training with Rebecca and was looking forward to helping in the birth process even to the point of taking pictures for their memories of a joyous time. Now they are worried that his not being at the birth may negatively influence Murray's relationship with his child. Your advice to them is to
    (a) be careful of his reaction when the child angers him because bonding has not taken place.
    (b) not worry because Murray's attitude toward the birth may be more important than his actually being there.
    (c) remember and use the breathing techniques they learned in Lamaze class when he has difficulty with the child.
    (d) try to obtain a hardship leave from the Navy for the birth under the grounds that Murray's not being there will negatively influence the child's first months of life.

8. Your friend has two children. She seems to interact with them very little, but their physical needs are taken care of. Your friend
    (a) will raise "A" children.
    (b) is a super mother.
    (c) will have children who are slow in language development.
    (d) is a zoo-keeper mother.
    (e) is called "Mommy Dearest" by her children.

9. Parents who take swimming classes with their very young children are told that if the child goes underwater and comes up sputtering with a frightened look on his/her face to smile at the child and make it look as if it is the greatest fun in the whole world. This is a good example of the concept of
   (a) maturation.
   (b) a paternal influence.
   (c) turn taking.
   (d) social referencing.
   (e) parents taking advantage of young children.

10. You are sitting in a doctor's waiting room with your one-year-old son. A nurse calls your name and since you know the visit will take only about 30 seconds, you leave your son behind. He starts crying. It is likely that he is suffering from
   (a) attachment deprivation.
   (b) stranger anxiety.
   (c) attachment anxiety.
   (d) separation anxiety.

11. Joan's father died before she was born and her mother died in childbirth. She is now 1 month old and has been in two different foster homes waiting for adoption. She is going to be adopted by a couple who are infertile but have always wanted a child and will make every effort to meet all of her affectional needs. It is most likely that
   (a) Joan's lack of attachment at birth will result in antisocial behavior as an adult.
   (b) she has been experiencing separation anxiety from birth, but that it can be overcome with the proper care.
   (c) Joan will develop normal affectionate bonds with her new parents.
   (d) Joan's development will appear normal until such time, as an adult, she decides to have children.

12. Any subject can be taught to a child at any age if it is taught in an intellectually honest form. Piaget would likely
   (a) agree with the statement.
   (b) agree with the statement provided the child is beyond the sensorimotor stage.
   (c) disagree with the statement because there are some concepts that absolutely cannot be mastered until a certain stage of development is reached.
   (d) disagree with the statement because the child may not be emotionally ready to master the concept.

13. "I won't steal that bicycle because I might get caught." This statement is an example of the _____ level of moral reasoning.
   (a) conventional
   (b) postconventional
   (c) preconventional
   (d) pleasure-seeking

14. Most children begin walking around the age of one year. Your child begins walking at six months of age. In this regard your child is a good example of
   (a) the effects of practice.
   (b) the statistical child.
   (c) the effects on an enriched environment.
   (d) the particular child.

15. Which of the following is the *best* example of the concept of responsiveness for a two-year-old child?
   (a) a chalkboard and a box of multicolored chalk
   (b) a box that unfolds and refolds itself completely automatically
   (c) a doll that walks, talks, wets, etc.
   (d) a videotape player

Chapter Review

1. The study of _____ is the heart of developmental psychology. However, developmental psychology is more accurately defined as the study of progressive changes in _____ and abilities from _____ to _____.

2. The human _____ (newborn) possesses a number of reflexes which improve its chances for survival. For example, an object pressed to its palm will be grasped tightly. This reflex is appropriately call the _____ reflex.

3. The _____ reflex occurs when a neonate is touched on its cheek and turns its head in that direction. When a nipple touches the neonate's mouth, the _____ reflex helps the baby obtain food. The _____ reflex involves a baby's making movements similar to an _____ when his or her head is dropped.

4. Neonates are probably much smarter than people think. Research indicates that newborns are able to _____ another person's facial expressions. Tests of infant vision indicate that the neonate prefers _____ patterns and human _____, especially _____ ones. The preference for familiarity _____ at about age two.

5. _____ refers to growth and development of the body. It underlies the orderly _____ observed in the unfolding of many basic responses. Its _____ varies from child to child, but its _____ is virtually universal.

6. The principle of _____ _____ states: "Until the necessary physical structures are mature, no amount of _____ will be sufficient to establish a skill."

7. The nature-nurture controversy refers to the relative contributions to development of _____ (nature) and _____ (nurture).

8. Hereditary instructions are carried by the _____. Smaller areas on these are called _____. When many of these latter units work in combination, a characteristic is called _____.

9. Genes may either be _____ or _____. The latter must be paired with a similar gene in order for its characteristic to be expressed. To be female, an organism must have two ____ chromosomes. To be male, there must be an ____ and a ____.

10. The broad outlines of the _____ _____ _____ are universal. In actuality, heredity and environment are _____; as a person grows there is a constant _____ between the forces of nature and nurture.

11. Children can be classified into three different temperamental categories: _____ children, _____ children, and _____-_____-_____-_____ children. A person's developmental level is determined by _____, _____, and the individual's own _____.

12. Damage that occurs to an unborn child because of environmental influences is referred to as _____. These problems are sometimes referred to as _____ _____. Problems that are inherited are called _____ problems.

13. Many drugs may pass through the mother and reach the fetus even though there is no direct mixing of _____ between the two. Evidence for this comes from the fact that if the mother is addicted to a drug, the infant may be born with a drug _____. Repeated heavy drinking by a pregnant woman can produce a variety of congenital problems including low _____ _____, retardation, and physical (facial) _____. _____ or _____ births are also common.

14. In addition, heavy smokers run a higher risk of _____ _____ and tend to give birth to babies who are _____.

15. Some form of _____ is used in 95% of all deliveries in the U.S. Many women and men are now going through _____ childbirth using such methods as the _____ method. This typically shortens labor and reduces pain. Having the father present can make a difference in his willingness to later _____ for the child. Yet, while participation by the father is valuable, a father's _____ toward the birth seems more important.

16. The French obstetrician _____ advocates a _____ way of birth. He claims that babies born in this fashion are _____ and _____. Skeptics say that one can't _____ well enough to spot complications. Research shows that there is _____ _____ after the first twenty minutes or so between babies born like this or more conventionally.

17. Differing maternal styles have been related to whether a child is unusually competent (A) or possesses little competence (C). _____ mothers produce A children and go out of their way to provide educational experiences for the child. The _____-_____ mother produces C or lower children and interacts with them very little but provides for their physical needs.

18. Optimal caregiving is related to the _____ of _____ between the temperaments of parents and children. Fathers contribute significantly to an infant's social and intellectual growth. Whereas mothers typically emphasize _____, fathers tend to function as a _____ for the infant.

19. Two important areas of social development are _____ - _____ and _____ - _____. The former depends upon _____ of the nervous system and begins to form the core of social development. It _____ as the child develops. When a child glances at its parent in order to decide how to respond to something, this is called _____ - _____.

20. A _____ _____ is a time when susceptibility to environmental influences is increased. The rapid and relatively permanent establishment of a behavior pattern is called _____. Even this behavior pattern is subject to a _____ _____.

21. Emotional _____ of human infants to their caretaker is a very important event. There is a _____ _____ during which this must occur for healthy development, but it is *not* essential that this occur within the first few _____ after birth.

22. Around 8 to 12 months babies display _____ _____ when their parents leave them which demonstrates that an _____ _____ has been formed. The quality of the attachment is revealed by how _____ act when their _____ return after a brief separation: _____ _____ infants seek to be near their mothers when they return; _____ - _____ infants turn away when their mothers return; _____ - _____ infants both seek to be near and yet resist contact with their mothers. The key to a _____ attachment is a mother who is accepting and sensitive to her baby's signals and rhythms.

23. High quality _____ - _____ does not appear to have _____ effects on preschoolers unless it exceeds _____ hours per week.

24. According to Klaus and Kennel, mother-child pairs who spend extra time together after birth form a stronger _____ _____. However, because _____ children, _____ babies and those born by cesarean section all develop normal bonds with their mothers, it is unlikey that emotional attachments depend _____ on the first few hours of life. In any event, meeting a baby's _____ _____ is every bit as important as meeting more obvious needs for food, water, and physical care.

25. The first stage of language acquisition is _____. Babies do this from the moment of _____. Around six to eight weeks babies begin repeating certain vowel sounds. This is called _____. Next the child begins to _____. The child then begins to form _____ _____. Last, simple two-word sentences called _____ speech are formed.

26. Infants move their arms and legs in synchrony to the rhythms of human_____. This is called _____ _____. Chomsky believes that language recognition is _____, and that humans have a _____ _____ to develop language.

27. Other specialists in the psychology of language (called _____) have recently shown that _____ and _____ are an important part of language learning.

28. A child's thinking is less _____ than that of an adult, for example children appear to be unable to make _____ before the "_____ of _____" (about age 7). Piaget believed that the growth of intellect proceeds through fixed _____. There are two processes which help the intellect grow. _____ refers to using existing patterns in new situations. In _____, existing ideas are modified to fit new requirements.

29. The first stage is the _____ stage. During this time the infant's movements become _____ and the concept of _____ _____ begins to emerge. The second stage is the _____ stage and is marked by development of the ability to think _____ and to use _____. The child's thinking is still _____ and the child is quite _____.

30. The next stage is the _____ _____ stage and is marked by the mastery of the concepts of _____ and _____. The last stage is called the _____ _____ stage. Now thinking is based more on _____ principles, and the child can consider _____ possibilities.

31. Some research suggests that cognitive development is not as strictly _____-and- _____-related as Piaget claimed. Many psychologists are convinced that he gave too little credit to _____. Conversely, researchers have recently found evidence that cycles of _____ growth at times that correspond with Piaget's stages.

32. To study moral development, Kohlberg posed _____ _____ to children of different ages. Kohlberg identified three levels and six stages of moral development. In the first level, the _____ level, moral development is determined by the _____ of actions (punishment, reward, or exchange of favors).

33. In the second or _____ level of morality, actions are directed by a desire to _____ to the expectations of others or to uphold socially accepted _____ and _____. The third or _____ level represents advanced moral development. Behavior is directed by _____-_____ moral principles.

34. According to Kohlberg, the preconventional stages of morality are most typical of young children and _____; the conventional stages are typical of older children and most of the _____ population; and, postconventional morality is achieved by only about _____ percent of the adult population.

35. Gilligan has pointed out that Kohlberg's system is concerned with the ethics of _____. However, morality should also include an ethic of _____ and _____ to others.

36. In development, the loss or withholding of _____ stimulation consittutes a condition of _____. Lack of _____ and lack of _____ _____ are two major factors in _____.

37. Harlow's research with monkeys confirms the effects of a lack of stimulation in infancy. Monkeys separated from their mothers preferred _____ mothers with a soft terrycloth surface. Harlow concluded from this that an important dimension of early stimulation is _____ _____ supplied by touching, holding, and stroking an infant.

38. On the other hand, _____ of the environment has been found to have a beneficial effect on a child's development. Rats raised in _____ environments have been found to have larger brains with thicker _____ than rats raised in _____ environments. Likewise, early education programs with children show a _____ relationship between early stimulation and _____ in various "intellectual" abilities.

39. Because parents want to see their children's _____ develop fully, some practical advice for effective parenting is as follows:
    (1) give an infant a feeling of being _____ which will help build a _____ mother-infant bond;
    (2) avoid _____ by giving age-appropriate limits and guidelines for acceptable behavior;
    (3) encourage a child to _____ the outside world;
    (4) remember that developmental norms are based on _____ (the concept of the _____ child) and that there is always a wide range of variation around each average which may encompass individual differences (the concept of the _____ child);
    (5) provide an _____ environment for the child;
    (6) create a world that _____ to the infant not one that bombards the infant with _____; and finally,
    (7) keep in mind that _____ _____ can bore a child.

40. Piaget suggests that in order to promote intellectual development, experiences should be provided that are only _____ novel or challenging. Experiences that are too unfamiliar may cause _____ and withdrawal.

41. There have been many recent advances in medicine and genetics. If a husband is sterile, a woman can undergo _____ _____. If the woman's eggs are harvested and then mixed with the man's sperm, this is called _____ _____ _____. It is also possible to have an influence on the _____ of the child.

42. Prospective parents who suspect that they may have a genetic disorder may seek _____ _____. This may include prenatal testing like _____. _____ is selective breeding for desirable characteristics. Removing defective genes and replacing them with normal ones is called _____ _____.

ANSWER KEYS

Do You Know the Information?

Multiple Choice

1. (d) obj. 1, p. 380
2. (a) obj. 2, p. 381
3. (b) obj. 2, p. 381
4. (a) objs.2-3, pp. 381-382
5. (d) obj. 4, p. 382
6. (a) obj. 4, p. 383
7. (c) obj. 5, p. 385
8. (a) objs.6-7, p. 384
9. (b) obj. 8, p. 385
10. (d) obj. 9, p. 387
11. (d) obj. 11, p. 388
12. (d) obj. 12, p. 388
13. (c) obj. 12, p. 388
14. (d) obj. 13, p. 389
15. (b) objs.14-15, pp. 389-390
16. (a) obj. 16, p. 391
17. (d) obj. 17, p. 391
18. (d) obj. 18, p. 392
19. (b) obj. 19, p. 392
20. (c) objs.20-21, pp. 393-394
21. (d) obj. 22, p. 394
22. (a) obj. 23, p. 395
23. (b) obj. 24, p. 395
24. (b) obj. 24, p. 395
25. (b) obj. 24, p. 396

26. (d) objs.25-26, pp. 397-398
27. (b) obj. 26, p. 398
28. (a) obj. 26, p. 398
29. (c) obj. 26, p. 399
30. (b) obj. 26, p. 399
31. (d) obj. 26, p. 400
32. (b) obj. 27, p. 402
33. (a) obj. 27, p. 403
34. (b) obj. 28, p. 404
35. (a) obj. 28, p. 404
36. (a) obj. 29, p. 404
37. (c) obj. 29, p. 405
38. (d) obj. 32, p. 408
39. (d) obj. 33, p. 408
40. (b) obj. 34, p. 411
41. (c) obj. 34, p. 411

True-False

1. T, obj. 3, p. 382
2. T, obj. 4, p. 382
3. F, obj. 7, p. 385
4. T, obj. 9, p. 387
5. T, obj. 10, p. 388
6. F, obj. 11, p. 388
7. T, obj. 12, p. 389
8. T, obj. 14, p. 389

9. T, obj. 17, p. 391
10. F, obj. 19, p. 393
11. F, obj. 21, p. 394
12. T, obj. 21, p. 394
13. F, obj. 24, pp. 395-396
14. T, obj. 27, p. 402
15. T, obj. 30, p. 405
16. F, obj. 32, p. 407

Can You Apply the Information?

1. (c) obj. 2, p. 381
2. (a) objs.3-4, p. 382
3. (c) obj. 4, p. 383
4. (b) obj. 5, p. 386
5. (a) obj. 9, p. 387
6. (b) obj. 11, p. 388
7. (b) obj. 14, p. 389
8. (d) obj. 16, p. 391
9. (d) obj. 18, p. 392
10. (d) obj. 19, p. 393
11. (c) obj. 21, p. 394
12. (c) obj. 26, pp. 398-400
13. (c) obj. 27, p. 402
14. (d) obj. 32, p. 407
15. (a) obj. 32, p. 408

Chapter Review

1. children, behavior, conception, death (p. 380)
2. neonate, grasping (p. 381)
3. rooting, sucking, Moro, embrace (p. 381)
4. imitate (p. 381); complex, faces, familiar, reverses (p. 382)
5. Maturation, sequence, rate, order (p. 382)
6. motor primacy, practice (p. 383)
7. heredity (p. 384); environment (p. 386)
8. chromosomes, genes (p. 384); polygenetic (p. 385)
9. dominant, recessive, X, X, Y (p. 385)
10. human growth sequence (p. 385); inseparable, interplay (interacting) (p. 386)
11. easy, difficult, slow-to-warm-up (p. 387); heredity, environment, behavior (p. 388)
12. congenital, birth defects, genetic (p. 388)
13. blood, addiction (p. 388); fetal alcohol syndrome, birth weight, malformations, Miscarriages, premature (p. 389)
14. premature births, underweight (p. 389)
15. painkiller, prepared, Lamaze, care, attitude (p. 389)
16. Leboyer, gentle, healthier, happier, see, no difference (p. 390)
17. Super, zoo-keeper (p. 391)
18. goodness, fit, caregiving, playmate (p. 391)
19. self-awareness (p. 391); social referencing, maturation, increases, social referencing (p. 392)
20. critical period (p. 392); imprinting, critical period (p. 393)
21. attachment, critical period (p. 393); hours (p. 394)
22. separation anxiety, emotional bond, babies, mothers, securely attached, insecure-avoidant, insecure-ambivalent, secure (p. 393)
23. day-care, harmful, 20 (p. 394)
24. emotional bond, adopted, premature, solely, affectional needs (p. 394)
25. crying, birth, cooing, babble, single words, telegraphic (p. 395)
26. speech, language dance, innate, biological predisposition, (p. 395)
27. psycholinguists, imitation, reward (p. 396)
28. abstract, transformations, age reason, (p. 397);stages, Assimilation, accommodation (p. 398)
29. sensorimotor, purposeful, object permanence, preoperational, symbolically, language, intuitive, egocentric (p. 398)
30. concrete operational, conservation, reversibility (p. 380); formal operations, abstract, hypothetical (p. 399)
31. age, stage, learning, brain (p. 400)
32. moral dilemmas, preconventional, consequences (p. 401)
33. conventional, conform, rules, values, post-conventional (p. 401); self-accepted (p. 402)
34. delinquents, adult, 20 (p. 402)
35. justice, caring, responsibility (p. 403)
36. normal, deprivation (p. 403); attachment, perceptual stimulation, deprivation (p. 404)
37. surrogate, contact comfort (p. 404)
38. enrichment, enriched, cortexes, positive, improvements (p. 405)
39. potential (p. 406); loved, secure, overindulgence, explore, averages, statistical, particular (p. 407); enriched, responds, stimuli, forced teaching (p. 408)
40. slightly, frustration (p. 408)
41. artificial insemination, in vitro fertilization, sex (p. 410)
42. genetic counseling, amniocentesis, Eugenics, genetic engineering (p. 411)

Chapter 15

From Birth to Death: Life-Span Development

KEY TERMS, CONCEPTS, AND INDIVIDUALS

life stage
developmental task
Erik Erikson — psychosocial dilemmas
   trust vs. mistrust
   autonomy vs. shame and doubt
   initiative vs. guilt
   industry vs. inferiority
   identity vs. role confusion
   intimacy vs. isolation
   generativity vs. stagnation
   integrity vs. despair
styles of parenting
   authoritarian
   overly permissive
   effective (authoritative)
stress — a normal childhood process
   overprotection
normal childhood problems
significant childhood problems
   enuresis, encopresis
   overeating, anorexia, pica
   delayed speech, stuttering
   learning disabilities
     dyslexia
     ADHD
       stimulant drugs
       behavior modification
     autism
child abuse
   characteristics of abusers
   preventing child abuse
adolescence
   puberty
     peak growth spurt
   early and late maturation
   hurried childhood development
   imaginary audience

parent/teenager conflict
   identity foreclosure
     minority youth
vocational choice
   exploration phase
     fantasy, tentative, realistic stages
   establishment phase
   midcareer phase
   later career phase
vocational counseling
career decision styles
Gould's adult challenges
   midlife crisis
   middle age
     menopause vs. climacteric
biological aging
   maximum life span vs. life expectancy
   fluid vs. crystallized abilities
   activity vs. disengagement theories
ageism
myths about aging
death and dying
   fear and reactions
   thanatologist
grief
parenting — two key areas
   techniques of discipline
     power assertion, withdrawal of love
     child management
   self-esteem
   guidelines for punishment
four ingredients of effective parenting
communication
   accepting feelings, encouragement,
   "I" message
natural and logical consequences
alternative paths approaching death

LEARNING OBJECTIVES

To demonstrate mastery of this chapter you should be able to:

1. List the life stages experienced by all people.
   a. infancy
   b. childhood
   c. adolescence
   d. young adulthood
   e. middle adulthood
   f. old age

2. Define developmental task. → skills that must be acquired or personal changes that must take place for optimal development

3. Explain according to Erikson how the resolution of the psychosocial dilemmas affects a person's adjustment to life. Resolving each dilemma creates a new balance between a person and the social world. An unfavorable outcome throws us off balance and makes it harder to deal with later crisis. A string of "successes" produces healthy development and a satisfying life.

4. State the nature of the psychosocial crisis and the nature of an adequate or inadequate outcome for each of Erikson's eight life stages. Match each crisis with the corresponding age.

   a. trust vs. mistrust → first year of life
   * Trust established when babies are given adequate warmth, touching, love and physical care. Mistrust is caused by inadequate or unpredictable care and by parents who are cold, indifferent, or rejecting. Mistrust may lead to insecurity, suspiciousness, or inability to relate to others.

   b. autonomy vs. shame and doubt → 1-3 years
   children grow self-control, expressed by climbing, touching, exploring, general desire to do things for themselves. Parents help a sense of autonomy by encouraging new skills. However, results of spilling, falling, wetting and other accidents. Parents who ridicule or overprotect them may cause doubt or shame.

   c. initiative vs. guilt → 3-5 years
   Child moves from simple self-control to an ability to take initiative. Parents reinforce initiative by giving the child the freedom to play, to ask questions, to use imagination, and choose activities. Children learn to feel guilty about the activities they initiate by parents who criticize severely, prevent play, or discourage questions.

   d. industry vs. inferiority → 6-12 years
   World is expanded beyond family. face a whole series of new challenges. Elementary school years are "entrance into life". Begin to learn skills. Valued by society, and success or failure has lasting effects on feelings of adequacy. Sense of industry occurs from a sense of praise for building, cooking, reading, studying, and productive activities. Efforts messy, childish or inadequate, feelings of inferiority result.

   e. identity vs. role confusion → Adolescence
   Caught btwn. childhood and adulthood, the adolescent faces some unique problems. Question "Who Am I?" Mental and physical maturation brings to the individual new feelings, a new body, and new attitudes. Must build a consistent identity out of self-perceptions and relationships with others. Persons who fail to develop a sense of identity suffer from role confusion, an uncertainty about who they are + where they are going.

   f. intimacy vs. isolation → Young Adulthood
   After establishing a stable identity, a person is prepared to share meaningful love or deep friendship with others. "Intimacy" means an ability to care about others and to share experiences with them.
   Failure to establish intimacy with others leads to a deep sense of isola. The person feels alone and uncared for in life.

g. generativity vs. stagnation → Middle Adulthood

Generativity is expressed by caring about oneself, one's children, and the future. May be achieved by guiding one's own children or by helping other children. Failure in this is marked by a stagnant concern with one's own needs and comforts. Life loses meaning, and the person feels bitter, dreary and trapped.

h. integrity vs. despair → Late Adulthood

The previous seven stages of life become the basis for successful aging. A person richly and responsibly develops a sense of integrity which allows the person to face aging and death with dignity. If previous life events are viewed with regret, the elderly person falls into despair, which there is a feeling that life has been a series of missed opportunities, that one has failed, and that it is too late to reverse what is done. Age + death become a source of fear + depression.

5. Compare and contrast the following three parenting styles and their effects on children:

a. **authoritarian** - parents view their children as having few rights but adult-like responsibilities. Tends to demand strict adherence to rigid standards of behavior. (Do it because I say so!) The child is expected to stay out of trouble and to accept ~~what~~ without question what the parents regard as right or wrong behavior. The children are typically obedient + self-controlled. Tend to be emotionally stiff, withdrawn, apprehensive, and lacking in curiosity.

b. **overly permissive** → (Do what you want!) view children as having few responsibilities but rights similar to adults. Require little responsible behavior from their children. Rules are not enforced, and the child usually gets his or her way. TENDS to Produce dependent, immature children who misbehave frequently.

c. **effective (authoritative)** those parents who balance their own rights with those of their children. They are demanding but not authoritarian. Control their children's behavior, but they are also loving, caring, and responsive. Approach discipline in a way that is firm and consistent, not harsh or rigid. Encourage the child to act responsibly. Produces children who tend to be competent, self-controlled, independent, assertive, and inquiring

6. Discuss the positive and negative aspects of stress on a developing child.

Overprotection can be damaging as overly stressful

7. List and describe (where applicable) nine "normal" childhood problems.

a. sleep disturbances

b. Specific fears

c. overly timid

d. general dissatisfaction

e. general negativism

f. clinging

g. reversals or regressions

h. sibling rivalry

i. rebellion

8. Give a brief description of the following childhood disorders and their possible causes:

both can be a means of expressing frustration or pent-up hostility

a. **enuresis** lack of bladder control, more common than encopresis and more common amongst males than females. Some have difficulty because they become extremely relaxed when asleep.

b. **encopresis** lack of bowel control

c. **overeating** is sometimes encouraged by a parent who feels unloved and compensates by showering the child with "love" in the form of food. Overfed children develop eating habits and conflicts that have lifelong consequences.

d. **anorexia nervosa** is a serious case of undereating, or self starvation (nervous loss of appetite.) Victims are mostly adolescent females. May reflect conflicts about maturing sexually. Can limit figure development and prevent menstruation. Delays the time when they must face adult responsibilities

e. **pica** childhood eating difficulty. A period of intense appetite during which they chew or eat on all sorts of inedible substances. Two most common substances are plaster and chalk.

f. **delayed speech** sometimes caused by too little intellectual stimulation in early childhood. Other possible causes are parents who discourage the child's attempts to grow up, childhood stresses, mental retardation, and emotional disturbances

g. **stuttering** In the past, it was held to be a psychological disturbance. Now, is of physical origin. Learned fears, anxieties, and speech patterns probably add to the problem. Is most likely to occur when a person fears they are going to stutter.

9. **Describe what the label "learning disability" includes.** Include problems with thinking, perception, language, attention or activity levels.

10. **Briefly describe the following disorders in terms of symptoms, causes, and treatments:**
a. **dyslexia** - An inability to read with understanding. When trying to read, they often reverse letters and words. Some try to read from left to right. Caused by a malfunction of language processing areas on the left side of the brain. Typically treated by special educational programs

b. **ADHD** – Attention-deficit hyperactivity disorder – constantly in motion and cannot concentrate. Talks rapidly, cannot sit still, rarely finishes work, acts on impulse, cannot pay attention. Can be primarily cognitive or behavoral. Believed to result from a brain condition present at birth. Areas of the brain associated w/ language, motor control, and attention are smaller than normal. Treatment is through drugs, behavioral management approaches, and family counseling

11. **Describe childhood autism in terms of symptoms, causes and treatments.**
The autistic child is locked into a private world and appears to have no need for affection or contact with others. May throw gigantic temper tantrums – self destructive behavioral. Many children are mute. If they speak at all they parrot back everything, called echolalia. Also engage in frequent repetative actions. Also may show no response to loud noise (sensory blocking) or they may spend hours watching a water faucet drip (sensory "spin-out")
– Recognized that autism is caused by congenital defects in the nervous system. Defect may lie in the cerebellum.
– treatment : behavioral modification

12. **Describe the characteristics of abusive parents and the conditions likely to foster abusive behavior.**

13. Describe what can be done to prevent child abuse.

14. Define and differentiate between the terms adolescence and puberty.

Adolescence – the socially defined period btwn. childhood and adulthood

Puberty – the biologically defined period during which a person matures sexually and becomes capable of reproduction.

15. Discuss the advantages and disadvantages of early and late puberty for males and females.

males	females
early: enhances their self-image and gives them an advantage socially and athletically. –tend to be more poised, relaxed, dominant, self assured, and popular.	early: In element. school, tend to have less prestige among peers. By junior high, includes secondary sexual characteristics leads to a more positive body image, greater peer prestige, and adult approval. date sooner, in trouble at school
late: anxious about being behind. however, when they catch up they tend to be more eager, talkative, self assertive, and tolerant of themselves	late: advantage of growing taller + thinner

16. Explain what Elkind means by children being "hurried into adulthood." Explain how social markers are related to "hurried" adolescence. Parents are forcing their children to attempt new things, to excel themselves as early and as fast as possible.

For example, a parent may flash cards, read and have a child take swimming lessons before 3 months of age.

Social markers are related in that they tell where a person stands socially. For example, teenagers wearing seductive clothes.

17. With regards to the adolescent search for identity,
   a. explain what that means; ~~puberty signals a new~~

   b. discuss the importance of imaginary audiences;

   c. describe the interactions between an adolescent and his/her parents and peers as identity formation occurs; and,

   increased conflict w/ parents
   increased identification amongst peer groups

d.   explain how being a member of a minority influences the identity search.

experience a barrage of prejudice and negative stereotypes from the majority groups.

18.   List and describe the four broad phases (and any stages therein) of career development.

a.   *exploration phase → an initial search for career possibilities is made*

1.   *fantasy stage - children under 10 imagine what they want to be when they grow up. Roles may be unrealistic*

2.   *tentative stage - (ages 10-18) begin to form more realistic views of what they want to do. May shift plans many times. by end of highschool*

3.   *realistic stage - after high school, narrow their range of vocational options. what jobs are like and prepare for them.*

b.   *establishment phase → person finds a job, enters a career, develops competence, and gains status.*

c.   *midcareer phase → a time of high productivity and acceptance by co-workers.*

d.   *later career phase → the individual serves as a respected expert and often as a mentor for younger workers*

19.   State the single best predictor of the job category a person will enter. In addition, describe the two steps which aid a person in selecting a realistic and rewarding vocation. Include in your answer the influence of vocational counseling. *The best single predictor of what job category you will enter is your vocational aspiration, which is simply what you tell yourself you would like to do.*

→ Two steps: ① gain an accurate understanding of various occupations. ② get a clear picture of your own interests, needs, and goals.

→ A vocational counselor can help you clarify your career goals, and he or she can administer vocational interest

20.   Generally describe the pattern of adult life stages proposed by Roger Gould.

✳16-18: Escape from dominance = struggle to escape from parental dominance on cause anxiety about the future and conflicts about continuing dependence on parents.

✳ 18-22: Leaving the family: majority leave in 20's. Building new friendships with other adults. Serve as substitutes for the family

✳ 22-28: Building a workable life: striving for accomplishment and reaching out to others. Married couples place high value on "togetherness."

✳ 29-34: Crisis of Questions: what life is all about? search for a style to bring meaning to half of life remaining

✳ 35-43: Crisis of Urgency: more aware of reality of death. Attempts to succeed at a career or to achieve one's life goals.

21. Describe what a midlife crisis is and how it can be both a danger and an opportunity. Explain what a transition period is.

22. Distinguish between menopause and the male climacteric, and describe the typical reactions to each.

23. Contrast biological aging with our society's expectation of aging. Include a description of the differences between fluid and crystallized abilities.

24. Differentiate the concepts maximum life span and life expectancy. List six suggestions for increasing life expectancy.

25. Describe and distinguish between the disengagement and activity theories of aging.

26. Describe what is meant by the term ageism.

27.   List the myths of aging refuted by Neugarten's research as well as Ryff's criteria of well-being in old age.

28.   With regards to our emotional reactions concerning death,
a.   explain what people fear about death and how they cope with that fear;

b.   list and briefly characterize the five emotional reactions typically experienced by people facing death; and,
1. denial + isolation

2. anger

3. bargaining

4. depression

5. Acceptance

c.   explain how knowledge of the reactions to coping with death is important.

29.   Discuss the general characteristics of each stage of the bereavement process. Explain how suppressing the grieving process is related to later problems.

The following objectives are related to the material in the "Applications" and "Exploration" sections of your text.

30. Name the two most important areas of parent-child relationships.

    a.

    b.

31. Explain the importance of consistency in disciplining children.

32. Give a brief description of each of the following childrearing techniques and describe their effects on children:

    a.   power assertion

    b.   withdrawal of love

    c.   child management (include the concept of self-esteem)

33. List seven guidelines that should be followed if physical punishment and/or withdrawal of love are used in disciplining a child.

    a.

    b.

    c.

    d.

    e.

    f.

    g.

34. Briefly describe each of the four basic ingredients of a positive parent-child relationship.

  a.

  b.

  c.

  d.

35. Describe the four methods which can be used to improve communication between parents and children.

  a.

  b.

  c.

  d.

36. Describe the philosophy and functions of hospices.

37. Explain the purpose of a "living will."

38. Define the terms active euthanasia, passive euthanasia, and cryonics.

SELF-QUIZZES

Do You Know the Information?

Multiple Choice

1. Which of the following is *not* one of the universal life stages?
   (a) infancy
   (b) adolescence
   (c) mid-life crisis
   (d) old age

2. According to Erikson, successfully resolving the psychosocial dilemmas at each stage of life results in
   (a) a heightened sense of oneness with the universe.
   (b) a balance between a person's integrity and his or her selfhood.
   (c) healthy development and a satisfying life.
   (d) a reduction of a person's need to self-actualize.

3. During the first year of life, a favorable outcome to the life crisis discussed by Erikson would be
   (a) faith in the environment and others.
   (b) ability to begin one's own activities.
   (c) feelings of self-control and adequacy.
   (d) ability to form bonds of love and friendship with others.

4. According to Erikson, a major conflict in the first year of life is between
   (a) trust vs mistrust.
   (b) initiative vs guilt.
   (c) autonomy vs shame and doubt.
   (d) relatedness vs isolation.

5. Which psychosocial stage is the one in which a person's feelings of adequacy are shaped by his or her successes or failures in learning skills valued by society?
   (a) initiative vs guilt
   (b) industry vs inferiority
   (c) identity vs role confusion
   (d) autonomy vs shame and doubt

6. A favorable outcome to the life crisis of adolescence would include
   (a) an ability to feel intimate.
   (b) concern for family, society, and future generations.
   (c) an integrated image of oneself as a unique person.
   (d) confidence in productive skills, learning how to work

7. According to Erikson, the need to develop a sense of identity is the principal task of
   (a) middle childhood.
   (b) later adulthood.
   (c) early adulthood.
   (d) adolescence.

8. If the psychosocial dilemma of middle adulthood is favorably resolved, the outcome is a(n)
   (a) concern for family, society, and future generations.
   (b) confidence in productive skills, learning how to work.
   (c) feelings of self-control and adequacy.
   (d) ability to form bonds of love and friendship with others.

9. Which of the following would be *most* characteristic of authoritative parents?
   (a) The child usually gets his or her own way.
   (b) The parents tend to demand strict adherence to rules.
   (c) Discipline is firm and consistent but not rigid and harsh.
   (d) The children are usually obedient and self-controlled but they are also emotionally stiff, withdrawn, and apprehensive.

10. Which of the following statements regarding stress is *false*?
    (a) Confronting some problems can prepare a child to later tackle the demands of life.
    (b) Most children will do a good job of keeping stress at a comfortable level in activities *they* initiate.
    (c) Overprotection is generally viewed as more damaging to a child than too much stress.
    (d) Too much stress can result in certain childhood problems.

11. Of the following, which are considered normal reactions to the unavoidable stress of growing up?
    (a) sleep disturbances
    (b) sibling rivalry
    (c) autism
    (d) specific fears of the dark, school, etc.
    (e) clinging
    (f) enuresis
    (g) rebellion
    (h) hyperactivity
    (i) reversals to more infantile behaviors
    (j) general dissatisfaction

12. Lack of bowel control is called
    (a) bulimia.
    (b) MBD.
    (c) encopresis.
    (d) enuresis.

13. Anorexia nervosa is probably caused by
    (a) conflicts about sexual maturation.
    (b) striving for perfection or having a distorted body image.
    (c) getting attention from refusing to eat.
    (d) all of the above.

14. Which of the following is a type of eating disorder in which inedible objects are chewed or eaten?
    (a) pica
    (b) bulimia
    (c) overeating
    (d) compulsion

15. Most researchers now believe that stuttering is due to
    (a) physical problems.
    (b) angry, critical parents.
    (c) anxiety.
    (d) all of these.

16. Which of the following statements is *true*?
    (a) Learning disabilities include such things as problems with language, attention, and activity level.
    (b) Dyslexia is an inability to understand certain kinds of spoken language.
    (c) Dyslexia is probably caused by some minimal brain dysfunction.
    (d) Dyslexia is probably caused by left hemispheric dominance for language.

17. The most widely accepted theory of hyperactivity states that it is the result of
    (a) poor diet.
    (b) parental detachment.
    (c) small brain areas associated with language, motor control and attention.
    (d) too many stimulating drugs.

18. Which of the following does *not* characterize childhood autism?
    (a) language deficiencies
    (b) difficulties in forming social relationships
    (c) inability to sit still, encopresis, and overeating
    (d) violent temper tantrums and repetitive actions

19. Which of the following is a behavior in which spoken words are simply repeated in parroting, stereotyped manner?
    (a) encopresis
    (b) stuttering
    (c) echolalia
    (d) idioglossia

20. A therapy which has been an effective form of treatment for both hyperactivity and autism is
    (a) drug therapy.
    (b) withdrawal of love.
    (c) restraint or seclusion.
    (d) behavior modification.

21. Which of the following statements about child abuse is *incorrect?*
    (a) Abusive parents often have a high level of stress and frustration in their lives.
    (b) Most abused children are between the ages of three and eight.
    (c) Abusive parents are typically under 30 and from lower income levels.
    (d) Abusive mothers are likely to believe that their children are acting intentionally to annoy them.

22. With regards to preventing child abuse, which of the following is *not* a good idea?
    (a) finding a legal "cure" for this problem
    (b) attending a self-help group staffed by former child abusers
    (c) changing the attitudes of people so that physical punishment is less accepted
    (d) specific training to help parents curb violent impulses

23. Which of the following statements about puberty and adolescence is *false?*
    (a) Puberty refers to rapid physical growth and hormonal changes.
    (b) Adolescence refers to a period of time when we move from childhood to acceptance as adults.
    (c) For boys, early maturation is generally beneficial because it enhances their self-image.
    (d) Girls who are developmentally advanced in elementary school tend to have more prestige among their peers.

24. Which of the following statements about adolescence are *false?*
    (a) The conflicts between adolescents and their parents are usually over issues such as morals, religion, marriage, etc.
    (b) Elkind feels that our society is hurrying adolescents into adulthood and that the net effect is that they are left without sufficient guidance to make a healthy transition into adulthood.
    (c) Conformity to peer values peaks in early adolescence.
    (d) Many teenagers feel that they have an imaginary audience that is constantly evaluating them.
    (e) Minority teenagers are no different than those in mainstream society because they all share the same aspirations and the means to attain them.

25. According to Elkind and his overview of the social markers of our society,
    (a) it has become easier for adolescents to make the transition into adulthood.
    (b) children are being hurried into adulthood resulting in serious stress symptoms.
    (c) violence and youth crime have now become two of the new social markers.
    (d) teenagers are given adequate guidance today, more so than in times past.

26. In the _____ phase of career development productivity and acceptance by co-workers would probably be at their highest.
    (a) midcareer
    (b) establishment
    (c) later career
    (d) exploration

27. What is the single best predictor of the job category a person will enter?
    (a) father's profession
    (b) educational level
    (c) vocational aspiration
    (d) socioeconomic history

28. According to Gould, adults are striving for accomplishment during the _____ challenge.
    (a) crisis of questions
    (b) building a workable life
    (c) crisis of urgency
    (d) leaving the family

29. The midlife crisis may take the form of
    (a) breaking out of a seriously flawed life structure.
    (b) a serious midlife decline due to having chosen a dead-end job or lifestyle.
    (c) a last-chance effort to achieve goals.
    (d) all of the above.

30. Concerning menopause and the climacteric
    (a) during the latter, men suffer decreases in male hormone which produces many significant and varied physical symptoms.
    (b) most menopausal women report that the experience was worse than they expected because of the anxiety over not knowing what was going to happen.
    (c) most men suffer a decrease in fertility when their level of hormones drops.
    (d) none of the above statements are true.

31. Which of the following statements concerning aging is (are) *correct*?
    (a) IQ scores do not begin a rapid decline until a person is 80-85 years of age.
    (b) Biological aging begins in midlife or after.
    (c) The prime for most abilities occurs around ages 30-35.
    (d) Most older people prefer to live apart from their children.
    (e) Most elderly people eventually show signs of senility.

32. Which of the following statements is *true*?
    (a) Life expectancy refers to the boundary that limits the length of our lives.
    (b) It is important to remain socially and economically active in retirement.
    (c) It is possible to extend the human life span by following certain principles.
    (d) The actual number of years a person lives is called the maximum life span.

33. Which of the following postulates that people who remain psychologically, physically, and socially involved are better able to adjust to the aging process?
    (a) activation-arousal theory
    (b) engagement theory
    (c) disengagement theory
    (d) activity theory

34. In studies with adults concerning their fears about death,
    (a) 1/4 showed evidence of directly fearing their own death.
    (b) young and old alike feared the circumstances of their own death.
    (c) their responses reflected a deeply ingrained denial of death.
    (d) young and old alike feared the occurrence of their own death.

35. The first emotional reaction in dealing with death is usually
    (a) anger.
    (b) depression.
    (c) bargaining.
    (d) denial.

36. Which of the following statements regarding coping with death and dying is *incorrect*?
    (a) Knowing about the reactions to coping with death can help one deal with a dying person who may need to share feelings.
    (b) In general, one's approach to dying will be similar to the way the person handled other major problems in life.
    (c) The desire for silent companionship is indicative of depression in either the dying individual or a relative.
    (d) Knowledge of the stages of death and dying can help the survivors deal with the denial.

37. Regarding the process of bereavement, which of the following statements is *correct?*
     (a) A period of shock occurs when the survivor accepts the reality of their loss.
     (b) Signs of apathy in normal life may continue for months following the death of a friend or relative.
     (c) Pangs of grief occur with intense shock or numbness.
     (d) Suppressing grief leads to more severe and lasting depression.

38. The two most important areas of parent-child relationships are.
     (a) discipline and communication.   (c) communication and autonomy
     (b) discipline and autonomy.   (d) love and attention.

39. When rearing children, it is important to remember that
     (a) discipline can be as important as love.
     (b) the goal is to socialize a child without undue frustration.
     (c) consistency of parental standards is more important than the "strictness" of limits.
     (d) all of the above statements are true.

40. Withdrawal of love as a technique of discipline tends to produce children who are all of the following *except*
     (a) self-disciplined.   (c) defiant and rebellious.
     (b) anxious and insecure.   (d) dependent upon adult approval.

41. High self-esteem is related to the use of which style of discipline?
     (a) management techniques   (c) physical punishment
     (b) withdrawal of love   (d) guilt-oriented approaches

42. For punishment to be effective,
     (a) the act should be disapproved, not the child.
     (b) the use of physical punishment should be minimized before age 2 and after age 5.
     (c) it should be administered immediately after the misdeed.
     (d) all of the above must occur.

43. A positive parent-child relationship includes which of the following?
     (a) understanding of discipline limits   (c) shared enjoyment of each other
     (b) mutual respect   (d) using physical restraint instead of punishment

44. An "I" message is one which
     (a) tells children what effect their behavior has had on you.
     (b) sometimes takes the form of threats.
     (c) tell children what is wrong with them.
     (d) all of the above.

45. Which of the following statements is *false?*
     (a) Hospices try to give specialized care to the dying individual and improve their quality of life.
     (b) In active euthanasia, steps are actually taken to hasten death.
     (c) Cryonics is the science of extending a person's life.
     (d) A hospice is like a traditional hospital except that patients have much more freedom of choice over certain matters.

True-False

_____ 1. Pretend play during Erikson's stage 3 helps children practice identity achievement.

_____ 2. Most children do a good job of keeping stress at comfortable levels when they initiate an activity.

_____ 3. Evidence for stuttering being hereditary is the fact that it is four times more common in females than in males.

_____ 4. Puberty tends to dramatically increase body awareness and concerns about physical appearance.

_____ 5. Conformity to peer values peaks in late adolescence.

_____ 6. To find out beforehand what an occupation is like, it is best to consult with a vocational counselor.

_____ 7. Even though adult development is complex, Erikson's, Gould's, and Levinson's stages of development fit for nearly all people.

_____ 8. Although fluid abilities may decline with age, crystallized abilities appear to improve at least into the 70's.

_____ 9. Positive stereotypes of the elderly can be as much of a problem as negative ones.

_____10. At present, hospices are rarely found in large cities because hospitals there can provide those services.

_____11. Living wills are designed to allow death with dignity and are made out when the person is still healthy.

Can You Apply the Information?

1. Ralph decides to give up his high-paying job to join VISTA (Volunteers in Service to America). He is probably in which of Erikson's psychosocial crises?
    (a) generativity versus stagnation   (c) integrity versus despair
    (b) intimacy versus isolation   (d) autonomy versus shame and doubt

2. Mary is 85 years old and is trying to justify why she never went to work when she wanted to early in her marriage. She is also struggling with her atheistic views. She is probably
    (a) in Erikson's stage of initiative versus guilt.   (c) becoming senile.
    (b) in Erikson's stage of integrity vs. despair.   (d) suffering from ageism.

3. As a 23-year-old, Robert is very shy and has very few friends. He is socially withdrawn whenever he goes out, which in itself is rare. At work, he does what he is told even if he doesn't like it and always keeps his emotions in check. His unemotional nature has meant that he has never had a long-term relationship. His current personality may be a by-product of having had _____ parents.
    (a) authoritarian   (c) authoritative
    (b) permissive   (d) effective

4. Your 4-year-old has recently started asking for a light to be left on in her room at night because she is scared. You are concerned that this could be the beginning of either a bad habit or an all-consuming fear of the dark. What is your pediatrician *most* likely to tell you about the situation when you ask?
    (a) Specific fears are very common and you should not worry unless it lasts for a long time or worsens.
    (b) The next problem that will surface will be an excessive amoung of clinging.
    (c) This is a sign of regression to more infantile behavior.
    (d) If you let her have her way she will start showing a defiance of all adult authority.

5. Gail is 13 years old and is in the 8th grade. She is constantly on a diet and worried about her figure. She weighs 70 pounds and is 5 feet tall. Gail's problem is
    (a) a normal reaction of adolescence.
    (b) pica.
    (c) anorexia nervosa.
    (d) related to her dislike of school which is considered a normal reaction of childhood.

6. Paul reads the word "stop" as "tsop." Paul is probably suffering from
    (a) autism.
    (b) delayed speech.
    (c) bulimia.
    (d) dyslexia.

7. Roberta and Robert are both 11 years old and both of them just started puberty. Therefore, we could expect
    (a) Roberta to be taller than Robert.
    (b) Robert to have a better self-image than Roberta.
    (c) Roberta to have better relationships than Robert.
    (d) Robert to be less poised and dominant than Roberta.

8. Shannon is a 13-year-old adolescent. Her mother buys her a pair of jeans from a discount store. When she wears these jeans, she is sure that everyone knows they are cheap. Shannon is preoccupied with
    (a) social markers.
    (b) her imaginary audience.
    (c) her social network.
    (d) growth of her separate identity.

9. Bill and Christine have been married for a number of years and they have no children. They used to feel that togetherness was most important but are now starting to be unsure. In fact, both of them are secretly considering reaching out to others in an extramarital sort of way. Gould would describe them as
    (a) trying to build a workable life.
    (b) being in a crisis of questions.
    (c) being in a crisis of urgency.
    (d) failing to attain stability.

10. Stuart is 60 years old and worried about the inevitable overall decline in all abilities during old age. Which of the following statements apply?
    (a) He will probably become senile by age 90 as do most 90-year-olds.
    (b) Although his psychological functioning will decline his physical abilities need not change substantially if he stays physically fit.
    (c) His physical abilities will steadily decline as will his intellectual functioning.
    (d) None of the above apply.

11. Harriet is 70 years old and has been forced to retire from her job of 30 years. According to the disengagement theory she will probably
    (a) be depressed.
    (b) go out and get another job.
    (c) adapt reasonably well to the new situation.
    (d) do none of the above.

12. About 2 months ago Charles discovered that he has inoperable cancer and only a short time left. At this point, he envies his wife for her good health and is trying to make life miserable for her. He is probably in the _____ emotional reaction.
    (a) denial
    (b) anger
    (c) bargaining
    (d) depression

13. Anne, a 38-year-old mother of two, has terminal breast cancer which has metastasized to her brain. She has always been viewed as an extroverted person, the life of the party. Her impending death has been hard to accept for her family and close friends. What might be an important consideration in her situation?
    (a) that her friends and family will overcompensate and upset her by wanting to talk too much about her impending death
    (b) that expressing anger over the situation will have no real effect and serve no purpose for either her or the family
    (c) that the family help her through the five stages of emotional reaction to her impending death in the correct order
    (d) that people close to her will have a great deal of difficulty with the idea of her death and will end up making her feel isolated and alone

14. You receive a call from your daughter's third grade teacher. She is concerned about an incident that just occurred on the playground in which your daughter struck another girl. What is the best thing to do?
    (a) Spank your daughter when she comes home from school and take away her privileges.
    (b) Tell the teacher to spank your daughter since punishment should be immediate to be effective.
    (c) Tell your daughter what a bad girl she has been.
    (d) Tell your daughter that her behavior makes you feel ashamed and embarrassed.

15. Your 16-year-old son has been driving the family car all day against your wishes. You informed him that if he took the car without your permission he would be grounded for two weeks. When he returns home he will be subject to the
    (a) logical consequences of his actions.
    (b) natural consequences of his actions.
    (c) withdrawal of love discipline technique.
    (d) power assertion consequence of his actions.

16. Your 75-year-old grandfather has had a heart attack and three strokes. He is completely paralyzed and in pain. He begins to have fever and you and the doctors mutually agree not to treat the obvious infection. This is an example of
    (a) active euthanasia.
    (b) cryonics.
    (c) passive euthanasia.
    (d) putting him in a hospice.

Chapter Review

1. Even though every person is an individual, all people go through the broad universal _____ _____ of _____, childhood, _____, _____ adulthood, middle adulthood, and old age. Each stage confronts a person with a new set of _____ _____ to be mastered for optimal development.

2. Personality theorist Erik Erikson suggests that we face a specific _____ dilemma at each stage of life. Resolving these crises creates a new _____ between a person and the social world. An unfavorable outcome throws one off balance and makes it harder to deal with later _____.

3. During the first year of life, Erikson believes that a basic attitude of _____ or _____ is formed. A favorable outcome of this stage is faith in the _____.

4. During stage two (1-3 years), the life crisis involves _____ vs _____ and _____. Parents foster _____ by encouraging children to try new skills. Parents who _____ their children foster feelings of _____. Successful resolution of this stage would include the development of feelings of _____-_____ and _____.

5. During stage three (3-5 years), the child moves from simple self-control to an ability to take initiative. Thus, this stage involves the conflict of _____ vs _____. During stage three, parents can reinforce _____ by giving freedom to play, to ask questions, to use imagination, and to choose activities.

6. During stage four (6-12 years) the major crisis involves the development of _____ vs _____. If a child develops confidence in _____ skills, this stage has been resolved successfully.

7. During stage five, Erikson believes that _____ vs _____
    _____ is the major developmental task facing the individual. A child should complete this
    stage with an _____ self-image.

8. Stage six involves the psychosocial crisis of developing _____ or _____.
    The person should be able to form bonds of love or friendship with others if this stage has a favorable
    outcome.

9. During stage seven, _____ vs _____ is the major conflict. This
    period involves broadening one's concern and energies to include the welfare of others and society as a whole.

10. During the final life phase, old age, Erikson sees _____ vs _____ as the psycho-
    logical crisis that must be resolved. A person should leave this stage with a sense of
    _____ and _____.

11. Parents who view children as having few rights but adultlike responsibilities and who demand strict adherence
    to rules are called _____. In contrast _____ _____
    parents view children as having few responsibilities but rights similar to adults. _____
    parents are those who balance their rights with those of their children. They tend to encourage the child to act
    _____.

12. Although too much _____ may be harmful, too little may also be harmful. Parents should
    not be too _____. Most children do a good job of keeping _____
    at comfortable levels when they initiate activities.

13. There are several childhood problems which can be considered a normal part of growing up. One of these,
    _____ _____, is a common problem. All children experience
    occasional wakefulness, frightening dreams, or a desire to get into the parents' bed.

14. Specific _____ of the dark, dogs, school, or of a particular room or person are also common
    childhood problems. Most children will be overly _____ at times, allowing themselves to be
    bullied by other children. There may also be temporary periods of general _____ when
    nothing pleases the child. Children also normally display periods of general _____
    marked by tantrums or refusal to do anything requested.

15. Another normal problem is _____, in which the child refuses to leave his mother's
    side. Development does not always advance smoothly. Every child will show occasional
    _____ or _____ to more infantile behavior. Two additional
    problems common to the elementary school years are _____ _____ (not
    getting along with brothers and sisters) and _____ against rules and
    limitations of the adult world.

16. Severe emotional disturbances do affect children. Emotional difficulties may develop during
    _____-_____ or over bowel and bladder habits. The two most common prob-
    lems are _____ (lack of bladder control) and _____ (lack of bowel
    control). Both problems can be a means of expressing pent-up _____.

17. Feeding disturbances is another area of emotional difficulty. _____ may be encouraged
    by a parent who compensates for feeling unloved by showering the child with "love" in the form of food.

18.   Serious cases of undereating are called _____ _____ (nervous loss of appetite). Most people who suffer this disorder are usually adolescent _____. This disorder may represent conflicts about _____ maturity.

19.   Another childhood problem associated with eating difficulties is a condition called _____, during which children go through a period of intense appetite and eat or chew on all sorts of inedible substances.

20.   Two common speech problems are _____ _____ and _____. A child may fail to learn language because of a general lack of _____. Stuttering was once held to be primarily a psychological disturbance; it is now believed to be more _____ in origin. However, learned _____, _____, and _____ patterns probably add to the problem as well.

21.   Learning disabilities include problems with _____, _____, _____, _____, or _____ levels. An inability to read with understanding is called _____. Researchers suspect that this disorder is related to a malfunction of _____ processing areas on the left hemisphere.

22.   A child may experience difficulties in learning for many reasons. One of the most significant problems is attention-deficit _____ disorder (___ ___ ___ ___), a condition in which the child is constantly in motion and cannot concentrate. The most widely accepted theory of this condition states that it is the result of smaller than normal brain areas associated with _____, _____ _____, and _____. Medical authorities advocate the use of _____ drugs. However, a number of psychologists have objected to the blanket use of these drugs and instead advocate the use of _____ _____.

23.   _____ is one of the most severe childhood problems. In addition to extreme _____, the child may throw gigantic _____ _____ including self-destructive behavior. _____ learning is usually so retarded that the child is mute. If these children speak at all, they often parrot back everything said, a reaction known as _____.

24.   Experts used to blame parents for autism. It is now recognized that autism is caused by _____ defects in the _____ _____ probably in the area of the _____. The therapy which has had the greatest success in treating autism is _____ _____.

25.   Abusive parents are usually under _____ years of age and are from _____ income levels. They often have a high level of _____ and _____ in their lives. The typical abused child is generally under _____ years of age. Abusive mothers are more likely to believe that their children are acting _____ to annoy them.

26.   There are _____ cures for child abuse including _____ homes and court _____ for the _____ while living with their _____. Also, there are _____-_____ groups. A third way of helping is through changing the _____ of our society toward _____ _____.

27. The period during which we move from childhood to acceptance as an adult is called
_____. _____ is a biological event. The growth spurt occurs roughly
two years earlier for _____ than it does for _____. For boys, early maturation is generally
_____. For girls in elementary school, those who are developmentally
_____ seem to have less prestige among peers, but this is reversed by junior high school.

28. Many teenagers believe that everyone seems to be watching everything he or she does. This is called their
_____ _____.

29. Elkind feels that we are _____ teenagers too much and that they will be left without
sufficient _____ to make a healthy transition to adulthood. This has occurred
because the traditional _____ _____ of adolescence have
disappeared.

30. The adolescent search for identity often results in increased _____ with parents, but usually
only in _____ areas of importance. Adolescents from minority cultures face a
barrage of _____ and _____ stereotypes from the
majority culture. Even though they share the hopes, dreams, and _____ of the
mainstream society, minority youth do not share the same _____ to attain their goals.

31. Career development tends to go through four phases: (1) the _____ phase during which
an initial search for a career possibilities is made; (2) the _____
phase when the person settles in; (3) the _____ phase which is the time of
highest productivity and acceptance by co-workers; and (4) the _____
_____ phase when the person may serve as a respected expert.

32. The best single predictor of what job category you will enter is your _____
_____, which is simply what you tell yourself you would like to do.

33. To make sure your vocational choice will be realistic and personally rewarding, you must: (1) gain an
accurate _____ of various occupations and (2) get a clear picture of your
own _____, _____, and _____.

34. The easiest way to improve occupational choice is to consult a _____
counselor. If one is not available, most libraries carry the _____
_____ Handbook which includes job descriptions, requirements, and earnings for
most jobs available in the marketplace. Another option is to talk to people in that line of work and
_____ people in an occupation that interests you.

35. Certain relatively consistent events, according to Roger Gould, mark adult development in our society. These
range from escaping _____ _____ in the late teens to a
noticeable acceptance of one's _____ in the late forties. Some research indicates that a
_____ _____ affects many people in the 37-41 age range. This is just
another time at which a person undergoes a _____ period when one life pattern is
ended and the door to new possibilities is opened.

36. Adjustment to later middle age may be complicated for women by _____ and for men
by a _____. For women, the level of the hormone _____ drops.
Males do not undergo such dramatic physical changes. Decreases in male _____
output may cause _____ symptoms similar to a woman's. Many of a male's symptoms are probably due to _____-_____.

37. _____ _____ is a gradual process that begins early in life. Peak functioning in most physical capacities reaches a maximum by about _____ to _____ years of age and then
gradually declines. For those who are still young, the prospect of physical aging may be the largest threat of
old age. However, only about _____ percent of the elderly are in nursing homes.

38. The length of our lives is limited by a boundary called the maximum _____ _____.
For most people, _____ _____ (the actual number of years the average person
lives) is shorter.

39. _____ (those who study aging) believe that only about _____ percent
of the disability of old people is medically based. For example, regarding intelligence, _____
abilities (those requiring speed) may decline with age, yet _____ abilities
(such as vocabulary) seem to improve with age.

40. The _____ theory of aging assumes that it is normal and desirable for
people to withdraw from society as they age. The second view, the _____
theory, predicts that people who remain active physically, mentally, and socially will adjust better to aging.

41. Discrimination or prejudice on the basis of age is called _____. Studies of the elderly
generally contradict most of the misconceptions about them. Studies show them to be
_____, _____, and _____
healthy. Generally, the six criteria of well-being in old age are as follows: (1) self-
_____; (2) positive _____ with others; (3)
_____ (personal freedom); (4) environmental _____; (5) a
purpose in life; and, (6) continued personal _____.

42. People often _____ their fears of death or fear the _____ of the dying
rather than the death itself. Elisabeth Kubler-Ross has found that the dying person tends to have five basic
emotional reactions. They are (in order) _____, _____,
_____, _____, and
_____.

43. Not all terminally ill individuals display these reactions, and they may not occur in this
_____. Knowledge of these reactions is important because it can help both the dying
individual and the survivors cope with the emotional upheaval. It is also important to note that a dying person
may need to share _____ and talk about _____ openly.
Someone who does not have all of these reactions is not somehow
_____.

44. Bereavement and grief generally begins with _____. This is followed by
pangs of _____. This gradually gives way to weeks or months of
_____, _____, and _____.
Little by little, the pangs of grief diminish and the person is said to be moving toward
_____. Research has shown that a lack of intense _____
does not usually predict later problems.

45. As a single problem area in development, the question of how to be a good parent has probably attracted more
attention than any other. Much of the answer can be found in _____ and
_____.

46. Discipline and _____ appear essential for healthy development with effective discipline being both _____ and _____. On the other hand, the strictness of the limits is less important than the _____ of parental standards.

47. Parents tend to base discipline on one or more of the following techniques: _____ _____, _____ of _____, or _____ _____.

48. Power-oriented techniques are associated with _____ and _____ of parents, and a lack of spontaneity and warmth. Severely punished children also tend to be _____, _____, and _____.

49. Withdrawal of love produces children who tend to be _____-_____. As a side-effect they are also frequently _____, _____, and _____ on adults for approval.

50. High _____-_____ was related to management techniques which emphasized strict and consistent discipline coupled with high parental interest and concern for the child.

51. If punishment is to be used parents should separate disapproval of the _____ from disapproval of the _____. They should state specifically what _____ is being punished. Punishment should never be _____ or _____ to a child. Punishment is most effective if it is delivered _____. Physical punishment is not particularly effective before age _____ or after age _____. Reserve _____ punishment for situations that pose danger for the child. Remember that it is usually more effective to _____ good behavior.

52. There appear to be four ingredients of a positive parent-child relationship: _____ _____, _____ _____, _____ and _____.

53. In helping to establish good communication between parents and children it is important to help children understand that all feelings are _____; only _____ are subject to disapproval. Supportive parents also _____ their children.

54. Dr. Thomas Gordon, who has developed a program called Parent Effectiveness Training (PET), believes that parents should send _____ messages instead of _____ messages.

55. Children are greatly influenced by the _____ of their _____. Some of these are _____ which means that they follow naturally from the behavior, whereas some are _____ meaning that they are _____ and _____ as well as being defined by the parents.

56. A _____ is basically a hospital for the terminally ill, modeled after a pioneering English facility. It is different from a hospital in several ways. For one, there are many _____ present. Second, the _____ is pleasant, informal, and has a sense of continued living. And third, the patient is allowed freedom of _____ concerning diet, drugs, etc.

57. The intent of a _____ _____ is to free the terminally ill from a slow and cruel death, allowing death with _____.

58.   When death is allowed to occur naturally but is not actively caused this is called
_____ _____. When death is actively caused the act
is called _____ _____. Freezing a person's body upon death
with the idea of thawing it out later when a cure is found for whatever killed him or her is called
_____.

ANSWER KEYS

Do You Know the Information?

Multiple Choice

1.   (c) obj. 1, p. 416
2.   (c) obj. 3, p. 416
3.   (a) obj. 4, pp. 416, 419
4.   (a) obj. 4, p. 416
5.   (b) obj. 4, p. 417
6.   (c) obj. 4, pp. 417, 419
7.   (d) obj. 4, p. 417
8.   (a) obj. 4, pp. 417, 419
9.   (c) obj. 5, p. 420
10. (c) obj. 6, p. 420
11. (a,b,d,e,g,i,j) obj. 7, pp. 420–421
12. (c) obj. 8, p. 421
13. (d) obj. 8, p. 421
14. (a) obj. 8, p. 421
15. (d) obj. 8, p. 421
16. (a) obj. 9, p. 422
17. (c) obj. 10, p. 422
18. (c) obj. 11, p. 423
19. (c) obj. 11, p. 423
20. (d) objs.10–11, pp. 422–423
21. (b) obj. 12, p. 424
22. (a) obj. 13, p. 424
23. (d) objs.14–15, p. 426
24. (a,e) objs.16–17, pp. 426–428
25. (b) obj. 16, pp. 426–427

26. (a) obj. 18, p. 428
27. (c) obj. 19, p. 429
28. (b) obj. 20, p. 430
29. (d) obj. 21, pp. 431–432
30. (d) obj. 22, p. 432
31. (d) objs.23,27, pp. 433–436
32. (b) obj. 24, p. 434
33. (d) obj. 25, p. 434
34. (c) obj. 28, p. 436
35. (d) obj. 28, p. 436
36. (c) obj. 28, p. 437
37. (d) obj. 29, p. 438
38. (a) obj. 30, p. 439
39. (d) obj. 31, p. 439
40. (c) obj. 32, p. 440
41. (a) obj. 32, p. 440
42. (d) obj. 33, pp. 440–441
43. (b,c) obj.34, p. 441
44. (a) obj. 35, p. 442
45. (c) objs.36,38, pp. 443–445

True-False

1.   F, obj. 4, p. 417
2.   T, obj. 6, p. 420
3.   F, obj. 8, p. 421
4.   T, obj. 14, p. 426

5.   F, obj. 17, p. 428
6.   F, obj. 19, p. 429
7.   F, obj. 21, p. 432
8.   T, obj. 23, p. 434
9.   T, obj. 27, p. 435
10. F, obj. 36, p. 444
11. T, obj. 37, p. 444

Can You Apply the Information?

1.   (a) obj. 4, p. 417
2.   (b) obj. 4, p. 418
3.   (a) obj. 5, p. 419
4.   (a) obj. 7, p. 420
5.   (c) obj. 8, p. 421
6.   (d) obj. 10, p. 422
7.   (b) objs.14–15, pp. 425–426
8.   (b) obj. 17, p. 427
9.   (b) obj. 20, p. 430
10. (d) objs.23, 27, pp. 433–436
11. (c) obj. 25. p. 434
12. (b) obj. 28, p. 436
13. (d) obj. 28, p. 437
14. (d) obj. 35, pp. 441–442
15. (a) obj. 35, p. 442
16. (c) obj. 38, p. 445

Chapter Review

1.   life stages, infancy, adolescence, young, developmental tasks (p. 416)
2.   psychosocial, balance, crises (p. 416)
3.   trust, mistrust (p. 416); environment (p. 419)
4.   autonomy, shame, doubt, autonomy, ridicule (overprotect), shame (doubt) (p. 416); self-control, adequacy (p. 419)
5.   initiative, guilt, initiative (p. 417)
6.   industry, inferiority (p. 417); productive (p. 419)
7.   identity, role confusion (p. 417); integrated (p. 419)
8.   intimacy, isolation (p. 417)
9.   generativity, stagnation (p. 417)

10.   integrity, despair (p. 418); dignity, fulfillment (p. 419)
11.   authoritarian, overly permissive, Authoritative (p. 419); responsibly (p. 420)
12.   stress, overprotective, stress (p. 420)
13.   sleep disturbances (p. 420)
14.   fears, timid, dissatisfaction, negativism (p. 420)
15.   clinging, reversals, regressions, sibling rivalry (p. 420); rebellion (p. 421)
16.   toilet-training, enuresis, encopresis, hostility (frustration) (p. 421)
17.   Overeating (p. 421)
18.   anorexia nervosa, females, sexual, (p. 421)
19.   pica (p. 421)
20.   delayed speech, stuttering, stimulation, physical, fears, anxieties, speech (p. 421)
21.   thinking, perception, language, attention, activity, dyslexia, language (p. 422)
22.   hyperactivity, language, motor control, attention, stimulant, behavior modification (p. 422)
23.   Autism, isolation, temper tantrums, Language, echolalia (p. 423)
24.   congenital, nervous system, cerebellum, behavior modification (p. 423)
25.   30, lower, stress, frustration (p. 423); three, intentionally (p. 424)
26.   legal, foster, supervision, children, parents, self-help, attitudes, physical punishment (p. 424)
27.   adolescence, Puberty, girls, boys (p. 425); beneficial, advanced (p. 426)
28.   imaginary audience (p. 427)
29.   hurrying, guidance (direction, support), social markers (p. 426)
30.   conflict, superficial (p. 427); prejudice, negative, aspirations, means (p. 428)
31.   exploration, establishment, midcareer, later career (p. 428)
32.   vocational aspiration (p. 429)
33.   understanding, interests, needs, goals (p. 429)
34.   vocational, *Occupational Outlook* (p. 429); observe (p. 430)
35.   parental dominance (p. 430); fate, midlife crisis, transition (p. 431)
36.   menopause, climacteric, estrogen, hormone (p. 432); psychological, self-doubt (p. 433)
37.   Biological aging, 25, 30, 5 (p. 433)
38.   life span (p. 433); life expectancy (p. 434)
39.   Gerontologists, 25, fluid, crystallized (p. 434)
40.   disengagement, activity (p. 434)
41.   ageism (p. 435); integrated, active, psychologically, acceptance, relations, autonomy, mastery, growth (p. 436)
42.   deny, circumstances, denial, anger (p. 436); bargaining, depression, acceptance (p. 437)
43.   order, feelings, death, deviant (immature), (p. 437)
44.   shock, grief (p. 437); apathy, dejection, depression, resolution, grief (p. 438)
45.   communication, discipline (p. 439)
46.   love, authoritative, sensitive, consistency (p. 439)
47.   power assertion, withdrawal, love, child management (p. 440)
48.   fear, hatred, defiant, rebellious, aggressive (p. 440)
49.   self-disciplined, anxious, insecure, dependent (p. 440)
50.   self-esteem (p. 440)
51.   act, child, misbehavior, harsh, injurious, immediately, two, five, physical, reinforce (p. 441)
52.   mutual respect, shared enjoyment, love, encouragement (p. 441)
53.   appropriate, actions (behaviors) (p. 441); encourage (p. 442)
54.   I, you (p. 442)
55.   consequences, actions, natural, logical, rational, reasonable (p. 442)
56.   hospice, people, atmosphere, choice (p. 444)
57.   living will, dignity (p. 444)
58.   passive euthanasia, active euthanasia, cryonics (p. 445)

Chapter 16

Dimensions of Personality

KEY TERMS, CONCEPTS, AND INDIVIDUALS

personality defined
character, temperament
trait vs. type approach
self-concept
personality theory
trait defined
types of traits
   common vs. individual
   cardinal, central, secondary (Allport)
   surface vs. source (Cattell)
      factor analysis
      16 PF, trait profile
five-factor model of personality
trait-situation interaction
ordinal position effects
parental emotional set
androgyny
   adaptability
personality assessment

interview — structured vs. unstructured
   halo effect
   direct observation
   rating scale
behavioral assessment
   situational testing
   personality questionnaire
      MMPI
projective tests
   ambiguous stimulus
   Rorschach Inkblot
   Thematic Apperception
limits of assessment techniques
sudden murderers
shyness
   elements, causes, dynamics
overcoming shyness
behavioral genetics
   twin studies — the influence of heredity

LEARNING OBJECTIVES

To demonstrate mastery of this chapter you should be able to:
1. Define the term personality, distinguishing it from character and temperament. Explain how personality is a hypothetical construct.

2.   Define the term trait. (pp. 450-452) Distinguish between "trait" and "type" approaches to personality, and explain the shortcoming of the type approach.

3.   Explain what the self-concept is and how it affects behavior and personal adjustment.

4.   Define the term personality theory. Discuss the functions of personality theories.

5.   Distinguish common traits from individual traits.

6.   Define, differentiate, and give examples of Allport's cardinal traits, central traits, and secondary traits.

7.   Distinguish between surface traits and source traits, and state how Cattell measures source traits.

8.   Explain how Cattell's approach to personality traits differs from Allport's approach.

9.   Discuss the five-factor model of personality.

10.   Discuss the relationship of personality traits and external circumstances to behavior (i.e., the trait-situation interaction).

11.   Explain how environment affects personality as evidenced by studies of birth order.

12.   Describe the possible outcomes of being a firstborn child versus a later-born child, and explain the reasons for the differences associated with birth order.

13.   Explain the meaning of the term "androgyny" and its relationship to masculinity, femininity, and adaptability.

14.   Discuss the following assessment techniques in terms of purpose, method, advantages, and limitations:
   a.   structured and unstructured interviews

   b.   direct observation combined with rating scales, behavioral assessment and situational testing.

   c.   personality questionnaires (MMPI).

   d.   projective tests Rorschach, TAT.

15.   Describe the personality characteristics of sudden murderers, and explain how their characteristics are related to the nature of their homicidal actions.

* * * * * * * * * *

The following objectives are related to the material in the "Applications" and "Exploration" sections of your text.

16.   With regards to the dynamics of shyness,
   a.   list and describe the three elements of shyness. State what usually causes shyness.
      1.

      2.

      3.

   b.   compare the personality of the shy and the nonshy. Include the concepts of labeling and self-esteem.

   c.   list four self-defeating beliefs that maintain, and six attitudes which combat, shyness.
      beliefs
      1.
      2.
      3.
      4.

      attitudes
      1.
      2.
      3.
      4.
      5.
      6.

17.   Describe how social skills can be developed by opening lines and conversation.

18.   Define the term behavioral genetics.

19.   Explain how twin studies are used to assess the relative contributions of heredity and environment to a person's personality. Discuss how the similarities in the personalities of twins can be explained. Assess the relative contributions of heredity and environment to the makeup of personality.

SELF-QUIZZES

Do You Know the Information?

Multiple Choice

1.   Personality is
     (a) a person's unique and enduring behavior patterns.
     (b) best typified by the type approach.
     (c) made up of surface and cardinal traits.
     (d) the same as temperament.

2.   Of the following, which implies an evaluation of the person?
     (a) temperament   (c) hypothetical construct
     (b) character   (d) personality

3.   A hypothetical construct
     (a) is something which does not really exist.
     (b) refers to things which are impossible to measure.
     (c) is used to establish the basis of temperament.
     (d) is not directly observable.

4.   Which of the following statements about types and traits is *incorrect*?
     (a) The trait approach attempts to specify those traits which best describe a particular individual.
     (b) The trait approach tends to oversimplify personality.
     (c) Personality traits are relatively permanent and enduring qualities that a person shows in most situations.
     (d) A personality type represents a category of individuals who have a number of traits in common.

5. A person's self-concept
   (a) determines what he/she pays attention to, remembers, and how events are interpreted.
   (b) represents a person's perception of how others view him or her.
   (c) has a minor influence on our behavior.
   (d) is built out of how we imagine other people view us.

6. Which of the following is a *correct* match?
   (a) trait theories — inner workings of personality as they relate to behavior
   (b) psychodynamic theories — importance of the external environment
   (c) behavioristic theories — personal growth as an extension of conditioning and learning
   (d) humanistic theories — private, subjective experience

7. Traits which are shared by most members of a culture are classified by Allport as _____ traits.
   (a) cardinal
   (b) central
   (c) secondary
   (d) common

8. According to Allport some traits are so basic that all of a person's activities can be traced to existence of these traits. Allport calls such traits
   (a) central traits.
   (b) cardinal traits.
   (c) source traits.
   (d) secondary traits.

9. Cattell attributes _____ traits to more basic underlying characteristics called _____ traits.
   (a) individual, common
   (b) surface, source
   (c) common, cardinal
   (d) central, cardinal

10. Cattell's Sixteen Personality Factor Questionnaire is designed to measure
    (a) cardinal traits.
    (b) central traits.
    (c) source traits.
    (d) surface traits.

11. Cattell's approach to personality differs from Allport's approach in that Cattell
    (a) asked random subjects to rank order what they considered to be the most important personality traits.
    (b) classified traits subjectively.
    (c) used a more circular research procedure than Allport did.
    (d) tried to be more objective by using factor analysis to reduce surface traits to source traits.

12. The five-factor theory of personality is an attempt to
    (a) relate the MMPI to a trait profile.
    (b) uncover the most basic dimensions of personality.
    (c) use the 16PF as a diagnostic tool.
    (d) identify the most salient cardinal traits.

13. Trait-situation interactions would predict that
    (a) although your behavior might be different in different situations, your underlying personality traits would still be apparent.
    (b) your behavior would probably be about the same in most situations because of your personality traits.
    (c) the situation is more important than the relevant personality trait.
    (d) your behavior would be different in different situations because traits cannot predict a person's behavior.

14. Which of the ordinal positions of birth is *most* likely to produce a child with high self-expectations, anxiety, and conformity?
    (a) first
    (b) middle
    (c) last
    (d) they are all about equal

15. A man who is androgynous
    (a) would be more nurturant than a masculine man.
    (b) would have a higher feminine score than a masculine score on the BSRI.
    (c) would be less adaptable than other males.
    (d) would have a higher masculine score than a feminine score on the BSRI.

16. Which is *not* considered a limitation of interviewing?
    (a) The interviewer may overlook certain qualities in his own personality.
    (b) The interviewer may affect what is said.
    (c) The interviewer can be swayed by preconceptions.
    (d) The interviewer may uncover relevant body language cues.

17. A valuable technique for improving the accuracy of direct observation is the use of
    (a) personality questionnaires.   (c) projective devices.
    (b) introspection.   (d) rating scales.

18. "Shoot—Don't Shoot" training is a good example of
    (a) a behavioral assessment.   (c) the halo effect.
    (b) situational testing.   (d) rating scales.

19. Probably the best known and the most widely used objective test of personality is the
    (a) 16 PF.   (c) Rorschach.
    (b) MMPI.   (d) TAT.

20. Which of the following statements about the MMPI is *incorrect*?
    (a) The answer to a single item usually reveals something important about a person's personality.
    (b) By comparing a person's profile with scores produced by normal adults, various disorders can be identified.
    (c) There are validity scales to detect if a person is trying to look better or worse than he/she really is.
    (d) One of the problems with the MMPI is that people other than psychologists may use it.

21. Of the following, which is designed to uncover deep-seated or unconscious wishes, thoughts, and needs?
    (a) personality questionnaires   (c) behavioral assessments
    (b) projective tests   (d) direct observation

22. Ambiguous stimuli are part of which type of assessment technique?
    (a) direct observation   (c) projective tests
    (b) personality inventories   (d) situational testing

23. Projective tests of personality
    (a) are considered almost worthless by most clinicians.
    (b) are computer scored.
    (c) are extremely reliable.
    (d) are low in validity.

24. Sudden murderers have been found to
    (a) be masculine and undercontrolled.
    (b) be shy, restrained, and inexpressive.
    (c) be aggressive and impulsive and become violent because of their unrestrained impulses.
    (d) not show any significant pathology on personality tests.

25. Which of the following is *not* one of the three elements of shyness?
   (a) self-defeating mental bias
   (b) social anxiety
   (c) lack of eye contact
   (d) underdevelopment of social skills

26. Which of the following statements about shyness is *incorrect?*
   (a) Shy people tend to consider their social anxiety to be caused by external situations.
   (b) People who are shy are high in public self-consciousness.
   (c) Nonshy persons tend to have higher self-esteem than shy persons.
   (d) Nonshy persons give themselves credit for successes.

27. Behavioral genetics refers to the
   (a) study of genetically determined physical characteristics.
   (b) selective breeding of characteristics like intelligence and personality.
   (c) effect of genes on personality.
   (d) study of inherited behavioral traits.

28. Which of the following statements regarding the influence of heredity on personality is *false?*
   (a) Identical twins who are reared apart are used to compare the similarity of their personality traits.
   (b) Identical twins usually are similar in traits such as dominance and extroversion.
   (c) Separated twins tend to share similar talents such as art, music, or dance.
   (d) A number of studies suggest that heredity may account for as much as 40 to 50 percent of the variation in personality traits.
   (e) The fallacy of positive instances may explain some of the astounding similarities between twins.

True-False

_____ 1. Temperament implies that a person has been evaluated, not just described.

_____ 2. Psychologists are hesitant to speak of personality "types" because this approach tends to oversimplify personality.

_____ 3. A system of assumptions, ideas, and principles used to explain personality is called a hypothetical construct.

_____ 4. Birth order effects are probably caused by increased parental attention, concern, anxiety, and expectations.

_____ 5. A person who is androgynous can be more adaptable and flexible according to what the situation demands.

_____ 6. The interview is called structured if the interviewee is allowed to determine what subjects are discussed.

_____ 7. Personality questionnaires are more subjective than interviews or observation.

_____ 8. The MMPI investigates patterns of responses rather than relying upon single items to assess personality.

_____ 9. "Sudden murderers" are likely to be habitually violent and impulsive individuals who feel cheated or betrayed.

_____10. Shyness is most often triggered by novel or unfamiliar social situations.

_____11. "I don't need to pretend to be someone I'm not; it just makes me more anxious" is an example of an innocuous opening line.

Can You Apply the Information?

1. A proud father is talking about his new son. "That kid was born with lots of personality." Technically, his statement is
   (a) True   (b) False

2. David views himself as a person who can't cope with the world. He believes that almost everyone thinks that he is stupid. If he was warmly welcomed into a room by nine people and the tenth person was rather cool toward him, he would interpret the situation as having been totally rejecting and that nobody liked him. It is probable that David
   (a) would score poorly on the MMPI.
   (b) would be evaluated as not having much character.
   (c) has a very poor self-concept.
   (d) has fewer positive personality traits than the average person.

3. The Scottish are thrifty. This is a _____ trait.
   (a) central   (c) cardinal
   (b) source   (d) common

4. Bill is considered timid. This is a _____ trait.
   (a) central   (c) common
   (b) secondary   (d) cardinal

5. At the end of football practice today, Edgar "high-fived" all of his teammates as they left the locker room. Tonight as he leaves his church choir practice, Edgar will probably also "high-five" the other choir members.
   (a) True   (b) False

6. Bob is tough, ambitious, competitive, and creative at work. When he gets home he is tender and loving to his children and warm and affectionate to his wife. These traits
   (a) are common traits.   (c) can be considered cardinal traits.
   (b) reveal that Bob is probably a firstborn child.   (d) indicate that Bob is probably androgynous.

7. Sigmund is a college professor but also operates a business on the side. He hires Susan, one of his best students, because he figures if she is such a good student she'll make a great oyster shucker. Sigmund is
   (a) confusing central traits and source traits.   (c) assuming that Susan is androgynous.
   (b) suffering from the halo effect.   (d) in need of a personality questionnaire.

8. Regina is obsessive-compulsive and washes her hands up to 300 times per day. In order to show her how often she engages in this behavior and to accurately inform her therapist of the exact magnitude of the problem, the nurses on the ward decide to
   (a) do a rating scale.   (c) do a behavioral assessment on Regina.
   (b) give her a projective test.   (d) administer a personality questionnaire to Regina.

9. In order to see how a secretary performs under the pressure of the job, the corporation executives decide to give each job applicant a
   (a) situational test.   (c) trait factor test.
   (b) computer simulation.   (d) rating scale.

10. You suspect that your patient has repressed a traumatic event from childhood. Which personality assessment technique seems most appropriate for this situation?
    (a) direct observation   (c) a projective test
    (b) a personality questionnaire   (d) situational testing

11. John is 30 years old. He is very quiet and shy and keeps his emotions and actions under tight control. What might you expect when he gets angry and releases his rigid self-control?
   (a) an overreaction to the situation and perhaps violence
   (b) no more reaction than he ever shows because research indicates that these individuals do not lose control
   (c) an underreaction to the situation since this is his predominant mode of responding
   (d) guilt, embarrassment, and neurotic anxiety

Chapter Review

1. Personality is considered a _____ construct. Most psychologists regard personality as one's _____ and _____ _____ patterns. Personality is different from character, which implies that a person has been _____. The raw material from which personality is formed is called _____.

2. Psychologists think of _____ as lasting qualities within a person that are inferred from observed behavior. The study of personality _____ is a natural extension of interest in personality. We often speak of the executive type, the motherly type, the strong, silent type, etc. However, too frequently they represent an _____ of personality.

3. A person's perception of his or her own personality traits is called the _____-_____. It greatly affects personal adjustment by determining how we _____ events.

4. A system of assumptions, ideas, and principles proposed to explain personality is called a _____   _____.

5. Allport makes a distinction between _____ and _____ traits. _____ traits are those shared by most members of a culture and help reveal the similarities among people. _____ traits characterize unique personal characteristics.

6. Allport has also distinguished three other types of traits. _____ traits are so basic that all of a person's activities can be traced to the existence of the trait. _____ traits are the basic building blocks that make up the core of personality. _____ traits are less consistent and less important aspects of a person.

7. Cattell distinguishes between the visible portions of personality called _____ traits and the underlying personality characteristics called _____ traits. Allport classifies traits _____, whereas Cattell used _____ _____.

8. Cattell's list of _____ traits forms the basis of a personality test called the _____ _____ _____. The attempt to reduce Cattell's list down to five factors has resulted in the _____-_____ model of personality. The factors are _____, _____, _____, _____, and _____ to experience.

9. Personality traits show a degree of _____ over time, but also _____ can exert a powerful influence on behavior. This is called the _____-_____ interaction.

10. Birth order, or _____ _____, in a family can leave a lasting imprint on adult personality, the clearest differences being between firstborn and later-born children. The firstborn seem to have a higher chance of achieving _____ than later-born children, but are also _____, more conforming, and more likely to be _____ under stress than later-born persons. Later-born persons tend to excel in _____ relationships. They are affectionate, friendly, and at ease with others.

11. The reason for these differences seems to lie in the "_____ _____" parents bring to each child. The first born often get more _____, praise, and concern with high parental _____ translated into high self-expectations. However, the inexperienced parents of the firstborn are more _____ and _____, which results in higher levels of anxiety and a tendency to conform to adult values.

12. Sandra Bem developed the Bem Sex Role Inventory (BSRI) to classify individuals as traditionally masculine, feminine, or _____ (literally meaning "man-woman"). If a person is in the latter category, he/she would be considered _____ with respect to sex roles and could act as the _____ requires.

13. Psychologists use various tools to assess personality. A very direct way to learn about a person's personality is to engage in conversation. An _____ is described as _____ if the conversation is informal and the_____ is allowed to determine what subjects are discussed. In a _____ _____, information is obtained by asking a series of preplanned questions.

14. Interviews are used to identify personality _____, to select persons for _____, _____, or special programs, and for research on the dynamics of _____.

15. In addition to providing _____, interviews give rapid insight into _____. They also allow observation of a person's tone of voice, posture, and other body cues. They also have certain limitations. Interviewers can be swayed by _____.

16. The interviewer's own _____ may cause him to accentuate, overlook, or distort qualities of the interviewee. Another problem in interviewing is the _____ effect, the tendency to generalize a favorable or unfavorable impression to unrelated details of personality.

17. When used as an assessment procedure, _____ _____ is a simple extension of the natural interest in "people watching." It is a useful technique but, like interviewing, has limitations. For this reason, _____ _____ are used which limit the chance of overlooking some traits while exaggerating others.

18. An alternative to rating scales is to do a _____ _____ which records how often various _____ even including _____ occur. A specialized form of direct observation is _____ _____ which is based on the premise that the best way to learn how a person reacts to a certain situation is to _____ that situation.

19. Most personality _____ are paper-and-pencil tests requiring a person to answer questions about himself. As measures of personality, they are more _____ than interviews or observation. The best known and most widely used objective test of personality is the ____ ____ ____ ____ - 2.

20. The ____ ____ ____ ____ - 2 is composed of _____ (how many?) items to which a subject must respond _____, _____, or _____ _____. The answer to a _____ item tells nothing about personality. It is only through the _____ of responses that personality dimensions are revealed. One problem is that people other than _____ are using this test.

21. In contrast to personality assessments that provide information on observable traits, _____ tests are designed to uncover deep-seated or _____ wishes, thoughts, and needs.

22. A projective test provides an _____ stimulus which the subjects must describe or about which they must make up a story. People tend to structure their descriptions according to their own life experiences. One of the oldest and most widely used projective tests is the _____ _____ Test. It consists of a set of ten standardized inkblots. Scoring is complex. _____ is less important than what _____ of the inkblot are used and how the image is _____.

23. Another popular projective test is the _____ _____ Test. This test consists of twenty sketches depicting various scenes. Subjects are asked to make up a _____ about the people in each sketch. Scoring is restricted to analysis of the _____ of the stories.

24. The _____ of projective tests is considered lowest among tests of personality. The _____ of judgments is low. Despite the drawbacks of projective tests, many psychologists attest to their value, especially as part of a _____ of tests and interviews.

25. Researchers like Lee, Zimbardo, and Bertholf have investigated the personalities of "_____ _____"—those who explode and commit violent crimes without warning. They found that these people were _____, _____, and _____ individuals. These people attack _____ of their personality, not in spite of it.

26. Forty percent of American college students consider themselves to be shy. Shyness combines social _____ with a tendency to avoid others. There are three elements of shyness. The first involves an underdevelopment of _____ skills. The second is social _____, and the third is a confidence-lowering _____ - _____ _____ in their thinking.

27. Shyness is most often triggered by _____ or _____ social situations. Shyness is linked to public _____-_____. Shy people consider their social anxiety a lasting _____ _____, whereas nonshy people believe that _____ _____ cause their occasional feelings of shyness. Shy people have lower _____-_____ than nonshy people.

28. The study of inherited behavioral traits is called _____ _____. This area of study relies mainly on comparisons of _____ _____.

29. Psychologists study the effect of heredity on personality by studying identical twins who have been _____ at birth. Studies have shown that they are amazingly similar _____ and less so in terms of their _____. Even unrelated pairs of people are amazingly similar. It seems reasonable to conclude that there is a _____ factor involved, but _____ also plays a role. Perhaps many of the characteristics can be accounted for by the _____ of _____ _____.

ANSWER KEYS

Do You Know the Information?

Multiple Choice

1. (a) obj. 1, p. 449	19. (b) obj. 14, p. 461	8. T, obj. 14, p. 461
2. (b) obj. 1, p. 449	20. (a) obj. 14, p. 461	9. F, obj. 15, p. 465
3. (d) obj. 1, p. 449	21. (b) obj. 14, p. 463	10. T, obj. 16, p. 466
4. (b) obj. 2, p. 450	22. (c) obj. 14, p. 463	11. F, obj. 17, pp. 468-469
5. (a) obj. 3, p. 451	23. (d) obj. 14, p. 464	
6. (d) obj. 4, p. 451	24. (b) obj. 15, p. 465	*Can You Apply the Information?*
7. (d) obj. 5, p. 452	25. (c) obj. 16, p. 466	
8. (b) obj. 6, p. 453	26. (a) obj. 16, p. 466	1. (b) obj. 1, p. 449
9. (b) obj. 7, p. 453	27. (d) obj. 18, p. 469	2. (c) obj. 3, p. 451
10. (c) obj. 7, p. 453	28. (b) obj. 19, p. 470	3. (d) obj. 5, p. 452
11. (d) obj. 8, p. 453		4. (a) obj. 6, p. 453
12. (b) obj. 9, p. 453	**True-False**	5. (b) obj. 10, p. 455
13. (a) obj. 10, p. 455		6. (d) obj. 13, p. 456
14. (a) obj. 12, p. 455	1. F, obj. 1, p. 449	7. (b) obj. 14, p. 459
15. (a) obj. 13, p. 456	2. T, obj. 2, p. 450	8. (c) obj. 14, p. 459
16. (d) obj. 14, p. 458	3. F, obj. 4, p. 451	9. (a) obj. 14, p. 459
17. (d) obj. 14, p. 459	4. T, obj. 12, p. 455	10. (c) obj. 14, p. 463
18. (b) obj. 14, p. 459	5. T, obj. 13, p. 456	11. (a) obj. 15, p. 465
	6. F, obj. 14, p. 458	
	7. F, obj. 14, p. 458	

Chapter Review

1. hypothetical, unique, enduring behavior, evaluated, temperament (p. 449)
2. traits, types, oversimplification (p. 450)
3. self-concept, interpret (perceive) (p. 451)
4. personality theory (p. 451)
5. common, individual, Common, Individual (p. 452)
6. Cardinal, Central, Secondary (p. 453)
7. surface, source, subjectively, factor analysis (p. 453)
8. source, 16 PF, five-factor, extroversion, agreeableness, conscientiousness, neuroticism, openness (p. 453)
9. consistency, situations, trait-situation (p. 455)
10. ordinal position, eminence, shyer, anxious (neurotic), social (p. 455)
11. emotional set, attention, expectations, anxious, inconsistent (p. 455)
12. androgynous, flexible (adaptable), situation (p. 456)
13. interview, unstructured, interviewee, structured interview (p. 458)

14. disturbances, employment, college, personality (p. 458)
15. information, personality, preconceptions (p. 458)
16. personality, halo (p. 458)
17. direct observation, rating scales (p. 459)
18. behavioral assessment, actions, thinking, situational testing, simulate (p. 459)
19. questionnaires, objective, MMPI (p. 460)
20. MMPI, 567, true, false, cannot say, single, patterns (p. 461); psychologists (p. 462)
21. projective, unconscious (p. 463)
22. ambiguous, Rorschach Inkblot (p. 463); Content, parts, organized (p. 464)
23. Thematic Apperception, story, content (p. 464)
24. validity, objectivity, battery (p. 464)
25. sudden murderers, passive, shy, overcontrolled, because (p. 465)
26. inhibition, social, anxiety, self-defeating bias (p. 466)
27. novel, unfamiliar, self-consciousness, personality trait, external situations, self-esteem (p. 466)
28. behavioral genetics, identical twins (p. 469)
29. separated, physically, personality, genetic, environment, fallacy, positive instances (p. 470)

Chapter 17

Theories of Personality

KEY TERMS, CONCEPTS, AND INDIVIDUALS

psychoanalytic theory (Sigmund Freud)
  id
      pleasure principle, libido,
      life instinct (Eros),
      death instinct (Thanatos)
  ego
      reality principle
  superego
      conscience, ego ideal
  neurotic and moral anxiety
  levels of awareness
      unconscious, preconscious,
      conscious
  psychosexual stages
      oral, anal, phallic,
      latent, genital
  erogenous zone
  fixation
  critical evaluation of Freud
neo-Freudians
  reasons for theoretical differences
  Alfred Adler
      striving for superiority
      feelings of inferiority
  Karen Horney
      basic anxiety
      moving toward, away from, against
  Carl Jung
      persona
      personal and collective unconscious
      archetypes
         anima, animus, self

behaviorist view of personality
  learning theory
  situational determinants
  habits — drive, cue, response, reward
social learning theory
  psychological situation
  expectancy
  reinforcement value
Skinner's view of personality
  self-reinforcement
  behaviorist view of development
  critical situations
      feeding, toilet training
      sex training, anger expression
  identification, imitation
humanistic theory
  human nature
      subjective experience
  Maslow
      self-actualization
  Rogers
      fully functioning person
      phenomenal field
        incongruent
      self, ideal self,
      possible self
  conditions of worth
  organismic valuing
psychoanalytic, behavioral, humanistic —
  compared and contrasted
steps for self-actualization
self-monitoring

LEARNING OBJECTIVES

To demonstrate mastery of this chapter you should be able to:
1.   Explain why Freud became interested in personality.

2.   List and describe the three parts of the personality according to Freud.
      a.

      b.

      c.

3.   Describe the dynamic conflict among the three parts of the personality and relate neurotic and moral anxiety to the conflict.

4.   Discuss the relationships among the three parts of the personality (according to Freud) and the three levels of awareness.

5. Explain how a society socializes its children.

6. List and describe Freud's four psychosexual stages including an explanation of fixation and the corresponding age range for each stage.
    a.

    b.

    c.

    d.

7. Generally enumerate the causes underlying Freud's concept of fixation at any stage.

8. Discuss the positive and the negative aspects of Freud's developmental theory.

9. Define the term neo-Freudian and explain why many of Freud's followers eventually disagreed with him.

10. Describe Adler's view of personality by defining or describing the following concepts:
    a. feelings of inferiority

    b. striving for superiority

c. compensation

d. style of life

e. creative self

11. Describe Horney's view of neurosis and emotional health including the concept of basic anxiety.

12. Describe Jung's view of personality by defining or explaining the following terms:
a. persona

b. introversion/extroversion

c. personal unconscious

d. collective unconscious

e. archetype

anima

animus

f. self archetype

13.   Explain how behaviorists view personality.

14.   Explain how learning theorists view the structure of personality. Include in your discussion the terms habit, drive, cue, response, and reward.

15.   Explain how learning theory and social learning theory differ. Include in your discussion an explanation of the terms psychological situation, expectancy, reinforcement value, and self-reinforcement. Explain how self-reinforcement may be related to self-esteem and depression.

16.   Explain how Skinner views personality.

17.   Using the behaviorist view of development, explain why feeding, toilet training, sex training, and learning to express anger or aggression may be particularly important to personality formation.

18.   Describe the roles of imitation and identification in personality development.

19.   Briefly explain how the humanists set themselves apart from the Freudian and behaviorist viewpoints of personality.

20.   Describe the concept of self-actualization and list ten characteristics of self-actualizers.
   a.   self-actualization

   b.   characteristics
      1.   6.

      2.   7.

      3.   8.

      4.   9.

      5.   10.

21.   Distinguish between Freud's and Rogers' views of the normal or fully functioning individual.

22.   Explain Roger's concept of self and "phenomenal field."

23.   Describe Rogers' view of an incongruent person. Include an explanation how "possible selves" help to translate our hopes, dreams, and fears as well as ultimately directing our future behavior.

24.   Explain how "conditions of worth" and "organismic valuing" may affect personality formation.

25.   Compare and contrast in general terms the strengths and weaknesses of the psychoanalytic, behavioristic, and humanistic theories of personality.

* * * * * * * * *

The following objectives are related to the material in the "Applications" and "Exploration" sections of the text.
26.   List and briefly explain or describe (where applicable) ten steps to promote self-actualization.
   a.

   b.

   c.

   d.

   e.

   f.

g.

h.

i.

j.

27. Define the term self-monitoring and differentiate high self-monitoring behavior from low self-monitoring behavior. Explain the advantages and disadvantages of each.

SELF-QUIZZES

Do You Know the Information?

Multiple Choice

1. In the Freudian view of personality, the _____ is totally unconscious and dominated by the pleasure principle.
   (a) ego.
   (b) id.
   (c) superego.
   (d) libido.

2. According to Freud any behavior that is aggressive or destructive in nature
   (a) originated in the superego.
   (b) reflects the influence of Eros .
   (c) is learned.
   (d) is derived from Thanatos.

3. In Freud's theory the aspect of the personality that acquires the values and ideals of the parents and the society is the
   (a) id.
   (b) superego.
   (c) ego.
   (d) life instinct.

4. According to Freudian theory, the basic conflict within an individual's psyche is between
   (a) psychic and physical energy.
   (b) the id and superego.
   (c) the ego and the id.
   (d) the ego and superego.

5. According to Freud, which part or parts of the personality operate at all three levels of consciousness?
   (a) id
   (b) ego
   (c) superego
   (d) id, ego, and superego

6. According to Freud, the Oedipus and Electra conflicts occur during the
    (a) phallic stage.   (c) oral stage.
    (b) anal stage.   (d) genital stage.

7. According to Freud, a person whose personality is characterized as obstinate, stingy, orderly, and compulsively clean would be classified as
    (a) oral-aggressive.   (c) anal-compulsive.
    (b) anal-expulsive.   (d) anal-retentive.

8. In the view of Alfred Adler, the main force in personality is
    (a) the libido.   (c) feelings of inferiority.
    (b) striving for superiority.   (d) basic anxiety.

9. According to Horney, when people feel isolated and helpless in a hostile world the result is
    (a) incongruence.   (c) basic anxiety.
    (b) organismic devaluing.   (d) feelings of inferiority.

10. Experiences that people have had with birth, death, power, and god figures, etc., led Jung to postulate the existence of the
    (a) collective unconscious.   (c) persona.
    (b) ego.   (d) mandalas.

11. The behaviorist position is that personality is
    (a) a collection of learned behavior patterns.
    (b) dominated by the self-concept.
    (c) an expression of the life instincts and the death instinct.
    (d) best understood in terms of subjective experiences.

12. Learning theorists
    (a) consider personality to be made up of traits.
    (b) believe personality is made up of responses to specific situations.
    (c) see man's personality as basically good.
    (d) closely reflect sociological thought regarding personality.

13. According to the social learning theorists, in order to understand a person's personality and his or her responses in a situation
    (a) the different values attached to activities must be understood.
    (b) it must be known if the person expects reinforcement.
    (c) it is important to know how the person interprets the situation.
    (d) all of the above.

14. Who says that "personality" is a fiction which is invented to pretend that behavior has been explained?
    (a) Freud   (c) Skinner
    (b) Rogers   (d) Maslow

15. Feeding is a developmental situation, from a behaviorist viewpoint, where a child learns
    (a) attitudes toward cleanliness.   (c) associations that will affect later social relationships.
    (b) to get pleasure from asserting him/herself. (d) none of the above.

16. Learning sex-appropriate behavior is greatly influenced by
    (a) toilet-training and early feeding contacts.
    (b) self-reinforcement and resolution of unconscious conflicts.
    (c) identification and imitation.
    (d) organismic valuing and self-regard.

17. The humanistic viewpoint emphasizes
    (a) the effects of reinforcement and prior learning.
    (b) biological instincts and unconscious forces.
    (c) subjective experience and self-actualization.
    (d) identification and imitation.

18. Maslow believed that all humans strive for this. These people are spontaneous, autonomous, task-centering, etc. The term is
    (a) self-actualization.
    (b) growth fulfillment.
    (c) conditions of worth.
    (d) congruence.

19. Whereas Freud thought the normal personality was adjusted to internal conflict, Rogers thought the fully functioning person
    (a) was able to symbolize the phenomenal field.
    (b) would find the self-image incongruent.
    (c) achieved an openness to feelings and experiences.
    (d) learned to trust other's expectations for him or her.

20. A person's total subjective experience of reality is called
    (a) self-image.
    (b) feelings of congruence.
    (c) conscious understanding.
    (d) phenomenal field.

21. In Carl Roger's view, information or feelings inconsistent with the self-image are said to be
    (a) separated from "not me" experiences.
    (b) incongruent .
    (c) symbolized.
    (d) a source of meta-needs.

22. Rogers believes that congruence and self-actualization are encouraged by substituting organismic valuing for
    (a) positive self-regard.
    (b) imitation.
    (c) conditions of worth.
    (d) self-image.

23. Of the following approaches, which has done the *most* in terms of rigorous testing and verification of concepts?
    (a) humanism
    (b) psychoanalysis
    (c) behaviorism
    (d) Freudian theory

24. Which theory presents a negative view of humans, sees their behavior as determined, and emphasizes motives for sex and aggression?
    (a) behavioristic theory
    (b) psychoanalytic theory
    (c) humanistic theory
    (d) neo-Freudian theory

25. The view of personality which gives the most encouragement for self-awareness and personal growth is the
    (a) humanistic theory.
    (b) neo-Freudian theory.
    (c) psychoanalytic theory.
    (d) behavioristic theory.

26. Which of the following is *poor* advice for a person who wishes to promote self-actualization?
    (a) Seek peak experiences.
    (b) Take responsibility for your life.
    (c) Try to live up to the positive expectations others may hold for you.
    (d) Be willing to change.

27.   Which of the following characteristics would be most typical of low self-monitors? You may choose more than one.
      (a) keenly interested in the actions of others.
      (b) tend to declare who they are by listing their roles and memberships.
      (c) prefer jobs where their roles are very clearly defined.
      (d) match their public behavior to their private attitudes, feelings, and beliefs.

True-False

_____ 1. Freud became interested in personality because there were no complete theories that explained healthy personality development to his satisfaction.

_____ 2. The actions of the id operate completely at the unconscious level.

_____ 3. Freud's insistence on the ego as the final director of behavior caused many of his followers to disagree and break away from him.

_____ 4. Threats of punishment from the superego cause neurotic anxiety.

_____ 5. Fixation early in the oral stage tends to produce people who are passive, gullible, and need lots of attention.

_____ 6. Freud's theory of the development of personality has been influential partly because it was the first theory to propose the idea that the first years of life help shape adult personality.

_____ 7. Freud's portrayal of the latency stage as free from sexuality and unimportant for personality development has been shown to be true.

_____ 8. With the concept of situational determinants, learning theorists have entirely removed the "person" from personality.

_____ 9. The existence of the self-archetype causes a gradual movement toward balance, integration, and harmony within the personality.

_____ 10. A basic active or passive orientation toward the world may be established by early feeding experiences.

_____ 11. Freud viewed a normal person as one who has learned to be open to the defense mechanisms resulting from internal conflict.

Matching *(Use the letters on the right only once.)*

_____ 1.	pleasure principle	A. archetype
_____ 2.	energy for the personality	B. neurotic anxiety
_____ 3.	punishment from superego	C. preconscious
_____ 4.	can be brought to awareness	D. high self-monitors
_____ 5.	moving toward, away from, and against others	E. anima
		F. libido
_____ 6.	mask; public self	G. Horney
_____ 7.	storehouse for experiences, feelings and memories	H. Thanatos
		I. Adler
_____ 8.	original idea or pattern	J. animus
_____ 9.	archetype which represents male principle	K. low self-monitors
_____ 10.	flexible, adaptable; display different behavior in different situations; think it is possible to love 2 people at once	L. ego
		M. persona
		N. id
		O. personal unconscious
		P. ego-ideal
		Q. moral anxiety
		R. conscious

Can You Apply the Information?

1. Fred really wants to have a package of Twinkies but he knows they will add to his weight problem. Impulses such as these probably come from the
   (a) collective unconscious.
   (b) superego.
   (c) ego.
   (d) id.

2. If a person unconsciously wants to kill someone but feels anxiety because of the impulse, which part of the personality decides on a socially acceptable response?
   (a) superego
   (b) ego
   (c) id
   (d) ego-ideal

3. Louise went home to see her parents for the weekend. Driving back to college on Sunday night she had a vague feeling of guilt. She figured she must have done something wrong. Her feelings probably came from
   (a) conventional moral thinking.
   (b) the preconscious.
   (c) the superego.
   (d) organismic valuing.

4. Fred is still struggling with the Twinkie problem. He's visiting the Twinkie factory with his college marketing class. He doesn't want to look ridiculous, but he has an almost irrestible urge to jump into a bowl of Twinkie batter. Fred is probably experiencing
   (a) pangs of extroversion.
   (b) moral anxiety.
   (c) images from the anima.
   (d) neurotic anxiety.
   (e) Weight Watchers' condemnation.

5. Brenda is 15 years old. She loves to be the center of attention and is always looking in mirrors because she says she's concerned about her appearance. Freud would likely say that Brenda is fixated at the _____ stage.
   (a) anal
   (b) genital
   (c) phallic
   (d) oral

6. Mary has barely passed each of her last three psychology tests and she doesn't have much hope of getting a higher score on her final exam even though she has studied. She is most likely to
   (a) resign herself to do better, put her nose to the grindstone, and get a good final score.
   (b) spend a lot of time praising herself for at least doing as well as she has.
   (c) take the course over next term with the confidence that she could do better.
   (d) do only as well as she expects to do.

7. Bob was born in an inner city ghetto. All of his life he has worked to get ahead. Which personality theory would view Bob's urge to overcome his roots as the main driving force in his personality?
   (a) Horney's
   (b) Jung's
   (c) behavioristic
   (d) Adler's

8. "Rainy days are gloomy." "The airport is far from here." "My closest friend is my spouse." These statements are indicative of a person's
   (a) anima.
   (b) mandala.
   (c) incongruence.
   (d) phenomenal field.

9. Dick considers himself warm, sensitive, loving and intelligent. His close associates perceive him to be cold, insensitive, manipulative, and not so bright. Dick refuses to believe such feedback. Dick is
   (a) incongruent.
   (b) reducing his phenomenal field.
   (c) a fully functioning person.
   (d) symbolizing his experiences.

10. Steve is a struggling downhill skier who practices diligently because he pictures himself as someday receiving an Olympic gold medal. He is utilizing
    (a) congruent personality self-images.
    (b) a very positive possible self.
    (c) the key to self-actualization.
    (d) superego functioning.

11. Which of the following would *not* be conducive to self-actualization?
    (a) Try to allow enough time for contemplation and self-exploration.
    (b) Try to live up to other's expectations.
    (c) Act as if you are personally responsible for every aspect of your life.
    (d) Be prepared to be unpopular or different when your views don't agree with others.

Chapter Review

1. The first truly comprehensive approach to understanding personality was developed by
   _____. He became interested in the treatment of mental disorders when he determined that many of his patients' problems were without _____ cause. Starting about 1890 and continuing to his death in 1939 Freud evolved a theory of
   _____.

2. Freud conceived personality as a dynamic system of energies directed by three structures: the _____,
   _____, and _____. The _____ is made up of innate _____
   _____ and urges present at birth. It operates on the _____
   principle. The energy for the personality is called_____ and derives from
   _____.

3. The _____ is the executive and draws its energy from the _____. The
   _____ operates on the _____ principle. The
   _____ acts as a judge or censor.

4. The _____ demands immediate gratification but the _____ may place moral restrictions on the impulses. The _____ is left to make the decision. Impulses from the _____ which threaten a loss of control cause _____ anxiety. Threats of punishment from the _____ cause _____ anxiety.

5. The id works totally on the _____ level. The ego and the superego may also work on this level and also on the _____ and _____ levels.

6. Freud theorized that the core of personality is formed before age six in a series of _____ stages. These stages in order from earliest to latest are the _____, _____, _____, and _____.

7. At each stage a different part of the body becomes an _____ zone (an area capable of producing pleasure). It serves as the principle source of pleasure, frustration, and self-expression. Freud believes that many adult personality traits can be traced to _____ (an unresolved conflict or emotional "hang-up") in one or more of the stages.

8. Fixation early in the oral stage produces an oral-_____ personality who is gullible, passive and needs lots of attention. Fixation later in the oral stage causes an oral-_____ adult who is argumentative, cynical, and exploitive of others.

9. Fixation during the anal stage can lead to anal-_____ personality, who is obstinate, stingy, orderly, and compulsively clean. It may also lead to the anal-_____ personality who is disorderly, destructive, cruel or messy.

10. During the phallic stage, increased sexual interest causes the child to become physically attracted to the parent of the opposite sex. In males this generates the _____ conflict in which the boy feels rivalry with his father for the affection of the mother. The counterpart to this is the _____ conflict. Fixation during this stage produces the _____ personality who exhibits vanity, exhibitionism, sensitive pride, and narcissism.

11. During the genital stage, personality is marked by a growing capacity for mature and responsible social-sexual relationships. This last stage comes after a long period of _____ during which psychosexual development is temporarily interrupted.

12. Freud's theory has been influential for a number of reasons. First, it pioneered the idea that the first years of life help shape adult _____. Secondly, it identified _____, _____ training, and early _____ experiences as critical events in personality formation. Third, Freud was among the first to propose that development proceeds through a series of _____.

13. Some of Freud's ideas are not universally accepted. In some cases he was clearly _____. Most psychologists feel that much more is going on during _____ than Freud recognized. Freud also overemphasized _____ in personality development.

14. Many theorists disagreed with Freud on his emphasis on _____ _____ and _____. Those who stayed close to Freud's thinking are now called _____ - _____. Adler views the main driving force in personality as a striving for _____. Adler felt that everyone experiences feelings of _____.

15. Horney was among the first to counter the _____ bias in Freud's thinking. Horney viewed that neurosis occurred when _____ _____ builds up from people feeling isolated and helpless in a hostile world. According to Horney, each of us can move _____ others, _____ from others, or _____ others. Emotional health requires a balance of each. Emotional problems lock people into overuse of only one of the three modes.

16. Like Freud, Jung called the conscious part of the personality the _____. Between this and the outside world we often find a mask or _____. What Freud called the unconscious, Jung called the _____ unconscious. It is the _____ for personal experiences, feelings and memories. Jung also proposed a deeper _____ unconscious.

17. According to Jung, _____ (original ideas, patterns, or prototypes) are found in the _____ unconscious. They are unconscious _____ that cause us to respond emotionally to various symbols. Two important _____ are the _____ (representing the female principle) and the _____ (representing the male principle). The _____ - _____ is the most important of all. It represents _____.

18. Behaviorists believe that personality is a collection of _____ _____ patterns. Personality is acquired through _____ and _____ conditioning, observational learning, reinforcement, extinction, generalization, and discrimination. Learning theorists have kept the "person" in personality by drawing our attention to the _____ determinants of behavior.

19. A behavioral view of personality proposed by Dollard and Miller holds that _____ form the structure of personality. These theorists believe that _____ are governed by four elements of the learning process: _____, _____, _____, and _____.

20. Social learning theorists have expanded the original learning theory view to give added emphasis to _____ relationships and _____. Such theorists include _____, _____, and other _____ events in their view of personality. Such elements are exemplified by Rotter's concepts of the _____ situation, _____, and _____ value. The social learning theorists have also added _____ - _____ to the behavioristic view. This might be considered the equivalent of the Freudian _____. People who have high rates of _____ - _____ have been found to have high _____ - _____.

21. A more extreme view of personality known as radical _____ has been proposed by _____. For him "personality" is a fiction we invent to pretend we have explained behavior that is actually controlled by the _____. He believes that everything a person does is based on past and present _____ and _____.

22. Many of Freud's major points can be restated in terms of modern learning theory. Miller and Dollard consider four situations of critical importance. These are: _____, _____ or cleanliness training, _____ training, and learning to express _____ or _____. Behaviorists tend to stress two processes that contribute greatly to personality development in general, and particularly to sex training. They are _____ and _____.

23. Identification refers to the child's _____ _____ to admired adults especially to those the child depends upon for love and care. Many sex traits come from identification with the behavior patterns of the _____-_____ parent. Identification typically encourages _____.

24. _____ is a reaction to the _____ of psychoanalytic theory and the _____ of learning theory. The _____ view human nature as inherently _____ and that we are creative beings capable of free _____. This viewpoint leads to a greater emphasis being placed on immediate _____ experience than on prior learning. According to Maslow, people strive for_____-_____.

25. Self-actualizers have efficient perceptions of _____, and they have a comfortable _____ of self, others and nature. They are _____, task-_____, and _____. They have a continued freshness of _____ of life, a fellowship with _____, and profound interpersonal _____. They have an _____ sense of humor and _____ experiences.

26. One influential humanist, Rogers, saw the _____ _____ person as one who has achieved an openness to feelings and experiences, and who has learned to trust inner urges and intuitions. This is different from Freud's view of the "normal" personality as adjusted to internal _____.

27. The_____ is a flexible and changing perception of personal identity which emerges from the _____ field. This is the person's total _____ experience of reality. Information or feelings inconsistent with the self-image are said to be _____.

28. When we translate our hopes, fears, fantasies, and goals into personal images of who we could be, we are utilizing _____ _____. They may either be positive or negative and tend to direct future _____.

29. Rogers holds that positive and negative evaluations by others cause a child to develop internal standard of evaluation called _____ of _____. By this he means that we learn that some actions win our parents' love and approval while others are rejected. This is directly related to a later capacity for positive _____-_____.

30. He believes congruence and self-actualization are encouraged by substituting _____ _____ for conditions of worth. This process is a direct, gut-level response to life experiences that avoids the filtering and distortion of _____.

31.   One of the most telling criticisms of Freudian theory is that it can be used to explain any psychological event
       _____ it has occurred but offers little help in predicting _____
       behavior. Psychoanalytic theory seems to present an unnecessarily _____ view of
       human nature and potential. Also Freud has been particularly criticized for his preoccupation with conflicts
       related to _____ and _____.

32.   Of the three major perspectives, the _____ have made the best effort to rigor-
       ously test and verify their concepts. They have been criticized for underestimating the impact on personality
       of _____, _____, and _____
       experience.

33.   The chief criticism of the humanistic approach lies in the _____ of its concepts. Its
       real strength is the light they have shed on the _____ dimensions of personality.

34.   While self-actualization offers the promise of personal growth, creativity, and fullness of life, it requires hard
       work, patience, and commitment. It is primarily a _____, not a goal or an
       endpoint.

35.   Several suggestions can be gleaned from the writings of Abraham Maslow on how to promote self-actualiza-
       tion. One is to be willing to _____. You must learn to take
       _____. You can become an architect of self by acting as if you are person-
       ally responsible for every aspect of your life.

36.   Another point is to examine your _____. Use self-discovery to try to make each life
       decision a choice for growth, not a response to fear or anxiety. Try to see things as they are, not as you would
       like them to be. In other words, experience things _____ and
       _____.

37.   Make use of positive experiences to promote growth. You might actively repeat activities that cause
       "_____ _____" (temporary moments of self-actualization).
       Actualizing potentials may place you at odds with cultural expectations. This may produce fear which keeps
       many people from becoming what they might. You must be prepared to be
       _____.

38.   Maslow found that self-actualizers tend to have a _____ or
       "_____" in life. Therefore, get involved and committed to problems outside
       yourself. Self-awareness takes time to develop. Slow down and avoid
       _____ or _____ your time.

39.   A valuable means of promoting self-awareness is to start a _____. Keeping
       records of experiences, daily thoughts, feelings, and attitudes can help make growth-oriented life changes. As
       a final note, _____ your progress. It is important to gauge your progress and to renew
       your efforts. _____ is a good sign that you are in need of further growth and
       change.

40.   When people observe or try to control the image of themselves that they display to others, this is called
       _____-_____. People who are high in this characteristic are flexible
       and adaptable and display different _____ from situation to situation. In
       contrast, people who are low change very little from situation to situation and seek to match their public
       behavior to their private _____.

ANSWER KEYS

Do You Know the Information?

Multiple Choice

1. (b) obj. 2, p. 475
2. (d) obj. 2, p. 475
3. (b) obj. 2, p. 475
4. (b) obj. 3, p. 476
5. (b,c) obj. 4, p. 477
6. (a) obj. 6, p. 478
7. (d) obj. 6, p. 478
8. (b) obj. 10, p. 479
9. (c) obj. 11, p. 480
10. (a) obj. 12, p. 480
11. (a) obj. 13, p. 481
12. (b) obj. 14, p. 482
13. (d) obj. 15, p. 483
14. (c) obj. 16, p. 484
15. (c) obj. 17, p. 485
16. (c) obj. 18, p. 485
17. (c) obj. 19, pp. 486-487
18. (a) obj. 20, p. 487
19. (c) obj. 21, p. 487
20. (d) obj. 22, p. 487
21. (b) obj. 23, p. 488
22. (c) obj. 24, p. 490

23. (c) obj. 25, p. 490
24. (b) obj. 25, p. 490
25. (a) obj. 25, p. 490
26. (c) obj. 26, p. 492-493
27. (d) obj. 27, p. 494

True-False

1. F, obj. 1, p. 475
2. T, objs. 2,4, pp. 475, 477
3. F, objs. 2,9, pp. 475, 479
4. F, obj. 3, p. 476
5. T, obj. 6, p. 478
6. T, obj. 8, p. 479
7. F, obj. 8, p. 479
8. F, obj. 14, p. 482
9. T, obj. 12, p. 481
10. T, obj. 17, p. 485
11. F, obj. 21, p. 487

Matching

1. N, obj. 2, p. 475
2. F, obj. 2, p. 475

3. Q, obj. 3, p. 476
4. C, obj. 4, p. 477
5. G, obj. 11, p. 480
6. M, obj. 12, p. 480
7. O, obj. 12, p. 480
8. A, obj. 12, p. 480
9. J, obj. 12, p. 481
10. D, obj. 27, pp. 494-495

Can You Apply the Information?

1. (d) obj. 2, p. 475
2. (b) objs. 2-4, pp. 475-476
3. (c) objs. 2,3, pp. 475-476
4. (d) obj. 3, p. 476
5. (c) obj. 6, p. 478
6. (d) obj. 15, p. 483
7. (d) obj. 10, p. 480
8. (d) obj. 22, p. 487
9. (a) obj. 23, p. 488
10. (b) obj. 23, p. 489
11. (b) obj. 26, pp. 492-493

Chapter Review

1. Freud, physical, personality, (p. 475)
2. id, ego, superego, id, biological instincts, pleasure, libido, Eros (p. 475)
3. ego, id, ego, reality, superego (p. 475)
4. id, superego, ego, id, neurotic, superego, moral (p. 476)
5. unconscious, conscious, preconscious (p. 477)
6. psychosexual, oral, anal, phallic, genital (p. 478)
7. erogenous, fixation (p. 478)
8. dependent, aggressive (p. 478)
9. retentive, expulsive (p. 478)
10. Oedipus, Electra, phallic (p. 478)
11. latency (p. 479)
12. personality, feeding, toilet, sexual, stages (p. 479)
13. wrong, latency, sexuality (p. 479)
14. instinctual drives, sexuality, neo-Freudians, superiority, inferiority (p. 479)
15. male, basic anxiety, toward, away, against (p. 480)
16. ego, persona, personal, storehouse, collective (p. 480)
17. archetypes, collective, images (p. 480); archetypes, anima, animus, self-archetype, unity (p. 481)
18. learned behavior, classical, operant (p. 481); situational (p. 482)

19. habits, habits, drive, cue, response, reward (p. 483)
20. social, modeling, perception, thinking, mental, psychological, expectancy, reinforcement, self-reinforcement, superego, self-reinforcement (p. 483) self-esteem (p. 484)
21. behaviorism, Skinner, environment, rewards, punishments (p. 484)
22. feeding, toilet, sex, anger, aggression, identification, imitation (p. 485)
23. emotional attachment, same-sex, imitation (p. 485)
24. Humanism, pessimism, mechanism, humanists, good, choice, subjective, self-actualization (p. 486)
25. reality, acceptance, spontaneous, centering, autonomous, appreciation, humanity, relationships, unhostile, peak (p. 487)
26. fully functioning, conflict (p. 487)
27. self, phenomenal, subjective (p. 487); incongruent (p. 488)
28. possible selves, behavior (p. 489)
29. conditions, worth, self-regard (p. 489)
30. organismic valuing, incongruence (p. 490)
31. after, future, negative, sex, aggression (p. 490)
32. behaviorists, temperament, emotion, subjective (p. 490)
33. impreciseness, positive (p. 490)
34. process (p. 492)
35. change, responsibility (p. 492)
36. motives, honestly, directly (p. 492)
37. peak experiences, different (p. 492)
38. mission, calling, hurrying, overscheduling (p. 493)
39. journal, assess, Boredom (p. 493)
40. self-monitoring, behavior, attitudes (feelings, beliefs) (p. 494)

Chapter 18

Intelligence

KEY TERMS, CONCEPTS, AND INDIVIDUALS

savant syndrome
Alfred Binet
intelligence defined
    operational definition
reliability, validity, objectivity, standardization
Stanford-Binet Intelligence Scale
    mental and chronological age
    intelligence quotient (IQ), deviation scores
    stability of IQ scores, effect of aging
Wechsler scales
    verbal and performance scales
group vs. individual tests
normal curve
    sex differences in intelligence
    occupation, school, and intelligence
Terman's study of the gifted
    misconceptions about genius
    characteristics of the gifted

Gardner's real world success criteria
mental retardation
    levels of retardation
    causes of retardation
    organic vs. familial
        birth injuries, fetal damage,
        metabolic disorders, genetic abnormalities
        PKU, microcephaly, hydrocephaly
        cretinism, Down syndrome
heredity/environment in intelligence
    twin studies
effect of environment and family
effects of training on intelligence
culture-fair tests
    Jensen—the heritability of IQ
positive and negative aspects of
    standardized testing
SOMPA

LEARNING OBJECTIVES

To demonstrate mastery of this material you should be able to:

1. Explain what the savant syndrome is.

2. Describe Binet's role in intelligence testing.

3.   State Wechsler's definition of intelligence.

4.   Explain what an operational definition of intelligence is.

5.   Define the terms validity, reliability, objective, and standardization as they relate to testing.

6.   Generally describe the construction of the Stanford-Binet Intelligence Scale.

7.   Define the components of the Stanford-Binet intelligence quotient (IQ) and use an example to show how it was computed.

8.   Differentiate between Stanford-Binet and deviation IQs.

9.   Explain how age affects the stability of intelligence scores and how aging affects intelligence.

10.   With regards to the types of intelligence tests,
    a.   distinguish the Wechsler from the Stanford-Binet tests; and

    b.   distinguish between group and individual intelligence tests.

11.   Describe the pattern of distribution of IQ scores observed in the general population.

12.   Describe the sex differences in intelligence.

13.   Describe the relationship between occupation and intelligence.

14.   With regards to Terman's study of gifted children,
    a.   list five popular misconceptions concerning genius and their corrections; and
       1.

       2.

3.

4.

5.

b.   explain how successful subjects differed from the less successful ones.

15.   Explain why basing judgment of giftedness on IQ scores may be misguided.

16.   Describe Gardner's broader view of intelligence and list the seven different kinds he discusses.

17.   State the dividing line between normal intelligence and retardation (or developmental disability), and list the degrees of retardation.

18.   Differentiate between organic and familial retardation.

19. List and describe the four types of organic causes of retardation.

    a.

    b.

    c.

    d.

20. Briefly describe the cause and effects of the following conditions:

    a. PKU

    b. microcephaly

    c. hydrocephaly

    d. cretinism

    e. Down syndrome

21. Briefly describe the maze-bright, maze-dull rat study as evidence for and against the hereditary view of intelligence.

22. Explain how the twin (identical and fraternal) studies can be used to support either side of the heredity/environment controversy.

23.   Describe the evidence that most strongly supports the environmental view of intelligence.

24.   Describe the studies which indicate how much the environment can alter intelligence.

25.   Answer the question "Can training in thinking skills increase tested intelligence?" Explain your answer.

26.   Explain Zajonc's confluence model relating the IQ of the children to the size of the family.

27.   Discuss how the heredity/environment debate is resolved.

* * * * * * * * * *

The following objectives are related to the material in the "Applications" and "Exploration" sections of your text.
28.   Define the term culture-fair test, and explain how IQ tests may be unfair to certain groups.

29.   State four arguments against Jensen's claim that the IQ difference between blacks and whites can be attributed to genetic inheritance.

a.

b.

c.

d.

30.   Discuss the general validity of IQ testing and the advantages and disadvantages of standardized testing in public schools.

31.   Describe the overall controversy in the Larry P. case.

32.   Explain what SOMPA is and how it helps solve many of the problems of using standardized IQ tests to assess the abilities of minority children.

SELF-QUIZZES

Do You Know the Information?

Multiple Choice

1.   A person of sub-normal intelligence who shows highly developed mental ability in one or more very limited areas is displaying the
  (a) effects of a marked chromosome.
  (b) gifted retardate syndrome.
  (c) result of a congenital disorder.
  (d) savant syndrome.

2. In constructing his test of intelligence, Binet
    (a) chose items at each age level which could be passed by an average child of that chronological age.
    (b) selected the children in the French school system with average grades at each grade level and determined what intellectual skills they possessed.
    (c) chose items at each level that all French-speaking children of that age could correctly answer.
    (d) consulted with Stanford University.

3. According to Wechsler, intelligence is
    (a) that which an intelligence test measures.
    (b) the ability to succeed in school.
    (c) the capacity to act purposefully, think rationally and deal effectively with the environment.
    (d) regarded as a person's capacity to learn.

4. A test has _____ when it measures what it claims to measure.
    (a) reliability   (c) objectivity
    (b) validity   (d) standardization

5. The IQ test which uses a set of increasingly more difficult items to categorize age groups is the
    (a) Wechsler Adult Intelligence Scale.   (c) Wechsler Intelligence Scale for Children.
    (b) Stanford-Binet Intelligence Scale.   (d) MGM Scale.

6. Of the following, which are associated with the Stanford-Binet Intelligence Scale?
    (a) chronological age   (d) separate subscales
    (b) morphological age   (e) overall IQ score
    (c) mental age   (f) intelligence quotient

7. The formula for figuring IQ is
    (a) $\dfrac{M}{A} \times 100 = IQ$ (c) $\dfrac{MA}{CA} \times 100 = IQ$

    (b) $\dfrac{CA}{MA} \times 100 = IQ$ (d) $\dfrac{MA}{CA(100)} = IQ$

8. First, it is determined how far above or below average a person's score is relative to others taking the test. Then, tables are used to convert the person's relative standing in the group to an IQ score. This process is used to calculate
    (a) an IQ score.   (d) a performance score.
    (b) a mental age score.   (e) the person's age + weight.
    (c) a deviation IQ score.

9. Which is *not* true of IQ scores?
    (a) Scores based on speed, rapid insight, or flexibility decline after middle age.
    (b) IQ test scores show a small, gradual increase until about age forty.
    (c) Twenty-five point changes on retesting are not unusual.
    (d) The younger the child when IQ is measured, the poorer the correlation with adult IQ scores.

10. Which of the following statements is *incorrect?*
    (a) The WAIS-R is a group intelligence test.
    (b) The WAIS-R is specifically designed to measure adult intelligence.
    (c) The WISC-III and the WAIS-R rate performance and verbal intelligence.
    (d) The Stanford-Binet gives one overall IQ score.

11. Women score higher than men on the portions of intelligence tests
    (a) adapted to the female mentality.
    (b) requiring verbal ability, vocabulary, and rote learning.
    (c) emphasizing spatial relationships and arithmetic reasoning.
    (d) which emphasize manual dexterity and other clerical skills.

12. Which of the following was *not* a conclusion reached from Terman's study of the mentally gifted?
    (a) The gifted are socially well-adjusted.
    (b) High IQ in childhood is associated with high adult IQ.
    (c) The highly intelligent person is more susceptible to mental illness.
    (d) Highly successful subjects were more persistent and more motivated than less successful subjects.

13. Gardner's broader view of intelligence
    (a) is supportive of studies which suggest that IQ test scores mainly reflect a general intelligence factor.
    (b) has been the basis of much of the search for culture-fair tests.
    (c) encompasses abilities including art, music, and athletics.
    (d) hopes to be able to make the most accurate prediction of school success.

14. What IQ score has traditionally been used as the dividing line between retardation and normal intelligence?
    (a) 60   (c) 80
    (b) 70   (d) 100

15. Which of the following is *not* a cause of organic retardation?
    (a) genetic abnormalities   (c) deprivation
    (b) prenatal infection   (d) metabolic disorders

16. Which of the following statements is *incorrect?*
    (a) Microcephaly is an inherited disorder in which the skull is extremely small.
    (b) A very significant factor in the causation of Down's syndrome is the age of the mother *and* the father.
    (c) Cretinism is a form of retardation that develops in infancy due to insufficient secretion of the hormone thyroid.
    (d) PKU can be controlled by manipulation of the diet.

17. A form of retardation caused by an excess production of fluid within the brain is called
    (a) Down's syndrome.   (c) PKU.
    (b) microcephaly.   (d) hydrocephaly.

18. In the study comparing maze-bright and maze-dull rats
    (a) eugenics was used.
    (b) the results suggest that some traits are highly influenced by heredity.
    (c) the "bright" rats were less easily distracted during testing and more motivated by food.
    (d) all of the above are true.

19. The correlation of intelligence test scores of identical twins
    (a) is only slightly lower when they are raised apart than when they are raised together.
    (b) is only slightly lower than that of parents and children.
    (c) is higher than for any other blood relatives except siblings.
    (d) is lower when they are raised together than that of siblings reared together.

20.   In the studies of families having one biological child and one adopted child,
      (a)   the adopted child's IQ is more like the biological mother's than the adoptive mother's.
      (b)   children reared by the same mother resemble her in IQ to the same degree.
      (c)   the adoptive child's IQ is more like the biological mother's if her educational level is higher than the adoptive
            mother's.
      (d)   the children were more alike in IQ than ordinary siblings were.

21.   In the Skeels study children who were considered retarded were moved from an orphanage to a more stimulating
      environment where
      (a)   their IQ test scores improved slightly.
      (b)   their IQ test scores rose an average of 29 points.
      (c)   they became better adjusted and happier but not intellectually superior.
      (d)   their IQs rose sufficiently to allow reclassification from mildly to moderately retarded.

22.   Tests developed so that they will not place certain groups at a disadvantage
      (a)   include the Dove test.   (c)   are best exemplified by the Wechsler scales.
      (b)   are called culturally balanced.   (d)   are culture-fair.

23.   Arguments against Jensen's contention concerning the heritability of intelligence in blacks and whites include
      (a)   standard IQ tests do not allow meaningful comparisons between ethnic, cultural, or racial groups.
      (b)   environment can correct any small hereditary differences in the races.
      (c)   blacks live in more impoverished environments.
      (d)   all of the above.

Matching (*Use the letters on the right only once.*)

_____ 1. procedures used to measure it have been   A.   cretinism
            specified   B.   SAT
_____ 2. if test yields same score when given   C.   valid
            repeatedly to same individual   D.   Kamin
_____ 3. person's score compared to the average   E.   savant syndrome
            score; tables then used to figure an IQ   F.   standardization
            score   G.   operational definition
_____ 4. example of a group intelligence test   H.   reliable
_____ 5. intellectual and educational level of home   I.   Down's syndrome
            is low   J.   PKU
_____ 6. inherited disorder   K.   Jensen
_____ 7. intelligence inherited   L.   deviation IQ
_____ 8. test measures what it purports to measure   M.   familial retardation
_____ 9. an island of brilliance in a sea of retarda-   N.   confluence model
            tion   O.   SOMPA
_____ 10. a new way of looking at children that   P.   giftedness
            takes cultural differences into account
_____ 11. find norm made by a large group of people
            like those for whom the test was designed
_____ 12. larger number of children in a family
            results in lower IQs
_____ 13. early fascination with explanations and
            problem solving

True-False

_____ 1. A test is said to be objective if it yields the same score when corrected by different people.

_____ 2. In the general population fewer people score above average than score below average on IQ tests.

_____ 3. Women tend to excel on IQ test items that require arithmetic reasoning, verbal ability, and rote learning.

_____ 4. People who hold "high-status" occupational positions have higher average IQs than those in "lower status" jobs.

_____ 5. A child who shows cooperation toward others is less likely to be gifted than one with a good memory.

_____ 6. Environmentalists argue that separated identical twins are almost always placed in homes socially and educationally similar to their biological parents. This artifically inflates the similarity in the separated twins' IQ scores.

_____ 7. Strong evidence of the environmental view of intelligence comes from studies of children who were separated at birth.

_____ 8. Training in thinking skills has not been shown to increase IQ scores.

_____ 9. There is probably no limit to how far down intelligence can go in an impoverished environment, but heredity may impose some limits on how far up IQ can go, even under ideal conditions.

_____ 10. One positive aspect of IQ testing in schools is that a bright child may be identified who has other overriding problems.

Can You Apply the Information?

1. Carl is mentally retarded but can memorize the Chicago telephone book in its entirety. Carl would be classified as
   (a) gifted but not genius.   (c) borderline retarded.
   (b) having the savant syndrome.   (d) a cretin.

2. "The temperature at sea level at 6:58 a.m. was 20 degrees Celsius." This is an example of an operational definition.
   (a) True   (b) False

3. When we administer a test to a large group of people and then retest them at a later date, we are investigating
   (a) validity.   (c) reliability.
   (b) objectivity.   (d) the normal curve.

4. You're looking at a patient's chart trying to figure out her age on the date of her intelligence testing. You can't read the number written down for her age. You know her IQ was 83 and her MA was 10. What was her CA on the date of testing?
   (a) 8   (c) 12
   (b) 9   (d) 10

5. The average twelve-year-old child has a mental age of
   (a) 10.   (c) 12.
   (b) 120.   (d) 100.

6. If a college professor's grade distribution "fit" her classes the way the normal curve fits randomly selected people, most students would make a(n) _____ in her class
   (a) A
   (b) B
   (c) C
   (d) D
   (e) F
   (f) insufficient data to choose an answer

7. You are more likely to find higher IQs among bankers than among truck drivers because banking requires more intelligence than truck driving.
   (a) True
   (b) False

8. Which of the following forms of retardation is the *most* easily prevented and treated?
   (a) phenylketonuria
   (b) microcephaly
   (c) Down's syndrome
   (d) all of these are equally difficult to work with

9. Providing extra stimulation and special attention can raise the IQ of young children above that of children not receiving such special treatment.
   (a) True
   (b) False

Chapter Review

1. A person of sub-normal intelligence who shows highly developed mental abilities in one or more very limited areas possesses the _____ syndrome.

2. Perhaps the first person to use an "intelligence" test was _____, whose approach gave rise to modern intelligence tests.

3. A general description of intelligence by David Wechsler defines it as the global capacity of the individual to act _____, to think _____, and to deal effectively with the _____.

4. A(n) _____ definition of intelligence is one that specifies the procedures used to _____ it.

5. For a test to be _____ it must yield the same score, or close to the same score, each time it is administered to the same individual. A test has _____ when it measures what it claims to measure. A test is said to be _____ if it gives the same score when different people correct it. Test _____ refers to two things. First, it means that the same _____ are used in giving the test to all people. Second, it means finding the _____ made by a large group of people like those for whom the test was designed.

6. One example of intelligence tests is the Stanford-Binet Intelligence Scale which uses a set of increasingly more difficult items to categorize _____ _____. These types of questions allow a person's _____ age to be determined.

7. To know the meaning of _____ age one must also consider _____ age. Using these two age values, an _____ or _____ _____ can be determined. This is defined as _____ age divided by _____ age multiplied by 100.

8. On tests currently in use, there is no longer any need to calculate IQ scores. Instead, a
    _____ _____ score is used. To compute this score, we determine how far above
    or below _____ a person's score is compared to others taking the test. Tables are then
    used to convert the person's _____ _____ in the group to an IQ score.

9. IQ scores do not become dependable until age _____, after which they correspond quite closely to adult
    IQ. The average change in IQ on retesting is approximately _____ points in either direction.

10. Studies of IQ have shown a gradual increase in intellectual ability until about age _____. Recent
    findings suggest that only certain kinds of intellectual abilities are affected by aging. When
    _____ _____ or _____ is
    emphasized, there is little decline until advanced age. On the other hand, test items requiring
    _____, rapid _____, or perceptual _____
    show earlier losses and a rapid decline after middle age.

11. A widely used alternative to the Stanford-Binet is the _____
    _____ Intelligence Scale—Revised. This test has a form adapted for use with children
    called the _____ Intelligence Scale for _____—
    III.

12. The Stanford-Binet only gives an overall IQ, whereas both the WISC-III and WAIS-R rate
    _____ intelligence in addition to _____ intelligence. Both
    the Stanford-Binet and the Wechsler tests are _____ intelligence tests.
    _____ intelligence tests are designed for use with large groups of people.

13. The distribution of IQs in the population approximates a _____ curve in which the
    majority of scores fall close to the _____, and relatively few at the
    _____.

14. It seems safe to assume that men and women do not differ in _____ intelligence. However,
    on the WAIS-R women do better on _____ ability, _____,
    and _____ learning, whereas men are best in visualization of _____
    _____ and _____ reasoning.

15. There is a relationship between IQ and _____ classification. Persons holding
    _____-_____ positions average much higher IQs than those in
    _____-_____ occupational settings.

16. Terman's study of the very _____ shows that there are many misconceptions
    about genius. Terman's subjects were not _____. They maintained their high IQ score.
    They were not physically _____. They had better than average
    _____ health. Two factors that greatly influence eventual success for the gifted
    are parental _____ and intellectual _____.
    The highly successful gifted subjects tend to be those who are more _____
    and _____ to succeed.

17. Gardner feels that the definition of intelligence needs to be _____ so that it can
    predict "_____ _____" success and not just success in
    _____. He feels that intelligence should include such things as language, logic and
    _____, visual and _____ thinking, music, _____ skills,
    _____ skills (self-knowledge), and _____
    skills (social skills).

18. An IQ of _____ or below has traditionally been the dividing line between normal intelligence and _____. The degrees of _____ are _____, _____, _____, and _____.

19. In 30 to 40% of the cases of retardation, no known biological problem can be identified. _____ retardation, as this is called, occurs most often in very poor households or impoverished environments.

20. About 50 percent of all cases of mental retardation are _____, or related to known physical disorders. These can be traced to one or more of the following conditions:
 (1) _____ injuries (such as lack of oxygen);
 (2) _____ damage caused by maternal drug abuse, disease, or infection;
 (3) _____ disorders; and
 (4) _____ abnormalities.

21. There are several distinctive forms of organic retardation, including _____ _____ _____ which results from the build-up of phenylpyruvic acid. The _____ suffers a rare abnormality in which the skull is extremely small or fails to grow, thus forcing the brain to develop in a severely limited space. _____ is caused by excess production of cerebrospinal fluid within the brain which forces the brain against the skull, grossly enlarging the head and damaging brain tissue. _____ results in stunted physical and intellectual growth due to an insufficient secretion of _____ hormone during infancy.

22. _____ _____ is characterized by almond-shaped, slanted eyes and an overly-large, protruding tongue. It is known that these individuals have an extra _____. The most significant factor in this disorder appears to be the _____ of the _____ at the time of the child's birth.

23. In a classic study of genetic factors and learning ability, Tryon managed to breed separate strains of _____-_____ and _____-_____ rats. The rats were actually just shown to be more _____ by food and less easily _____ during testing.

24. In assessing the relative importance of heredity and environment on the development of intelligence, studies have looked at the similarity in IQ between various relatives. It is typically found that as the genetic similarity increases, the similarity in IQ _____.

25. For example, _____ twins when reared together have virtually identical IQs. When reared apart, the correlation _____ but only _____. This tends to support the _____ side of the controversy. However, the _____ argue that the separated twins are nearly always put into _____ homes.

26. There is increasing evidence that extended, in-depth training in thinking skills can _____ measured intelligence.

27. The strongest evidence for the environmentalist view comes from families in which there is one _____ child and one _____ child. Studies show that children reared by the same mother resemble her in IQ to the same degree.

28. The environment can have considerable impact on a person's intelligence. One study showed that when 25 children who were considered mentally retarded were transferred to a more _____ environment, the result was an average gain of _____ IQ points. In that same study, a second group of initially less retarded children who remained in the orphanage lost an average of _____ IQ points.

29. Psychologist Robert Zajonc believes that IQ tends to _____ as family size _____. The brightest children come from the _____ families and are _____ in ordinal position. This is called the _____ model.

30. Most psychologists agree that _____ and _____ are inseparable, interacting factors in determining intelligence. There is probably no _____ to how far _____ intelligence can go in an impoverished environment. Heredity may impose some _____ on how far _____ IQ can go, even under ideal conditions.

31. There are many problems involved in the use and interpretation of IQ tests. One such problem lies in the test _____ which tends to be biased in favor of the white, middle-class background. In recognition of this problem, some psychologists are trying to develop _____- _____ tests that will not disadvantage certain groups.

32. Although his views are not widely accepted, Arthur Jensen believes that blacks have lower IQ scores than whites because of _____ _____. Criticisms against Jensen's view include the idea that blacks may live in _____ environments, that the difference in scores is small enough to be corrected by _____, that standard IQ tests can't make meaningful comparisons between racial or other groups, and that Jensen's _____ is faulty.

33. Criticism of intelligence tests used in public schools has also become an issue. David McClelland compared a group of college students with straight A's to another group with poor grades; he found no differences in later _____ _____.

34. In considering the positive and negative aspects of standardized tests such as the Scholastic Aptitude Test, Robert Glaser points out that they are now used primarily to select _____ rather than to adapt _____ to the strengths, weaknesses, and needs of each student.

35. In considering the use of IQ tests, it is wise for the individual to remember that IQ is not _____. It is only an _____. If you change the test, you change the score.

36. As a result of the Larry P. case, a federal judge ruled that _____ _____ alone (because of their _____) can no longer be used to place students in special classes for the educable mentally retarded. Instead, _____ is being used. It is not a _____ but a controversial new way of looking at children that takes _____ differences into account. _____ assesses children in three different ways: first, it looks for any _____ problems. Next, the child's _____ outside the classroom is evaluated. Last, the child's WISC-III score is compared to others from similar _____.

ANSWER KEYS

Do You Know the Information?

Multiple Choice

1. (d) obj. 1, p. 498
2. (a) obj. 2, p. 499
3. (c) obj. 3, p. 499
4. (b) obj. 5, p. 500
5. (b) objs.6, 10, p. 501
6. (a,c,e,f)objs. 6, 10, p. 501
7. (c) obj. 7, p. 501
8. (c) obj. 8, p. 502
9. (c) obj. 9, p. 503
10. (a) obj. 10, p. 504
11. (b) obj. 12, p. 505
12. (c) obj. 14, p. 507
13. (c) obj. 16, p. 508
14. (b) obj. 17, p. 509
15. (c) objs.18, 19, p. 510
16. (a) obj. 20, p. 510
17. (d) obj. 20, p. 510
18. (d) obj. 21, p. 511
19. (a) obj. 22, p. 512

20. (b) obj. 23, p. 512
21. (b) obj. 24, p. 513
22. (d) obj. 28, p. 516
23. (d) obj. 29, pp. 516-517

Matching

1. G, obj. 4, p. 500
2. H, obj. 5, p. 500
3. L, obj. 8, p. 502
4. B, obj. 10, p. 504
5. M, obj. 18, p. 509
6. J, obj. 20, p. 510
7. K, obj. 29, p. 516
8. C, obj. 5, p. 500
9. E, obj. 1, p. 498
10. O, obj. 32, p. 520
11. F, obj. 5, p. 501
12. N, obj. 26, p. 513
13. P, obj. 15, p .507

True-False

1. T, obj. 5, p. 500
2. F, obj. 11, p. 505
3. F, obj. 12, p. 505
4. T, obj. 13, p. 506
5. F, obj. 15, p. 507
6. T, obj. 22, p. 512
7. F, obj. 23, p. 513
8. F, obj. 25, p. 513
9. T, obj. 27, p. 514
10. T, obj. 30, p. 517

Can You Apply the Information?

1. (b) obj. 1, p. 498
2. (a) obj. 4, p. 500
3. (c) obj. 5, p. 500
4. (c) obj. 7, p. 501
5. (c) obj. 7, p. 501
6. (c) obj. 11, p. 506
7. (b) obj. 13, p. 506
8. (a) obj. 20, p. 510
9. (a) obj. 25, p. 513

Chapter Review

1. savant (p. 498)
2. Binet (p. 499)
3. purposefully, rationally, environment (p. 499)
4. operational, measure (p. 500)
5. reliable, validity, objective, standardization, procedures, norms (p. 500)
6. age groups, mental (p. 501)
7. mental, chronological, IQ, intelligence quotient, mental, chronological (p. 501)
8. deviation IQ, average, relative standing (p. 502)
9. 6, 5 (p. 503)
10. 40, general information, comprehension, speed, insight, flexibility (p. 503)
11. Wechsler Adult, Wechsler, Children (p. 504)
12. performance (verbal), verbal (performance), individual, Group (p. 504)
13. normal, average, extremes (p. 505)
14. overall, verbal, vocabulary, rote, spatial relationships, arithmetic (p. 505)
15. job, high-status, lower-status (p. 506)
16. bright, peculiar, inferior, mental, education, determination, persistent, motivated (p. 507)
17. broader, real world, school, math, spatial, bodily, intrapersonal, interpersonal (p. 508)
18. 70, retardation, retardation, mild, moderate, severe, profound (p. 509)
19. Familial (p. 509)
20. organic, birth, fetal, metabolic, genetic (p.510)

21. PKU, microcephalic, Hydrocephaly, Cretinism, thyroid (p. 510)
22. Down syndrome, chromosome, age, parents (p. 510)
23. maze-bright, maze-dull, motivated, distracted (p. 511)
24. increases (p. 511)
25. identical, decreases, slightly, heredity, environmentalists, similar (p. 512)
26. increase (p. 513)
27. biological (adopted), adopted (biological) (p. 512)
28. stimulating, 29, 26 (p. 513)
29. decline, grows, smallest, first, confluence (p. 513)
30. heredity, environment, limit, down, limits, up (p. 514)
31. language, culture-fair (p. 516)
32. genetic heritage, impoverished, environment, logic (p. 516)
33. career success (p. 517)
34. people, instruction (p. 518)
35. intelligence, index (p. 518)
36. IQ scores, bias (p 519); SOMPA, test, cultural, SOMPA, medical, behavior, backgrounds (p. 520)

Chapter 19

Maladaptive Behavior: Deviance and Disorder

KEY TERMS AND CONCEPTS

psychopathology
DSM-III-R
psychological disorders
    organic mental,
    psychoactive substance abuse
    psychotic, mood, anxiety
    somatoform, dissociative
    personality, psychosexual
neurosis
insanity
views of normality
    subjective discomfort
    statistical
    social nonconformity
    context
    cultural relativity
    male bias in DSM-III-R
borderline personality
antisocial personality (sociopath)
    characteristics and causes
sexual deviances
    types, causes
    pedophilia
rape and sexual stereotyping

definition of anxiety
    adjustment disorder (nervous breakdown)
anxiety disorders
    generalized anxiety
    panic
    phobic
        agoraphobia
    obsessive-compulsive
    post-traumatic stress
dissociative disorders
    amnesia, fugue,
    multiple personality
somatoform disorders
    hypochondriasis
    somatization disorder
    somatoform pain disorder
    conversion disorders
understanding psychopathology
    psychodynamic, humanistic,
    behavioristic
Rosenhan — pseudopatients,
    danger of labels
insanity defense

LEARNING OBJECTIVES

To demonstrate mastery of this chapter you should be able to:

1. Present information to indicate the magnitude of mental health problems in this country including the proportion of the population which will require hospitalization at some point in his or her lifetime.

2. Define psychopathology.

3. Generally describe each of the following categories of mental disorders found in the DSM-III-R:
    a. psychotic disorders

    b. organic mental disorders

    c. psychoactive substance use disorders

    d. mood disorders

    e. anxiety disorders

    f. somatoform disorders

    g. dissociative disorders

    h. personality disorders

    i. sexual disorders

4. Explain why "neurosis" as a category was omitted from the DSM-III-R and list the three categories which now comprise that former disorder.

    a.

    b.

    c.

5. Differentiate psychosis from insanity.

6. Describe the following ways of viewing normality including the shortcoming(s) of each:
    a. subjective discomfort

    b. statistical definitions (norms)

    c. social nonconformity

    d. situational context

    e. cultural context

7. Explain why more women than men are treated for psychological problems.

8. State the conditions under which a person is usually judged to need help.

9.   With regards to personality disorders,
   a.   list and briefly describe the eleven different types (see Table 19-3)
        1.

        2.

        3.

        4.

        5.

        6.

        7.

        8.

        9.

        10.

        11.

   b.   describe the distinctive characteristics, causes, and treatment of the antisocial personality.

10. Explain what sets true sexual deviations apart from other sexual activity, and explain what generally causes sexual deviations.

11. Describe exhibitionism including who the offenders are, why they do it, and how one should react to them.

12.   Describe the typical child molester. Characterize the effect of single versus repeated episodes, and how parents should react to an incident of it.

13.   Explain how one can recognize signs of molestation from a child's behavior.

14.   Explain why rape is viewed by experts as primarily an aggressive rather than a sexual act.

15.   Explain how sex role stereotyping may encourage the act of rape.

16.   Differentiate anxiety from fear.

17.   List the three general characteristics common to anxiety disorders, dissociative disorders, and somatoform disorders.
      a.

      b.

      c.

18.   State what is usually meant when the term "nervous breakdown" is used. Differentiate this category from an anxiety disorder.

19.   Differentiate generalized anxiety disorders from panic disorders.

20.   Describe the following conditions:
        a.   phobic disorder

              differentiate a social phobia from a simple phobia

        b.   agoraphobia

        c.   obsessive-compulsive disorder

        d.   post-traumatic stress disorder

        e.   dissociative reactions:
              amnesia

              fugue

              multiple personality

        f.   somatoform disorders

              hypochondriasis

somatization disorder

somatoform pain disorder

g.   conversion reactions

21.   Discuss how each of the three major forces (theories) in psychology views non-psychotic disorders.

* * * * * * * * * *

The following objectives are related to the material in the "Applications" and "Exploration" sections of your text.
22.   Briefly describe Rosenhan's pseudo-patient study, and explain how his results relate to the idea of labeling.

23. Explain how legal sanity or insanity is determined and present an argument for and against the existence of an insanity plea.

SELF-QUIZZES

Do You Know the Information?

Multiple Choice

1. About _____ out of every 100 people will become so severely disturbed in his/her lifetime as to require hospitalization.
   (a) five
   (b) one
   (c) ten
   (d) three

2. _____ disorders are problems caused by known and verifiable brain pathology.
   (a) Substance use
   (b) Organic mental
   (c) Dissociative
   (d) Anxiety

3. The presence of physical symptoms suggesting disease or injury for which there are no identifiable causes is an indication of _____ disorders.
   (a) organic
   (b) dissociative
   (c) anxiety
   (d) somatoform

4. Neurosis as a category was omitted from the DSM-III-R because
   (a) it was too close to the term insanity.
   (b) it was actually the basis of personality disorders.
   (c) it was vague and lumped together too many separate problems.
   (d) of the legal implications of the term.

5. A problem with the statistical definition of normality is
   (a) the line between normality and abnormality is not specified.
   (b) subjective discomfort is overemphasized.
   (c) the method is not objective.
   (d) all of the above.

6.   Which of the following statements is *incorrect?*
(a)   A lack of subjective discomfort indicates that there are no psychological problems present.
(b)   Before any behavior can be defined as abnormal we must consider the context in which it occurs.
(c)   Before the judgment that a person needs help is made, a person in a position of power must notice the behavior and then do something about it.
(d)   There may be a damaging male bias to traditional conceptions of normality.

7.   The sociopath (psychopath)
(a)   usually gives a bad first impression.
(b)   tends to be selfish and impulsive.
(c)   is relatively easy to treat by psychotherapy.
(d)   avoids other people as much as possible.

8.   The early history of sociopaths is usually marked by
(a)   parental double-bind communication.
(b)   tension and stress.
(c)   emotional deprivation and neglect.
(d)   sexual perversion and obscenity.

9.   A lack of interest in close relationships with other people is a characteristic of a(n) _____ personality disorder.
(a)   narcissistic
(b)   schizotypal
(c)   schizoid
(d)   avoidant

10.   From a psychological point of view, the mark of true sexual maladjustments is that they are
(a)   against the law.
(b)   compulsive and a source of guilt or discomfort for one or both partners.
(c)   practiced by few people.
(d)   listed in the DSM-III-R.

11.   Which of the following statements about exhibitionism and pedophilia is *incorrect?*
(a)   Most exhibitionists are repeat offenders and are dangerous.
(b)   The impact of molestation is affected by how long the abuse lasts and whether genital sex acts are involved.
(c)   Parents are encouraged not to overreact to an incident of molestation because this may make a merely frightening episode a traumatic event.
(d)   Most exhibitionists have a deep sense of inadequacy and a need to prove their manhood.

12.   Which of the following is *not* a sign of child molestation?
(a)   fears of being seen in the nude
(b)   becoming markedly emotional and irritable
(c)   revealing self-destructive thoughts
(d)   having no loss of self-esteem

13.   Forcible rape is now considered by experts to be
(a)   primarily a sexual act.
(b)   an act designed to humiliate and degrade the victim.
(c)   an act that reveals the sexual immaturity of the rapist.
(d)   all of the above.

14.   Concerning rape and sex role socialization, it has been found that
(a)   women are reared to be more emotional than men and this makes them more susceptible to rape.
(b)   college males who were low in sex role stereotyping were more aroused by a rape story than those who were high in sex role stereotyping.
(c)   men are taught that women should show no direct interest in sex, but that they (the men) should take the initiative and in fact persist in their efforts.
(d)   none of the above is true.

15. Anxiety
   (a) is a response to an unclear or ambiguous threat.
   (b) is usually associated with psychosis.
   (c) is another term for fear.
   (d) is both a and b.

16. Which of the following is *not* a characteristic of disruptive anxiety?
   (a) self-defeating behaviors
   (b) elaborate defense mechanisms to maintain minimal functioning
   (c) dissatisfaction with life
   (d) amount of anxiety is proportional to the situation

17. A nervous breakdown is *not* the same as an anxiety disorder because
   (a) a nervous breakdown is really an adjustment disorder whose symptoms disappear when life circumstances improve.
   (b) an anxiety disorder has lower levels of anxiety than do adjustment disorders.
   (c) a nervous breakdown is self-defeating.
   (d) a person having a nervous breakdown shows a greater loss of contact with reality.

18. The behavioral pattern characterized by continuous tension and occasional attacks in which the person thinks he or she is going insane or is about to die is called
   (a) phobic disorder.
   (b) generalized anxiety disorder.
   (c) panic disorder.
   (d) conversion reaction.

19. Irrational and exaggerated fears that persist even when there is no real danger to a person are called
   (a) phobias.
   (b) anxieties.
   (c) delusions.
   (d) obsessions.

20. Avoiding speaking in public for fear of being evaluated could be a symptom of a(n)
   (a) agoraphobia.
   (b) simple phobia.
   (c) social phobia.
   (d) panic disorder.

21. Thoughts or images that intrude into consciousness against a person's will and which cause anxiety or extreme discomfort are called
   (a) phobias.
   (b) obsessions.
   (c) compulsions.
   (d) hallucinations.

22. Compulsions
   (a) give rise to obsessions.
   (b) make a person feel more secure by keeping activities highly structured.
   (c) tend to increase immediate anxiety but reduce it in the long run.
   (d) are all of the above.

23. The story of Sybil, a woman who had sixteen separate personalities, illustrates multiple personality which is a rare form of
   (a) fugue.
   (b) dissociative disorder .
   (c) schizophrenia.
   (d) psychosis.

24. _____ _____ are said to occur when anxiety or severe emotional conflicts are manifested as physical symptoms resembling disease or disability.
   (a) Dissociative reactions
   (b) Hypochondrial disorders
   (c) Somatosensory disorders
   (d) Conversion reactions

25. Which of the following *best* characterizes Carl Rogers' interpretation of the cause of dissociative, anxiety, and somatoform disorders?
    (a) a learned response
    (b) a form of avoidance learning
    (c) an attempt to handle guilt generated by the superego
    (d) the end product of a faulty self-image

26. In the behavioristic explanation of self-defeating behavior, the paradox is an example of
    (a) avoidance learning.
    (b) observational learning.
    (c) classical conditioning.
    (d) latent learning.

27. The psychodynamic, humanistic-existential, and behavioristic explanations of disordered behavior agree that
    (a) such behavior is made up of reinforced habits.
    (b) guilt underlies most of it. ·
    (c) self-image is a central issue.
    (d) it is paradoxical and self-defeating.

28. David Rosenhan's research on the fate of pseudo-patients in psychiatric hospitals indicates that
    (a) pseudo-patients recover more slowly than those given drugs.
    (b) psychiatric labels can be dangerous.
    (c) pseudo-patients are easily detected by hospital staff.
    (d) madness can be a breakthrough as well as a breakdown.

True-False

_____ 1. Psychopathology may be defined as the inability to behave in ways that conform to other's expectations.

_____ 2. Organic mental disorders are problems caused by brain pathology.

_____ 3. Because Robert is psychotic he is also, by definition, insane.

_____ 4. The context in which a behavior occurs is unimportant when evaluating if that behavior is abnormal

_____ 5. Sexual offenders are usually sexually immature and inhibited and choose a relatively infantile method of sexual expression because it is less threatening.

_____ 6. Exhibitionism is displaying the genitals to voyeurs.

_____ 7. Anxiety is more focused and intense than fear and is the result of a specific, identifiable threat.

_____ 8. The presence of intense anxiety attacks characterizes panic disorders whereas a generalized anxiety disorder is characterized by chronic, free floating anxiety.

_____ 9. The goal of therapy for a person suffering from multiple personality disorder is integration and fusion of the various personalities into a single entity.

_____10. According to Freud, neurosis represents a raging conflict between conscious and unconscious thought patterns.

_____11. When dealing with psychiatric labels, it is more productive to label the problem rather than the person.

_____12. Persons suffering from a mental illness that prevents them from knowing right from wrong are considered insane.

Matching (*Use the letters on the right only once.*)

_____ 1. psychotic disorder
_____ 2. somatoform disorder
_____ 3. personality disorder
_____ 4. legal term
_____ 5. agoraphobia
_____ 6. post-traumatic stress disorder
_____ 7. dissociative reaction
_____ 8. fugue
_____ 9. pseudo-patients
_____ 10. diminished capacity

A. brought about by stress beyond the range of normal experience
B. Rosenhan
C. fear of public places
D. escape
E. kind of insanity plea
F. hypochondriasis
G. fleeing to escape extreme conflict or threat
H. caused by senility
I. deeply ingrained maladaptive personality problems
J. most severe form of psychopathology
K. statistical definition
L. amnesia
M. insanity

Can You Apply the Information?

1. Tom has trouble controlling his thoughts and has hallucinations. He probably has a(n) _____ disorder.
    (a) mood
    (b) anxiety
    (c) psychotic
    (d) somatoform

2. You are sitting in a room full of convicted murderers. You are not a murderer. According to which definition of normality could you be considered abnormal in this situaion?
    (a) social nonconformity
    (b) statistical
    (c) subjective discomfort
    (d) all of these

3. You are a psychiatrist talking to a patient who thinks he has a sexual problem. Your patient only likes the missionary position but feels guilty because his wife wants a little variety. Can this situation be considered abnormal or a sexual deviation?
    (a) Yes
    (b) No

4. Ralph is a con-artist. He is a pro at pulling scams. He feels no guilt after bilking little old widows out of their savings. Ralph is probably suffering from
    (a) an anxiety disorder.
    (b) a psychotic problem.
    (c) sociopathy.
    (d) an adjustment disorder.

5. Thinking about going to college makes you nervous. In this case you would be feeling
    (a) anxiety.
    (b) fear.

6. Susan has lost the job she held for eighteen years. She really loved going to work. Now she has insomnia, she can't eat, she cries for no reason at all, and she feels worthless. It is likely that Susan is experiencing
    (a) a psychosis.
    (b) obsessions.
    (c) an adjustment disorder.
    (d) an organic mental disorder.

7. You are deathly afraid of giving an oral report in front of class. Shortly before you are due to give your report you feel your heart pounding, you feel like you're dizzy, and you feel like you might fall over dead. You're having the classic symptoms of a(n)
    (a) generalized anxiety disorder.
    (b) phobic attack.
    (c) panic disorder.
    (d) adjustment disorder.

8. Herman is afraid to leave the familiar surroundings of his home. He would be diagnosed as having
   (a) a social phobia.
   (b) claustrophobia.
   (c) acrophobia.
   (d) agoraphobia.

9. A househusband, whose dedication to household cleanliness is so great that he runs the vacuum cleaner five times a day whether or not the house needs it, probably has a(n) _____ disorder.
   (a) mood
   (b) phobic dosorder
   (c) conversion reaction
   (d) obsessive-compulsive disorder

10. Barbara witnesses her father committing a homosexual act. She immediately becomes blind and does not remember the event. Doctors can find nothing organically wrong with her eyes. The doctors diagnose her blindness as
   (a) a conversion reaction.
   (b) fugue.
   (c) amnesia.
   (d) a phobic disorder.

Chapter Review

1. _____ may be defined as the inability to behave in ways that foster the well-being of the individual and ultimately of society. _____ out of every 100 persons will become so severely disturbed in his or her lifetime as to require hospitalization.

2. The most widely accepted system of classification of disorders is the _____-III-R. Some of the disorders which are included in it follow. _____ disorders are the most severe type of psychopathology, often requiring hospitalization. Here there is a loss of contact with shared views of _____ and a major loss of ability to control thoughts and actions.

3. _____ mental disorders are problems caused by brain pathology. Psychological dependence on mood- or behavior-altering drugs results in a _____ _____ use disorder. _____ disorders involve significant disturbances in mood or emotion.

4. _____ disorders may take the form of _____ (irrational fear of objects, activities, or situations), panic (in which the person suffers unexplainable feelings of total panic), or _____ _____ (chronic and persistent anxiety). Also associated with this disorder is a pattern known as _____-_____be-havior.

5. _____ disorders are indicated when a person has physical symptoms suggesting physical disease or injury (paralysis, blindness, chronic pain, etc.) for which there is no identifiable cause. _____ disorders include cases of sudden temporary amnesia, fugue, and instances of _____ personality.

6. _____ disorders are deeply ingrained, maladaptive personality patterns, usually recognizable by adolescence and continued throughout most of the individual's adult life.

7. _____ disorders include gender identity disorders, transsexualism, and other problems.

8. DSM-III-R omits neurosis because it is too _____ a term and lumps together too many separate problems. Behavior that was once considered "neurotic" is now separated into _____ disorders, _____ disorders, and _____ disorders.

9. Insanity is a _____ term. Psychosis is a _____ term.

10. Defining normality is difficult. We can begin by saying that _____ _____ is characteristic of psychopathology and accounts for most instances in which a person makes a decision to voluntarily seek professional help. However, a problem with this definition of abnormality is that in some cases a person's behavior may be quite _____ without producing any discomfort. Additionally, in some cases a _____ of discomfort may indicate a problem.

11. Some psychologists have tried to define normality more objectively by using _____ definitions. Unfortunately this kind of definition of abnormality tells us nothing about the meaning of _____ from the _____. Another major problem with a statistical definition is the question of where to draw the line between _____ and _____.

12. _____ _____ may also serve as a basis for judgments of normality. Abnormal behavior can sometimes be viewed as a failure in _____. Before any behavior can be defined as normal or abnormal we must consider the _____ in which it occurs. One of the most influential _____ in which any behavior is judged is that of _____. There is always a high degree of _____ _____ in perceptions of normality and abnormality.

13. It should be clear that all definitions of abnormality are _____. In practice, the judgment that a person is abnormal or needs help usually occurs when the person does something that annoys or gains the _____ of a person in a position of _____ who then does something about it. If doing something about it includes giving a label, some psychologists believe that the DSM-III-R has a distinct male _____.

14. The individual with an antisocial personality, known as a _____ or _____, is irresponsible, impulsive, selfish, lacking in judgment, and unable to learn from _____. The sociopath's childhood is usually a history of _____ deprivation and neglect, thus they are unable to form a healthy emotional attachment to a caregiver.

15. Sociopathy is _____ treated with any success since the sociopaths _____ therapy as they might any other situation. There is, however, some evidence that antisocial behavior declines somewhat after age _____.

16. The mark of true sexual deviations is that they are _____ and _____, or that they cause guilt, anxiety, or discomfort for one or both participants. In characterizing sexual offenders, the picture of sexual deviance that usually emerges is one of sexual _____ and _____. The outlet for sexual expression is selected because it is less _____ than normal sexuality.

17. The category of sexual offenses that has the highest rate of repeaters is _____. Most of these offenders have a deep sense of _____. A woman should try not to become visibly _____ when confronted by one of these men.

18. In one-half to two-thirds of all cases of _____, the offender is known to the child. A single incident of _____ is unlikely to psychologically harm a child, but _____ incidents especially by someone the child knows, can cause problems. The impact varies and is affected by the _____ of the incidents and whether _____ sex acts are involved.

19. Many psychologists no longer think of _____ as a sexual act; rather it is an act of _____. The goal of the act is not sexual intercourse, but to attack, subordinate, humiliate, and degrade the victim. Many people learn to believe that women are not supposed to show any direct _____ in sex and men are taught to take the _____ and even _____ in their attempts at sexual intimacy. For these reasons our culture may _____ rape.

20. Anxiety is similar to fear except anxiety is a response to an _____ or _____ threat. Fear is more _____ and intense. What were formally called the neuroses are now classified separately as _____ disorders, _____ disorders, and _____ disorders. In general these disorders involve high levels of _____ and/or restrictive, self-defeating _____ patterns, a tendency to use elaborate _____ _____ or _____ responses, and pervasive feelings of _____ and dissatisfaction with life.

21. The term nervous breakdown has no formal meaning. It is best described as an _____ disorder. This disorder is the result of obvious environmental _____ that pushes people beyond their ability to cope effectively.   In a generalized _____ disorder there is at least 6 months of excessive _____. In a _____ disorder the affected person feels heart _____, _____ sensations, or feels that he or she is about to _____ because of the tremendous _____.

22. _____ are irrational fears that persist even when there is no real danger to a person. For this disorder to exist, the person's fear must _____ his or her daily life. The most common and disruptive phobic disorder is _____, a fear of leaving _____ and losing _____ in public places.

23. _____ are thoughts or images that intrude into consciousness against a person's will. These usually give rise to _____, irrational acts a person feels driven to repeat which may help to lessen the associated _____. Such phenomena are characteristic of _____-_____ disorders.

24. Most anxiety disorders are relatively lasting patterns. An exception to this is _____-_____ _____ disorder. These problems occur when_____ (like disasters or war) outside the range of normal human experience cause a disturbance. Symptoms may include _____ the traumatic event and a _____ of emotions.

25. A _____ reaction is marked by striking episodes of _____ (the inability to recall one's name, address, or past), _____ (fleeing to escape threat or conflict), or _____ _____ (a rare condition in which two or more separate personalities exist in an individual). The latter condition is aided by _____ which allows contact with the various personalities.

26. The person who has multiple physical complaints for which medical attention is sought but for which no clear physical cause can be found suffers from what is called _____ (one of the _____ disorders). Persons who have a _____ disorder express their anxieties in the form of various bodily complaints. A person suffering from _____ pain disorder is disabled by pain that has no identifiable physical basis. Another form of this, _____ reactions, is said to occur when anxiety or severe emotional conflicts are converted into physical symptoms resembling disease or disability.

27. At least three major psychological perspectives on the causes of dissociative, anxiety, and somatoform disorders can be identified. The first explanation was proposed by _____ and is called the _____ approach. According to this view, these disorders represent a raging conflict between the three subparts of the personality: the _____, _____, and _____.

28. Psychologist _____ _____, exemplifying the humanistic approach, interprets these disorders as the end-product of a faulty _____-_____. A more existential view stress that unhealthy anxiety reflects a loss of _____ in one's life. _____ have generally rejected previous explanations. They stress that such behavior is _____ just like any other behavior.

29. All theorists agree that this behavior is ultimately _____-_____ and _____. This means the behavior makes the person more miserable in the long run, but its immediate effect is to make him feel temporarily less _____.

30. The behavioristic explanation is that self-defeating behavior begins with _____ learning. Anxiety has been conditioned to various situations, and the immediate reinforcement of relief keeps the behavior pattern alive. This is called the _____ _____ hypothesis.

31. David Rosenhan gained entrance to mental hospitals by complaining of hearing voices. In 11 out of 12 tries, he and his colleagues were admitted with a diagnosis of _____.

32. Rosenhan and the others spent from one to seven weeks in hospitals before being discharged and found that contact between staff and patients was very limited. Attendants and staff only spent an average of _____ percent of their time out of the glassed-in central compartment in the ward; daily therapist contact averaged about _____ minutes.

33. These findings carry an important message: _____ can be dangerous. It is more productive to label _____ than to label people.

34. In Western law, the insanity defense evolved from the _____ rule. Insanity is closely related to claims of diminished _____ or that the person had an irresistible _____.

ANSWER KEYS

Do You Know the Information?

Multiple Choice

1. (b) obj. 1, p. 524
2. (b) obj. 3, p. 526
3. (d) obj. 3, p. 526
4. (c) obj. 4, p. 526
5. (a) obj. 6, p. 528
6. (a) objs.6-8, pp. 527-529
7. (b) obj. 9, p. 530
8. (c) obj. 9, p. 530
9. (c) obj. 9, p. 531
10. (b) obj. 10, p. 531
11. (a) objs.11-12, pp. 531-532
12. (d) obj. 13, p. 532
13. (b) obj. 14, p. 532
14. (c) obj. 15, pp. 532-533
15. (a) obj. 16, p. 533
16. (d) obj. 17, pp. 533-534
17. (a) obj. 18, p. 534
18. (c) obj. 19, p. 534
19. (a) obj. 20, p. 535
20. (c) obj. 20, p. 535
21. (b) obj. 20, p. 536

22. (b) obj. 20, p. 536
23. (b) obj. 20, p. 537
24. (d) obj. 20, p. 538
25. (d) obj. 21, p. 539
26. (a) obj. 21, p. 540
27. (d) obj. 21, p. 540
28. (b) obj. 22, p. 542

True-False

1. F, obj. 2, p. 524
2. T, obj. 3, p. 526
3. F, obj. 5, p. 527
4. F, obj. 6, p. 528
5. T, obj. 10, p. 532
6. F, obj. 11, p. 531
7. F, obj. 16, p. 533
8. T, obj. 19, p. 534
9. T, obj. 20, p. 537
10. F, obj. 21, p. 539
11. T, obj. 22, p. 542
12. T, obj. 23, p. 543

Matching

1. J, obj. 3, p. 526
2. F, objs.3,20,pp. 526, 538
3. I, obj. 3, p. 526
4. M, obj. 5, p. 527
5. C, obj. 20, p. 535
6. A, obj. 20, p. 536
7. L, obj. 20, p. 537
8. G, obj. 20, p. 537
9. B, obj. 22, p. 541
10. E, obj. 23, p. 543

Can You Apply the Information?

1. (c) obj. 3, p. 526
2. (b) obj. 6, p. 527
3. (a) objs.6,10,pp. 527, 531
4. (c) obj. 9, p. 530
5. (a) obj. 16, p. 533
6. (c) obj. 18, p. 534
7. (c) obj. 19, p. 535
8. (d) obj. 20, p. 535
9. (d) obj. 20, p. 536
10. (a) obj. 20, p. 538

Chapter Review

1. Psychopathology, One (p. 524)
2. DSM (p. 525); Psychotic, reality (p. 526)
3. Organic, psychoactive substance, Mood (p. 526)
4. Anxiety, phobias, generalized anxiety, obsessive-compulsive (p. 526)
5. Somatoform, Dissociative, multiple (p. 526)
6. Personality (p. 526)
7. Sexual (p. 526)
8. vague, anxiety, somatoform, dissociative (p. 526)
9. legal, psychiatric (p. 527)
10. subjective discomfort, maladaptive (abnormal), lack (p. 527)
11. statistical, deviations, norm, normality, abnormality (p. 527)
12. Social nonconformity, socialization, context (p. 528); contexts, culture, cultural relativity (p. 529)
13. relative, attention, power, bias (p. 529)
14. sociopath, psychopath, experience (p. 530); emotional (p. 531)
15. rarely, manipulate, 30 (p. 531)
16. compulsive, destructive, (p. 531); inhibition, immaturity, threatening (p. 532)
17. exhibitionism, inadequacy, upset (p. 531)
18. molestation, molestation, repeated, length, genital (p. 532)
19. rape, aggression (brutality), interest, initiative, persist, encourage (p. 532)

20.   unclear, amgiguous, focused, anxiety, dissociative, somatoform, anxiety, behavior, defense mechanisms, avoidance, stress (insecurity, inferiority, unhappiness) (p. 533)
21.   adjustment, stress, anxiety, anxiety (p. 534); panic, palpitations, choking (smothering), die, anxiety (p. 535)
22.   Phobias, disrupt, agoraphobia, home, control (p. 535)
23.   Obsessions, compulsions, anxiety, obsessive-compulsive (p. 536)
24.   post-traumatic stress, stresses, reliving, numbing (p. 536)
25.   dissociative, amnesia, fugue, multiple personality, hypnosis (p. 537)
26.   hypochondriasis, somatoform, somatization, somatoform, conversion (p. 538)
27.   Freud, psychodynamic, id, ego, superego (p. 539)
28.   Carl Rogers, self-image, meaning (p. 539); Behaviorists, learned (p. 540)
29.   self-defeating, paradoxical, anxious (p. 540)
30.   avoidance, anxiety reduction (p. 540)
31.   schizophrenia (p. 541)
32.   11, 7 (p. 541)
33.   labels, problems (p. 542)
34.   M'Naghten, capacity, impulse (p. 543)

Chapter 20

Major Mental Disorders

KEY TERMS, CONCEPTS, AND INDIVIDUALS

psychosis
features of psychosis
    delusions
        depressive, somatic,
        grandeur, influence,
        persecution, reference
    hallucination
    disturbed emotions
    disturbed communication
    personality disintegration
brief reactive psychosis
organic psychosis
    general paresis, Alzheimer's disease,
    senile dementia
functional psychosis
    delusional disorder
        paranoid psychosis
schizophrenia
    disorganized, catatonic,
    paranoid, undifferentiated
schizotypal personality
causes of schizophrenia
    environment
        trauma, family environment,
        double-bind and deviant communication
    heredity
    brain chemistry

dopamine
CT scan, PET scan
mood disorders
    manic
    depressive
        dysthmia, cyclothymia,
        reactive, postpartum
major mood disorder
    bipolar, manic, mixed,
    depressive, unipolar,
    affective psychosis
        endogenous
causes of mood disorders
Seasonal Affective Disorder
treatment
    psychotherapy
    somatic therapy
        chemotherapy
            taredive dyskinesia
        ECT
        psychosurgery
    hospitalization
        revolving-door policy
community mental health center
    prevention, paraprofessional
suicide — who, why, how to prevent
Szasz — the myth of mental illness

LEARNING OBJECTIVES

To demonstrate mastery of this chapter you should be able to:

1. List and explain the five major characteristics of a psychosis.

   a.

   b.

   c.

   d.

   e.

2. Define delusion. List and describe the six different types of delusions.

   a.

   b.

   c.

   d.

   e.

   f.

3. Define hallucination and name the most common type.

4. Explain how a brief reactive psychosis differs from other psychoses.

5.   Differentiate an organic from a functional psychosis.

6.   Describe the following types of organic psychoses:
     a.   general paresis

     b.   thoses from lead and mercury poisoning

     c.   senile dementia

     d.   Alzheimers disease

7.   List the three major types of functional psychoses.
     a.
     b.
     c.

8.   Describe what a delusional disorder is including the most common, paranoid psychosis.

9.   Generally describe schizophrenia.

10. Distinguish between schizophrenia and a schizotypal personality disorder.

11. List and describe the four major types of schizophrenia.
    a.

    b.

    c.

    d.

12. Explain how paranoid delusional disorder (psychosis) and paranoid schizophrenia differ.

13. Describe the roles of the following three areas as causes of schizophrenia:
    a. Environment

        1. trauma

        2. disturbed family environment

            a. double-bind communication

            b. deviant communication

    b. Heredity

c.   Brain chemistry

1.   dopamine (include a description of recent studies on dopamine receptors in the brain)

14.   Explain how CT and PET scans contribute to the study of abnormal brain activity.

15.   Summarize the relationship among inheritance, stress, and body chemistry as causes of schizophrenia. Explain why the Genain sisters case supports both genetic and environmental explanations of psychosis.

16.   State the incidence and characteristics of mood disorders, expecially depression, in the general population.

17.   Explain the differences between dysthymia and cyclothymia as well as a description of reactive depression.

18.   Differentiate maternity blues from postpartum depression. Describe what may predict the occurrence of the latter and the best way to treat it.

19.   Describe the following major mood disorders:
       a.   bipolar

       b.   unipolar

       c.   major depression

       d.   affective psychosis

20.   Differentiate between manic behavior and depressive reactions.

21.   Explain how major mood disorders differ from dysthymia and cyclothymia (include the concept of endogenous).

22.   Describe six possible explanations for the occurrence of depression.
       a.

       b.

       c.

       d.

       e.

       f.

23.   Explain seasonal affective disorder (SAD) and how it can be helped.

24.   Distinfuish between the two basic kinds of treatment for psychosis.

25.   Define chemotherapy. List and describe the three classes of drugs used to treat psychopathology.

26.   Discuss the advantages and disadvantages of the use of chemotherapy in the treatment of psychosis. (Include the term tardive dyskinesia in your discussion.)

27.   Describe the roles, advantages, and disadvantages of electroconvulsive therapy. Include a discussion of how the ECT debate is resolved.

28.   Describe the past and current uses of psychosurgery in the treatment of psychosis.

29.   Describe the role of hospitalization in the treatment of psychological disorders.

30.   Explain what deinstitutionalization is and how community mental health centers have attempted to help in the treatment of mental health.

* * * * * * * * * *

The following objectives are related to the material in the "Applications" and "Exploration" sections of your text.

31.   Discuss how each of the following factors affects suicide rate.

    a.   season

    b.   sex

    c.   age

    d.   income

    e.   marital status

32.   Discuss why people try to kill themselves.

33.   Name/identify the eight warning signs of suicide.
       a.

       b.

       c.

       d.

       e.

       f.

       g.

       h.

34.   List 4 common characteristics of suicidal thoughts and feelings.
       a.

       b.

       c.

       d.

35.   Explain how you can help prevent suicide.

36.   Describe Thomas Szasz's view of mental illness and treatment.

SELF-QUIZZES

Do You Know the Information?

Multiple Choice

1. Psychosis is a break in contact with reality typically characterized by
   (a) self-pity and other schizophrenic symptoms.
   (b) delusions, disturbed communication, hallucinations, personality disturbances, and disturbed emotions.
   (c) increased anxiety, mounting tensions, loneliness, and despair.
   (d) mania and depression.

2. Extremely psychotic behavior typically occurs
   (a) without flat affect.
   (b) without involving personality disintegration.
   (c) when word salad is present.
   (d) in brief episodes.

3. A delusion is
   (a) a false belief that is held even though the facts contradict it.
   (b) sensory experience that occurs in the absence of a stimulus.
   (c) seeing insects that are not really there crawling on your arm.
   (d) characterized by all of the above.

4. Among psychotics, the most common hallucination is
   (a) hearing voices.
   (b) seeing objects fly around the room.
   (c) seeing places or people related to the source of the psychosis.
   (d) feeling insects crawling under the skin.

5. A psychosis based on unknown or psychological factors is termed a(n)
   (a) organic psychosis.
   (b) affective disorder.
   (c) senile psychosis.
   (d) functional psychosis.

6. A psychosis resulting from an advanced stage of syphilis in which the disease attacks brain cells is called
   (a) general paresis.
   (b) affective psychosis.
   (c) functional psychosis.
   (d) senile psychosis.

7. Which of the following statements about Alzheimer's disease is *false*?
   (a) It is the most common form of organic brain damage.
   (b) It is the major cause of senility.
   (c) It is thought to be caused by a subtle buildup of toxins in certain areas of the brain.
   (d) It eventually involves serious physical as well as psychological problems.

8. The major symptom of paranoid psychosis is
   (a) hallucinations.
   (b) flat affect.
   (c) delusions of persecution.
   (d) depression.

9. Delusional disorders marked by a belief that one's body is infested with insects would be of the _____ type.
   (a) grandiose
   (b) somatic
   (c) erotomanic
   (d) persecutory

10. Schizophrenia involves
    (a) the delusions, hallucinations, and thought abnormalities found in other types of psychosis.
    (b) a withdrawal from contact with others; an inability to deal with daily events.
    (c) a split between thought and emotion.
    (d) all of the above.

11. Which personality disorder develops gradually and is characterized by isolation and withdrawal?
    (a) schizotypal
    (b) dependent
    (c) catatonic
    (d) paranoid

12. The most common form of schizophrenic disorder is
    (a) undifferentiated.
    (b) disorganized.
    (c) catatonic.
    (d) paranoid.

13. In paranoid schizophrenia there is _____ that is not evident in paranoid delusional disorder.
    (a) depression
    (b) personality disintegration
    (c) delusional thought
    (d) persecution

14. Families of persons likely to become disturbed have been found to interact in which of the following ways?
    (a) confusion, conflict, guilt, emotional attacks
    (b) much anger and prying but laced with love
    (c) love and much dependency
    (d) efforts to try to raise the person's level of achievement

15. Studies with identical twins show that
    (a) knowing the mental health of one has no predictive value for knowing the mental health of the other.
    (b) if one twin is schizophrenic the other will be no more likely to be schizophrenic than another sibling.
    (c) if one twin is diagnosed schizophrenic, the other twin has about a 50-50 chance of becoming schizophrenic.
    (d) none of the above are true.

16. Research into the possible dopamine connection as a cause of schizophrenia has indicated that
    (a) schizophrenics are on a constant "dopamine high."
    (b) antipsychotic drugs have no effect on dopamine action in the brain.
    (c) schizophrenics have double the normal number of dopamine receptors in their brains.
    (d) dopamine levels fluctuate depending on diet.

17. The use of which of the following techniques has indicated that the left hemisphere is overactive in schizophrenics?
    (a) PET scans
    (b) dopamine receptor mapping
    (c) CT scans
    (d) disturbed family measurement scale

18. The history of the Genain sisters and their respective schizophrenias has shown that
    (a) hereditary influences are more important than environmental influences in the development of schizophrenia.
    (b) environmental influences are more important than heriditary influences in the development of schizophrenia.
    (c) hereditary and environmental influences play different roles in the development of schizophrenia.
    (d) the family environment is the most crucial element in the development of schizophrenia.

19. In view of current research, choose the best summary statement concerning the causes(s) of schizophrenia.
    (a) Extremely traumatic experiences early in childhood cause the first split in personality to form.
    (b) The right combination of inherited potential and environmental stress brings about important changes in brain chemicals.
    (c) A by-product of adrenaline called dopamine accumulates in the schizophrenic's body.
    (d) Schizophrenics are really adapting to an impossible environment created by double-bind communication.

20. Depression can be termed to _____ if a person is intensely depressed following a major failure.
    (a) dysthymic
    (b) cyclothymic
    (c) reactive
    (d) delusional

21. High levels of anxiety during a pregnancy increase the risk of _____ following the birth of the baby.
    (a) dysthymia
    (b) postpartum depression
    (c) cyclothymia
    (d) reactive mania

22. Major mood disorders are characterized by
    (a) feelings that someone is out to get you.
    (b) a state of total panic which results in a stuporous condition.
    (c) lasting extremes of emotion.
    (d) a heightened state of anxiety.

23. A person with a major mood disorder who is continuously loud, inappropriately elated, hyperactive, and energetic would be classified as which of the following types?
    (a) manic-depressive
    (b) unipolar disorder
    (c) bipolar disorder, manic type
    (d) bipolar disorder, mixed type

24. Major mood disorders appear to be endogenous meaning that they
    (a) are depressive in nature.
    (b) are usually manic in nature with only periodic depressive episodes.
    (c) appear to be produced from within.
    (d) are a response to external events.

25. Women are twice as likely to experience depression than men. Researchers attribute this difference to
    (a) social and environmental conditions which place greater stresses on women.
    (b) biochemical differences in the brains of men and women.
    (c) the fact that women repress anger more than men.
    (d) the genetic superiority of men in dealing with their own family pressures.

26. Therapy which emphasizes two people talking about a person's problems is called
    (a) somatic therapy.
    (b) hospitalization.
    (c) bodily therapy.
    (d) psychotherapy.

27. The minor tranquilizers
    (a) improve the mood of those who are depressed.
    (b) are used to treat flat affect.
    (c) lessen anxiety and calm patients.
    (d) help control hallucinations.

28. Which of the following is a neurological side effect of extended major tranquilizer usage?
    (a) tardive dyskinesia
    (b) loss of memory
    (c) senility
    (d) dry mouth and constipation

29. Which one of the following statements about chemotherapy is *incorrect*?
    (a) Chemotherapy is often overused and keeps patients docile and easy to manage.
    (b) Drugs generally cure mental illness.
    (c) Drugs provide symptomatic relief and may allow patients to benefit more fully from psychotherapy.
    (d) Drugs have greatly improved the chances for recovery from a psychiatric disorder.

30. ECT is primarily used in treating
    (a) mania.
    (b) psychosis.
    (c) depression.
    (d) neurosis.

31. Most experts seem to agree that ECT
    (a) produces permanent improvement.
    (b) only causes temporary memory loss.
    (c) be used primarily for depression.
    (d) can now be used in lieu of drug therapy.

32. Psychosurgery is rarely used for the treatment of mental illness because
    (a) it is irreversible and unpredictable.
    (b) chemotherapy has made the procedure worthless.
    (c) regrowth of brain cells occurs very slowly.
    (d) it has been shown to have little or no effect on personality.

33. Which of the following statements about hospitalization are *true*?
    (a) Long-term hospitalization has better results than short-term.
    (b) It works best when it is the treatment of choice.
    (c) It does nothing to improve a troubled individual by itself.
    (d) None of the above statements are true.

34. Which set of factors would be *most* likely to increase the odds that suicide will occur?
    (a) being a poor woman at Christmas time
    (b) being a student with a need for recognition during final exams
    (c) being a divorced male psychiatrist over the age of 45
    (d) being a mentally retarded woman with strong religious convictions

35. Which of the following is *not* one of the common characteristics of suicidal thoughts and feelings?
    (a) Frustrated psychological needs.
    (b) Reduced behavioral output.
    (c) Constriction of options.
    (d) Unbearable psychological pain.

36. Which of the following statements reflects Thomas Szasz's views on mental illness and its treatment?
    (a) Although many brain diseases have been identified and empirically demonstrated which cause mental illness, they are of little explanatory value.
    (b) Emotional disturbances (problems in living) are really more appropriately labeled mental illness.
    (c) The only legitimate reason for committing a person is for being "dangerous to others" but only if he or she has committed violence or is threatening to do so.
    (d) The medical model is adequate for explaining mental illness.

True-False

_____ 1. Communication difficulties are nearly universal among all psychoses.

_____ 2. Paranoids are rarely treated or admitted to mental hospitals.

_____ 3. Schizophrenia is the psychotic version of a multiple personality disorder.

_____ 4. The term undifferentiated is used to describe many schizophrenic disorders because patients may shift from one pattern of behavior to another.

_____ 5. The diagnosing of schizophrenia is fairly objective and straightforward.

_____ 6. There is a greater than average degree of stress in the childhood of those who develop schizophrenia.

_____ 7. Mood disorders include manic behavior, but depression is by far the most common problem.

_____ 8. The risk of postpartum depression is increased by high levels of anxiety during pregnancy and negative attitudes toward childrearing.

_____ 9. Manic behavior can be viewed as a reaction of individuals trying to escape feelings of worthlessness and depression.

_____10. The fact that major mood disorders appear to be endogenous implies that genetics may be involved in their cause.

_____11. A person who gets severely depressed only in the winter is probably suffering from unipolar depression.

_____12. "Fly-catching" is symptomatic of tardive dyskinesia.

_____13. The advantage of using ECT is that it can easily be done first before beginning a long program of drug therapy.

_____14. Psychiatric patients recover better the longer they stay in the hospital (up to 3-4 months.)

_____15. Hospitalization is a form of therapy since it removes a disturbed person from a stressful environment.

_____16. Community mental health centers emphasize curing mental illness.

_____17. More women than men attempt suicide, but more men complete the act due to the techniques selected.

_____18. Generally, suicide is more common among lower socioeconomic status individuals than those higher in material wealth.

_____19. People who try to kill themselves have often suffered a break in communication with others, there may be sexual problems, job problems, and they are considered mentally ill.

_____20. In order to help a suicidal person it is important to accept his or her feelings and even the idea of the act of suicide itself.

Matching *(Use the letter on the right only once)*

_____ 1.	unrelated events given personal significance	A. Szasz
_____ 2.	sensory experience but no stimulus	B. somatic therapy
_____ 3.	most common of organic problems	C. endogenous
_____ 4.	waxy flexibility	D. CT scan
_____ 5.	silliness, laughter, bizarre behavior	E. delusion of reference
_____ 6.	produced from within	F. minor tranquilizer
_____ 7.	may contribute to the later development of schizophrenia	G. undifferentiated schizophrenia
_____ 8.	nearly double the normal number of these receptors in the brains of schizophrenics	H. dopamine
		I. energizers
_____ 9.	measures how much sugar is used in each area of the brain	J. flat affect
		K. PET scan
_____ 10.	chemotherapy, ECS, and psycho-surgery	L. psychotherapy
_____ 11.	improves mood of depressed person	M. phototherapy
_____ 12.	treatment for SAD	N. trauma like sexual abuse, etc.
_____ 13.	label for overlap among the types	O. halfway houses
_____ 14.	may live on fringe of society as vagrant, eccentric, or derelict	P. catatonic schizophrenic
		Q. delusion of influence
_____ 15.	mental illness is a myth	R. disorganized schizophrenic
_____ 16.	lacking signs of emotion	S. schizotypal personality
_____ 17.	eases a psychotic patient's return to the community	T. hallucination
		U. senile dementia

Can You Apply the Information?

1. Tim says he hears a radio inside his head. The CIA is speaking to him through the radio and telling him what to do. Tim is having delusions of
    (a) reference.   (c) grandeur.
    (b) persecution.   (d) influence.

2. Mary and Frank have an apartment in a very old building. They also have a two year old child. From an organic psychosis point of view regarding their child, Mary and Frank should be most concerned about
    (a) whether the elevator works or not in their building.
    (b) whether one of them might be carrying syphilis.
    (c) the possibility that the child might develop senile dementia.
    (d) whether the paint on the walls might contain lead or not.

3. Antonio is extremely hard to live with. He is convinced that he is Jesus and will not tolerate any doubt or word to the contrary. He is not actively hallucinating and his personality seems to be intact. Antonio is probably suffering from
    (a) schizophrenia.   (c) a delusional disorder.
    (b) paranoid psychosis.   (d) a psychotic mood disorder

4. The medical record of Pamela reveals that she was admitted to the hospital complaining of being chased by the Mafia. Her parents noted that she seemed to be a completely different person than she was a year ago. Pamela probably has
   (a) paranoia.
   (b) a schizoaffective disorder.
   (c) paranoid schizophrenia.
   (d) schizotypal personality.

5. On your first visit to a psychiatric ward you notice a patient sitting motionless and in an odd position on a couch. He holds the position for the full 30 minutes you are there. The patient probably is
   (a) manic-depressive.
   (b) catatonic.
   (c) disorganized.
   (d) schizotypal .

6. Steve breaks into uncontrollable laughter when told of his mother's death. Steve is probably suffering from
   (a) undifferentiated schizophrenia.
   (b) paranoid schizophrenia.
   (c) catatonic schizophrenia.
   (d) disorganized schizophrenia.

7. The father who says "I love you. Come give me a hug," to his daughter but then stiffens and nonverbally rejects her when she gets into his lap is probably
   (a) experiencing a schizophrenic break.
   (b) paranoid.
   (c) manic-depressive.
   (d) communicating with her in a double-bind fashion.

8. Sara's mother and father were both schizophrenic. If you're playing the odds, do you think Sara will also become schizophrenic?
   (a) Yes
   (b) No

9. Flat affect would be least likely in which of the following disorders?
   (a) major mood disorder
   (b) senile psychosis
   (c) catatonic schizophrenia
   (d) paranoid schizophrenia

10. Betsy has unlimited energy but cannot keep her mind on one thing for more than a few seconds. She talks constantly and is easily distracted. Eventually she becomes incoherent and disorganized. She probably is
    (a) in the manic phase of a major mood disorder.
    (b) paranoid.
    (c) a disorganized schizophrenic.
    (d) suffering from an organic psychosis.

11. David feels worthless. He has lost 25 pounds in the last three months and he can't sleep at night. His boss is on the verge of firing him because he has missed so much work, and when he is there, his performance is far below average. David had a manic episode one year ago. Now he appears to be suffering from
    (a) bipolar disorder, mixed.
    (b) bipolar disorder, depressed.
    (c) bipolar disorder, manic.
    (d) unipolar disorder, major depression.

12. Frank is in the hospital, but drugs haven't diminished his severe depression. He is now talking about suicide. As a psychiatrist, the next form of therapy you might consider would be
    (a) psychosurgery.
    (b) psychotherapy.
    (c) ECT.
    (d) none of these.

13. Which person would probably be the *greatest* proponent of the "medical model" of mental illness?
    (a) a psychiatrist
    (b) a clinical psychologist
    (c) a social worker
    (d) a psychoanalyst

Chapter Review

1. Psychosis — a major loss of contact with shared views of _____ — is among the most serious of all mental problems. It is characterized by the presence of _____ and _____, disturbed _____ and _____, and personality _____.

2. _____ are false beliefs that are held even when the facts contradict them.

3. One common form of delusion is a _____ delusion in which people feel they have committed some horrible crime or sinful deed.

4. Also common in psychosis are _____ delusions, such as belief that one's body is "rotting" away or emitting foul odors. Delusions of _____ may occur as well. Here the individuals think they are extremely important persons. Delusions of _____ occur when individuals feel that they are being controlled by other persons or unseen forces.

5. Delusions of _____ in which the people feel others are "out to get them" are also common. Finally, there may be delusions of _____, in which unrelated events are given personal significance.

6. _____ are sensory experiences that occur in the _____ of a stimulus. The most common psychotic hallucination is _____ _____.

7. Psychotic speech tends to be _____ and _____ sometimes sounding like a "_____."

8. Most psychotic patients are aware of their _____ (such as insomnia or feeling "high") and try to ward off a coming _____ _____. An exception is a pattern called a _____ _____ _____ where the symptoms appear after an extremely stressful event. The psychosis tends to have a _____ onset and rarely lasts more than a _____.

9. A psychosis based on known brain pathology caused by disease, gunshot wound, accident, etc., is termed an _____ psychosis. A psychosis based on unknown or psychological factors is called a _____ psychosis.

10. One example of organic psychosis is _____ _____, which occurs in a small number of cases of untreated syphilis. Probably the most common of organic problems is _____ _____, premature deterioration of the brain. Its most common cause is _____ disease, but it is also caused by circulatory problems, repeated strokes, or general shrinkage and atrophy of the brain. It is typically marked by disturbances in _____, abstract reasoning, _____, _____ control, and personality, leaving the individual confused, suspicious, apathetic, or withdrawn.

11. The major cause of senility is _____ disease. Initially victims have trouble remembering _____ events. Slowly, they become more _____. Eventually they are mute, bedridden, and unable to walk, sit up, or smile. Two brain areas seem to be implicated. They are the _____ and the _____ _____.

12. The three major types of functional psychoses are _____ disorders, psychotic _____ disorders, and _____.

13. People with delusional disorders usually do not suffer from _____, _____ excesses, or personality _____. This disorder's main feature is the presence of deeply held false _____. The most common delusional disorder is called _____ psychosis and centers on delusions of _____.

14. Besides paranoid psychosis, five other types of delusional disorders exist:
(1) _____ (marked by erotic delusions that one is loved by someone _____);
(2) _____ (where one believes in their having some great unrecognized talent);
(3) _____ (where one has an all-consuming, unfounded belief that their lover is _____);
(4) _____ (believing that one is being conspired against); and,
(5) _____ (believing that one's body is diseased).

15. Another major type of functional psychosis is _____. The word refers to a split between _____ and _____. The latter may become _____ or very _____. Recent studies suggest schizophrenic symptoms are related to an inability to maintain _____ _____.

16. _____ personality disorder develops gradually, usually starting in adolescence. The individual becomes _____ and _____, and they are often considered _____, _____, or _____. Problems of this type resemble _____ but do not involve a break with _____.

17. In _____ schizophrenia, the individual's personality disintegrates almost completely, resulting in silliness, laughter, bizarre and often obscene behavior. Chances of improvement are limited and social impairment is usually extreme.

18. In _____ schizophrenia, the person seems to be in a state of total panic. This brings about a stuporous condition in which odd positions may be held for hours or days. In this condition _____ _____ occurs in which the person can be arranged into any position like a mannequin.

19. _____ schizophrenia is the most common form of schizophrenic disorder. This type of schizophrenia, like paranoid delusional disorder, centers around delusions of _____ and _____, but in the schizophrenic disorder there is major personality _____ not evident in paranoia.

20. There is considerable overlap among the types of schizophrenia, with patients often shifting from one pattern of behavior to another at different times during the course of the psychosis. Many are simply classified as suffering from _____ schizophrenia.

21.   Some psychologists suspect that early _____ _____ may contribute to
the later development of schizophrenia. There seems to be a greater than average degree of
_____ in the childhood of those who develop schizophrenia. Many psychologists theorize
that a disturbed _____ environment is a causal factor in schizophrenia.

22.   R. D. Laing suggests that the families of schizophrenics frequently engage in _____-
_____ communication, where messages place the listener in a "no-win situation." Similarly,
the chance of developing schizophrenia appears to be related to patterns of _____
communication in families. People more likely to become disturbed had families whose communication
patterns were laden with _____.

23.   Although attractive, environmental explanations of schizophrenia are incomplete. When the children of
schizophrenic parents are raised away from their home environment, they are just as likely to become
psychotic. Thus children may at least inherit a _____ for schizophrenia.
This is shown by studies with twins. If one identical twin becomes schizophrenic, there is a
_____ percent chance the other will also.

24.   Many scientists believe that psychosis may be based on _____ abnormalities
which cause the body to produce some substance similar to a psychedelic drug. The most likely candidate is
_____. Rather than being on a "_____
_____" the brains of schizophrenics have been found to contain nearly _____
the normal number of dopamine receptors in the brain. Hence, schizophrenics get
_____ effects from normal levels of dopamine in their brains.

25.   Medical researchers are now able to directly observe the schizophrenic by looking at an x-ray picture of the
brain called a _____ scan. Researchers can also measure how much sugar is used in each area
of the brain. This is called a _____ scan.

26.   Although no single cause fully accounts for psychosis, it appears that anyone subjected to enough
_____ may be pushed to a psychotic break. Some people _____ a
difference in bodily _____ or _____ structure
and this makes them more susceptible.

27.   In _____ disorders sadness and despondency are exaggerated and prolonged for
unreasonable periods of time. If the depression lasts more days than not for at least 2 years then the person
has _____, but if it alternates with elevated mood periods then it is said to
_____. Sometimes a person's depression represents an
_____ _____ which is completed within a
reasonable time. However, if a person is unprepared to cope with a major loss on top of a previous series of
_____, then a _____ depression may occur.

28.   A temporary disturbance in mood after childbirth is called _____ _____. A
more serious disorder called _____ _____involves mood swings, despondency,
and feelings of inadequacy. It appears to be related to high levels of _____ during pregnancy. The amount of _____ support a person receives seems to be related to the
problem.

29.   Another major type of functional disorder is major _____ disorder which accounts for
about 14 percent of the patients admitted to mental hospitals. These types of disorders often appear to be
produced from within (which is called _____). This implies that
_____ has a role in the cause of these disorders.

30. In these disorders one of the following patterns predominates: In _____ disorders, persons go up or down emotionally. Individuals may be continually loud, inappropriately elated, hyperactive and energetic (_____ type) or may swing between this and deep depression (_____ type). Even when a person is sad and guilt-ridden, the problem is considered a _____ disorder (_____ type) if the person has ever been _____ in the past. The person who only goes down emotionally suffers from a _____ disorder. If the severe depression occurs without any history of _____, it is called a _____ depression. When a major mood disorder has psychotic symptoms, then a person is said to have an _____ _____.

31. The major mood disorders differ from other affective disorders in that the former usually involves more severe _____ changes. Also, psychotic _____ and _____ are present. _____ _____ disorder (SAD) is a depressive disorder which appears to be related to an increased release of _____ during the winter. The most efficacious treatment appears to be _____.

32. Depression and other _____ disorders have resisted adequate explanation and treatment. Some researchers are focusing on the biology of mood changes with some success. For example, the chemical named _____ _____ can be effective in treating some cases of depression, particularly those also showing manic behavior. Others have sought psychological explanations for depression. Psychoanalytic theory, for instance, holds that depression is caused by repressed _____ that is displaced and turned inward as self-blame and self-hate. Behavioral theories of depression emphasize learned _____.

33. Two basic forms of treatment for psychosis can be distinguished. The first, called _____, can be described as two people talking about one person's problems. A second major approach to treatment is _____ (or bodily) therapy.

34. One of the principal somatic treatments is _____, the use of drugs to control or alleviate the symptoms of emotional disturbance. This therapy is most often used to combat _____ but may also be used to relieve the anxiety attacks and other discomforts of nonpsychotic disorders.

35. _____ tranquilizers calm anxious or agitated persons, _____ improve the mood of those who are depressed, and _____ control hallucinations and other symptoms of psychosis.

36. While drugs have improved the chances of recovery from a psychiatric disorder, there are some drawbacks. First of all, drugs generally do not _____ mental illness. Patients may separate temporary improvement caused by a drug from improvement they consider genuine.

37. Also, there is the problem of _____ _____. For example, as many as 10 percent of patients taking major tranquilizers for extended periods develop _____ _____, a neurological condition where patients develop rhythmical facial and mouth movements, as well as unusual movements of the limbs and other parts of the body. Perhaps the most valid criticism of chemotherapy is the simple observation that it is easily _____.

38. Another somatic treatment is _____ therapy in which convulsions are produced by electric current. This is a rather drastic medical treatment used mainly for _____.

39. Critics of ECT claim that _____ _____ is often permanent and that there is evidence of occasional _____ _____ from its use. Proponents argue that detailed _____ scans show no evidence of damage. Also, it has been reported that if the electrodes are applied to only one side of the head, _____ loss is greatly reduced. Others argue that ECT done in this way may not _____ depression.

40. In summary, ECT probably only gives _____ improvement, but it does produce some _____ loss. It should be used for _____ as a last resort after _____ therapy has failed.

41. The most extreme type of somatic therapy is _____, a general term applied to any surgical alteration of the brain. The best known of these treatments is the _____ _____, where the frontal lobes are surgically disconnected from other areas of the brain.

42. The original goal of this procedure was to _____ a person who had not responded to any other type of treatment. Unfortunately, studies indicate it has very unpredictable results, and at the very least is _____, since damage to the brain is permanent.

43. Most neurosurgeons now use a technique called _____ _____ in which small areas in the brain's interior are destroyed electrically.

44. In the last 20 years, the resident population in large mental hospitals has been reduced by two-thirds (a process called _____). Hospital stays are now held to a minimum through use of _____ - _____ policies in which patients are released as soon as possible and readmitted only if necessary. Recent research indicates that patients do as well with _____-_____ hospitalization as they do with _____ periods.

45. A bright spot in the area of mental health care has been the passage of federal legislation to encourage creation of _____ _____ _____ centers. The most distinctive feature of these centers is an emphasis on _____. These centers have made mental services more accessible than ever before. Much of their work is made possible by _____, individuals who work under the supervision of more highly trained staff.

46. Several factors appear related to suicide; other popular beliefs appear untrue. For example, there is little connection between major holidays and the suicide rate. The peak actually occurs in _____ _____.

47. More _____ actually complete suicide, but _____ make more attempts. More than half of all suicides are committed by individuals over _____ years old, although there has been a recent increase in rates for adolescents and young adults. Studies also show that the person who is likely to commit suicide is in a _____ line of work and in terms of marital situation is probably _____.

48. There are many factors which cause suicide. There is usually a history of _____ troubles, a _____ problem, a _____ problem, or _____ difficulties. There is usually a break in _____ and the _____-_____ becomes very negative. Severe feelings of _____ are a warning of a high suicide risk.

49. There are several common characteristics of suicidal thoughts or feelings. Most people who want to kill themselves believe that this is the ultimate _____ from unbearable psychological _____. These people also usually have frustrated psychological _____ and they feel that this is the only _____ to their problems.

50. To help a suicidal person you should _____ their feelings and the idea of _____, try to get day-by-day _____ from them, don't end your efforts too soon, put the person in touch with a suicide _____ center, and if the suicidal person has a concrete _____, ask him or her to accompany you to a local emergency ward.

51. Thomas Szasz has charged that medical concepts of disease have been wrongly applied to emotional problems. The "_____ _____" as this is called, treats such problems as diseases with symptoms that can be cured. He believes that clearly demonstrated _____ diseases may eventually be found, but at the present time, they only apply to a small percentage of the cases.

52. Szasz prefers to view emotional disturbances as "_____ in _____," making _____ the goal of therapy. He believes that the only justification for involuntary commitment is for being _____ to others and only if the person has broken the _____ or is threatening to do so.

ANSWER KEYS

Do You Know the Information?

Multiple Choice

1. (b) obj. 1, pp. 548-549	18. (c) obj. 15, p. 555	**True-False**
2. (d) obj. 1, p. 549	19. (b) obj. 15, p. 556	
3. (a) obj. 2, p. 548	20. (c) obj. 17, p. 559	1. T, obj. 1, p. 548
4. (a) obj. 3, p. 548	21. (b) obj. 18, p. 559	2. T, obj. 8, p. 551
5. (d) obj. 5, p. 549	22. (c) obj. 19, p. 560	3. F, obj. 9, p. 552
6. (a) obj. 6, p. 549	23. (c) obj. 19, p. 560	4. T, obj. 11, p. 553
7. (c) obj. 6, p. 550	24. (c) obj. 21, p. 561	5. F, obj. 11, p. 553
8. (c) obj. 8, p. 550	25. (a) obj. 22, p. 561	6. T, obj. 13, p. 554
9. (b) obj. 8, p. 551	26. (d) obj. 24, p. 562	7. T, obj. 16, p. 559
10. (d) obj. 9, p. 551	27. (c) obj. 25, p. 563	8. T, obj. 18, p. 559
11. (a) obj. 10, p. 552	28. (a) obj. 26, p. 563	9. T, obj. 20, pp. 560-561
12. (d) obj. 11, p. 553	29. (b) obj. 26, p. 563	10. T, obj. 22, p. 561
13. (b) obj. 12, p. 553	30. (c) obj. 27, p. 563	11. F, obj. 23, p. 561
14. (a) obj. 13, p. 554	31. (c) obj. 27, p. 564	12. T, obj. 22, p. 563
15. (c) obj. 13, p. 554	32. (a) obj. 28, p. 564	13. F, obj. 27, p. 564
16. (c) obj. 13, p. 556	33. (d) obj. 29, pp. 564-565	14. F, obj. 29, p. 564
17. (a) obj. 14, p. 556	34. (c) obj. 31, pp. 566-567	15. T, obj. 29, p. 564
	35. (b) obj. 34, p. 568	16. F, obj. 30, p. 565
	36. (c) obj. 36, pp. 570-571	17. T, obj. 31, p. 566

True-False (continued)

18. F, obj. 31, p. 567
19. F, obj. 32, p. 567
20. T, obj. 35, pp. 567-568

Matching

1. E, obj. 2, p. 548
2. T, obj. 3, p. 548
3. U, obj. 6, p. 550
4. P, obj. 11, p. 553
5. R, obj. 11, p. 552

6. C, obj. 21, p. 561
7. N, obj. 13, p. 554
8. H, obj. 13, p. 556
9. K, obj. 14, p. 556
10. B, obj. 24, p. 562
11. I, obj. 25, p. 563
12. M, obj. 23, p. 561
13. G, obj. 11, p. 553
14. S, obj. 10, p. 552
15. A, obj. 36, p. 570
16. J, obj. 1, P. 548
17. O, obj. 30, p. 565

Can You Apply the Information?

1. (d) obj. 2, p. 548
2. (d) obj. 6, p. 550
3. (c) obj. 8, p. 550
4. (c) objs.10-12, pp. 552-553
5. (b) obj. 11, p. 553
6. (d) obj. 11, p. 552
7. (d) obj. 13, p. 554
8. (b) obj. 13, p. 554
9. (a) obj. 19, p. 560
10. (a) obj. 19, p. 560
11. (b) obj. 19, p. 560
12. (c) obj. 27, p. 564
13. (a) obj. 36, p. 570

Chapter Review

1. reality, delusions, hallucinations, emotions, communications (p. 548); disorganization (disintegration) (p. 549)
2. Delusions (p. 548)
3. depressive (p. 548)
4. somatic, grandeur, influence (p. 548)
5. persecution, reference (p. 548)
6. Hallucinations, absence, hearing voices (p. 548)
7. garbled, chaotic, "word salad" (p. 548)
8. symptoms, "high," psychotic break, brief reactive psychosis, sudden month (p. 549)
9. organic, functional (p. 549)
10. general paresis (p. 549); senile dementia, Alzheimer's, memory, judgment, impulse (p. 550)
11. Alzheimer's, recent, disoriented (suspicious, confused), hippocampus, nucleus basalis (p. 550)
12. delusional, mood, schizophrenia (p. 550)
13. hallucinations, emotional, disintegration, beliefs, paranoid, persecution (p. 550)
14. erotomanic, famous, grandiose, jealous, unfaithful, persecutory, somatic (p. 551)
15. schizophrenia, thought, emotion, blunted, inappropriate, selective attention (p. 551)
16. Schizotypal, isolated (listless), withdrawn (apathetic), odd, shiftless, eccentric, schizophrenic, reality (p. 552)
17. disorganized (p. 552)
18. catatonic, waxy flexibility (p. 553)
19. Paranoid, grandeur, persecution, disintegration (p. 553)
20. undifferentiated (p. 553)
21. psychological trauma, stress, family (p. 554)
22. double-bind, deviant, confusion (conflict, etc.) (p. 554)
23. potential, 46 (p. 554)
24. biochemical, dopamine, "dopamine high," double, psychedelic (p. 556)
25. CT, PET (p. 556)
26. stress, inherit, chemistry, brain (p. 556)
27. depressive, dysthymia, syslothymia, emotional adjustment, disappointments, reactive (p. 559)
28. maternity blues, postpartum depression, anxiety (p. 559); social (p. 560)
29. mood (p. 560); endogenous, genetics (p. 561)
30. bipolar, manic, mixed, bipolar, depressed, manic, unipolar, mania, major, affective psychosis (p. 560)
31. emotional, delusions, hallucinations, seasonal affective, melatonin, phototherapy (p. 561)
32. mood, depression, lithium carbonate, anger, helplessness (p. 561)
33. psychotherapy, somatic (p. 562)

34.   chemotherapy, psychosis (p. 563)
35.   Minor, energizers, antipsychotics (p. 563)
36.   cure (p. 563)
37.   side effects, tardive dyskinesia, overused (p. 563)
38.   electroconvulsive, depression (p. 563)
39.   memory loss, brain damage, brain, memory, end (p. 564)
40.   temporary, memory, depression, drug (p. 564)
41.   psychosurgery, prefrontal lobotomy (p. 564)
42.   calm, irreversible (p. 564)
43.   deep lesioning (p. 564)
44.   deinstitutionalization, revolving-door, short-term, longer (p. 564)
45.   community mental health, prevention, paraprofessionals (p. 565)
46.   early spring (p. 566)
47.   men, women (p. 566); 45, professional, divorced (p. 567)
48.   interpersonal, drinking, sexual, job, communication, self-image, hopelessness (p. 567)
49.   escape, pain, needs, solution (p. 568)
50.   accept, suicide (p. 568); commitments, prevention, plan (p. 569)
51.   medical model, brain (p. 570)
52.   problems, living, change, dangerous, law (p. 570)

Chapter 21

Insight Therapy

KEY TERMS, CONCEPTS, AND INDIVIDUALS

psychotherapy defined
what can be expected from therapy
dimensions of therapy
    individual, group,
    insight, action,
    directive, nondirective, time-limited
history (origins) of therapy
    trepanning
    demonology, exorcism
    ergotism
    Philippe Pinel
psychoanalysis — Sigmund Freud
    techniques of psychoanalysis
        free association, analysis of
        dreams, resistance, & transference
    short-term dynamic therapy
    spontaneous remission
humanistic therapy — Carl Rogers
    client-centered therapy — essentials
        unconditional positive regard,
        empathy, authenticity,
        no interpretations or advice
existential therapy — Victor Frankl
    free will, logotherapy
    confrontation, encounter

Gestalt therapy — Fritz Perls
    connected wholes,
    emphasis on present
group therapy
psychodrama
    role reversals, mirror technique, role plays
family therapy
group awareness training
    sensitivity vs. encounter groups
    large group awareness training
    therapy placebo effect
transactional analysis
    ego states — parent, adult, child
    transactions — crossed, ulterior,
        complementary
    games
effectiveness of therapy
goals of therapy
commonalities in therapy
how to know when to seek help
where to get help
how to help a friend
cultural barriers
    culturally skilled counselor

LEARNING OBJECTIVES

To demonstrate mastery of this chapter you should be able to:
1.   Define psychotherapy.

2. Distinguish between individual and group therapies.

3. Distinguish between insight and action therapies.

4. Distinguish between directive and non-directive therapies.

5. Explain what is meant by time-limited therapy.

6. Evaluate what a person can expect as possible outcomes from psychotherapy.

7. Briefly describe the history of the treatment of psychological problems, including in your description trepanning (trephining), demonology, exorcism, ergotism, and Pinel.

8. Describe Freud's development of psychoanalysis.

9.   List the four basic techniques used in psychoanalysis, and explain their purpose.
     a.

     b.

     c.

     d.

10. Explain how short-term dynamic therapy differs from psychoanalysis. Describe the criticism that helped promote the use of short-term dynamic therapy.

11. Contrast client-centered (humanistic) therapy and psychoanalysis.

12. Describe client-centered therapy including the four conditions that should be maintained for successful therapy.

13. Explain the approach of existential therapy and compare and contrast it with client-centered therapy. Generally describe logotherapy as an example of existential therapy.

14. Briefly describe gestalt therapy.

15. Describe the advantages of group therapy.

16. Briefly describe each of the following group therapies:
   a. psychodrama

   b. family therapy

   c. group awareness training (including sensitivity groups, encounter groups, and large group awareness training)

17. Distinguish between and evaluate the effectiveness of encounter and sensitivity groups. Include a description of the positive and negative results of each and a discussion of the therapy placebo effect.

18. Discuss the pros and cons of phone-in radio psychologists and describe what the APA recommends should be the extent of their activities.

19. Describe the following concepts from transactional analysis:
    a. parent ego-state

    b. adult ego-state

    c. child ego-state

    d. crossed transaction

    e. ulterior transaction

    f. games

20. Discuss the effectiveness of psychotherapy. Describe the rate at which typical doses of therapy help people improve.

21. List the six goals of psychotherapy, and state the four means used to accomplish the goals.
    Goals:
    a.

    b.

    c.

    d.

    e.

    f.

    Means:
    a.

    b.

    c.

    d.

* * * * * * * * * *

The following objectives are related to the material in the "Applications" and "Exploration" sections of your text.

22. List and describe four indicators that may signal the need for professional psychological help.
    a.

    b.

    c.

    d.

23. Explain the methods available for finding psychological help in your community. Include a description of other options that might be available as well as how to evaluate a therapist.

24.   List and briefly describe nine points or tips which can help a person when counseling a friend.
a.

b.

c.

d.

e.

f.

g.

h.

i.

25.   List the four main cultural barriers to effective counseling as stated by Sue and Sue.
a.
b.
c.
d.

26.   Enumerate and explain the characteristics of a culturally skilled counselor.

SELF-QUIZZES

Do You Know the Information?

Multiple Choice

1. Psychotherapy is defined as
   (a) a technique used to cure mental illness.
   (b) a psychological technique that facilitates positive changes in a person's adjustment, behavior, or personality.
   (c) two people facilitating each other's personal growth.
   (d) any technique which provides an understanding of one's problems.

For questions 2-5 use a letter from the following list:

   (a) individual therapy   (e) directive therapy
   (b) group therapy   (f) nondirective therapy
   (c) insight therapy   (g) time-limited therapy
   (d) action therapy

_____ 2. one-to-one basis between client and therapist

_____ 3. focuses on directly changing troublesome habits and behavior

_____ 4. fosters a deeper understanding of the assumptions, beliefs, emotions, and conflicts underlying a problem

_____ 5. places responsibility for the course of therapy on the client

6. Which of the following statements about psychotherapy is *incorrect?*
   (a) Chances of improvement are fairly good for circumscribed problems such as phobias, sexual problems, marital conflicts, etc.
   (b) Therapy's major benefit is that it provides comfort, support, and a way to make positive changes.
   (c) Therapy usually helps bring about a dramatic end to a person's suffering.
   (d) Therapy is not just done to solve problems but also to encourage personal growth and enrichment.

7. Trepanning was the technique in which
   (a) a hole was bored into a person's skull to release evil spirits.
   (b) a person was tortured as a part of a religious ritual.
   (c) a person was chained to a wall to prevent injury.
   (d) a person's system was purged of the ergot fungus.

8. During the Middle Ages, treatment for the mentally ill in Europe focused on
   (a) demonology.   (c) unconscious motives.
   (b) poisoning.   (d) physiological abnormalities.

9. A compassionate view of the mentally ill slowly emerged after 1793, primarily as a result of the efforts of
   (a) Freud.   (c) Rogers.
   (b) Pinel.   (d) Frankl.

10. The first psychotherapy was developed because Freud
    (a) could not understand his dreams.
    (b) believed that deeply hidden unconscious conflicts caused hysteria.
    (c) became convinced that the driving forces of personality were conscious ideas that needed controlling.
    (d) found the symptoms of hysteria were caused by dreams.

11. A patient in psychoanalysis does not wish to talk about her ideas and thoughts during free association or dream analysis. This problem is known as
    (a) transference.
    (b) empathy.
    (c) resistance.
    (d) identification.

12. Which of the following statements about psychotherapy is *incorrect*?
    (a) Most therapists who use psychoanalytic theory have switched to short-term dynamic therapy.
    (b) The success of psychoanalysis may be attributable to spontaneous remission.
    (c) Some people in psychoanalysis improve with the mere passage of time.
    (d) The number of therapists practicing psychoanalysis has increased.

13. The goal of psychoanalysis is
    (a) adjustment.
    (b) self-knowledge.
    (c) self-actualization.
    (d) to rebuild connected wholes.

14. Which of the following statements concerning client-centered therapy and psychoanalysis is *incorrect*?
    (a) The client-centered therapist tends to take a position of authority from which he or she offers interpretations.
    (b) Psychoanalysts delve into childhood, dreams, and the unconscious.
    (c) Client-centered therapy and the other humanistic therapies view therapy as a means of giving a person's natural tendencies toward mental health a chance to emerge.
    (d) In client-centered therapy the client determines what will be said in each session.

15. The terms unconditional positive regard and empathy are most closely associated with _____ therapy.
    (a) psychoanalytic
    (b) client-centered
    (c) existential
    (d) rational-emotive

16. The idea of existential therapy is to
    (a) probe hidden desires that relate to the nature of one's being.
    (b) confront a person's unrealistic expectations.
    (c) eliminate undesirable behavior by manipulating reinforcers.
    (d) promote self-knowledge and self-actualization and emphasize free will.

17. Which of the following therapies stresses confrontation between client and therapist?
    (a) psychoanalysis
    (b) logotherapy
    (c) transactional analysis
    (d) client-centered therapy

18. A therapist who tries to help an individual rebuild thinking, feeling, and acting into connected wholes would most likely be a
    (a) Gestalt therapist.
    (b) transactional analyst.
    (c) encounter group therapist.
    (d) sensitivity group therapist.

19. According to Perls, the founder of Gestalt therapy, emotional health comes from getting in touch with what you
    (a) should do.
    (b) ought to do.
    (c) want to do.
    (d) should want to do.

20. An advantage of group therapy is that it
    (a) provides an important link between the real world and therapy.
    (b) enables patients to have more individual time with the therapist to talk over personal problems.
    (c) provides a more protected atmosphere than individual therapy.
    (d) is all of the above.

21. In which of the following therapies would a person role play incidents resembling those which cause problems in real life?
    (a) TA
    (b) encounter groups
    (c) psychodrama
    (d) sensitivity groups

22. The therapy in which a person is encouraged to get rid of his or her psychological defenses and to be totally honest and confronting is
    (a) TA.
    (b) encounter groups.
    (c) psychodrama.
    (d) sensitivity groups.

23. Which of the following statements is *incorrect?*
    (a) The APA recommends that radio psychologists discuss only problems of a general nature and not discuss the particular problem of an individual caller.
    (b) Many radio psychologists stress that their work is educational, not therapeutic.
    (c) Many of the claimed benefits of sensitivity and encounter groups are the result of a therapy placebo effect.
    (d) The therapy placebo effect is related to things such as the therapist's theoretical orientation, the number of years of schooling, etc.

24. Of the following therapies, which focuses on the analysis of personality ego-states?
    (a) Gestalt
    (b) psychodrama
    (c) family therapy
    (d) transactional analysis

25. Which ego-state is the internal record of all of the messages received from one's parents?
    (a) Child
    (b) Parent
    (c) Adult
    (d) none of these

26. According to TA, _____ transactions form the basis of _____.
    (a) crossed, life scripts
    (b) crossed, games
    (c) crossed, ulterior transactions
    (d) ulterior, games

27. Which of the following statements about psychotherapy is *incorrect?*
    (a) In a study of the rate of improvement, half of the patients reported feeling better after one month.
    (b) In the above study, the majority of patients had improved after 6 months.
    (c) The typical "dose" of therapy is one hour per week.
    (d) In hundreds of studies of the effectiveness of therapy, a modest but consistent positive effect was found.

28. Which of the following is *not* a goal of psychotherapy?
    (a) better interpersonal relations
    (b) resolution of conflicts
    (c) a more pleasant personality
    (d) insight

29. To accomplish part or all of the goals of psychotherapy, the different therapies offer
    (a) an explanation or a rationale for the suffering the client has experienced.
    (b) a protected setting in which emotional catharsis can take place.
    (c) a therapeutic alliance between client and therapist.
    (d) a new perspective about self and their situation.
    (e) all of the above.

30. Which of the following would *not* be considered an important indicator that a person needs professional psychological help?
    (a) significant change in observable behavior
    (b) inability to meet the expectations of others
    (c) persistent suicidal thoughts or impulses
    (d) high level of psychological discomfort

31. Which of the following is considered to be the therapist's most basic tool?
    (a) a peer-led self-help group
    (b) a crisis hotline
    (c) the fact that all therapies are about equally effective
    (d) the relationship between the client and the therapist

32. In choosing a psychotherapist, it is best to
    (a) choose a psychologist instead of a psychiatrist.
    (b) start with a short consultation first for evaluation purposes.
    (c) avoid paraprofessionals at all costs.
    (d) be sure you have enough money to cover the costs of a long therapeutic interaction.

33. Which of the following is *not* good to keep in mind when comforting someone in distress?
    (a) Focus on feelings to avoid making the person defensive.
    (b) Resist the temptation to contradict the person with your point of view.
    (c) Show your understanding and support by giving your advice freely.
    (d) Encourage free expression through open questions.

34. Culturally skilled counselors need to
    (a) set aside their own cultural values and biases.
    (b) realize that cultural barriers are rarely transcended.
    (c) avoid thinking of clients in terms of stereotypes.
    (d) mentally take the role of the ethnic or racial group.

True-False

_____ 1. Time-limited therapy is used when each therapy session is to last no more than one hour.

_____ 2. Therapy is about equally effective for all problems.

_____ 3. Ergotism, which occurred in the Middle Ages, was poisoning from a fungus that produced psychotic-like symptoms.

_____ 4. Psychoanalysis as originally conducted by Freud is still in widespread use today.

_____ 5. Psychoanalysis is usually better than no treatment at all.

_____ 6. Client-centered therapy emphasizes the idea of free will whereas existential therapy seeks to uncover a "true self" hidden behind an artificial screen of defenses.

_____ 7. In psychodrama an individual role-plays dramatic incidents resembling those that cause problems in real life.

_____ 8. Family therapists believe that problems are rarely limited to a single family member, but that is the person who should receive therapy.

_____ 9. Encounter groups are usually more confrontive and emotionally intense than sensitivity groups.

_____10. Because there is a danger of psychological damage, encounter group participation is safest when members are carefully screened and when groups are professionally led.

_____11. According to TA, games may become emotionally or physically destructive.

_____12. Psychotherapy techniques tend to be about equally successful in helping clients with emotional/behavioral problems.

_____13. At this point psychotherapy is an art, not a science.

_____14. Whether a client likes their therapist or not seems to have no relationship to the success of the therapy.

_____15. When counseling a friend, contradict his or her opinion of a situation if you feel it is wrong.

_____16. Even though clients and therapists may come from different cultural backgrounds, misunderstandings are relatively rare.

Can You Apply the Information?

1. Alex is going to a therapist in hopes of breaking his smoking habit. The therapy which would most likely be best for him would be _____ therapy.
    (a) nondirective
    (b) action
    (c) insight
    (d) group

2. In the above question, if Alex were going to a therapist to find out why he smokes, he would probably be participating in _____ therapy.
    (a) action
    (b) insight
    (c) nondirective
    (d) none of these

3. In a psychoanalytic session the patient is talking about her relationship with her father. She begins to get angry with the psychoanalyst when he makes comments. It is likely that the therapist would begin to concentrate on
    (a) analysis of resistance.
    (b) dream interpretation.
    (c) analysis of transference.
    (d) free association.

4. Which of the following therapists would be *least* likely to give you suggestions on how to solve an emotional problem?
    (a) Perls (Gestalt therapy)
    (b) Frankl (logotherapy)
    (c) Berne (TA)
    (d) Rogers (client-centered therapy)

5. You are a humanistic therapist doing client-centered therapy. What is probably your *first* step with most of your clients?
    (a) Convince your client that you are a competent therapist capable of guiding them to good adjustment.
    (b) Reflect upon the client's mistakes and tell them what you would do to improve behavior.
    (c) Offer the client unconditional positive regard and strive to be authentic in your relationship.
    (d) None of the above choices would be first.

6. David's therapist is emphasizing the idea that David is totally free to make his own choice concerning his future. David is probably in
    (a) existential therapy.
    (b) transactional analysis.
    (c) client-centered therapy.
    (d) Gestalt therapy.

7. With the help of her therapist, Rebecca is now able to decide what she wants to do for herself rather than dwelling on what others may want her to do or on what she feels she ought to be doing. Rebecca has probably been in
   (a) existential therapy.
   (b) logotherapy.
   (c) client-centered therapy.
   (d) Gestalt therapy.

8. Frank is in group therapy. During one session he and the rest of the group act out his latest confrontation with his alcoholic wife. Frank is probably engaged in
   (a) logotherapy.
   (b) sensitivity training.
   (c) Gestalt therapy.
   (d) psychodrama.

9. Betty is depressed and suicidal. Her best friend Linda has asked her to go to an encounter group as her guest and consider this type of therapy. Betty should
   (a) go with Linda because the group will probably help her understand her problem in a nonthreatening manner.
   (b) stay away because she is probably not psychologically suited for the brutal honesty.
   (c) go with Linda to better understand her ego-states.
   (d) not do anything now and expect to improve with time.

10. Mary is having trouble sleeping at night, and she believes that she can get help by calling her local radio psychologist. It takes 30 minutes of constant dialing to finally get through. Even though the psychologist only talks about insomnia in a general manner and not about her specific problem, Mary's insomnia is alleviated and she can now sleep normally. What would account for this apparent "relief"?
   (a) the therapy placebo effect
   (b) the indepth discussion of Mary's personal life
   (c) the psychologist's unconditional positive regard for Mary and her situation
   (d) the use of awareness training during the call

11. Karen and Ted are at the dinner table. Ted comments about their lawn by saying, "Why can't you ever remember to water the grass? I've had to remind you twice in the past week." What ego-state is Ted in?
   (a) Parent
   (b) Adult
   (c) Child
   (d) California

12. Tony (the therapist) and Bob (the client) are trying to come to grips with Bob's deep feelings of hurt and rejection because of the physical abuse Bob suffered as a child. They are working together to see how this has affected Bob's relationships with his children. Which of the four "means to accomplish the goals of psychotherapy" are they employing?
   (a) a new perspective
   (b) a protected setting
   (c) a therapeutic alliance
   (d) an explanation or rationale

Chapter Review

1. _____ is any psychological technique designed to facilitate positive changes in a person's _____, _____, or _____. There are many different kinds of therapy.

2. _____ therapies foster a deeper understanding of the assumptions, beliefs, emotions, and conflicts underlying a problem. _____ therapies focus on directly changing troublesome habits and behavior. In _____ therapies, the therapist guides the client strongly, sometimes even making important decisions for the client.

3. _____ approaches place responsibility for the course of therapy on the client; it is up to the client to discover his or her own solutions. _____ therapies proceed on a one-to-one basis between client and therapist. In _____ therapy, individual problems are resolved by making use of the special characteristics of the group setting. If therapy is begun with the expectation that it will last only a limited number of sessions then the therapy is known as _____-_____.

4. Therapy is not equally effective for all problems. Chances of improvement are fairly good for _____, low _____-_____, some _____ problems, and _____ complaints. People who enter therapy should not expect _____ results.

5. During the Stone Age, spirits were released from the head by a process called _____, where a hole was bored, chipped, or bashed into the skull. During the Middle Ages, treatment for the mentally ill in Europe focused on _____ with the major technique being _____. Some psychotic-like behavior was probably caused by _____, the eating of bread made from grain infected with a fungus.

6. Finally, a more compassionate view of the mentally ill emerged after 1793 when _____ changed the Bicetre Asylum in Paris from a "mad house" to a mental hospital by personally _____ the inmates. The first true psychotherapy was developed around the turn of the century by _____.

7. Freud sought to understand and treat cases of _____, where physical symptoms like paralysis or numbness occur without known physical cause. Freud slowly became convinced that the symptoms of this disorder were caused by hidden _____ _____. Freud's form of therapy was called _____.

8. Freud relied on four basic techniques to uncover the unconscious roots of neurosis. One of these, _____ _____, required the patient to say whatever came to mind without regard for whether it made sense, was painful, or embarrassing. The purpose of this technique was to lower _____ so that unconscious material may emerge.

9. Another technique, _____ analysis, was considered by Freud to be an unusually good means of tapping the unconscious. Freud felt that forbidden _____ and unconscious _____ are freely expressed in dreams and that the hidden (_____) content of dreams can be revealed by interpreting _____ _____.

10. When free associating or describing dreams, the patient may _____ talking or thinking about certain topics. Such _____ are said to reveal particularly important unconscious conflicts. The individual undergoing psychoanalysis may also _____ feelings to the therapist that relate to important past relationships with others.

11. Because of the huge amounts of _____ and _____ required for psychoanalysis, this type of therapist has become relatively _____. In its place has come _____-_____ _____ therapy. Eysenck has suggested that psychoanalysis takes so long that patients improve due to the mere passage of time. This improvement is called _____ _____. Recent research reveals that _____ is better than no treatment at all.

12. The goal of Freudian therapy is _____. The humanistic therapies seek to help people make full use of their _____.

13. Carl Rogers has developed a therapy called _____-_____ therapy. Rogers believes that the psychoanalyst tends to take a position of _____ about what is wrong with the patient. He believes that the psychoanalyst's _____ of what is right or valuable may not be so for the client. Thus, Rogers uses a _____ approach in that the client determines what will be discussed during each session.

14. According to Rogers, the therapist's job is to create an "atmosphere of growth" by maintaining four basic conditions. First the therapist offers the client _____ _____ _____ — the client is accepted totally. Second, the therapist attempts to achieve genuine _____ for the client by trying to view the world through the client's eyes.

15. As a third condition, the therapist strives to be _____ in his or her relationship with clients. Fourth, rather than making interpretations, posing solutions, or offering advice, the therapist _____ the client's thoughts and feelings. Client-centered therapy is based on drawing insights from conscious _____ and _____ and accepting one's true _____.

16. _____ therapy focuses on problems of existence or "being in the world." Its goals are self-knowledge and self-actualization. This therapy emphasizes _____ _____. Through choices one can become the person he or she wants to be. An example of this therapy is _____ which is centered around _____. This therapy is considered successful when clients regain a strong sense of purpose and _____ in life.

17. Another approach called _____ therapy is built around the idea that perception or awareness becomes _____ and _____ in the maladjusted individual. The therapy developed by Perls emphasizes that emotional health comes from getting in touch with what you _____ to do — not what you should do, ought to do, or should want to do. The therapist seeks to help the individual rebuild thinking, feeling, and acting into connected _____. Above all else, the therapy emphasizes _____ experience.

18. In _____ therapy a person can act out or experience problems in addition to talking about them. Also, support is provided by other members who share similar problems. This form of therapy helps form a _____ between therapy and real-life problems.

19. One of the first group approaches was developed by J. L. Moreno, who called his technique _____. Through this an individual play-acts roles and dramatic incidents resembling those that cause problems in real life.

20. The basic belief of _____ therapists is that problems are rarely limited to a _____ family member. Thus, family members work together to improve _____, to change destructive patterns, and to see themselves and each other in new ways.

21. _____ groups tend to be less confrontive than _____ groups. Participants in the former take part in experiences that gently enlarge_____ of oneself and others. The emphasis in the latter is on tearing down _____ and facades through discussion that can be brutally honest.

22. There has recently been a shift away from sensitivity and encounter groups to _____ _____ _____ training. Many people feel that all such groups are not really therapy-based, but that the derived benefits may simply result from a kind of _____ _____ effect.

23. Many people turn to _____ psychologists for help. There is much concern about this practice, but these psychologists defend themselves by saying that listeners learn from other people's problems and that their work is primarily _____, not _____. The APA takes the position that only problems of a _____ nature should be discussed and not a specific caller's problem.

24. Another example of group therapy is _____ _____, which seeks to help people become more aware of themselves and their interactions with others. The personality scheme of this therapy proposed by Eric Berne postulates three basic parts or _____-_____.

25. The _____ is a carry-over from youth that can be primitive, impulsive, demanding, creative, playful, or manipulative. According to Berne we also carry another product of our past, the _____ ego-state which is an internal record of all the messages received from one's parents as personality developed. The _____ is a mature and rational decision-making part of the personality.

26. Using this ego-state system, troubled relationships develop when _____ or _____ transactions occur. In a _____ transaction, a message sent from one ego-state is answered by statements from another ego-state.

27. Also, in a(n) _____ transaction, the exchange appears to take place on one level, but actually takes place on another. This transaction forms the basis of _____, indirect ways of communicating such as the "if it weren't for you" game that is very common in marriage.

28. In many studies of the effectiveness of psychotherapy, a modest but consistent _____ effect was found to exist. Half of the patients felt better in just _____ month(s).

29. All therapies have in common some combination of the following goals: _____, resolution of _____, an improved sense of _____, a change in unacceptable patterns of _____, better _____ relations, and an improved picture of _____ and the world.

30. To accomplish these goals, all psychotherapies offer four qualities. The first is a _____ _____ between client and therapist (sometimes called the therapeutic _____). Therapists also offer a _____ _____ in which emotional catharsis or release can take place. All therapies to some extent offer an _____ or _____ for the suffering the client has experienced and propose action which if followed will end this suffering. Therapy also provides patients with a new _____ about themselves and their situation.

31.   In determining when you should seek professional help, several guidelines can be suggested. The first is: if your level of psychological discomfort becomes comparable to a level of _____ discomfort that would cause you to see a dentist or physician. Another sign is the occurrence of _____ _____ in observable behavior.

32.   If you find friends or relatives making suggestions that you seek professional help, they may be seeing things more _____ than you. Definitely seek help if you have persistent or disturbing _____ thoughts or impulses.

33.   One can find a therapist to talk to through a variety of sources: psychologists are listed in the _____ _____; community _____ _____ centers offer services directly or can provide referrals; _____ _____ associations keep lists of qualified therapists in their local communities; _____ provide counseling services to their students; psychologists also advertise in _____; and, by calling a _____ _____.

34.   The decision over which type of therapist to use is often _____. For example, the amount of money one has available or whether one has health _____ may influence the decision. Some communities utilize the services of _____ or peer counselors which are usually free or at very low cost. Likewise, one should not overlook _____ - _____ self-help groups which can often support professional treatment.

35.   A balanced look at psychotherapies suggests that all _____ are about equally successful, but all _____ are not.

36.   Several points may help you when a friend wants to talk about a problem. First, you should practice _____ _____; a person with a problem needs to be heard. If you try to understand the person's problem, you may help him or her _____ it. By focusing on the person's _____ you can avoid making him or her defensive. This helps permit the free outpouring of emotion that is the basis for _____.

37.   Avoid giving _____. It is not unreasonable to do so when asked but beware of the trap described by Eric Berne, "Why don't you? Yes, but." Accept the person's frame of _____. This will encourage freedom to examine and question his or her point of view objectively.

38.   One of the most productive things you can do is to give feedback by simply _____ thoughts and feelings said by the person. You may find it helpful to be _____ so that the other person has plenty of opportunity to talk. To encourage free expression you should ask _____ questions. Your efforts to help should include maintaining _____. Avoid the temptation to gossip.

39.   When a client and therapist come from different _____ backgrounds, _____ are common. There appear to be four cultural _____ to effective counseling which include differences in _____, social class, cultural _____, and non-verbal communication.

40.   A _____ skilled counselor is aware of their own cultural biases and values, avoids thinking in _____, and sees minority cultural beliefs and values as different but not _____. Essentially, cultural barriers are _____ on a regular basis by counselors who achieve _____ with their clients by being able to mentally take the _____ of the client.

ANSWER KEYS

Do You know the Information?

Multiple Choice

1. (b) obj. 1, p. 575
2. (a) obj. 2, p. 575
3. (d) obj. 3, p. 575
4. (c) obj. 3, p. 575
5. (f) obj. 4, p. 576
6. (c) obj. 6, p. 576
7. (a) obj. 7, p. 576
8. (a) obj. 7, p. 576
9. (b) obj. 7, p. 577
10. (b) obj. 8, p. 577
11. (c) obj. 9, p. 578
12. (d) obj. 10, p. 579
13. (a) obj. 11, p. 580
14. (a) obj. 11, p. 580
15. (b) obj. 12, p. 580
16. (d) obj. 13, p. 581
17. (b) obj. 13, p. 581
18. (a) obj. 14, p. 582
19. (c) obj. 14, p. 582
20. (a) obj. 15, p. 583
21. (c) obj. 16, p. 583
22. (b) obj. 16, p. 584
23. (d) objs.17-18, p. 584
24. (d) obj. 19, p. 585
25. (b) obj. 19, p. 585
26. (d) obj. 19, p. 586
27. (a) obj. 20, p. 586
28. (c) obj. 21, p. 587
29. (e) obj. 21, p. 587-588
30. (b) obj. 22, p. 589
31. (d) obj. 23, p. 590
32. (b) obj. 23, p. 590
33. (c) obj. 24, pp. 590-591
34. (c) obj. 26, p. 594

True-False

1. F, obj. 5, p. 576
2. F, obj. 6, p. 576
3. T, obj. 7, p. 576
4. F, obj. 10, p. 579
5. T, obj. 10, p. 579
6. F, obj. 13, pp. 580-582
7. T, obj. 16, p. 583
8. F, obj. 16, p. 584
9. T, obj. 16, p. 584
10. T, obj. 17, p. 584
11. T, obj. 19, p. 586
12. T, obj. 23, p. 590
13. T, obj. 23, p. 590
14. F, obj. 23, p. 590
15. F, obj. 24, p. 591
16. F, obj. 25, p. 593

Can You Apply the Information?

1. (b) obj. 3, p. 575
2. (b) obj. 3, p. 575
3. (c) obj. 9, p. 576
4. (d) objs.11-14, pp. 580-582
5. (c) obj. 12, p. 580
6. (a) obj. 13, p. 581
7. (d) obj. 14, p. 582
8. (d) obj. 16, p. 583
9. (b) objs.16-17, p. 584
10. (a) objs.17-18, p. 584
11. (a) obj. 19, p. 585
12. (c) obj. 21, p. 587

Chapter Review

1. Psychotherapy, personality, behavior, adjustment (p. 575)
2. Insight, Action, directive (p. 575)
3. Nondirective (p. 576); Individual, group (p. 575); time-limited (p. 576)
4. phobias, self-esteem, sexual, marital, dramatic (p. 576)
5. trepanning, demonology, exorcism, ergotism (p. 576)
6. Pinel, unchaining, Freud (p. 577)
7. hysteria, unconscious conflicts (p. 577) psychoanalysis (p. 578)
8. free association, defenses (p. 578)
9. dream, desires, feelings, latent, dream symbols (p. 548)
10. resist, resistances, transfer (p. 578)
11. time, money, rare, short-term dynamic, spontaneous remission, psychoanalysis (p. 579)
12. adjustment, potentials (p. 580)
13. client-centered, authority, interpretations, nondirective (p. 580)
14. unconditional positive regard, empathy (p. 580)
15. authentic, reflects, thoughts, feelings, self (p. 580)
16. Existential, free will, logotherapy, confrontation, meaning (p. 581)
17. Gestalt, disjointed, incomplete, want, wholes, present (p. 582)
18. group, bridge (p. 583)
19. psychodrama (p. 583)
20. family, single, communication (p. 584)

21. Sensitivity, encounter, awareness, defenses (p. 584)
22. large group awareness, therapy placebo (p. 584)
23. radio (media), educational, therapeutic, general (p. 585)
24. transactional analysis, ego-states (p. 585)
25. Child, Parent, Adult (p. 585)
26. crossed, ulterior (p. 585); crossed (p. 586)
27. ulterior, games (p. 586)
28. positive, two (p. 586)
29. insight, conflict, self, behavior, interpersonal, oneself (p. 587)
30. caring relationship, alliance, protected setting (p. 587); explanation, rationale, perspective (p. 588)
31. physical, significant changes (p. 589)
32. objectively, suicidal (p. 589)
33. yellow pages, mental health, mental health, colleges (universities), newspapers, crisis hotline (p. 589)
34. arbitrary, insurance (p. 589); paraprofessionals, peer-led (p. 590)
35. techniques, therapists (p. 590)
36. active listening, clarify, feelings, catharsis (p. 591)
37. advice, reference (p. 591)
38. reflecting, quiet, open, confidentiality (p. 592)
39. cultural, backgrounds, language, values (p. 593)
40. culturally, stereotypes, inferior, transcended, empathy, role (p. 594)

Chapter 22

Behavior Therapy

KEY TERMS AND CONCEPTS

behavior modification — assumptions
cognitive behavior therapy
classical and operant conditioning
aversion therapy
    response-contingent shock
    rapid smoking
    transference/generalization
desensitization
    hierarchy
    reciprocal inhibition
    vicarious desensitization
    eye-movement desensitization
operant principles
    positive reinforcement, nonreinforcement
    extinction, punishment, shaping,
    stimulus control, time out
tokens

target behaviors
token economy
social rewards
self-defeating thoughts
selective perception
overgeneralization
all-or-nothing thinking
rational-emotive therapy
    faulty (irrational) beliefs
    A-B-C
covert sensitization
thought stopping
covert reinforcement
relaxation
using behavior modification principles
positive and negative aspects of behavior mod

LEARNING OBJECTIVES

To demonstrate mastery of this chapter you should be able to:
1. Contrast the goal of behavior modification with the goal of insight therapies.

2. Define behavior modification and state its basic assumption.

401

3.   Relate basic principles of classical conditioning to behavior modification.

4.   Describe aversion therapy and explain how it can be used to stop smoking and drinking.

5.   Explain the relationship of aversion therapy to classical conditioning.

6.   State two problems associated with aversion therapy.

7.   Explain how adaptation, relaxation, reciprocal inhibition, and use of a hierarchy are combined to produce desensitization.

8.   State what desensitization is used for and give an example of desensitization therapy or vicarious desensitization therapy.

9.   Explain the relationship between the basic principles of operant conditioning and behavior modification.

10.   Explain how nonreward and time out can be used to bring about extinction of a maladaptive behavior.

11.   Describe a token economy including its advantages and possible disadvantages. Include the terms token and target behavior in your description.

12.   Describe what distinguishes a cognitive behavior therapist from other behavior therapists.

13.   List and describe the three thinking errors which underlie depression and explain what can be done to correct such thinking.
        a.

        b.

c.

14.   Describe rational-emotive therapy. Identify the three core ideas (ABC's) which serve as the basis of most irrational beliefs.

* * * * * * * * * *

The following objectives are related to the material in the "Applications" and "Exploration" sections of your text.

15.   Describe how covert sensitization, thought-stopping, and covert reinforcement can be used to reduce unwanted behavior.

16.   Give an example of how you can overcome a common fear or break a bad habit using the steps given for desensitization.

17.   Describe the possible positive and negative aspects of using behavior therapy.

SELF-QUIZZES

Do You Know the Information?

Multiple Choice

1. The goal of insight therapies is _____, whereas the goal of behavior therapy is to _____.
    (a) insight; allow the person to achieve his or her full potential
    (b) understanding; alter troublesome thoughts and behavior
    (c) understanding; discover the cause of the behavior
    (d) self-actualization; improve the negative behavior

2. Behavior modification is based upon which of the following principal assumptions?
    (a) Conflicts between the conscious and unconscious produce maladaptive behaviors.
    (b) Habits that cause problems are learned and therefore can be unlearned.
    (c) The thwarting of self-actualization processes produces abnormal ego-states.
    (d) Insight is the key to normal adjustment.

3. The basic idea of aversion therapy is
    (a) a person learns to associate a strong aversion with an undesirable habit.
    (b) behavior is extinguished by punishment.
    (c) maladaptive behavior is eliminated or decreased by rewarding desirable behavior.
    (d) not included in any of the above answers.

4. Of the following, which is a problem in the use of aversion therapy?
    (a) ineffectiveness with some personality types
    (b) lack of a sound theoretical base
    (c) poorly defined connections between applications and basic research
    (d) difficulties of generalization of results from the therapy setting to the real world

5. Desensitization is based on the principle of
    (a) retroactive inhibition.
    (b) proactive inhibition.
    (c) reactive inhibition.
    (d) reciprocal inhibition.

6. Desensitization is used ***primarily*** for
    (a) diminishing hallucinations and delusions.
    (b) treating depression.
    (c) hysteria.
    (d) alleviating phobias and anxieties.

7. When constructing a hierarchy for desensitization, care should be taken to insure that the situations
    (a) do not provide any reinforcement.
    (b) are ordered from the least disturbing to the most disturbing.
    (c) do not provoke undue anxiety.
    (d) are balanced between situations that are perceived as disturbing and those that are not.

8. Eye-movement desensitization appears to work
    (a) because of the rapid pencil movement.
    (b) because people are ready to change by this stage of therapy.
    (c) because of the side-to-side movement matching the normal nystagmus of the eye.
    (d) because of some as yet unknown reason.

9. _____ prevents reward from following an undesirable response.
   (a) Punishment
   (b) Extinction
   (c) Time out
   (d) Nonreinforcement

10. When a child misbehaves in order to gain attention, an effective way of decreasing this misbehavior is to
    (a) ignore the child's misbehavior.
    (b) be reinforcing and kind to the child when he or she misbehaves.
    (c) direct negative statements at the child when he or she misbehaves.
    (d) give the child what he or she desires so he or she will no longer misbehave.

11. One advantage of a token economy is
    (a) it often works on seemingly hopeless cases.
    (b) it overcomes the problem of generalization by using tokens.
    (c) target behaviors can be more easily identified than in aversion therapy.
    (d) not in any of the above answers.

12. As compared to a behavior therapist, a cognitive behavior therapist
    (a) uses less relaxation training.
    (b) has been generally more concerned with why certain thoughts or behavior occur.
    (c) is interested in thoughts instead of just visible behavior.
    (d) uses more tokens in therapy.

13. Which of the following statements about cognitive behavior therapy is *incorrect*?
    (a) Cognitive therapy has been especially effective in the treatment of depression.
    (b) To combat depression clients are asked to collect information to test the beliefs that cause the depression.
    (c) Cognitive therapists look for the presence of effective coping skills and thought patterns, not for self-defeating thinking.
    (d) According to Beck depressed people engage in selective perception, over-generalization, all-or-nothing thinking, and magnification of the importance of undesirable events.

14. The basic idea of rational-emotive therapy is that
    (a) people who exhibit psychotic behavior should just try to live more rationally.
    (b) emotions cause people to hold irrational thoughts about themselves.
    (c) therapists who use desensitization will not get good generalization to the outside world.
    (d) people develop self-defeating habits because of unrealistic or faulty beliefs.

15. Which of the following methods could be misconstrued as "playing a game with yourself"??
    (a) Thought Stopping.
    (b) Covert Sensitization.
    (c) Covert Reinforcement.
    (d) Relaxation.

16. Which of the following statements about behavior modification is *incorrect*?
    (a) There are some ethical concerns about using behavior modification on "captive" audiences.
    (b) Behavior modification has no peer in some areas such as classroom management.
    (c) All psychotherapies modify behavior in one way or another.
    (d) Studies have shown behavior therapists to be less warm and caring than traditional therapists.

True-False

_____ 1. The idea of aversion therapy is to associate something like alcohol (the CS) with something aversive (the CR) like vomiting.

_____ 2. Constructing a hierarchy is not essential to the desensitization process.

_____ 3. A variation of nonreinforcement is the time-out procedure whereby an individual is removed from a situation in which reinforcement occurs.

_____ 4. In the A-B-C of rational-emotive therapy the "B" stands for behavior.

_____ 5. One of the core ideas which forms the basis of irrational beliefs is that a person must perform well and be approved of by significant others.

_____ 6. Covert sensitization involves associating very unpleasant thoughts or images with a habit you wish to diminish.

_____ 7. The simplest thought-stopping technique makes use of mild punishment to suppress upsetting mental images and internal "talk."

Can You Apply the Information?

1. For which of the following would behavior modification be *inappropriate*?
   (a) making an autistic child more socially responsive
   (b) losing weight
   (c) understanding why you smoke
   (d) overcoming procrastination

2. A pedophile (a person who achieves sexual gratification through contact with children) desperately wants to overcome his problem. To help you show him slides of naked children and every time he begins to get an erection you give him a severe shock. This therapy is an example of
   (a) desensitization.
   (b) implosive therapy.
   (c) covert sensitization.
   (d) aversion therapy.

3. Donald has been offered a job as a janitor in the reptile house at the local zoo but he is deathly afraid of snakes. Which of the following therapies would probably be most appropriate for him?
   (a) desensitization
   (b) nonreinforcement
   (c) insight therapy
   (d) cognitive behavior therapy

4. Your husband has started telling you jokes that you really don't like. The best "therapy" for him would be
   (a) desensitization.
   (b) nonreinforcement.
   (c) insight therapy.
   (d) covert sensitization.

5. Benjamin is argumentative and belligerent with his parents. To correct the behavior his parents make him sit on the stairs by himself for three minutes. Benjamin's parents are using
   (a) desensitization.
   (b) cognitive behavior therapy.
   (c) time out.
   (d) a token economy.

6. Bob is very depressed. He was accepted at the college of his choice, he has a good summer job, and has a great date for the prom, but all he can think about is the one college which rejected his application. He seems to be suffering from
    (a) all-or-nothing thinking.   (c) thought stopping.
    (b) selective perception.   (d) target behaviors.

7. "I can't take it anymore. I've tried to be the perfect mother, the perfect lawyer, and the perfect wife, and I'm blowing all three. I want to be the best in everything I do." This person is probably a good candidate for
    (a) covert sensitization.   (d) rational-emotive therapy.
    (b) time out.   (e) a padded room.
    (c) behavior modification.

8. Pat wants to reduce the amount of red meat she eats. When she thinks about eating a hamburger she envisions cholesterol clogging her arteries. This is an example of
    (a) covert sensitization.   (d) covert reinforcement.
    (b) thought stopping.   (e) the origins of the dance known as "clogging."
    (c) desensitization.

9. Bill suffers from an incredible level of anxiety because of the quality of his cognitive activity. For example, whenever he is driving he envisions himself having a terrible accident and smashing himself all over the inside of the car. Bill might benefit from which of the following types of therapy?
    (a) desensitization   (d) time out
    (b) aversion   (e) Driver's Education
    (c) thought-stopping

10. Simon has been labelled a paranoid schizophrenic. Although medication has diminished his hallucinations and delusions, he still suffers from intrusive self-deprecating thoughts. In bed at night before he falls asleep, he seems to concentrate on all of the negative things which have happened to him in his life. His therapist gave him a rubber band to put on his wrist and snap whenever he starts thinking such thoughts. Simon's therapist is using
    (a) thought stopping which employs aversion therapy.
    (b) reciprocal inhibition.
    (c) insight therapy.
    (d) desensitization.
    (e) rational-emotive therapy.

Chapter Review

1. Behavioral approaches include _____ _____ (the use of _____ principles to change behavior) and _____ _____ therapy (the use of learning principles to change upsetting _____ and _____).

2. Psychologists called _____ _____, who use behavior modification, feel that _____ or _____ of one's problems is unnecessary. Instead these therapists try to directly change _____. Behavior modification is based on one principal assumption: people have _____ to be the way they are. Consequently, they can _____ behavior, or _____ more appropriate habits.

3. Behavior modification is a term referring to any attempt to use the learning principles of _____ or _____ conditioning to change human behavior.

4.   Behavior therapists may use the principles of classical conditioning to associate discomfort, called an
_____, with a bad habit. Use of this technique is called _____
therapy and is one form of behavior modification. When an _____ is paired with a
bad habit so that the habit no longer occurs or is replaced by a competing response, a
_____ _____ has developed.

5.   Psychologist Roger Vogler uses aversion therapy with alcoholics who have tried almost everything to stop
drinking. Vogler associates painful, but non-injurious _____ with the intake of
alcohol. This _____-_____ _____ takes
the immediate pleasure out of drinking and causes the patient to develop a conditioned aversion to drinking.
In this example, alcohol would be a _____ _____ and the
aversion would be the _____ _____.

6.   Similar aversion therapy can be done with smoking, but in this case the aversion is caused by
_____ _____.

7.   One problem with successful treatment is getting the conditioned aversion to _____
or _____ from the therapy situation to the real world. For that reason, aversion
therapy is often used as a _____ _____.

8.   A reduction in fear, brought about by gradually approaching a feared stimulus while maintaining complete
relaxation, is called _____. An ordered set of steps called a
_____ is used to allow the individual to adapt to gradual approximations of the end, desired behavior.

9.   Desensitization is based on the principle of _____
_____, which means that one emotional state can _____
the occurrence of another. Desensitization is primarily used to help people unlearn
_____ or strong _____.

10. Desensitization usually involves three steps. First, the patient and therapist construct a
_____, a list of fear-provoking situations involving the phobia and ranging from
the least disturbing to the most disturbing situation. Second, the patient is taught exercises that produce total
_____. Once the patients are _____ they proceed to the
third step by trying to perform the _____ disturbing item on their
_____.

11. In situations where it is impractical for the patient to practice the steps, desensitization is accomplished when a
patient vividly _____ each of the steps in the hierarchy. In some cases the problem can
be handled by having clients observe models who are performing the feared behavior. This is known as
_____ desensitization.

12. Dr. Francine Shapiro's technique of _____ - _____ desensitization utilizes a
pencil rapidly moved in front of a person's eyes while they concentrate on the
_____ that trouble or upset him/her most. Without knowing the reason why, a
single session of this technique lowers _____ and takes the _____ out
of traumatic memories.

13. The principles of _____ conditioning have been developed by Skinner
and his associates mostly through laboratory research with animals. There are several principles used with
humans.

14.   The operant principles most frequently used by behavior therapists to deal with human behavior are:
   (1) _____ _____ where an action
          followed by a reward will occur _____ frequently;
   (2) _____-_____ where an action not followed by a reward will
          occur _____ frequently;
   (3) _____ where an action repeatedly not followed by a reward will go away;
   (4) _____ where an action followed by _____ will be
          suppressed;
   (5) _____ where actions that are closer and closer _____
          of a desired response are rewarded;
   (6) _____ _____ whereby responses tend to come under the
          control of the situation in which they occur; and,
   (7) _____ _____ where an individual is removed feom a situation where
          _____ usually occurs.

15.   Most frequently occurring human behaviors lead to some form of reward. An undesirable response can be
       eliminated by identifying and _____ the rewards which maintain it. Most of
       the rewards which maintain human behavior are more subtle than food, money, etc. Rather they include
       _____, _____, and
       _____.

16.   This can be demonstrated in classroom situations where teachers give attention in various forms when
       misbehavior occurs. When attention takes the form of saying things such as "Sit down!" the frequency of
       misbehavior _____. Non-reward and extinction can eliminate many of these
       problem behaviors. For example, in the classroom example when misbehaving children are
       _____ and attention given to children not misbehaving, misbehavior
       _____.

17.   A strategy used in institutions is called _____ _____, and involves refusing to
       reward maladaptive responses by refusing to play the attention game. Another form of this is to
       _____ an individual immediately from the setting in which an undesirable
       response occurs so that the response will not be _____.

18.   An approach to help the severely disturbed is based on the use of _____, symbolic rewards
       that can be exchanged for real rewards. So that incentives and rewards will have maximum impact, the
       therapist selects specific _____ _____ that could or
       should be improved.

19.   Full-scale use of tokens in an institutional setting produces a _____
       _____. As with aversion therapy, lack of _____
       to the outside world can be a problem. The most effective _____ _____ are
       those that gradually switch from tokens to _____ _____ such as
       recognition and approval.

20.   The results of token economies have sometimes been dramatic. The effects can be a radical change in a
       patient's overall _____ and _____.
       Many "_____" retarded, mentally ill, and delinquent people have been
       returned to a productive life by means of token economies.

21. _____ _____ therapists are interested in thoughts as well as visible behavior. They try to help clients change _____ _____ that lead to trouble. This type of therapy has been especially effective in the treatment of _____.

22. According to Beck, depressed persons engage in many forms of negative thinking including _____ _____, the _____ of the importance of undesirable events, and _____ or _____ thinking. Cognitive therapists make a step-by-step effort to correct negative thoughts.

23. According to Ellis, people become unhappy and develop self-defeating habits because of unrealistic _____. His therapy is called _____-_____ therapy.

24. Ellis' A-B-C analysis goes like this: The person assumes the cause of the emotional _____ to be the _____ experience. In between the two is the client's irrational and unrealistic _____ and expectations which are the true cause of the difficulty.

25. Most irrational beliefs come from three unrealistic core ideas: I must perform well and be _____ of by significant others. You must _____ me fairly. _____ must be the way I want them to be.

26. In _____ _____ disturbing or disgusting thoughts or images are associated with a behavior or habit to make a person less likely to want to do it. Therapists have found that upsetting or disturbing thoughts can be decreased by using a technique called _____-_____. The simplest technique uses mild _____ to suppress the thoughts.

27. The key to desensitization is _____. One way to learn this is to practice tightening different muscles for five seconds and then letting go.

28. In developing a _____, make a list of situations related to the fear that makes you anxious. If you can vividly imagine yourself in the first situation of your hierarchy without a noticeable increase in _____ _____ at least twice, proceed to the next card you have constructed.

29. Stop when you reach a card that you cannot visualize without _____ after three attempts. On each successive day, begin one or two cards before the one on which you stopped the previous day. Eventually you can learn to control the fear.

30. There is no ethical problem with modifying behavior when the person does it _____. When behavior modification was first introduced, observers feared that it would be used to _____ people against their will. This fear has proved unfounded. It is now clear that all psychotherapies _____ _____ in one way or another.

31. Studies show that behavior therapists are rated just as _____ and _____ as traditional therapists. In view of the demonstrated effectiveness of behavioral techniques, many behavior therapists would consider it _____ to withhold treatment from some mental patients in state hospitals.

ANSWER KEYS

Do You Know the Information?

Multiple Choice

1. (b) obj. 1, p. 599
2. (b) obj. 2, p. 599
3. (a) obj. 4, p. 600
4. (d) obj. 6, p. 600
5. (d) obj. 7, p. 601
6. (d) obj. 8, p. 602
7. (b) obj. 8, pp. 602-603
8. (d) obj. 8, p. 604
9. (c) obj. 9, p. 604
10. (a) obj. 10, p. 605
11. (a) obj. 11, p. 606
12. (c) obj. 12, p. 606

13. (c) objs.12,13, pp. 606-608
14. (d) obj. 14, p. 608
15. (b) obj. 15, pp. 610-611
16. (d) obj. 17, p. 614

True-False

1. T, obj. 5, p. 600
2. F, obj. 8, p. 602
3. T, obj. 10, p. 605
4. F, obj. 14, p. 608
5. T, obj. 14, p. 608
6. T, obj. 15, p. 610
7. T, obj. 15, p. 611

Can You Apply the Information?

1. (c) obj. 1, p. 599
2. (d) obj. 4, p. 600
3. (a) obj. 8, p. 602
4. (b) obj. 10, p. 605
5. (c) obj. 10, p. 605
6. (b) obj. 13, p. 607
7. (d) obj. 14, p. 608
8. (a) obj. 15, p. 610
9. (c) obj. 15, p. 611
10. (a) objs.4, 15, pp. 600, 611

Chapter Review

1. behavior modification, learning, cognitive behavior, thoughts, beliefs (p. 598)
2. behavior therapists, insight, understanding, behavior, learned, unlearn, relearn (p. 599)
3. classical, operant (p. 599)
4. aversion, aversion, aversion (p. 600); conditioned aversion (p. 599)
5. shocks, response-contingent shock (p. 600); conditioned stimulus, conditioned response (p. 599)
6. rapid smoking (p. 600)
7. transfer, generalize (p. 600); last resort (p. 601)
8. desensitization, hierarchy (p. 601)
9. reciprocal inhibition, prevent (p. 601); phobias, anxieties (p. 602)
10. hierarchy, relaxation, relaxed, least, list (p. 602)
11. imagines, vicarious (p. 602)
12. eye-movement, thoughts (p. 603); anxieties, pain (p. 604)
13. operant (p. 604)
14. positive reinforcement, more, non-reinforcement, less, extinction, punishment, discomfort, shaping, approximations, stimulus control, time out, reinforcement (p. 604)
15. removing, attention, approval, concern (p. 605)
16. increases, ignored, decreases (p. 605)
17. time out, remove, rewarded (p. 605)
18. tokens, target behaviors (p. 606)
19. token economy, generalization (tranference), token economies, social rewards (p. 606)
20. adjustment, morale, hopelessly (p. 606)
21. Cognitive behavior, thinking patterns (p. 606); depression (p. 607)
22. selective perception, overgeneralization, magnification, all, nothing (p. 607)
23. beliefs, rational-emotive (p. 608)
24. consequence, activating, beliefs (p. 608)
25. approved, treat, Conditions (p. 608)
26. covert sensitization (p. 610); thought-stopping, punishment (p. 611)
27. relaxation (p. 611)
28. hierarchy, muscular tension (p. 612)
29. tension (p. 612)
30. voluntarily, control, modify behavior (p. 614)
31. warm, caring, unethical (p. 614)

Chapter 23

Social Psychology I

KEY TERMS, CONCEPTS, AND INDIVIDUALS

social psychology
culture
   groups
      structure, cohesiveness
   roles
      ascribed, achieved, conflict, status
norms
   autokinetic effect
proxemics — personal space (zones)
   intimate, personal, social, public
attribution
   external vs. internal
   consistency, distinctiveness,
   actor-object-setting, discounting,
   situational demands, consensus
self-handicapping
fundamental attributional error
need to affiliate
social comparison theory
interpersonal attraction
   physical proximity, physical
   attraction, competence, similarity

factors in selecting a mate
self-disclosure
   reciprocity vs. over disclosure
social exchange theory
romantic love, mutual absorption
   attachments
social influence
conformity — Asch's experiment
   groupthink
   group factors
social power — reward, coercive,
   legitimate, referent, expert
obedience — Milgram's experiment
compliance
   foot-in-the-door effect
   door-in-the-face effect
   low-ball technique
passive compliance
assertiveness training — rehearsal,
   overlearning, broken record
traps — social, collective social, tragedy of
   the commons

LEARNING OBJECTIVES

To demonstrate mastery of this chapter you should be able to:

1. Define social psychology. *Scientific study of how people behave, think, and feel in social situations.*

2. Define the following terms:
   a. culture - *An ongoing pattern of life that is passed on from one generation to the next.*

b. **role** — patterns of behavior expected of persons in various social positions.

c. **ascribed role** — roles that are not under the individual's control: male/female, son, inmate

d. **achieved role** — roles attained voluntarily or by special effort: spouse, teacher, band leader

e. **role conflict** — a person occupying two or more conflicting roles.
ex. traffic court judge whose son is brought before her with a violation

f. **status** — position in a group

g. **group structure** — the organization of roles, communication pathways, and power in the group.

h. **group cohesiveness** — an indication of the degree of attraction among group members.
*closely coordinated

i. **norm** — standards of conduct for appropriate behavior in various situations

3. **Explain how norms are formed using the idea of the autokinetic effect.**
"self-moving"
* Ideas vary widely from person to person! However, when two or more people give estimates at the same time, their judgements rapidly converge. A similar convergence of attitudes, beliefs, and behaviors takes place among members of most groups.
ex. personal space

4. **Define proxemics.**
The study of rules for the personal use of space.

5. **List and describe the four basic interpersonal zones and describe the nature of the interactions which occur in each.**
a. Intimate → space extends about 18 inches out from the skin
*entry within this space is reserved for special people or circumstances. (sex, cuddling children, comforting others)
b. Personal → maintained in comfortable interaction with friends. 1½ to 4 ft. from the body.
c. Social → Impersonal Business and Casual social gatherings range of 4ft. to 12. eliminates touching and formalizes conversation.
d. Public → more than 12ft. look "flat" and voices must be raised (formal speeches, lectures, business meetings)

6. **Define attribution and state the difference between external and internal attribution.**
attribution is the process of making inferences about behavior.
Internal → A cause of behavior that is assumed to lie within a person.
External → A cause of behavior that is assumed to lie outside a person.

7. **Explain how the consistency and distinctiveness of a person's behavior affect his or her attributions.**

Consistency - a basis for making casual attributions, noticing that a behavior changes very little in similar situations on different occasions.

Distinctiveness - a basis for making casual attributions, noticing that a behavior occurs only under a specific (distinct) set circumstances.

8. **Explain how self-handicapping protects a person who has a fragile self-image.**

People sometimes arrange to be evaluated while "handicapped." That way, they can attribute failure to the handicap.

9. **Explain what the fundamental attributional error is.** Attributing the actions of others to internal causes, while attributing our own behavior to External (causes) situations.

10. **State the needs that appear to be satisfied by affiliation and describe the research indicating humans have a need to affiliate.** Affiliation helps meet needs for approval, support, friendship, and information. We also seek company to alleviate fear or anxiety.

* The women who were told that the shock would be painful wanted to be with others, but those told it would tickle didn't mind to be alone.
* A later experiment with women expecting to be shocked were asked whether they wanted to wait with other subjects, with those waiting to see their advisors, or alone. Most chose to wait with future "victims"

11. **Describe the social comparison theory.** When there are no objective standards, we must turn to others to evaluate our actions, feelings, opinions, or abilities.

* A desire for self-evaluation provides a general motive for associating with others and influences which groups we join.

12. **List and describe the factors which affect interpersonal attraction. (Include a description of the similarities and differences in what men and women look for in a date.)**

Physical Proximity: Nearness plays a powerful role. It increases the frequency of contact between people (There does seem to be a "boy-next-door" or "girl-next-door" effect in romantic attraction, and a "folks-next-door" effect in friendship.

Physical Attractiveness: Basically, it is "what is beautiful is good." Physical attractiveness has more of an influence on a woman's fate than on a man's in romance. Looks, for women, are related to their dating frequency. Men are the opposite. This is temporary because it takes more to have a lasting relationship

Competence: We like competent but human people.

Similarity: People with similar backgrounds, interests, attitudes, beliefs and personalities are attracted to each other.

13.   **Explain self-disclosure and discuss the effects of varying degrees of disclosure on interpersonal relationships.**
Refers to the process of letting yourself be known to others. The ability to reveal your thoughts and feelings to others is a basic skill for developing close relationships. Lack of self-disclosure is frequently associated with unhappiness and loneliness. Most often we reveal ourselves to persons we like. Also to those we trust. Moderate self-disclosure leads to reciprocity (a return in kind.) Overdisclosure gives rise to suspicion and reduced attraction. When self-disclosure proceeds at a moderate pace, it is accompanied by growing trust and intimacy. When it is too rapid or inappropriate, we are likely to "back off" and wonder about the person's motives.

14.   **Describe the social exchange theory as it relates to interpersonal relationships.**
As relationships progress, quite often they can be understood in terms of maximizing rewards while minimizing "costs". Break-ups: costs — in terms of effort, irritation, or lowered self-esteem — have exceed their rewards.
We unconsciously weigh such rewards and costs.
*Personal standard used to evaluate rewards and costs is called comparison level. High for a person who has had a history of satisfying and rewarding relationships. Vice-Versa

15.   **Describe Rubin's studies of romantic love. Discuss the differences between loving and liking and between male and female friendships (including the term mutual absorption and the different love/attachment styles).**
Romantic Love usually involves deep mutual absorption of the lovers. In other words, lovers attend almost exclusively to one another.
*Dating couples liked and loved their partners but mostly liked their friends. Women were a little more "loving" of their friends than were men.
* There is a growing evidence that early attachments to caregivers can have a lasting impact on how we relate to others.
   * Those who are secure find it relatively easy to get close to others.
   * Those who are avoidant are suspicious, aloof, and skeptical about love. find it hard to completely trust and depend on others. Basically, want to avoid intimacy.
   * Those who are ambivalent regard themselves as misunderstood and unappreciated. want to be close to partner, but are preoccupied with doubts.

16.   **State the meaning of social influence.**
When people interact, they almost always affect one another's behavior.

17.   **Describe Asch's experiment on conformity.** A group of six students were sitting at a table and asked to identify/match lines. The first few trials one individual seemed to agree upon the answers everyone else gave. On the final guess everyone said 1, but the single individual was about to say 3. He obviously conformed to saying 1, because of the group pressures.

18.   Explain how group sanctions and unanimity affect conformity.

19.   Define groupthink and explain how it may contribute to poor decision-making.

20.   Describe four ways to prevent groupthink.
      a.

      b.

      c.

      d.

21.   List and describe the five sources of social power.
      a.

      b.

      c.

      d.

      e.

22.   Describe Milgram's study of obedience.

23.   Identify the factors which affect the degree of obedience.

24.   Explain how compliance differs from simple conformity.

25.   Describe the following methods of compliance:
a.   foot-in-the-door

b.   door-in-the-face

c.   low-ball technique

26.   Describe the research that deals with passive compliance and briefly explain how it applies to everyday behavior.

* * * * * * * * *

The following objectives are related to the material in the "Applications" and "Exploration" sections of your text.
27.   Distinguish among assertive behavior, non-assertive behavior, and aggressive behavior.

28. Describe how a person can learn to be more assertive using rehearsal, role playing, overlearning, and the broken record technique.

29. Explain what a social trap, a collective social trap, and the tragedy of the commons are. Explain how they can be avoided or escaped.

SELF-QUIZZES

Do You Know the Information?

Multiple Choice

1. The study of how people behave in the presence of others is called
    (a) conformity.
    (b) social psychology.
    (c) groupthink.
    (d) proxemics.

2. The ongoing pattern of life that is passed from one generation to the next is called
    (a) norms.
    (b) roles.
    (c) culture.
    (d) group structure.

3. The autokinetic effect
    (a) occurs when people experience role conflict.
    (b) demonstrates that when people interact, norms are formed and attitudes, beliefs, and behaviors tend to converge.
    (c) is subject to the presence of group sanctions.
    (d) is not affected by cultural stereotypes.

4.   The study of the personal use of space is called
     (a) spaceology.   (c) kinesics.
     (b) kinesthetics.   (d) proxemics.

5.   The distance maintained in comfortable interactions with friends is called _____ distance.
     (a) personal   (c) intimate
     (b) public   (d) social

6.   When making an attribution we should be *most* aware of
     (a) the situational demands.   (c) any consensus that might be present.
     (b) the setting in which the behavior occurs. (d) all of the above conditions.

7.   Which of the following statements about attribution theory is *incorrect?*
     (a) When situational demands are strong, we tend to discount claims that a person's actions are internally caused.
     (b) If someone's behavior is very consistent, we tend to assume that his/her behavior is externally caused.
     (c) A consensus in the behavior of a number of people implies that the behavior has an external cause.
     (d) If the situational demands are strong, we may know little about a person's motives.

8.   When a person does not feel confident about succeeding or to protect a fragile self-image, people may engage in
     (a) discounting.   (c) self-handicapping.
     (b) proxemics.   (d) consistency.

9.   The fundamental attributional error
     (a) often leads to role conflict.
     (b) occurs when we attribute the actions of others to internal causes while attributing our own behavior to external causes.
     (c) results from the actor, the object, or the setting responding to situational demands.
     (d) is attributing the actions of others to situations while attributing our own behavior to internal causes.

10. When threatened with a series of painful electric shocks women generally chose to wait
     (a) with calmer students not taking part in the experiment.
     (b) alone.
     (c) with other shock subjects.
     (d) with whomever was closest .

11. Often we must turn to others to evaluate our actions, feelings, or abilities. This idea is the basis for
     (a) self-disclosure.   (c) social exchange theory.
     (b) social comparison theory.   (d) Aronson's theory of social evaluation.

12. Of the following, which are factors that determine interpersonal attraction between individuals?
     (a) physical proximity   (e) competence
     (b) physical attractiveness   (f) similarity
     (c) inherent goodness   (g) group status
     (d) morality   (h) cultural compatibility

13. In selecting a mate it has been found that
     (a) kindness and understanding are ranked first by almost all men and women.
     (b) people tend to choose someone who is different but complementary.
     (c) men rank a good earning capacity higher than women do.
     (d) women rank attractiveness higher than men do.

14. It is apparent that self-disclosure
    (a) leads to reciprocity when the amount of self-disclosure is moderate.
    (b) is a major step toward friendship.
    (c) gives rise to suspicion and reduced attraction if it is excessive.
    (d) encompasses all of the above.

15. According to social exchange theory, a relationship must be _____ to endure.
    (a) meaningful
    (b) reasonable
    (c) profitable
    (d) positive

16. Rubin's study of romantic love revealed that
    (a) mutual absorption was important for both liking and romantic love.
    (b) mutual absorption almost always led to sexual intimacy.
    (c) dating couples liked and loved their partners but mostly liked their friends.
    (d) all of the above are true.

17. When psychologists study how people affect each other's behavior, they are generally examining the area of
    (a) social influence.
    (b) conformity.
    (c) group pressures.
    (d) normative biasing.

18. In his experiment, Asch found that _____ percent of all subjects involved yielded to group judgment at least once.
    (a) 50
    (b) 75
    (c) 90
    (d) 100

19. Having at least one person who agreed with the subject's judgment (in Asch's experiment)
    (a) greatly reduced the pressures to conform.
    (b) was not as influential as the number of people who disagreed with you.
    (c) often increased the group sanctions against the subject.
    (d) increased conformity but only in isolated situations.

20. Decision making which becomes so compulsive in maintaining personal status and conformity that it minimizes critical thinking is called
    (a) proxemics.
    (b) obedience.
    (c) role conflict.
    (d) groupthink.

21. Which of the following is *not* an antidote for the problem of groupthink?
    (a) defining each group member's role as a critical evaluator
    (b) stating the problem being examined in an unbiased fashion, i.e., factually.
    (c) getting each member's personal preferences aired at the outset of discussion
    (d) inviting a group member to take the "devil's advocate" role

22. Of the following, which are types of social power?
    (a) reward
    (b) coercive
    (c) noble
    (d) expert
    (e) legitimate
    (f) business
    (g) referent
    (h) group

23. In his original study of obedience to authority, Milgram found that _____ percent of those tested obeyed completely by going all the way up to the 450 volt shock level.
    (a) 25
    (b) 50
    (c) 65
    (d) 75

24. Which of the following was *least* important in affecting the degree of compliance in Milgram's study?
    (a) the distance between the "learner" and the "teacher"
    (b) the opportunity to imitate two other teachers who resisted orders and walked out
    (c) the location of the experiment or the experimenter's appearance
    (d) the distance between the "teacher" and the "authority"

25. Which of the following statements is *true*?
    (a) In conformity situations the pressure to get in line is usually indirect.
    (b) Compliance is when a person with little or no authority makes a direct request of another person.
    (c) Obedience is when a person of authority gives an order and the pressure is direct and difficult to resist.
    (d) All of the above statements are true.

26. If I get a person committed to act in a certain way and then make the terms of acting less desirable, this technique of compliance is called
    (a) passive compliance.   (c) the low-ball technique.
    (b) the door-in-the-face.   (d) the foot-in-the-door technique technique.

27. In Moriarty's experiment in which subjects were subjected to very loud music
    (a) many subjects were angry but only asked the culprit twice to turn off the music.
    (b) the accomplice was instructed to turn off the music at the first request, but no one asked.
    (c) about half of the subjects glared at first but only requested that the music be turned down when this did not work.
    (d) most subjects said nothing.

28. Which of the following statements is *correct* concerning assertion, aggression, and non-assertion?
    (a) People who are nonassertive are usually patient to a fault.
    (b) Assertion is exclusively self-serving.
    (c) Although very negative, aggression takes into account the other person's feelings.
    (d) Assertion usually leads to loss of self-respect.

29. Convincing yourself that you have the right to refuse, to request, and to right a wrong is a basic principle of
    (a) conformity.   (c) groupthink.
    (b) assertiveness training.   (d) proxemics.

30. Restating your request repeatedly until it is heeded is an example of
    (a) the rehearsal technique.   (c) intimidation.
    (b) aggressive behavior.   (d) the broken record technique.

31. Any social situation that rewards actions that have undesirable effects in the long run is called a
    (a) social problem.   (c) social trap.
    (b) non-assertive behavior.   (d) compliant behavior.

Can You Apply the Information?

1. Which of the following is an ascribed role?
   (a) teacher   (c) daughter
   (b) mother   (d) doctor

2. You are a college professor and your husband decides to enroll in your class. This could develop into
    (a) role conflict.
    (c) an ascribed role.
    (b) group cohesiveness.
    (d) attribution.

3. Vickie is a typical college student. In class she is quiet, attentive, and intelligent. In the college cafeteria she acts like the rest of her group. She can be rather loud, boisterous, and sometimes very lewd. The difference in her behavior can be attributed to
    (a) group structure.
    (c) ascribed roles.
    (b) obedience.
    (d) group norms.

4. At a cocktail party most people stand within touching distance while talking. What is this distance called?
    (a) public distance
    (c) intimate distance
    (b) personal distance
    (d) social distance

5. When talking about proxemics as being the study of rules for the personal use of space, we are talking about the _____ of personal space use within a given culture.
    (a) norms
    (c) achieved roles
    (b) cohesiveness
    (d) structure

6. Bob has a drinking problem. For the past few months, he has appeared to be on a roller coaster. His life seems to hit rock bottom, and then he slowly seems to get better. His family and friends always seem to be willing to rescue him. They will even set him up with a new job, but every time he is supposed to show up for these really good jobs (considering Bob's present state), he gets drunk and "can't" show up. It appears that Bob is engaging in
    (a) the fundamental attributional error.
    (c) self-handicapping.
    (b) discounting.
    (d) social comparison theory .

7. Audrey and Lisa are looking at the grades posted outside of their class. They have both made a "D." Lisa says to herself that the reason her grade is so low is that she had to get a second job to make ends meet, but that Audrey just isn't as smart as her. This is an example of
    (a) social exchange theory.
    (c) passive compliance.
    (b) fundamental attributional error.
    (d) group cohesiveness.

8. You have a chance to find out how much money your close friend makes. One reason you might want to find out could be because of
    (a) social exchange theory.
    (c) proximity.
    (b) social comparison theory.
    (d) the liking/loving dimension.

9. John and Jane are planning a June wedding. Their parents are thrilled because the parents have been best friends since high school and get together often. The original reason for John and Jane's relationship was probably
    (a) similarity.
    (c) proximity.
    (b) physical attraction.
    (d) competence.

10. Sam is very reserved and quiet. He never tells others about himself or his feelings. It is likely that people respond to him by
    (a) asking a lot of questions.
    (b) telling him a lot about themselves.
    (c) comparing his possible feelings to their feelings.
    (d) disclosing little about themselves.
    (e) treating him like a houseplant.

11. Bart and Bernice have been married for twelve years. From Bart's point of view Bernice is now overweight, a nag, and unstimulating. Bart believes that he is getting very little from the relationship even though he is still putting a lot into it. He wants a divorce. Bart's feelings can easily be explained from the point of view of
   (a) social comparison theory.
   (b) social influence.
   (c) social exchange theory.
   (d) conformity.

12. As a child, Richard was never really sure whether his parents loved him or not. Many times he felt loved one minute and rejected the next. Now as an adult he is most likely to have a(n) _____ attachment style in relationships.
   (a) secure
   (b) avoidant
   (c) ambivalent
   (d) absorbed

13. Although the speed limit now on some major highways is 55, Ray remembers when it was 70. He figures it was safe then and it is safe now, so he ignores the 55 m.p.h. rule. His behavior shows a blatant disregard for
   (a) coercive power.
   (b) legitimate power.
   (c) referent power.
   (d) reward power.

14. Paul goes to the library with his Walkman turned so loud that it bothers other people. According to the findings from Moriarity's study, most people will probably
   (a) do nothing.
   (b) leave his vicinity.
   (c) ask him politely to turn it down.
   (d) ask someone in authority to speak to Paul about the noise.
   (e) use sign language to try to communicate with Paul.

15. The setting is the coast of Florida. It is August and the National Weather Service is predicting that a hurricane will strike Miami. There is plenty of food in the stores, but a minority of people go out and buy much more than they could possibly eat in a month. This creates a shortage for the rest of the population that has decided to stay and ride out the storm. This situation is called
   (a) a social problem.
   (b) the tragedy of the commons.
   (c) assertive behavior.
   (d) low-balling.

Chapter Review

1. _____ _____ is the study of how people behave in the presence (real or implied) of others. _____ is the ongoing _____ ____ _____ that is passed on from one generation to another.

2. In your day-to-day life your immediate social environment includes many _____ such as your family and your classmates. In each _____ you meet expectations associated with playing _____. Some of these are _____ _____ and you have no control over them. Others which you attain voluntarily are _____ _____. When actual behavior is inconsistent with expected behavior you may be caught in a _____ _____.

3. The organization of roles, communications, pathways, and power in the group is _____ _____, and the degree of attraction among group members is _____ _____. The position in a group determines one's _____, and the standards of conduct which indicate appropriate behavior are called _____.

4. Pressures toward conformity affect the perception of movement of a stationary pinpoint of light in a completely darkened room. This illusion is called the _____ effect.

5. People maintain and regulate personal _____ which forms an invisible spatial area around each individual. _____ is the study of rules for the personal use of space.

6. Hall has identified four basic zones which relate to comfortable or acceptable distances. The first, _____ distance, extends about _____ inches out from the skin. The second, _____ distance, is the distance maintained in comfortable interaction with friends. This extends from about _____ to _____ feet from the body. The third is _____ distance which includes impersonal business and casual social gatherings and covers a range of about _____ to _____ feet. Speeches and lectures are carried out at _____ distance when people are separated by more than 12 feet.

7. The process of making inferences about behavior is called _____. Two factors that greatly influence it are _____ and _____. We are also very sensitive to _____ demands. If we have _____ it makes us feel much more assured about our inferences.

8. When a person does not feel confident about succeeding or to protect a fragile self-image, people sometimes arrange to be evaluated while engaging in _____-_____. That way, they can attribute the failure to the _____. One of the most popular and effective ways to do this is to use _____.

9. The fundamental attributional error is when we attribute the behavior of others to _____ causes and our own behavior to _____ causes. One facet of the fundamental attribution error is that the success of men is often attributed to _____ and that of women to _____.

10. The need to _____ helps people meet needs for approval, friendship, and support. Women waiting to be given painful _____ tended to want to wait with _____.

11. Group membership fills the need for _____ _____ which gives people a chance for self-evaluation. _____ _____ theory holds that a desire for self-evaluation determines what groups are joined. People also affiliate because of _____ _____ which is the basis for most voluntary social relationships.

12. Attraction is influenced by physical _____ because it increases the frequency of contact between people. In addition physical _____, talent or _____, and _____ of backgrounds, interests and attitudes influence choice of friends. When selecting a mate, people tend to marry those who are very similar — a pattern called _____.

13. Engaging in _____-_____ is a major step toward friendship. This process requires a degree of _____. There are definite _____ about when it is acceptable and when it is not. Moderate _____-_____ leads to _____ _____, however, gives rise to suspicion and reduced attraction.

14. People select a mate in a variety of ways. The thing which is most similar in married couples is _____. The two most important qualities picked by men and women were _____ and _____. However, physical attractiveness was ranked higher by _____ and earning capacity was ranked higher by _____.

15. According to the _____ _____ theory we want to maximize profitable, rewarding relationships.

16. Rubin has found that dating couples _____ and _____ their partners, but mostly _____ their friends. Women, however, were a little more "_____" toward their friends than were men. "Passionate" or romantic love is often associated with _____ _____. In addition, early _____ to caregivers during childhood impact on how we relate to others as adults. Specifically, the _____, _____, and _____ attachment patterns seen in early childhood translate to similar patterns with affectionate relationships as adults.

17. In Asch's experiment on conformity, subjects conformed to the group on about _____-_____ of the critical trials. Of those tested _____ percent yielded at least once. Subjects were most influenced by the group when it was _____.

18. A compulsion by decision-makers to maintain each other's approval even at the cost of critical thinking is called _____. The core of it is misguided group _____ where group members believe that there is more _____ and _____ than actually exists. To prevent it group leaders should _____ each group member's _____, avoid stating his or her own _____ in the beginning, state the problem _____, and make sure there is a _____ _____.

19. _____ power differs from _____ power in that the first lies in the ability to punish whereas the second is based on respect. Of the three other types of social power, _____ power is based on acceptance of a person as a representative of an established social order, _____ power is based on the ability to reward compliance, and _____ power is based on knowledge or expertise.

20. Stanley Milgram studied _____ by investigating some of the factors which influenced whether or not an individual would administer _____ _____ to a stranger in an experimental situation.

21. In Milgram's study _____ percent of those tested obeyed by going all the way to a 450-volt level. Obedience decreased when the victim was in the _____ _____, when the _____ and _____ were face-to-face, when the authority figure was _____ and when others refused to _____.

22. In _____ situations the pressure to get in line is usually indirect as opposed to when an authority commands _____. The term _____ is used to describe situations in which a person with little or no authority makes a direct request.

23. A person who agrees to a small request is later more likely to comply with a larger demand. This is called the _____-_____-_____-_____ effect. The_____-____-_____-_____ effect is when a person agrees to a smaller request after having first denied a larger request. The _____-_____ technique consists of getting a person committed to act and then making the terms of acting less desirable.

24. In addition to excessive obedience, many people are surprisingly _____. This is demonstrated by _____ _____ to unreasonable requests and by failure to be assertive.

25. _____ is a direct, honest expression of feelings and desires and differs from _____ which is an attempt to get one's own way no matter what. In _____ _____ individuals learn that they have the right to stand up for their rights.

26. Assertiveness can be improved by _____ the behaviors that you will need to use is a situation. If possible, you should _____ _____ the scene with a friend. It may also help to use _____. The _____ _____ technique may prove helpful. To do this you simply _____ your request as many times and as many ways as necessary.

27. A _____ _____ is any situation that rewards actions which have undesired effects in the long run. If this situation is one in which if many people act alike collective harm is done then it is called a collective social trap. If a number of people share a common resource and each individual acts in his or her own best interest which causes the resource to be depleted, this is called the _____ of the _____. Sometimes these situations can be avoided if the _____ and _____ can be rearranged.

ANSWER KEYS

Do You Know the Information?

Multiple Choice

		Can You Apply the Information?
1. (b) obj. 1, p. 618	17. (a) obj. 16, p. 629	1. (c) obj. 2, p. 618
2. (c) obj. 2, p. 618	18. (b) obj. 17, p. 630	2. (a) obj. 2, p. 618
3. (b) obj. 3, p. 620	19. (a) obj. 18, p. 631	3. (d) obj. 2, p. 620
4. (d) obj. 4, p. 620	20. (d) obj. 19, p. 630	4. (b) obj. 5, p. 621
5. (a) obj. 5, p. 621	21. (c) obj. 20, p. 630	5. (a) objs.2&4, p. 620
6. (d) obj. 6, p. 622	22. (a,b,d,e,g)obj.21, p. 631	6. (c) obj. 8, p. 622
7. (b) objs.6-7, p. 622	23. (c) obj. 22, p. 632	7. (b) obj. 9, p. 623
8. (c) obj. 8, p. 622	24. (c) obj. 23, p. 633	8. (b) obj. 11, p. 624
9. (b) obj. 9, p. 623	25. (d) obj. 24, p. 634	9. (c) obj. 12, p. 625
10. (c) obj. 10, p. 624	26. (c) obj. 25, pp. 634-645	10. (d) obj. 13, p. 626
11. (b) obj. 11, p. 624	27. (d) obj. 26, p. 636	11. (c) obj. 14, p. 627
12. (a,b,e,f)obj. 12, pp. 625-626	28. (a) obj. 27, p. 637	12. (c) obj. 15, p. 628
13. (a) obj. 12, p. 626	29. (b) obj. 27, p. 637	13. (a) obj. 21, p. 631
14. (d) obj. 13, p. 626	30. (d) obj. 28, p. 638	14. (a) obj. 26, p. 636
15. (c) obj. 14, p. 627	31. (c) obj. 29, p. 639	15. (b) obj. 29, p. 640

Chapter Review

1. Social psychology, Culture, pattern of life (p. 618)
2. groups, group, roles, ascribed roles, achieved roles, role conflict (p. 618)
3. group structure, group cohesiveness (p. 619); status (p, 618); norms (p. 619)
4. autokinetic (p. 620)
5. space, Proxemics (p. 620)
6. intimate, 18, personal, 1 1/2, 4, social, 4, 12, public (p. 621)
7. attribution, consistency, distinctiveness, situational, consensus (p. 622)
8. self-handicapping, handicap, alcohol (p. 622)
9. internal, external, skill, luck (p. 623)
10. affiliate, shocks, others (p. 624)
11. social comparison, Social comparison (p. 624); interpersonal attraction (p. 625)
12. proximity, attractiveness (p. 625); competence, similarity, homogamy (p. 626)
13. self-disclosure, trust, norms, self-disclosure, reciprocity, Overdisclosure (p. 626)
14. attitudes (opinions), kindness, understanding, men, women (p. 626)
15. social exchange (p. 627)
16. liked, loved, liked, loving, mutual absorption (p. 627); attachments, secure, avoidant, ambivalent (p. 628)
17. one-third, 75, unanimous (p. 630)
18. groupthink, loyalty, agreement, unanimity, define, role, preferences, factually, devil's advocate (p. 630)
19. Coercive, referent, legitimate, reward, expert (p. 631)
20. obedience, electric shocks (p. 632)
21. 65, same room, victim ("learner"), subject ("teacher"), distant (absent), obey (p. 633)
22. conformity, obedience, compliance (p. 634)
23. foot-in-the-door, door-in-the-face (p. 634); low-ball (p. 635)
24. passive (compliant), passive compliance (p. 636)
25. Assertion, aggression, assertiveness training (p. 637)
26. rehearsing, role play (p. 637); overlearning, broken record, restate (p. 638)
27. social trap (p. 639); tragedy, commons, rewards, costs (p. 640)

Chapter 24

Social Psychology II

KEY TERMS, CONCEPTS, AND INDIVIDUALS

attitudes — components and formation
why behavior sometimes does not
    reflect attitudes
attitude measurement
groups — reference, membership
persuasion and how to do it
cognitive dissonance theory
    justification or reward
forced attitude change
    brainwashing and cults
prejudice versus discrimination
    scapegoating
personal and group prejudice
authoritarian personality
    ethnocentrism, dogmatism
social stereotypes
    symbolic prejudice
status inequalities

equal-status contact
superordinate goals
jigsaw classrooms
aggression — causes
    instinct (Konrad Lorenz)
    biology
    frustration-aggression hypothesis
    aversive stimuli
    social learning theory
    & pornography
anger control
prosocial behavior
bystander apathy
    factors of bystander intervention
empathic arousal
    empathy-helping relationship
multiculturalism
sociobiology

LEARNING OBJECTIVES

To demonstrate mastery of this chapter you should be able to :
1. Define attitude. Describe the belief, emotional, and action components of an attitude.

2.   List, describe, and give examples of six ways in which attitudes are acquired.
      a.

      b.

      c.

      d.

      e.

      f.

3.   Explain why people may exhibit discrepancies between attitudes and behavior and how conviction affects attitudes.

4.   Briefly describe the following techniques for measuring attitudes:
      a.   open-ended interview

      b.   social distance scale

      c.   attitude scale

5.   Differentiate between reference groups and membership groups.

6.   Define persuasion.

7.   List nine conditions bringing about attitude change.
      a.

      b.

      c.

      d.

      e.

      f.

      g.

      h.

      i.

8.   Describe the effects of role playing as a way to change attitudes.

9.   Explain cognitive dissonance theory.

10.   Indicate the influence of cognitive dissonance on attitude formation.

11.   Describe the effect of reward or justification on dissonance.

12.   Differentiate between brainwashing and other persuasive techniques.

13.   Explain how beliefs may unfreeze, change, and refreeze, and indicate how permanent the attitude changes brought about by brainwashing are.

14.   Describe how cults are able to recruit, convert, and retain their members.

15.   Define and differentiate prejudice and discrimination.

16.   Explain how scapegoating relates to prejudice.

17.   Distinguish between personal and group prejudices.

18.   Describe the characteristic beliefs (including ethnocentrism and dogmatism) and childhood experiences of the authoritarian personality.

19. Present the major characteristics of social stereotypes and indicate how they may lead to intergroup conflicts. (Include a description of symbolic prejudice.)

20. Explain how status inequalities may lead to the development of stereotypes and how equal-status contact may reduce intergroup tension. Give an example of each situation.

21. Define superordinate goals. (Include an explanation of how they can reduce conflict and hostility.)

22. Explain how a "jigsaw" classroom utilizes superordinate goals and helps reduce prejudice.

23. Discuss the roles of instincts and physiology in terms of aggression.

24.   State the frustration-aggression hypothesis, indicating why it may or may not be true.

25.   Discuss how frustration, in the form of aversive stimuli, can encourage aggression.

26.   Explain how the weapons effect encourages aggression.

27.   Discuss how social learning theory explains aggression.

28.   Briefly describe the results of studies on the relationship between aggressive pornography and aggression of males toward females.

29.   Explain the basic principle of anger control and list five strategies for controlling anger.

       a.

       b.

       c.

       d.

       e.

The following objectives are related to the material in the "Applications" and "Exploration" sections of your text.

30. Give an example of bystander apathy, and indicate the major factor which determines whether or not help will be given.

31. Describe four conditions that need to exist before bystanders are likely to give help. (Indicate how the presence of other people can influence apathy.)
     a.

     b.

     c.

     d.

32. Discuss how heightened and empathetic arousal affect helping behavior.

33. State three ways in which prosocial behavior can be encouraged.
     a.

     b.

     c.

34. Define the term multiculturalism.

35. Discuss six ways in which a person can become more tolerant.
     a.

     b.

c.

d.

e.

f.

36. Explain how a person can develop cultural awareness.

37. Explain the basic idea behind sociobiology and evaluate it in terms of its strengths and weaknesses.

SELF-QUIZZES

Do You Know the Information?

Multiple Choice

1. A(n) _____ is a mixture of belief and emotion that predisposes a person to respond to people, objects, or institutions in a positive or negative way.
    - (a) norm
    - (b) belief
    - (c) stereotype
    - (d) attitude

2. The influence that rock music videos appear to have is through the attitude formation process of
    - (a) direct contact.
    - (b) conditioning.
    - (c) group membership.
    - (d) interaction with others.

3. Often there are large differences between attitudes and behavior. This occurs because
    - (a) long-standing habits may take precedence.
    - (b) the immediate consequences of our actions may be more important.
    - (c) we may expect that others will negatively evaluate our actions.
    - (d) of all of the above.

4. Which technique for measuring attitudes indicates a person's willingness to have contact with another person?
    - (a) attitude scales
    - (b) open-ended interview
    - (c) liking/loving ratio
    - (d) social distance scale

5. Membership groups and reference groups differ in that
   (a) a person sees a reference group as holding values and attitudes relevant to his or her own.
   (b) to be a part of a membership group the membership need not be physical.
   (c) being part of membership group depends on who you identify with or care about.
   (d) none of the above are true.

6. Which of the following is *not* likely to be particularly persuasive?
   (a) The message is repeated as frequently as possible.
   (b) The message is presented rationally as opposed to appealing to the emotions.
   (c) The persuader appears to have nothing to gain if the message is accepted.
   (d) The message states clear-cut conclusions.

7. According to cognitive dissonance theory
   (a) there is usually an inconsistency between attitudes and behavior.
   (b) people tend to seek information which runs counter to previously established attitudes.
   (c) behavior which is inconsistent with attitudes may provoke attitude change.
   (d) a large reward will create more dissonance.

8. Persuasion resembles brainwashing except that the latter
   (a) is more effective.   (c) requires a captive audience.
   (b) is more effective for long-term attitude change. (d) involves confession.

9. Which of the following statements concerning brainwashing is *true*?
   (a) The effects are relatively permanent.
   (b) It typically begins with praise for correct behavior.
   (c) The person being brainwashed goes through a cycle known as unfreezing, changing, refreezing.
   (d) The "target" is allowed to exist independent of his captors.

10. Cults
    (a) tend to create guilt and fear in their members.
    (b) isolate potential members from noncult members and try to wear down physical and emotional resistance.
    (c) try to catch potential converts at a time of need.
    (d) do all of the above.

11. The difference between prejudice and discrimination is
    (a) prejudice leads to discrimination, but discrimination doesn't lead to prejudice.
    (b) prejudice refers to behavior and discrimination doesn't.
    (c) discrimination is always negative and prejudice is not.
    (d) discrimination refers to behavior, prejudice refers to an attitude.

12. People who have an authoritarian personality
    (a) are happy but rather prejudiced.
    (b) were raised as children to be independent and achievement oriented.
    (c) have attitudes and values marked by rigidity, inhibition, and oversimplification.
    (d) are prejudiced against all in-groups.

13. Oversimplified images of people who fall into a particular category are called
    (a) social stereotypes.   (c) group attitudes.
    (b) ethnocentrisms.   (d) status inequalities.

14. Which of the following statements is *incorrect?*
    (a) Status inequalities help to increase prejudice.
    (b) Superordinate goals are usually too difficult to reach and thus increase prejudice and discrimination.
    (c) Equal-status interaction between groups should reduce prejudice and stereotypes.
    (d) Prejudice and discrimination can be taught to children in as little as one day.

15. Aversive stimuli work to heighten hostility and aggression. The rationale for this falls under a more general
    _____ cause for aggression.
    (a) instinctual   (c) frustration
    (b) biological   (d) social-learning

16. The social learning theory states that
    (a) when we become frustrated, we become aggressive.
    (b) there are certain areas of the brain responsible for triggering aggression.
    (c) aggression is an instinct.
    (d) we become aggressive by observing aggression in others.

17. Concerning aggression and pornography it has been found that
    (a) pornography causes aggression.
    (b) exposure to an aggressive film after becoming angry helps reduce a person's level of anger.
    (c) the mass media has not had an appreciable effect on sex-related crimes.
    (d) none of the above are true.

18. A person will be likely to help someone when
    (a) there are few people around.
    (b) there is greater diffusion of responsibility.
    (c) there are many people around to provide emotional support.
    (d) status inequalities exist.

19. Which of the following statements concerning multiculturalism is *incorrect?*
    (a) Just-world beliefs assume that all discrimination and prejudice will disappear in time.
    (b) Seeking individuating information helps to eliminate stereotypes.
    (c) People tend to act in accordance with other's expectations of them.
    (d) Social competition tends to foster a feeling of "we're better than all the rest" in every major ethnic group.

20. Which of the following statements about sociobiology or its views is *incorrect?*
    (a) The core idea is that social behavior evolves in ways that maximize the fitness of a species for survival.
    (b) Genes manipulate our behavior to ensure their survival.
    (c) Evolution progresses too slowly to account for many behavioral adaptations.
    (d) Its major strength is that it helps relate human behavior to biology.
    (e) Sociobiology offers new possibilities and suggestions to help change human problems.

Matching (*Use the letters on the right only once.*)

_____ 1. ways to acquire attitudes
_____ 2. deliberate attempt to bring about attitude change by transmission of information
_____ 3. creating emotional experiences to alter attitudes
_____ 4. forced attitude change methods
_____ 5. behavior as opposed to attitude
_____ 6. form of displaced aggression
_____ 7. when members of another group represent a threat to individual security or comfort
_____ 8. consider members of own national, ethnic or religious group superior to others
_____ 9. rationalized or disguised prejudice
_____10. must cooperate in order to succeed
_____11. humans are naturally aggressive
_____12. according to the social learning theory, how to decrease aggression in children
_____13. key to anger control
_____14. one of the decision points for helping behavior to occur
_____15. social behavior evolves in ways to maximize fitness for survival

A. personal prejudice
B. turn off television
C. persuasion
D. see the upsetting situation as problem to be solved
E. biology
F. ethnocentric
G. brainwashing, cults
H. define emergency
I. sociobiology
J. childrearing, mass media, chance conditioning, etc.
K. scapegoating
L. dogmatism
M. role playing
N. instinct
O. equal status interaction
P. discrimination
Q. jigsaw classroom
R. frustration
S. symbolic prejudice

Can You Apply the Information?

1. Sally feels very strongly about uvulas and, in fact, went to the annual meeting of the National Uvula Foundation. Sally's attendance at that meeting was an example of the _____ component of her attitude.
    (a) emotional
    (b) belief
    (c) action
    (d) none of these

2. Juanita owns and operates a small manufacturing company in Alaska. She doesn't pay her workers much money and constantly has trouble finding help. It seems that the only people she can find are down-and-out white men who tend to be alcoholics or drug abusers. As a result of this she has tended to take a rather negative attitude toward all white people. It could be said that her prejudice is a result of
    (a) group membership.
    (b) child rearing.
    (c) interaction with others with the same attitude.
    (d) direct contact.

3. Jane and Bob have recently moved and have joined a new recreation club. They spend a lot of their time at the new club because they had to quit the recreation club in their old neighborhood. They still feel closer to the members in the old club. Their new club is a(n) _____ group.
    (a) equal-status
    (b) reference
    (c) membership
    (d) identification

4. Phil will have a better chance convincing his nuclear physicist audience that nuclear energy is a threat to Earth if
    (a) he appeals to their emotions.
    (b) he presents both sides of the argument.
    (c) he tells them that he has recently sold his stock in coal and gas companies.
    (d) he can do all of the above.

5. In which of the following situations will cognitive dissonance be *most* likely to occur?
    (a) Bill, a student, is asked to give a speech on why tuition at his college should be raised by $1000.
    (b) Bill has to give the same speech (as above) or get an "F" in his speech class.
    (c) Bill is paid $100 to give the speech.
    (d) Bill believes that tuition should be raised, and he wants to give the speech.

6. Betty works on an assembly line putting round doohickys in round doohicky holes. It is tedious, boring work. She has been asked to speak to a local high school class touring the plant in the hopes that many of them will want similar jobs. Betty will try to convince the students of the interesting nature of this job. Which compensation that the company could give her would result in the *greatest* dissonance?
    (a) a two-week all expenses paid vacation for two in Jamaica
    (b) making her a foreman with a substantial increase in pay
    (c) allowing her to set her own work schedule
    (d) giving her five additional minutes each coffee break

7. Fred has a great distrust and suspicion of the Japanese. He always expects Japanese people to be cunning and wiley. This is an example of discrimination.
    (a) True   (b) False

8. It is likely that most members of the Ku Klux Klan possess a high level of
    (a) ethnocentrism.   (d) both a and c.
    (b) dogmatism.   (e) all of the above.
    (c) personal prejudice.

9. Fred is riding on a bus to a football game. The bus has a flat tire, and in order to get to the game Fred helps the Japanese bus driver change the tire. Fred's attitudes have mellowed toward Japanese people slightly as a result of the incident. This is an example of using a(n) _____ goal to reduce hostility.
    (a) overriding   (c) authoritarian
    (b) ethnocentric   (d) superordinate

10. The phrase "misery loves company" would most closely relate to which of the following concepts?
    (a) diffusion of responsibility   (c) empathic arousal
    (b) bystander apathy   (d) prosocial behavior

Chapter Review

1. _____ are mixtures of beliefs and emotions that predispose a person to respond in a certain way. They have three major components, a _____ component, an _____ component, and an _____ component.

2. Attitudes are acquired in several basic ways, sometimes through _____
    _____ with the object of the attitude, through _____ with others holding the same attitude, through _____ _____ in which one becomes like his/her parents, through _____ _____,
    through the _____ _____, and through _____
    _____.

3. Many times there are discrepancies between our attitudes and our behavior because the immediate _____ of our actions weigh heavily on the choices we make. A second factor is our expectation of how others will _____ our actions. Finally, we must not overlook the effects of long-standing _____. However, attitudes which are held with passionate _____ often lead to major changes in personal behavior.

4. If you were asked, "How do you feel about drafting women?" you may be taking part in an _____ - _____ _____ designed to measure attitudes. Another approach to attitude measurement is the _____ _____ scale which measures the degree to which one person would be willing to associate with another. If you were asked to express agreement or disagreement with the concept of drafting women by using a five-point _____ ranging from "strongly agree" to "strongly disagree," you would be rated on an _____ _____.

5. A _____ group is one whose values and attitudes are seen by the individual as being relevant to his or her own. A _____ group is merely a group to which you belong.

6. A deliberate attempt to change attitudes by the imparting of _____ is called _____. Attitude change is most encouraged when (1) the communicator is _____; (2) the message appeals to _____; (3) the message presents a clear _____ of _____; (4) the message states clear-cut _____; (5) the message is backed up by _____; (6) both sides of the argument are presented for a _____-informed audience; (7) one side of the argument is presented for a _____-informed audience; (8) the persuader appears to have nothing to _____; and (9) the message is presented _____.

7. People who engage in _____ _____ about a topic are more likely to change their opinions than people who merely hear a lecture about the topic. This phenomenon can be partially explained by _____ _____ theory which states that the maintenance and change of attitudes is closely related to needs for _____ in attitudes and action.

8. Studies have indicated that the amount of dissonance is inversely related to the amount of _____ or _____ for acting _____ to one's real beliefs.

9. Two methods of forced attitude change are _____ and _____.

10. One difference between persuasion and brainwashing is that brainwashing requires a _____ audience. The target of brainwashing is _____ from other people, is made _____ on his captors for satisfaction of needs, and the captors are in a position to _____ changes in attitudes or behavior. All of these techniques serve to _____, change, and then _____ the target's attitudes.

11. _____ use high-pressure indoctrination techniques similar to those used in brainwashing. Members stay because of _____ and _____ and because they are _____ on the group.

12. _____ is a negative attitude which may contribute to _____, behavior that prevents individuals from doing things they would like, such as   buying a house or belonging to an organization.

13. Prejudice may represent a form of _____, a form of _____ aggression in which hostility and frustration cause aggression to be redirected to other targets. _____ prejudice occurs when an individual's comfort or security is threatened by members of another racial or ethnic group. _____ prejudice occurs through the individual's identifying with group norms.

14. One prejudice-prone personality is the _____ personality. They tend to be _____ (prejudiced against people who are not members of their own national, ethnic, or religious group) and _____ (unwarranted positiveness in matters of belief or opinion).

15. Prejudice may have its roots in positive or negative _____ _____ or oversimplified images of people who are in a particular category. When prejudice is expressed through opinions on issues such as busing, etc., this is known as _____ prejudice. To combat prejudice, changing the belief component of an attitude through education may be partially effective. In addition, increased _____-_____ interaction between groups in conflict should reduce prejudice and stereotyping.

16. On the other hand, merely bringing people together may increase negative stereotyping unless _____ _____ force members of each group to cooperate for mutual gain. Such goals are effective because they make people _____. "_____" classrooms force this type of interaction by requiring cooperation for students to do well on _____.

17. Some of the potential explanations for the occurrence of aggression include the theory of Konrad Lorenz, a prominent _____, who believes that aggression is an _____ behavior observed in all animals, including humans.

18. Other researchers feel that there is a _____ basis for aggressive behavior. Certain _____ areas may be capable of triggering or ending aggressive behavior. In addition, there may be a relationship between aggression and _____, allergies, specific _____ injuries and disorders, and between aggression and _____.

19. The _____-_____ hypothesis states that there is a close link between frustration and _____. However _____ does not always lead to aggression, and _____ can occur in the absence of _____, such as instances in which such actions are committed by trick-or-treaters on Halloween even after they have received treats.

20. Frustration encourages aggression because it is _____. Aversive _____ also heighten hostility by making us more sensitive to _____. Such is the case with the _____ effect, i.e., the sight of a weapon encourages _____.

21. The _____ _____ theory of aggression holds that we learn aggression by observing aggression in others. Among the most influential models for children were those observed on _____. Children learn _____ in this way. The implication of this research is that perhaps parents should monitor what their children watch on _____.

22. Recent studies indicate that there is a link between _____ and _____. Exposure to mass media stimuli that have _____ and _____ content increases the audience's aggressive-sexual fantasies, beliefs in _____ myths, and _____ behavior. Experts warn that it is media _____ which is most damaging.

23. _____ control can be taught. The key to it is the fact that people who respond calmly to upsetting situations tend to see them as _____ to be _____.

24. One factor which leads to bystander _____ is the presence of other people. When many other people are present, personal responsibility for helping is spread thin. Before people decide to give help, they must _____ that something is happening, they must _____ the event as an emergency, they must take _____ and finally, they must _____ a course of action. Groups limit helping by causing a _____ of _____. Studies show that when we see someone in trouble, this tends to cause an increase in two types of arousal: _____ arousal and _____ arousal. Empathic _____ gives a feeling of _____ to the victim which is important in helping. Hence there is a strong _____ - _____ relationship.

25. Learning to respect and appreciate our cultural differences is termed _____. To help ourselves break the _____ of prejudice we can:
    (1) beware of _____;
    (2) seek _____ information;
    (3) be careful of _____ - _____ beliefs as well as _____ - _____ prophecies;
    (4) avoid unnecessary _____ _____; and,
    (5) look for _____.

26. Living comfortably in a multicultural society means getting to know a little about other _____.

27. According to _____, many human social behaviors have roots in heredity. The core idea is that social behavior evolves in ways that maximize the fitness of a species for _____. It is almost as if our _____ manipulate our behavior to ensure their _____.

28. The major strength of this point of view is that it helps relate human behavior to _____. Its major weakness is that it _____ its case. Critics also point out that _____ moves too slowly to account for many behavioral adaptations.

ANSWER KEYS

Do You Know the Information?

Multiple Choice

1. (d) obj. 1, p. 645
2. (b) obj. 2, p. 646
3. (d) obj. 3, p. 647
4. (d) obj. 4, p. 647
5. (a) obj. 5, p. 647
6. (b) obj. 7, p. 648
7. (c) objs. 9-10, p. 649
8. (c) obj. 12, p. 650
9. (c) obj. 13, p. 651
10. (d) obj. 14, p. 651
11. (d) obj. 15, p. 652
12. (c) obj. 18, p. 653
13. (a) obj. 19, p. 654
14. (b) objs. 20-21, p. 656
15. (c) obj. 25, p. 659
16. (d) obj. 27, p. 660

17. (d) obj. 28, p. 660
18. (a) objs. 30-31, pp. 661-662
19. (a) objs. 34-35, pp. 664-666
20. (e) obj. 37, pp. 667-668

Matching

1. J, obj. 2, pp. 645-646
2. C, obj. 6, p. 648
3. M, obj. 8, p. 648
4. G, objs. 12,14, pp. 650-651
5. P, obj. 15, p. 652
6. K, obj. 16, p. 652
7. A, obj. 17, p. 652
8. F, obj. 18, p. 653
9. S, obj. 19, p. 655
10. Q, obj. 22, p. 657
11. N, obj. 23, p. 658

12. B, obj. 27, p. 660
13. D, obj. 29, p. 660
14. H, obj. 31, p. 662
15. I, obj. 37, p. 667

Can You Apply the Information?

1. (c) obj. 1, p. 645
2. (d) obj. 2, p. 645
3. (c) obj. 5, p. 648
4. (d) obj. 7, p. 648
5. (a) objs. 9-10, p. 649
6. (d) obj. 11, p. 649
7. (b) obj. 15, p. 652
8. (e) objs. 17-18, pp. 652-653
9. (d) obj. 21, p. 656
10. (c) obj. 32, p. 663

Chapter Review

1. Attitudes, belief, emotional, action (p. 645)
2. direct contact, interaction, child rearing, group membership (p. 645); mass media, chance conditioning (p. 646)
3. consequences, evaluate, habits, conviction (p. 647)
4. open-ended interview, social distance, scale, attitude scale (p. 647)
5. reference (p. 647); membership (p. 648)
6. information, persuasion, likeable (trustworthy, expert, similar), emotions, course, action, conclusions, facts (statistics), well, poorly, gain, frequently (p. 648)
7. role playing (p. 648); cognitive dissonance, consistency (p. 649)
8. reward, justification, contrary (p. 649)
9. brainwashing, cults (p. 650)
10. captive (p. 650); isolated, dependent, reward, unfreeze, refreeze (p. 651)
11. Cults, guilt, fear, dependent (p. 651)
12. Prejudice, discrimination (p. 652)
13. scapegoating, displaced, Personal, Group (p. 652)
14. authoritarian (p. 652); ethnocentric, dogmatic (p. 653)
15. social stereotypes (p. 654); symbolic (p. 655); equal-status (p. 656)
16. superordinate goals (p.656); mutually interdependent, Jigsaw, tests (p. 657)
17. ethologist, instinctive (p. 658)
18. biological, brain, hypoglycemia, brain, drugs (alcohol) (p. 658)
19. frustration-aggression, aggression, frustration, aggression, frustration (p. 659)
20. aversive (uncomfortable), stimuli, aggression cues (p. 659); weapons, aggression (p. 660)
21. social learning, television, aggression, television (p. 660)
22. aggression, pornography, violent, sexual, rape, aggressive, violence (p. 660)

23. Anger, problems, solved (p. 660)
24. apathy (p. 661); notice, define, responsibility, select, diffusion, responsibility (p. 662); general, empathic, arousal, connection, empathic-helping (p. 663)
25. multiculturalism, habit, stereotypes, individuating, just-world, self-fulfilling (p. 665); social competition, commonalities (p. 666)
26. groups (p. 666)
27. sociobiology, survival (p. 667); genes, survival (p. 668)
28. biology, overstates, evolution (p. 668)

Chapter 25

Gender and Sexuality

KEY TERMS AND CONCEPTS

primary and secondary sex characteristics
menarche, ovulation, menopause
sex hormones
    estrogens, androgens,
    testosterone
gonads
dimensions of gender
    genetic sex, gonadal sex,
    hormonal sex, genital sex,
    gender identity
androgen insensitivity, hermaphroditism,
    androgenital syndrome, biological
    biasing effect
sex role, sex role socialization
    sex role stereotypes
    instrumental, expressive behavior
causes of sexual arousal
    physical and emotional effects
sexual scripts
differences in sex drives
    castration, sterilization,
    masturbation
homosexuality

ego-dystonic
phases of sexual response — excitement,
    plateau, orgasm, resolution
    differences and similarities in male
    and female sexual response
ejaculation, refractory period
    multiple orgasm
sexual revolution
date rape
sexually transmitted diseases
    acquired immune deficiency
impotence — primary and secondary
    occasional
    organic and psychogenic
    causes and cures
premature and retarded ejaculation
female general sexual dysfunction
    causes and cures
    female orgasmic dysfunction
    causes and cures
vaginismus
improving communication skills
    touching

LEARNING OBJECTIVES

To demonstrate mastery of this chapter you should be able to:
1. Differentiate primary from secondary sex characteristics and state (in general) what causes them.

2.   Define or describe the following terms or concepts:
      a.   gonads

      b.   menarche

      c.   ovulation

      d.   menopause

      e.   estrogens

      f.   androgens

      g.   testosterone

3.   List and describe the five dimensions of gender.
      a.

      b.

      c.

      d.

      e.

4.   Explain how a person's gender develops. Include in your discussion a description of these conditions:

      a.   androgen insensitivity

      b.   hermaphroditism

   c.   androgenital syndrome

   d.   biological biasing effect

5.   Differentiate gender identity from sex role and explain how gender identity is formed.

6.   Describe the effects of socialization on sex roles and include a discussion of instrumental and expressive behaviors.

7.   Discuss the differences between males and females in their degree of arousal to erotic stimuli.

8.   Explain what a sexual script is and how it relates to sexual behavior.

9.   Explain what causes differences in sex drives in males and females.

10.   Describe the effects of alcohol, castration, and aging on the sex drive.

11.   Discuss the normality and acceptablility of masturbation.

12.   Discuss the combination of influences that appears to produce homosexuality.

13.   Characterize the mental health status of homosexuals and state under what conditions homosexuality is considered a problem.

14.   List in order and briefly describe the four phases of sexual response in men and women.

                 men   *women*

   a.

   b.

   c.

   d.

15.   State the two most basic differences in the sexual response styles of men and women.

   a.

   b.

16.   Describe the changes that have taken place in sexual attitudes and behavior in the last 50 years.

17.   Explain what is meant by the phrase, "slow death of the double standard."

18.   Define acquaintance or "date rape" and discuss its effects.

19.   Explain the cause, methods of transmission, and ways of preventing AIDS.

* * * * * * * * * *

The following objectives are related to the material in the "Applications" and "Exploration" sections of your text.

20.   Describe the following sexual problems including the nature, cause, and treatment of each:

a.   impotence — organic and psychogenic (primary and secondary)

b.   premature ejaculation

c.   retarded ejaculation

d.   general sexual dysfunction

e.   orgasmic dysfunction

    f.   vaginismus

21.   List eight techniques that can be used to encourage effective communication between husbands and wives.
       a.

       b.

       c.

       d.

       e.

       f.

       g.

       h.

22.   Discuss the cultural limitations of non-sexual touching.

SELF-QUIZZES

Do You Know the Information?

Multiple Choice

1.   In general, primary and secondary sex characteristics are caused by
      (a) socialization.   (c) sex hormones.
      (b) sexual activity.   (d) societal expectations.

2.   A female's gonads are (is) the
      (a) ovaries.   (c) vagina.
      (b) clitoris.   (d) uterus.

3.   Male hormones secreted by the gonads are
      (a) estrogens.   (c) adrenalins.
      (b) androgens.   (d) progesterones.

4. Which of the following is *not* a dimension of gender?
   (a) sex role
   (b) hormonal sex
   (c) gender identity
   (d) gonadal sex

5. A learned, self-perception of one's maleness or femaleness is referred to as
   (a) expressive behavior.
   (b) instrumental behavior.
   (c) sex-role socialization.
   (d) gender identity.

6. Dual or ambiguous sexual anatomy may result from hormonal problems before birth. This is known as
   (a) hermaphroditism.
   (b) androgenital syndrome.
   (c) general sexual dysfunction.
   (d) vaginismus.

7. When a genetic abnormality causes the adrenal glands to secrete excess amounts of androgen, it can produce a condition known as _____ in which a female child has male genitals.
   (a) gender misidentity
   (b) androgenital syndrome
   (c) primary sexual dysfunction
   (d) androgen insensitivity

8. Which of the following statements is *incorrect*?
   (a) Nature's primary impulse is to make a biological female.
   (b) The interplay of sex hormones before birth may "sex type" the brain.
   (c) Gender identity is essentially formed at age two when the child has mastered the rudiments of language.
   (d) Sex roles are public and observable while gender identity is a private inner feeling.

9. Because of sex role socialization
   (a) the female role appears to be definitely "not male."
   (b) girls are held less than boys at an early age.
   (c) natural male or female behavior is universally adopted.
   (d) boys are encouraged to adopt instrumental behaviors.

10. When comparing the responses of males and females to general erotic material we find that
    (a) women are less aroused than men.
    (b) men are less aroused than women.
    (c) men and women are equally aroused.
    (d) men are more aroused by romance than are women.

11. In males and perhaps in females the strength of the sex drive is related to the amount of _____ secreted.
    (a) gonadin
    (b) androgen
    (c) estrogen
    (d) testosterone

12. Castration leads to
    (a) a cessation of the sex drive in human males but not in females.
    (b) an immediate and drastic reduction of the female sex drive because of reduced estrogen levels.
    (c) a cessation of the sex drive in men over 85 years of age.
    (d) none of the above.

13. Which of the following statements about masturbation is *incorrect*?
    (a) Masturbation is considered a biologically healthy substitute for intercourse during adolescence.
    (b) A large percentage of people continue to masturbate after marriage.
    (c) Rhythmic self-stimulation has been observed in infants under one year of age.
    (d) Masturbation doesn't cause VD or insanity, but it can dull the pleasure of normal sexual intercourse after marriage.
    (e) There's nothing wrong with masturbation, you just don't meet a lot of nice people that way.

14. Which of the following is thought to be the *probable* cause of homosexuality?
    (a) hormonal imbalances
    (b) genetic and biological factors
    (c) social and psychological influences
    (d) all of these are involved

15. Which of the following statements about homosexuality is *incorrect*?
    (a) Ego-dystonic homosexuality is when the person feels lasting guilt and self-hate.
    (b) Although psychologically they are similar to heterosexuals, homosexuals show an overall poorer adjustment to life.
    (c) About 5 to 10 percent of all adult men are homosexuals.
    (d) Almost two-thirds of 76 cultures surveyed accept some form of homosexuality.

16. The *correct* ordering of the stages of the human sexual response cycle are
    (a) excitement, plateau, orgasm, and resolution.
    (b) plateau, resolution, excitement, and orgasm.
    (c) resolution, excitement, plateau, and orgasm.
    (d) excitement, resolution, orgasm, and plateau.

17. As compared to the male sexual response cycle, females
    (a) are more capable of multiple orgasms.
    (b) usually go through the sexual phases more slowly than men.
    (c) are more similar to males than they are different.
    (d) can be described by all of the above.

18. Which of the following changes in sexual attitudes and/or behavior have taken place?
    (a) Attitudes have become more tolerant.
    (b) The gap between sexual values and actual behavior has widened.
    (c) There has been no significant difference in the number of people having premarital intercourse.
    (d) Contrary to popular belief, males are engaging in sexual behavior earlier and girls are delaying their first participation.

19. Which of the following statements is *incorrect* with regards to AIDS?
    (a) AIDS can be spread without people knowing that they have it for as long as 7 years.
    (b) It is appropriate to call AIDS a "gay plague."
    (c) The majority of people infected with HIV are heterosexual.
    (d) Responsibility for avoiding HIV infection rests with the individual.

20. Primary impotence refers to
    (a) males who have had active sex lives but who can no longer achieve an erection.
    (b) men who cannot achieve orgasm.
    (c) the inability to control orgasm.
    (d) men who have never been able to achieve or maintain an erection.

21. A major sexual therapy technique which involves nongenital physical contact is
    (a) sensate focus.
    (b) squeeze technique.
    (c) sex role socialization.
    (d) orgasmic relearning.

22. Retarded ejaculation refers to an inability to
    (a) sustain erection.
    (b) feel physical pleasure.
    (c) achieve orgasm.
    (d) achieve erection promptly.
    (e) teach semen a thing.

23. The technique of choice in treating premature ejaculation is
    (a) sensate focus.
    (b) squeeze technique.
    (c) sex role socialization.
    (d) desensitization.

24. A condition in which muscle spasms make intercourse impossible for the female is known as
   (a) frigidity.
   (c) orgasmic dysfunction.
   (b) androgenital syndrome.
   (d) vaginismus.

True-False

_____ 1. When menarche occurs in a female, she is fertile and capable of becoming pregnant.

_____ 2. Nature's primary impulse is to make a male so as to assure abundant levels of sperm for procreation.

_____ 3. The biological biasing effect for females is caused by a prenatal exposure to androgen and results in an abnormal amount of masculine-type behaviors.

_____ 4. Acquiring a gender identity begins with the label "boy" or "girl" and thereafter is influenced by sex-role socialization.

_____ 5. There appear to be no "natural" male or female behaviors.

_____ 6. Attitudes toward sex, sexual experience, physical factors, and recency of sexual release are all important in determining a person's sex drive.

_____ 7. The depressant alcohol (even in small doses) depresses sexual desire.

_____ 8. The critical factor for an extended sex life appears to be regularity.

_____ 9. A combination of biological and social factors is responsible for the development of sexuality whether it be homosexuality, heterosexuality, or bisexuality.

_____10. Women ejaculate slightly when they reach orgasm.

_____11. Approximately one half of the female students who have been raped suffered acquaintance rape.

_____12. Impotence is almost always psychological in nature.

_____13. Although it is not necessarily constructive, in order to resolve differences it is important for disagreement to be solved by having a winner.

_____14. Compared with such countries as France and Puerto Rico, there is very little touching between individuals in our culture.

Matching *(Use the letters on the right only once.)*

_____ 1. primary sex characteristics
_____ 2. secondary sex characteristics
_____ 3. onset of menstruation
_____ 4. one of the androgens
_____ 5. predominance of androgen or estrogen
_____ 6. the favored pattern of behavior expected of
          individuals on the basis of gender
_____ 7. instrumental behaviors
_____ 8. "You know I like to make love in the dark."
_____ 9. no amount of continued stimulation will
          produce a second orgasm
_____10. "separate but not equal" position regarding
          sexual behavior of males and females
_____11. fatal STD
_____12. has previously performed successfully, but
          then became impotent
_____13. lack of erotic response to sexual stimulation

A.   estrogen
B.   general sexual dysfunction
C.   refractory period
D.   sexual script
E.   goal-directed
F.   double standard
G.   body hair, development of breasts
H.   AIDS
I.   hormonal sex
J.   secondary impotence
K.   sex role
L.   retarded ejaculation
M.   menarche
N.   scrotum, ovaries
O.   female orgasmic dysfunction
P.   testosterone
Q.   gender identity
R.   primary impotence
S.   emotionally oriented

Can You Apply the Information?

1. If you were a mad scientist and wanted to permanently eradicate a man's sex drive, which of the following would
    you do?
    (a) Castrate him.   (c) Decrease his supply of androgen.
    (b) Give him estrogen shots.   (d) None of the above would be sufficient.

2. John has been married for 18 years and masturbates about once a week. His masturbation is an indication that he
    and his wife do not have a satisfying sex life.
    (a) True   (b) False

3. Men are incapable of multiple orgasms.
    (a) True   (b) False

4. Bill has never had any sexual problems. However, shortly after he started his new job he has had trouble keeping
    his erection long enough to reach orgasm. Bill's problem would be diagnosed as
    (a) retarded ejaculation.   (c) primary impotence.
    (b) premature ejaculation.   (d) secondary impotence.

5. Ron has been married for 23 years. He has not been able to have an orgasm for almost a year. Ron is most likely
    suffering from
    (a) primary impotence.   (c) retarded ejaculation.
    (b) general sexual dysfunction.   (d) secondary impotence.

6. Janice feels that her sex drive is too low. She never feels any response when her husband kisses and caresses her.
    Janice's problem would probably be diagnosed as
    (a) female orgasmic dysfunction.   (c) female impotence.
    (b) vaginismus.   (d) female general sexual dysfunction.

7. Sylvia was raped at age 13. After that experience she has been unable to have intercourse due to vaginismus. A therapist might suggest any of the following procedures except
    (a) desensitization of fears of intercourse.   (c) masturbation.
    (b) progressive relaxation of the vaginal muscles. (d) sensate focus.

8. Bob and Betty have been married three years. They have about one explosive argument a month. This is the only time when Bob verbally releases his frustrations. This is an example of
    (a) gunnysacking.   (c) being open about feelings.
    (b) attacking the other person's character.   (d) winning a fight.

Chapter Review

1. Primary sexual characteristics refer to the _____ and _____ organs of males and females. _____ sexual characteristics appear at puberty in response to hormonal signals from the pituitary gland. In females, they include development of the _____, the broadening of the _____, and other changes in body shape. For males, they include development of facial and body _____, and the deepening of the _____.

2. Secondary sex characteristics signal physical readiness for reproduction. This is especially evident in the female _____ (onset of menstruation). Soon after this time, monthly _____ (the release of ova from the ovaries) begins. From then until _____, the end of regular monthly fertility cycles, women can potentially bear children.

3. Both primary and secondary sexual characteristics are closely related to the action of sex _____, chemical substances secreted by glands of the endocrine system. The _____ or sex glands affect sexual development by secreting hormones. These hormones include the female hormones (_____) and the male hormones (_____).

4. The gonads in the male are the _____ and in the female the _____. The _____ glands, located on top of the kidneys, also supply sex hormones in both males and females.

5. All individuals normally produce both _____ and _____, the balance of which influences sexual differences. The development of male or female genitals before birth is largely due to the presence or absence of _____, one of the _____.

6. _____ _____ is determined at the instant of conception. In the absence of a Y chromosome, the embryo will develop female reproductive organs. Nature's primary impulse, then, is to make a _____.

7. A genetic male will fail to develop male _____ if insufficient testosterone is formed during prenatal growth. Even if testosterone is present, an inherited _____ _____ may exist, again resulting in female development. Hormonal problems during early development may lead to _____ where dual or ambiguous sexual anatomy frequently occurs.

8.   Masculinization of a female can result when normal amounts of estrogen are produced, but a genetic abnormality causes the adrenal glands to secrete excess amounts of androgen. This is called the _____ syndrome and can produce a female child with male genitals.

9.   In addition to guiding physical development, the interplay of sex hormones before birth may also _____ _____ the brain. However, the evidence suggests that most sex-linked behavior is _____. Still, some researchers feel that prenatal exposure to androgens or estrogens exerts a biological _____ _____ on later psychosexual development in humans.

10. Some psychologists believe that _____ underlies the slight differences in male-female thinking abilities. Others do not support this idea and note that male-female differences in scores on the SAT are rapidly declining as the similarity of male-female _____ and _____ grows.

11. One's personal, private sense of maleness or femaleness is referred to as _____ _____ and appears to be a learned self-perception. In contrast _____ _____ are _____ traits and behaviors defined by one's culture as "male" or "female."

12. Gender identity begins with male-female labels and is then influenced by _____-_____ _____, that is the subtle pressure exerted by parents, peers, and cultural institutions that urge boys to "act like boys" and girls to "act like girls." In determining adult sexual behavior and sex-linked personality traits, _____ _____ are probably as important as chromosomal, genital or hormonal sex.

13. Sex role refers to the favored _____ of _____ that is expected of individuals on the basis of gender. The naturalness of sex roles is _____ based on cross-cultural observations.

14. Learning sex roles begins immediately after birth. Overall, parents tend to encourage their sons to engage in _____ (goal-directed) behaviors, to control their _____, and to prepare for the world of work. Daughters are encouraged in _____ (emotion-oriented) behaviors and to a lesser degree for the _____ role.

15. Research suggests that women are _____ _____ physically aroused by erotic stimuli than are men. However, compared to men, women more often have a negative _____ response to pictures of explicit sex. It has been found that sexual _____ tend to guide our sexual _____.

16. The sex drive is influenced by _____ toward sex, sexual _____, _____ of sexual release, and the amount of _____ present (for both men and women).

17. Alcohol is a _____. As such it may lower _____ that would normally keep any prohibited behavior in check. However, it often has a _____ effect on sexual response.

18. In humans, the effects of male or female castration vary. Some individuals show a decline in sex drive, but many others experience no change. However, after several years almost all subjects report a(n) _____ in sex drive. Sterilization does not _____ the sex drive and in fact may _____ it.

19.   Aging does not unavoidably end sexual activity. The crucial factor appears to be _____.

20.   Kinsey reports that _____ percent of the women he surveyed had masturbated at some time, and _____ percent of the males reported having masturbated. Hunt found that sizable number of married people masturbate at least occasionally — approximately _____ percent. The contemporary view is that masturbation is a _____ sexual outlet.

21.   It is estimated that _____ percent of all American adults are homosexual. A major survey of 76 cultures found that almost two-thirds _____ some form of homosexuality. Psychological testing consistently shows _____ _____ in personality or adjustment between homosexuals and heterosexuals. If homosexuals suffer lasting guilt or self-hate the homosexuality is described as _____-_____. Homosexuality (as well as heterosexuality and bisexuality) is probably caused by a combination of _____, _____, and _____, and _____ influences. Prejudice and fear aimed at homosexuals is usually refered to as _____.

22.   Masters and Johnson have classified sexual response in both males and females into four phases: _____, _____, _____, and _____.

23.   Sexual arousal in the male is signaled by _____ of the _____ during the excitement phase. In the mature male, orgasm is accompanied by _____ (release of seminal fluid) and is followed by a short _____ _____ during which no amount of continued stimulation will produce a second orgasm.

24.   Although the timing and intensity of the phases vary considerably for individual women, the basic pattern of response is the same as that for men. During the excitement phase, a complex pattern of changes prepares the vagina for intercourse. After orgasm, many females return to the _____ phase and may be stimulated to orgasm again.

25.   Masters and Johnson exploded the Freudian myth that clitoral orgasm is an immature form of female response. They showed there is _____ _____ in physical response no matter what form of stimulation produces orgasm. As a matter of fact, the _____ is relatively insensitive to touch. During love-making, _____ to _____ minutes are usually required for a woman to go from excitement to orgasm. Males may experience all four stages in as little as _____ minutes.

26.   The _____ in the male and female sexual responses outweigh the _____. Women generally go through the phases more _____ than men, and men are not generally capable of multiple _____.

27.   The gap between sexual values and actual behavior has _____. According to polls, there has been a dramatic drop in the number of people who disapprove of _____ sex and a large percentage of people have engaged in it by age 25. What is also apparent is the _____ participation in sexual behavior by both sexes.

28.   Roughly _____ _____ of the 15% of female college students who have been raped were raped by a(n) _____ or _____. The effects of the crime on the woman were no less devastating than if it had been done by a stranger. This underscores the fact that if a woman says "_____," she means it.

29. STD stands for _____ _____ disease. AIDS is just an STD but it is different in that it is _____. AIDS is caused by the human _____ virus (commonly called ____ ____ ____). Symptoms of AIDS may not show up for years making it possible for someone with AIDS to _____ others unknowingly. Even though AIDS has been called the "_____ _____" it can be spread by all forms of sexual intercourse.

30. _____ refers to a male's inability to maintain an erection for sexual intercourse. Those suffering from _____ _____ have never been able to produce or maintain an erection, while those who have previously performed successfully, but then lose the ability, are said to suffer from _____ _____.

31. Although impotence is more likely to be caused by _____ factors than _____ factors, _____ percent of the cases are _____ caused. Most cases are related to highly restrictive _____ training, early sexual experience with a seductive _____, or other experiences leading to guilt, fear, and sexual inhibition.

32. In _____ _____, a technique used in treating impotence and other sexual disorders, the couple is initially told to take turns stroking various parts of each other's bodies. Genital contact is avoided at first, with emphasis placed on giving pleasure and on signaling what is most gratifying.

33. Masters and Johnson define the problem of _____ _____ as one in which a man is unable to delay sexual climax long enough to satisfy his partner in at least one-half of their lovemaking attempts. The most common treatment for this problem is the _____ technique.

34. An inability to reach orgasm, or _____ ejaculation, may have many different causes. However, it too can be successfully treated using sensate focus, manual stimulation by the female, and work around personal conflicts and marital difficulties.

35. Women who show little or no physical arousal to sexual stimulation and persistently derive no pleasure from sexual stimulation suffer from _____ _____ dysfunction commonly referred to as _____.

36. Female general sexual dysfunction is similar to male impotence. It may be either primary or secondary. Also, it has similar causes. Treatment includes sensate focus, genital stimulation by the woman's partner, and "_____" intercourse controlled by the woman.

37. The most prevalent sexual complaint among women is _____ dysfunction, an inability to reach _____ during intercourse, the most common source being _____ of the sexual response. In the condition known as _____, muscle spasms make intercourse impossible. It is often accompanied by obvious fears of intercourse or at least high levels of anxiety.

38. Treatment of vaginismus is similar to what might be done for a nonsexual _____ including desensitization, implosive therapy, and hypnosis.

39. Several guidelines can be suggested to help facilitate communication. One of them is to avoid "_____," that is saving up feelings and complaints.

40. Another suggestion is to be open about _____. Happy couples not only talk more, they convey more personal feelings and show greater sensitivity to their partner's feelings. Don't attack the other person's _____. Expressions of negative feelings should be given as statements of one's own feelings, not as statements of _____.

41.   Don't try to _____ a fight; instead try to resolve the differences without focusing on who is right or wrong. Recognize that _____ is appropriate. However, constructive fights require than couples fight fair by sticking to the real issues and not "hitting below the belt." Hence, for good communication to occur it is appropriate to see things through your partner's _____, rather than assuming you know what your partner is thinking (i.e., being a "_____ _____").

42.   Sidney Jourard has conducted some intriguing studies in human touching, not only in our country, but cross-culturally. He discovered that, in American society, most regions of a young adult's body remain untouched unless one has a close friend of the _____ _____, and even that depends upon their relationship.

43.   Jourard also found interesting sex differences. Daughters are touched more right into their twenties. Mothers are allowed to touch a girl's hair frequently. One-_____ of the parents get to touch their daughters' lips, and one-_____ manage a literal pat on the back. Sons, on the other hand, receive considerably _____ touching. Also, parents stop touching boys much _____.

44.   Taboos do exist. Only _____ percent of the girls studied received a paternal pat on the bottom and _____ were touched by their fathers in the genital areas.

ANSWER KEYS

Do You Know the Information?

Multiple Choice

1. (c) obj. 1, p. 673
2. (a) obj. 2, p. 673
3. (b) obj. 2, p. 673
4. (a) obj. 3, p. 674
5. (d) objs. 3, 5, pp. 674,676
6. (a) obj. 4, p. 674
7. (b) obj. 4, p. 674
8. (c) obj. 5, p. 676
9. (d) objs. 6, p. 678
10. (c) obj. 7, p. 679
11. (b) obj. 9, pp. 679-680
12. (d) obj. 10, p. 680
13. (d) obj. 11, p. 681
14. (b,c) obj. 12, p. 681
15. (b) obj. 13, pp. 681-682
16. (a) obj. 14, p. 682
17. (d) obj. 15, p. 684
18. (a) obj. 16, p. 685
19. (b) obj. 19, pp. 687-688
20. (d) obj. 20, p. 689
21. (a) obj. 20, p. 690
22. (c) obj. 20, p. 690
23. (b) obj. 20, p. 690
24. (d) obj. 20, p. 691

True-False

1. F, obj. 2, p. 673
2. F, obj. 4, p. 674
3. T, obj. 4, p. 675
4. T, obj. 5, p. 676
5. T, obj. 6, p. 677
6. T, obj. 9, p. 679
7. F, obj. 10, p. 680
8. T, obj. 10, p. 680
9. T, obj. 12, p. 681
10. F, obj. 14, p. 683
11. T, obj. 18, p. 686
12. F, obj. 20, pp. 689-690
13. F, obj. 21, p. 692
14. T, obj. 22, p. 694

Matching

1. N, obj. 1, p. 673
2. G, obj. 1, p. 673
3. M, obj. 2, p. 673
4. P, obj. 2, p. 673
5. I, obj. 3, p. 673
6. K, obj. 5, p. 676
7. E, obj. 6, p. 678
8. D, obj. 8, p. 679
9. C, obj. 14, p. 682
10. F, obj. 17, p. 686
11. H, obj. 19, p. 686
12. J, obj. 20, p. 689
13. B, obj. 20, p. 691

Can You Apply the Information?

1. (d) objs. 9-10, pp. 679-680
2. (b) obj. 11, p. 681
3. (b) objs. 14-15, pp. 682, 684
4. (d) obj. 20, p. 689
5. (c) obj. 20, p. 690
6. (d) obj. 20, p. 691
7. (d) obj. 20, p. 691
8. (a) obj. 21, p. 692

Chapter Review

1. sexual, reproductive, Secondary, breasts, hips, hair, voice (p. 673)
2. menarche, ovulation, menopause (p. 673)
3. hormones, gonads, estrogens, androgens (p. 673)
4. testes, ovaries, adrenal (p. 673)
5. androgens, estrogens, testosterone, androgens (p. 673)
6. Genetic sex, female (p. 674)
7. genitals, androgen insensitivity, hermaphroditism (p. 674)
8. androgenital (p. 674)
9. sex type, learned, biasing effect (p. 675)
10. biology (brain differences), interests (p. 675); experiences (p. 676)
11. gender identity, sex roles, observable (p. 676)
12. sex-role socialization, sex roles (p. 676)
13. pattern, behavior (p. 676); questionable (p. 677)
14. instrumental, emotions, expressive, maternal (p. 678)
15. no less, emotional, scripts, behavior (p. 679)
16. attitudes, experience, recency, androgen (p. 679)
17. depressant, inhibitions, decreasing (negative) (p. 680)
18. decrease, decrease, increase (p. 680)
19. regularity (opportunity) (p. 681)
20. 60, 95, 70, normal (acceptable) (p. 681)
21. 5, accept, no differences (p. 681); ego-dystonic (p. 682); hereditary, biological, social, psychological (p. 681); homophobia (p. 682)
22. excitement, plateau, orgasm, resolution (p. 682)
23. erection, penis, ejaculation, refractory period (p. 682)
24. plateau (p. 684)
25. no difference, vagina, 10, 20, 4 (p. 684)
26. similarities, differences, slowly, orgasms (p. 684)
27. narrowed, premarital, earlier (p. 685)
28. one half, acquaintance, date, No (p. 686)
29. sexually transmitted, fatal, immunodeficiency, H I V (p. 686); infect, gay plague (p. 687)
30. Impotence, primary impotence, secondary impotence (p. 689)
31. psychological, physical, 40, physically, religious, mother (p. 689)
32. sensate focus (p. 690)
33. premature ejaculation, squeeze (p. 690)
34. retarded (p. 690)
35. general sexual (p. 691); frigidity (p. 690)
36. nondemanding (p. 691)
37. orgasmic, orgasm, overcontrol, vaginismus (p. 691)
38. phobia (p. 691)
39. gunnysacking (p. 692)
40. feelings, character, blame (p. 692)
41. win, anger, eyes (p. 692); mind-reader (p. 693)
42. opposite sex (p. 694)
43. half, half, less, earlier (p. 694)
44. 13, none (p. 694)

Chapter 26

Applied Psychology

LEARNING OBJECTIVES

To demonstrate mastery of this chapter you should be able to:

1. Define the term applied psychology.

2. Describe the work of a community psychologist.

3. List some of the areas of interest of industrial/organizational psychology and engineering psychology.

4.   Describe the typical activities of the engineering psychologist.

5.   Describe the activities of personnel psychologists by defining or describing the following areas:
      a.   job analysis

      b.   biodata

      c.   vocational interest test

      d.   aptitude test

      e.   assessment center

6.   Differentiate scientific management styles (Theory X) from human relations approaches (Theory Y) to management including work efficiency and psychological efficiency. Include the terms participative management, management by objectives, and quality circles.

7. List six factors which seem to contribute the most to job satisfaction.

    a.

    b.

    c.

    d.

    e.

    f.

8. Explain the purpose and results of job enrichment.

9. Explain the goals of environmental psychology.

10. Describe how people exhibit territoriality.

11. Discuss the results of animal experiments on the effects of overcrowding, and state the possible implications for humans.

12. Differentiate between crowding and density.

13.   Discuss the following types of overload: attentional, sensory, and cognitive.

14.   Explain how architectural psychology can be used to solve environmental problems.

15.   Describe the goals of educational psychology. Differentiate direct instruction from open teaching in your answer.

16.   Describe the activities and interests of a consumer psychologist.

17.   Discuss the psychology of law and identify topics of special interest.

18.   Explain the ways in which a sports psychologist might contribute to peak performance by an athlete.

* * * * * * * * * *

The following objectives are related to the material in the "Applications" and "Exploration" sections of your text.

19.   List and explain ten ways to improve communication skills.

    a.   f.

    b.   g.

    c.   h.

    d.   i.

    e.   j.

20.   List and describe six ways to be a good listener.

    a.   d.

    b.   e.

    c.   f.

21.   Describe several major human factors concerns that will have an impact on the success of future space missions and habitats.

SELF-QUIZZES

Do You Know the Information?

Multiple Choice

1. Which of the following *best* exemplifies the idea of flexitime?
   a) Workers' hours are staggered and rotated.
   b) Starting and quitting times are voluntarily adjustable within limits.
   c) Days off are rotated and made flexible.
   d) Twenty-five percent of the workers must arrive for the "core hours" during the day.

2. The inside light of an automobile that comes on when the door is open is an example of the principle of good design known as
   a) natural design.
   b) feedback.
   c) human factors design.
   d) compatibility.

3. Which of the following statements about biodata is *false*?
   a) Biodata is a good way to predict job success.
   b) The idea behind biodata is that past behavior predicts future behavior.
   c) Some useful items of biodata are past athletic interest, scientific interest, and religious activities.
   d) Biodata is used to help screen out job candidates who seem to have serious psychological problems.

4. At an assessment center
   a) one would be likely to receive vocational counseling.
   b) one might be likely to receive an in-basket test.
   c) candidates for assembly line positions would be screened and evaluated.
   d) management strategies such as Theory X are evaluated.

5. Theory Y is *most* closely associated with which of the following terms?
   a) scientific management
   b) work efficiency
   c) task analysis
   d) participative management

6. Which of the following factors is *not* closely associated with the highest job satisfaction?
   a) relative freedom from close supervision
   b) allowed ordinary social contacts with others
   c) pleasant working environment
   d) recognition for doing well

7. In comparing the results of experiments on crowding in rats and the behavior of humans living in crowded inner-city ghettos, the only viable conclusion is that
   a) there is a clear link between crowding and abnormal behavior in both species.
   b) laboratory studies with humans fail to produce the kinds of problems seen in rats.
   c) crowding and density mean the same thing for both species.
   d) crowding alone is a greater influence in humans than is either nutrition or education.

8. The term _____ refers to the number of people in a given space.
   a) crowding
   b) discrimination
   c) overload
   d) density

9. Sensory and cognitive overload (according to Milgram) may result in
   a) high blood pressure.
   b) brief, superficial interpersonal contacts.
   c) callousness.
   d) all of the above.

10. Which specialty would tend to work with people who design buildings?
    a) consumer psychology
    b) health psychology
    c) architectural psychology
    d) personnel psychology

11. When factual information is presented by lecture, discussion, and rote practice, this type of teaching is called
    a) open teaching.
    b) interactional persuasion.
    c) direct instruction.
    d) balanced education.

12. To pinpoint the factors which may influence consumer behavior, consumer psychologists conduct a type of public opinion polling called
    a) attitude change.
    b) promotional schemes.
    c) brand loyalty.
    d) marketing research.

13. Which of the following statements about juries is *incorrect* according to research?
    a) In selecting a jury which may be beneficial to one's case, it is important to know the potential juror's demographic characteristics and observe his or her nonverbal behavior.
    b) Most jurors are able to remain fairly neutral in order to make a judgment.
    c) Jurors are not very good at separating evidence from other information like their perceptions of the defendant.
    d) Jurors usually cannot suspend judgment until all evidence is in.

14. Which of the following is *not* an area of stress that psychologists have pinpointed as a key area of concern that future space residents will have to contend with?
    a) sensory restriction
    b) sexual deprivation
    c) need for privacy
    d) mental health problems

Matching *Use the letters on the right only once.)*

____	1.	use of psychological principles and research methods to solve practical problems	A. Theory Y
____	2.	make machines compatible with human capacities	B. job satisfaction
____	3.	concerned with work efficiency	C. environmental psychology
____	4.	removing some of the controls and restrictions promotes this	D. crowding
____	5.	how surroundings influence our behavior	E. applied psychology
____	6.	protecting your space	F. territorial behavior
____	7.	a psychological condition from being overstimulated	G. Theory X
____	8.	for example, concerned with why people buy the things they do	H. consumer psychologist
____	9.	a trance experience sometimes refered to as "flow"	I. engineering psychology
			J. job enrichment
			K. density
			L. peak performance
			M. attentional overload

Can You Apply the Information?

For questions 1 through 5, use the following choices to select who could best solve the problem which is presented.

a. environmental psychologist
b. counseling psychologist
c. consumer psychologist
d. architectural psychologist

e. educational psychologist
f. community psychologist
g. personnel psychologist
h. engineering psychologist

_____ 1. Company X needs to find out exactly who will best be able cope with the demands of a production line which uses robotics and other automation. For long periods there will be little social contact with co-workers.

_____ 2. NASA wants one of its suppliers to rearrange the instrumentation in the shuttle cockpit to reduce the response time during emergency situations.

_____ 3. The City Council wants to help county health officials reduce the number of admissions to their local community mental health facility. In short, they are trying to increase the level of primary prevention programs for mental health. They need someone to study the problem and make recommendations.

_____ 4. The library board receives complaints from patrons that they feel crowded and tense when using the library facilities. The Board is considering remodeling or building a new library.

_____ 5. A large advertising firm wants to design an ad campaign based on what features of soft drinks appeal to most buyers.

6. At Hoof-Hearted Horseshoe Factory there are no private offices for management, everyone wears the same overalls, and there are daily meetings that everyone attends to air differences, talk about production, etc. Which type of management does this factory operate under?
a) Theory X   b) Theory Y

7. Linda works in a large office area where each person has his/her own desk, but their are no walls or other dividers. She brings a couple of plants from home and a picture or two. Linda is most likely engaging in
a) personal space.   c) job enrichment.
b) job satisfaction.   d) territoriality.

8. Put eight people in a space the size of a hot tub, call it an elevator, and you'll probably find eight uncomfortable people. Put eight people in a hot tub and you'll probably find eight contented people. The difference is probably due to
a) density.   c) psychic "noise."
b) images.   d) crowding.

9. Dennis is teaching his class on the topic of euthanasia through guided, active teacher-student discussion. This type of instruction is called
a) balanced instruction.   c) open teaching.
b) direct instruction.   d) interactional persuasion.

10. Ralph is a professional basketball player who is concerned about his stress level and wants to learn to relax. It would be most appropriate for him to see a
a) engineering psychologist.   d) behavioral medicine specialist.
b) sports psychologist.   e) very tall psychologist.
c) health psychologist.

11.   You have been working on your taxes and have organized piles of receipts all over your dining room table. Your spouse enters and says, "Where did all this garbage come from?" thereby making what mistake to effective communication?
   a)   use of loaded words
   b)   excessive use of slang
   c)   overuse of big words
   d)   not using your name

Chapter Review

1.   The use of psychological principles to solve practical problems is called _____ psychology.

2.   _____ psychologists treat whole neighborhoods as their clients and tend to stress _____. An _____ psychologist seeks to make machines compatible with our sensory and motor capacities.

3.   Effective human factors engineering is refered to as _____ design. It makes use of _____ that are naturally understood without any additional learning. Effective design also provides clear _____. Hence, "human error" may actually be related to _____ design.

4.   The idea of _____ is that workers get to choose their starting and quitting times within limits. Benefits observed from this include increased job _____ and less _____.

5.   _____ psychologists try to match people with jobs. To do this they may use _____ _____ to find out exactly what workers do, or collect detailed biographical information called _____. The traditional _____ _____ is still used to select people for jobs even though it is subject to the _____ effect. In addition, personnel psychologists use _____ tests to rate a person's potential. Finally, _____ centers may be used to fill management and executive positions.

6.   Managers who are concerned with improving work efficiency as opposed to worker autonomy and participation in management believe in Theory _____. Theory _____ managers assume that workers enjoy independence and are willing to accept responsibility. The latter group often uses _____ management, management by _____, and quality _____.

7.   Job satisfaction appears to be closely related to the following factors: _____ contact with other workers, opportunity to use their own _____ and _____, recognition for doing well, chance to apply their _____, freedom from close _____, and opportunity for _____ and _____.

8.   Job enrichment involves removing some of the _____ and _____ on employees. As a result, there are usually lower production _____, increased job _____, reduced _____, and less _____.

9.   The speciality concerned with how our surroundings influence our behavior is called _____ psychology. This speciality is interested in _____ and _____ surroundings and _____ settings.

10. _____ refers to the tendency to identify a space as ours. This identification is accomplished through the use of specific territorial _____ such as "saving a place." We are likely to signal this through the use of obvious _____.

11. Overpopulation is a serious problem today. However, distress is caused by factors in addition to the _____, the sheer number of people in a given space.

12. _____ refers to subjective feelings of being overstimulated by loss of privacy or increased social input. At a party, a high _____ may be experienced as pleasurable whereas in another situation it may lead to stress. A consequence of this is cognitive and sensory overload also called _____ overload) which may lead to superficiality or callousness in interpersonal interactions.

13. The speciality concerned with the importance of designing buildings to maximize psychological comfort is called _____ psychology.

14. _____ psychology seeks to understand how people learn and how teachers instruct. When factual information is presented by lecture, demonstration, and/or rote practice, this is called _____ instruction. When discussion is emphasized, this is termed _____ teaching.

15. _____ psychology is an applied field that focuses on how and why people buy and spend as they do. Often this is done through a type of public opinion polling called _____ research.

16. Psychologists have also worked in the area of jury research. They have found that jurors rarely set aside their _____ in making decisions. Jurors are also not very good at separating _____ from other information.

17. _____ psychologists seek to understand and improve _____ performance and to enhance the benefits of participation. One phenomenon that they are interested in is _____ _____, an experience commonly called "flow."

18. Knowing how to communicate clearly can be very important. One should: state ideas _____ and decisively; not overuse _____ words; avoid excessive use of _____ or slang; avoid _____ words; use people's _____; be polite and _____; use an _____ tone of voice; speak fluently and _____; and use _____-_____ cues.

19. Being a good listener, on the other hand, requires paying _____, identifying the speaker's _____, suspending _____, checking your _____ of what is being said, looking out for _____-_____ messages, and accepting _____ for effective communication.

20. Psychologists have pinpointed several key areas that future space residents will have to cope with. One is the general _____ of the space station. There should be some flexibility concerning the use of _____ and _____ areas. _____ cycles will need to be carefully controlled to avoid disrupting bodily rhythms. It is also necessary to recognize the need for _____. Being in space may also leave astronauts with a problem of _____ restriction and social _____. There will also be the need to deal with _____ resolution and mental _____.

ANSWER KEYS

Do You Know the Information?

Multiple Choice

1. (b) obj. 3, p. 701
2. (b) obj. 4, p. 701
3. (d) obj. 5, p. 702
4. (b) obj. 5, p. 704
5. (d) obj. 6, p. 705
6. (c) obj. 7, p. 706
7. (b) obj. 11, p. 709
8. (d) obj. 12, p. 709
9. (d) obj. 13, p. 710
10. (c) obj. 14, p. 711
11. (c) obj. 15, p. 713
12. (d) obj. 14, p. 714
13. (b) obj. 17, pp. 715-716
14. (b) obj. 21, pp. 722-724

Matching

1. E, obj. 1, p. 699
2. I, obj. 3, p. 701
3. G, obj. 6, p. 704
4. J, obj. 8, p. 706
5. C, obj. 9, p. 707
6. F, obj. 10, p. 708
7. D, obj. 12, p. 709
8. H, obj. 16, p. 713
9. L, obj. 18, p. 717

Can You Apply the Information?

1. (g) obj. 5, p. 702
2. (h) obj. 3, p. 701
3. (f) obj. 2, p. 700
4. (a,d) objs. 9, 14, pp. 707, 711
5. (c) obj. 16, p. 713
6. (b) obj. 6, p. 705
7. (d) obj. 10, p. 708
8. (d) obj. 12, p. 709
9. (c) obj. 15, p. 713
10. (b) obj. 18, p. 716
11. (a) obj. 19, pp. 719-720

Chapter Review

1. applied (p. 699)
2. Community, prevention (education, consultation) (p. 700); engineering (p. 701)
3. natural, signals, feedback, poor (p. 701)
4. flexitime, satisfaction, absenteeism (p. 701)
5. Personnel, job analysis, biodata, personal interview, halo (p. 702); aptitude (p. 703); assessment (p. 704)
6. X (p. 704); Y, participative, objectives (p. 705); circles (p. 706)
7. social, judgment, intelligence, skills, supervision, promotion, advancement (p. 706)
8. controls, restrictions, costs, satisfaction, boredom, absenteeism (p. 706)
9. environmental, physical, social, behavioral (p. 707)
10. Territoriality, behaviors, markers (p. 708)
11. density (p. 709)
12. Crowding, density (p. 709); attentional (p. 710)
13. architectural (p. 711)
14. Educational (p. 712); direct, open (p. 713)
15. Consumer (p. 713); marketing (p. 714)
16. biases (attitudes, values), evidence (p. 715)
17. Sports, sports, (p. 716); peak performance (p. 717)
18. clearly, big (p. 719); jargon, loaded, names, respectful, expressive, quickly, non-verbal (p. 720)
19. attention (p. 720); purpose, evaluation, understanding, non-verbal, responsibility (p. 721)
20. environment (p. 722); living, work, Sleep, privacy, sensory (p. 723); isolation, conflict, health (p. 724)

Appendix B

KEY TERMS AND CONCEPTS

descriptive statistics
  graphical statistics
    frequency distribution
    histogram
    frequency polygon
  measures of central tendency
    mean, median, mode
  measures of variability
    range
    standard deviation
    Z-scores

inferential statistics
    sample vs. population
    representative, random
  normal curve
  significant difference
  correlation
    positive relationship
    zero relationship
    negative relationship
    prediction
  variance
  correlation vs. causation

LEARNING OBJECTIVES

To demonstrate mastery of this chapter you should be able to:

1. Distinguish between the purposes of descriptive and inferential statistics.

2. List the three basic techniques of descriptive statistics.
   a.

   b.

   c.

3. Explain the purpose of graphical statistics and give an example of a frequency distribution, a histogram, and a frequency polygon.

473

4. List and describe the three measures of central tendency. Explain why the mean is not always the best measure of central tendency.

    a.

    b.

    c.

5. Describe the use of the range, standard deviation, and z-score as measures of the variability of scores around the mean.

6. Describe the use of the normal curve and its relationship to the standard deviation (or z-score).

7. Explain the difference between a population and a sample.

8. Explain the importance of representativeness and randomness as they relate to a sample.

9.   Explain the purpose of a test of statistical significance.

10.   Describe how a correlation coefficient indicates the degree of relationship between two variables.

11.   Give an example of the useful information that correlations can provide. Explain how correlation coefficients are used to make predictions.

12.   Describe the limitations of correlation as it relates to causation.

SELF-QUIZZES

Do You Know the Information?

Multiple Choice

1.   Which of the following statements is *incorrect?*
      (a) Inferential statistics are used for decision-making.
      (b) Inferential statistics are used for drawing conclusions.
      (c) Descriptive statistics are used for generalizing to the population-at-large from a small sample.
      (d) Inferential statistics allow us to generalize from the behavior of small groups of subjects to that of the larger groups they represent.

2. Which of the following is *not* one of the three basic techniques of descriptive statistics?
    (a) measures of central tendency   (c) measures of variability
    (b) measures of reliability   (d) graphical statistics

3. The graphic display of frequency distributions which uses bars to indicate the frequency of scores within class intervals is the
    (a) frequency polygon.   (c) histogram.
    (b) histograph.   (d) frequency distribution.

4. Graphical statistics are used for the purpose of letting people "see" how a pattern of numbers looks.
    (a) True   (b) False

5. The measure of central tendency which is obtained by ranking scores from the highest to the lowest and selecting the middle score is the
    (a) mode.   (c) standard deviation.
    (b) mean.   (d) median.

6. The mean is not always the best measure of central tendency because it
    (a) is difficult to compute.
    (b) can't be used to help calculate a coefficient of correlation.
    (c) always distorts the population.
    (d) is sensitive to extremely high or low scores in a distribution.

7. The measure of central tendency which expresses the most frequently occurring score in a distribution is the
    (a) mode.   (c) standard deviation.
    (b) mean.   (d) median.

8. The number which represents the spread between the highest and the lowest score in a distribution is called the
    (a) range.   (c) z-score.
    (b) standard deviation.   (d) normal score.

9. An advantage of the standard deviation is that it can be used to "standardize" scores to give them more meaning.
    (a) True   (b) False

10. A z-score is a number which shows the relationship among a person's score, the mean, and the standard deviation.
    (a) True   (b) False

11. Psychological traits or events (like chance events) tend to approximate a normal curve where some outcomes have very little probability but occur frequently.
    (a) True   (b) False

12. In a normal curve, 68 percent of all cases fall between 3 SD above and below the mean.
    (a) True   (b) False

13. A sample
    (a) is composed of the entire group about which you wish to make inferences.
    (b) should be representative of the composition and characteristics of the larger population.
    (c) provides an estimate of how often experimental results could have occurred by chance alone.
    (d) is an example of descriptive statistics.

14. Tests of statistical significance
    (a) relate the mean to the mode.
    (b) are predictive of the coefficient of correlation.
    (c) provide an estimate of how often experimental results could have occurred by chance alone.
    (d) are an example of descriptive statistics.

15. When two variables are not related, they have a
    (a) positive correlation.
    (c) negative correlation.
    (b) zero correlation.
    (d) statistical significance.

16. If decreases in one measure (X) are matched by decreases in the other measure (Y), what we have is a
    (a) positive correlation.
    (b) negative correlation.

17. If we know two measures are correlated, and we know a person's score on one measure,
    (a) we can predict his or her score on the other.
    (b) we can assume the tests are representative.
    (c) the tests are probably causally related.
    (d) all of the above are true.

Can You Apply the Information?

1. You are an average student, and you have a test in your psychology class. Your instructor decides to give a passing grade to everyone over a certain grade and a failing grade to everyone under that grade. There is a really brilliant student in your class who always aces every test. How would you rather have your instructor compute that dividing point?
    (a) Mean
    (b) Median

2. Your instructor decides instead to report your score as a z-score. You get a +1.5. Are you happy with your score?
    (a) Yes
    (b) No

3. Gordon wants to do an election prediction for Chicago. Should he get a sample or a population?
    (a) Sample
    (b) Population

4. The first thing Gordon would do after polling everyone on his list would be to begin using _____ statistics.
    (a) descriptive
    (b) inferential

5. As the temperature increases the activity level of dogs decreases. Which of the following coefficients of correlation *best* expresses this observation?
    (a) +.86
    (c) 0
    (b) −.30
    (d) +.07

Chapter Review

1. One of the two major types of statistical methods is _____ statistics. They are used to summarize large amounts of data. The second major type is used for decision-making, for _____ from _____ samples, and for drawing conclusions. This type is called _____ statistics.

2. The three basic types of descriptive statistics are _____ statistics, measures of _____ _____, and measures of
_____.

3. One type of graphical statistics is the _____ distribution. It is formed by breaking down the entire range of possible scores into classes of equal size and then recording the number of scores falling in each class. This type of distribution is often expressed graphically using _____.
An alternative way of graphing a distribution of scores is the more familiar
_____ _____. Here, points are placed at the center of each class interval to indicate the number of cases. Then, the dots are connected by straight lines.

4. A measure of _____ _____ is simply a number describing a "middle score" around which other scores fall. One familiar measure is the _____ or average. It is sensitive to extremely _____ or _____ scores in a distribution and, consequently, does not always give the best measure of _____ _____. In such cases the "middle score" in a group of scores, called the _____, is used instead.

5. A final measure of central tendency is the _____. It simply represents the most frequently occurring score in a distribution.

6. When we want to know if scores are clustered closely about the mean or scattered widely, we use measures of _____ to attach a numerical value to the "spread of scores." The simplest way to describe variability is to use the _____, which is the spread between the highest and lowest scores. A better measure of variability is the _____
_____.

7. A particular advantage of the standard deviation is that it can be used to "standardize" scores in a way that gives them greater meaning. This is done using the _____-_____.

8. When chance events are recorded and graphed, they resemble what is called a _____
_____. Measures of psychological variables tend to approximate this curve.

9. A great deal is known about the mathematical properties of the normal curve. For example, there is a fixed relationship between the _____ _____ and the normal curve. The standard deviation measures off constant proportions of the curve above and below the mean. As an example of this principle, notice that _____ percent of all cases fall between one standard deviation above and below the mean. Similarly, _____ percent of all cases can be found between three standard deviations above and below the mean.

10. _____ statistics, the other major division of statistical methods, includes techniques that allow us to _____ from the behavior of small groups of subjects to that of the larger groups they represent.

11. In any scientific investigation, we would like to observe the entire set or
_____ of subjects, objects, or events being studied. However, this is usually impossible. Instead, _____ or small cross sections of a population are selected, and observations of this group are used to draw conclusions about the entire group.

12. The major requirement of any sample is that it be _____. It must truly reflect the composition and characteristics of the larger population. A very important aspect of representative samples is that their members are chosen at _____; that is, each member of the population must have an equal chance of being included in the sample.

13. When we compare results from different groups, we wish to know if they might have simply occurred by chance or if they represent a real difference. Tests of _____ _____ provide an estimate of how often experimental results could have occurred by chance alone.

14. The results of a test of statistical significance are stated as a probability, giving the odds that the observed difference was due to chance. In psychology, any experimental condition attributable to chance _____ times or less out of 100 is considered significant.

15. Many of the statements that psychologists make about behavior do not result from the use of experimental methods and are not analyzed using tests of statistical significance. Instead, they deal with the fact that two variables are _____-_____ (varying together in some orderly fashion).

16. We use _____ methods which give a number, called the _____ of _____, indicating the degree of relationship between two measures.

17. A _____ correlation occurs when there is no relationship between the two variables. With a _____ correlation, increases (decreases) in the scores of one variable are associated with increases (decreases) in the other. With a _____ correlation, increases (decreases) in the scores of one variable are associated with decreases (increases) in the other. The numerical value of a correlation coefficient may range from _____ for a perfect positive correlation to _____ for a perfect negative relationship.

18. Correlations often provide useful information. For instance, it is valuable to know that there is a correlation between _____ and lung cancer rates. Correlations are particularly valuable for making _____. If we know two measures are correlated, and we know a person's score on one measure, then we can predict the person's score on the other.

19. It is important to recognize that the existence of a correlation between two measures does not mean that one causes the other. This is expressed by the phrase, "_____ does not demonstrate _____."

ANSWER KEYS

Do You Know the Information?

Multiple Choice

1. (c) obj. 1, p. A-5
2. (b) obj. 2, p. A-5
3. (c) obj. 3, p. A-6
4. (a) obj. 3, p. A-6
5. (d) obj. 4, p. A-6
6. (d) obj. 4, p. A-6
7. (a) obj. 4, p. A-6
8. (a) obj. 5, p. A-7

9. (a) obj. 5, p. A-8
10. (a) obj. 5, p. A-8
11. (b) obj. 6, p. A-9
12. (b) obj. 6, p. A-9
13. (b) objs. 7-8, p. A-10
14. (c) obj. 9, p. A-10
15. (b) obj. 10, p. A-11
16. (a) obj. 10, p. A-11
17. (a) objs.11-12, pp. A-12—A-14

Can You Apply the Information?

1. (b) obj. 4, p. A-6
2. (a) obj. 6, p. A-10
3. (a) obj. 7, p. A-10
4. (a) obj. 1, p. A-5
5. (b) obj. 10, p. A-11

Chapter Review

1. descriptive, generalizing, small, inferential (p. A-5)
2. graphical, central tendency, variability (p. A-5)
3. frequency (A-5); histograms, frequency polygon (p. A-6)
4. central tendency, mean, high, low, central tendency, median (p. A-6)
5. mode (p. A-6)
6. variability, range (A-7); standard deviation (p. A-8)
7. z-score (p. A-8)
8. normal curve (p. A-9)
9. standard deviation, 68, 99 (p. A-10)
10. Inferential, generalize (p. A-10)
11. population, samples (p. A-10)
12. representative, random (p. A-10)
13. statistical significance (p. A-10)
14. five (p. A-10)
15. co-relating (p. A-11)
16. correlational, coefficient, correlation (p. A-11)
17. zero, positive, negative, +1.00, -1.00 (p. A-11)
18. smoking, predictions (p. A-12)
19. Correlation, causation (p. A-13)